Human–Computer Interaction Series

Editors-in-chief

Desney Tan
Microsoft Research, USA

Jean Vanderdonckt
Université catholique de Louvain, Belgium

HCI is a multidisciplinary field focused on human aspects of the development of computer technology. As computer-based technology becomes increasingly pervasive—not just in developed countries, but worldwide—the need to take a human-centered approach in the design and development of this technology becomes ever more important. For roughly 30 years now, researchers and practitioners in computational and behavioral sciences have worked to identify theory and practice that influences the direction of these technologies, and this diverse work makes up the field of human-computer interaction. Broadly speaking it includes the study of what technology might be able to do for people and how people might interact with the technology. The HCI series publishes books that advance the science and technology of developing systems which are both effective and satisfying for people in a wide variety of contexts. Titles focus on theoretical perspectives (such as formal approaches drawn from a variety of behavioral sciences), practical approaches (such as the techniques for effectively integrating user needs in system development), and social issues (such as the determinants of utility, usability and acceptability).

Titles published within the Human–Computer Interaction Series are included in Thomson Reuters' Book Citation Index, The DBLP Computer Science Bibliography and The HCI Bibliography.

More information about this series at http://www.springer.com/series/6033

Nadia Magnenat-Thalmann
Junsong Yuan · Daniel Thalmann
Bum-Jae You
Editors

Context Aware Human-Robot and Human-Agent Interaction

Editors
Nadia Magnenat-Thalmann
Institute for Media Innovation, SCE
Nanyang Technological University
Singapore
Singapore

Daniel Thalmann
Institute for Media Innovation, SCE
Nanyang Technological University
Singapore
Singapore

Junsong Yuan
Institute for Media Innovation, EEE
Nanyang Technological University
Singapore
Singapore

Bum-Jae You
Center of HCI for Coexistence
Korea Institute of Science and Technology
Seoul
South Korea

ISSN 1571-5035
Human–Computer Interaction Series
ISBN 978-3-319-37347-8   ISBN 978-3-319-19947-4 (eBook)
DOI 10.1007/978-3-319-19947-4

Springer International Publishing AG Switzerland is part of Springer Science+Business Media
(www.springer.com)

Preface

This book is the first book to describe how Autonomous Virtual Humans and Social Robots can interact with real people, be aware of these people and the environment and react to various situations. The book explains the main techniques for the tracking and the analysis of humans and their behaviour including facial expressions, body and hand gestures and sound localization. It explains how the virtual human and the social robot should react at the right time based on the perception they have from the real participants. It describes how to create socially interactive behaviour generation for virtual characters and social robots using the same modalities as human do: verbal, body gestures, facial expressions and gaze. The book also discusses how a virtual human or a social robot can replace a real human in a remote location.

The contributors of this book are international experts in the field. Several of them come from different institutes/schools in Nanyang Technological University (NTU) in Singapore: Institute for Media Innovation, School of Electrical and Electronic Engineering, and School of Art, Design and Media. Three chapters have contributors from the well-known Korea Institute of Science and Technology in Seoul. Other contributors are from France and China. In total, more than 100 researchers have contributed to this book.

This book is partly the result of two large ongoing projects developed in two main centres: the Centre of Human-centred Interaction for Coexistence in Seoul at Korea Institute of Science and Technology (KIST) and the BeingThere Center (BTC) in NTU in Singapore. The research done by the authors in the BeingThere Centre in NTU is supported by the Singapore National Research Foundation under its International Research Centre Funding Initiative and administered by the IDM Programme. The research done at the Korea Institute of Science and Technology (KIST) is supported by the Ministry of Education, Science and Technology in Korea.

Singapore

Nadia Magnenat-Thalmann

Singapore

Junsong Yuan

Singapore

Daniel Thalmann

South Korea

Bum-Jae You

January 2015

Contents

Contributors

Sang Chul Ahn Centre of Human-centred Interaction for Coexistence, Korea Institute of Science and Technology, Seoul, Korea

Aryel Beck BeingThere Centre, Nanyang Technological University, Singapore, Singapore

Junghyun Cho Centre of Human-centred Interaction for Coexistence, Korea Institute of Science and Technology, Seoul, Korea

Heeseung Choi Centre of Human-centred Interaction for Coexistence, Korea Institute of Science and Technology, Seoul, Korea

Xudong Jiang BeingThere Centre, Nanyang Technological University, Singapore, Singapore

Justin Dauwels BeingThere Centre, Nanyang Technological University, Singapore, Singapore

Andy W.H. Khong BeingThere Centre, Nanyang Technological University, Singapore, Singapore

Ig-Jae Kim Centre of Human-centred Interaction for Coexistence, Korea Institute of Science and Technology, Seoul, Korea

Jun Lee BeingThere Centre, Nanyang Technological University, Singapore, Singapore

Sang Hyoung Lee Hanyang University, Seoul, Korea

Sukwon Lee Korea Advanced Institute of Science and Technology, Daejon, Korea

Sung-Hee Lee Korea Advanced Institute of Science and Technology, Daejon, Korea

Samuel Lemercier BeingThere Centre, Nanyang Technological University, Singapore, Singapore

Hui Liang BeingThere Centre, Nanyang Technological University, Singapore, Singapore

Nadia Magnenat-Thalmann BeingThere Centre, Nanyang Technological University, Singapore, Singapore

Constable Martin BeingThere Centre, Nanyang Technological University, Singapore, Singapore

Mengyu Zhou BeingThere Centre, Nanyang Technological University, Singapore, Singapore

Rasheed Umer BeingThere Centre, Nanyang Technological University, Singapore, Singapore

Jianfeng Ren BeingThere Centre, Nanyang Technological University, Singapore, Singapore

Hyewon Seo CNRS-University of Strasbourg, Strasbourg, France

Shoko Dauwels BeingThere Centre, Nanyang Technological University, Singapore, Singapore

Il Hong Suh Hanyang University, Seoul, Korea

Daniel Thalmann BeingThere Centre, Nanyang Technological University, Singapore, Singapore

Kai Wu BeingThere Centre, Nanyang Technological University, Singapore, Singapore

Yang Xiao School of Automation, Huazhong University of Science and Technology, Wuhan, China

Yasir Tahir BeingThere Centre, Nanyang Technological University, Singapore, Singapore

Junsong Yuan BeingThere Centre, Nanyang Technological University, Singapore, Singapore

Zerrin Yumak BeingThere Centre, Nanyang Technological University, Singapore, Singapore

Juzheng Zhang BeingThere Centre, Nanyang Technological University, Singapore, Singapore

Jianmin Zheng BeingThere Centre, Nanyang Technological University, Singapore, Singapore

Zhang Zhijun BeingThere Centre, Nanyang Technological University, Singapore, Singapore

Introduction

Virtual humans have become very popular in the last 15 years, mainly through three-dimensional (3D) movies and games. In movies, they now have very realistic physical and emotional characteristics, including their facial expressions, hair, clothes and motions. In parallel, robotics has made considerable progress and new kinds of robots are available as social companions. Some of them have the appearance of humans. They are physically present, and in case of social robots, we can define them as artificial characters. These social robots share a lot of research in common with Virtual Humans. The high level research on awareness of a situation and the proper reaction to this situation can be addressed by both domains (Virtual Humans and Social robotics).

It is now possible, for example, to replace a real participant in a meeting or an event by its virtual or robotic counterpart. The virtual or robotic counterpart is supposed to give the illusion that the real person is present. This implies that they should look the same as the real human, speaks with the same intonation, and be aware of the real situation, the real participants, and the task currently performed. The virtual human and the robot should react at the right time based on the perception they have from the real participants. It implies to evaluate what each real participant is doing. Perception will be obtained by visual and audio input and recognition. The virtual participant reacts according to the input and its current knowledge. Its reactions encompass animation (body and facial gestures) and speech synthesis.

To tackle the issues on global awareness and proper reactions to real world given situation, the research is focused on three main areas:

- **Tracking of Gestures and Analysis of Real Humans' Behaviour**: This is important as it will give the virtual human and the social robot the capacity to sense and understand what is happening in their environment.
- **Facial and Body Modelling and Animation**: The virtual human or the social robot will need to react and respond appropriately considering the perception of the current situation and the users' state. They should use the same modalities as human does: verbal, body and hand gestures, facial expressions and gaze.

- **Modelling Human Behaviours**: It consists first in modelling personality, mood, and emotion in order to generate the appropriate behaviour; more complex situations correspond to multiple virtual humans interactions and multi-modal and multi-party social interactions.

This book is structured according to these three main research areas and we briefly now summarise the three parts and the corresponding chapters. Part I is dedicated to the analysis and recognition of the situation in order to make the Virtual Human or the Social Robot aware of this situation. First, Chap. 1 addresses the problem of face recognition and facial expression analysis as they are essential abilities of the human and provide the basic visual clues during human–computer interaction. In Chap. 2, it is explained how a social robot or a Virtual Human can understand the meaning of human upper body gestures and express itself by using a combination of body movements, facial expressions and verbal language. It is important to enable the virtual human/social robot such capabilities in order to achieve autonomous behaviour. The human–robot interaction system is based on a novel combination of sensors: the CyberGlove II is employed to capture the hand posture and this feature is combined with the head and arm posture information captured from the Microsoft Kinect. Based on the body posture data, an effective and real-time human gesture recognition method is proposed. Chapter 3 describes how sound source localization and tracking plays an important role in this global analysis of a situation and can support awareness for the virtual human or the social robot. Given the location of a sound, the social robot can be endowed with the capability of sound event awareness, which results in enhanced interaction with human beings.

Part II emphasises the methods for modelling and animating faces and bodies in order to generate the right motion. Chapter 4 is dedicated to conversation, which is clearly important in many applications. It describes the unsolved problem of how the non-verbal component of a conversation might be visualised in a concise yet effective manner that would be suitable for use in a communication skill training scenario. Functionally, conversation serves to deliver and exchange information. However, there is much of a conversation that lays outside of its verbal content yet impacts directly on those involved and in a manner that might be to their detriment or benefit. In Chap. 5, we show that combining 2D images and the range scanned measurement can lead to successful reconstruction results. The quality shape and collective knowledge from scanned dataset has been exploited to efficiently complement the geometric shape recovery from image inputs. More specifically, a set of 3D body scans that are put in correspondence have been used to parameterise the shape space, which we explore in order to find the optimising parameters that best fit the given image data. The aim of Chap. 6 is to give a comprehensive overview of current state-of-the-art parametric methods for realistic facial modelling and animation. Facial modelling is a fundamental technique in a variety of applications in computer graphics, computer vision and pattern recognition areas. As the 3D sensing technologies have been evolved, the quality of facial modelling has been greatly improved. To enhance the modelling quality and controllability of the model further, parametric methods, which represent or manipulate facial attributes (e.g., identity, expression, viseme) with a set of control parameters, have been proposed in recent years. Chapter 7 introduces several learning approaches to generate non-preprogrammed motions for a virtual human. To generate non-preprogrammed motions, a Virtual Human should possess the abilities to: (1) segment a whole movement into meaning segments; (2) learn motion primitives for their adaptation in a changing environment; (3) represent a combination of a motion primitive and its causalities by considering reusability; and finally, (4) swiftly and reasonably select a dependable motion primitive in accordance with current and goal situations. Chapter 8 presents how to generate natural behaviours of Virtual Humans responsive to the physical interaction with the user such as push and pull. These physical interactions play an important role for increasing the level of immersion of the user and lay foundations for more advanced level of interactions. One of the key components for physical interaction is the generation of suitable balancing behaviours of humanoids against user inputs. In Chap. 9, we introduce the concept of shared object manipulation between real and virtual humans. These can be applied to 3D telepresence applications such as computer-aided design and virtual simulation and training. It consists of three different and complex research domains: (1) virtual object grasping methods for intuitive behaviour (2) virtual object manipulation by virtual humans. (3) consistent management of shared objects to avoid conflicts from multiple simultaneous inputs.

The goal of Part III is to present all behavioural aspects of virtual humans and social robots, when they react to real people or to other virtual humans and social robots. Chapter 10 considers affect dynamics which simulates the relation among the emotions, mood and personality and updates emotional states for long-term human-agent interactions. We first examine basic psychological concepts and computational models for affect dynamics. Then we present a psychologically plausible affect dynamics algorithm in which the personality influences the updating of emotional states during the whole interactions. This makes affect dynamics characterised by the personality, which is shown to be important for long-term interactions. Chapter 11 is looking at motion control for the physically realistic robot Nadine. Robot controllers for such robot need to produce behaviours that match the physical realism of the robot. This chapter describes a robot controller that allows such a robot to fully use the same modalities as humans during interaction including speech, facial and bodily expressions. Chapter 12 presents a review about interactions between real and multiple virtual humans with a focus on virtual assistants and social phobia examples. Interactions between virtual humans are then addressed; particularly gaze attention of other characters and navigation interactions between multiple virtual humans. Chapter 13 focused on interaction of virtual characters and robots interacting with people in social contexts with emphasis on multi-modal and multi-party interactions. The challenges in this area are the estimation of high level user states fusing low level multi-modal sensory input, taking socially appropriate decisions using this partial sensory information and rendering synchronised and timely multi-modal behaviours based on taken decisions.

Part I
User Understanding Through Multisensory Perception

Chapter 1
Face and Facial Expressions Recognition and Analysis

Jianfeng Ren, Xudong Jiang and Junsong Yuan

Abstract Face recognition and facial expression analysis are essential abilities of humans, which provide the basic visual clues during human-computer interaction. It is important to enable the virtual human/social robot such capabilities in order to achieve autonomous behavior. Local binary pattern (LBP) has been widely used in face recognition and facial expression analysis. It is popular because of robustness to illumination variation and alignment error. However, local binary pattern still has some limitations, e.g. it is sensitive to image noise. Local ternary pattern (LTP), fuzzy LBP and many other LBP variants partially solve this problem. However, these approaches treat the corrupted image patterns as they are, and do not have an mechanism to recover the underlying patterns. In view of this, we develop a noise-resistant LBP to preserve the image micro-structures in presence of noise. We encode the small pixel difference as an *uncertain* state first, and then determine its value based on the other bits of the LBP code. Most image micro-structures are represented by uniform codes and non-uniform codes mainly represent noise patterns. Therefore, we assign the value of *uncertain* bit so as to form possible uniform codes. In such a way, we develop an error-correction mechanism to recover the distorted image patterns. In addition, we find that some image patterns such as lines are not captured in uniform codes. They represent a set of important local primitives for pattern recognition. We thus define an extended noise-resistant LBP (ENRLBP) to capture line patterns. NRLBP and ENRLBP are validated extensively on face recognition, facial expression analysis and other recognition tasks. They are shown more resistant to image noise compared with LBP, LTP and many other variants. These two approaches greatly enhance the performance of face recognition and facial expression analysis.

J. Ren (✉) · X. Jiang · J. Yuan
BeingThere Centre, Nanyang Technological University, Singapore, Singapore
e-mail: JFREN@ntu.edu.sg

X. Jiang
e-mail: EXDJiang@ntu.edu.sg

J. Yuan
e-mail: JSYUAN@ntu.edu.sg

© Springer International Publishing Switzerland 2016
N. Magnenat-Thalmann et al. (eds.), *Context Aware Human-Robot and Human-Agent Interaction*, Human–Computer Interaction Series,
DOI 10.1007/978-3-319-19947-4_1

1.1 Introduction

Humans can easily recognize the identity of other people through face images. In fact, face recognition provides an important visual clue for human–computer interaction. It enables the virtual human/social robot to have essential optical capabilities, i.e., to recognize who it is talking to. Then the virtual human/social robot can associate the identity with other information stored in its memory, and enable other high-level interactions. Face recognition is built into the human system as a functional module that provides the user's identity.

In addition to recognizing faces, humans also easily recognize the facial expressions of others. By analyzing facial expressions, we can understand the emotional mood of people and act accordingly. Thus, it is desirable to enable the virtual human/social robots to recognize the facial expressions of a user, determine the emotional state, and act accordingly to achieve autonomous behavior. Facial expression recognition is thus built into our system as a functional module to analyze the user's emotion.

Traditionally, holistic features were used in visual recognition, which were derived by vectorizing raw-image pixels. However, the performance of these approaches is often limited by rigorous image alignment and high computational cost. Recently, LBP has become one of the most popular feature representations in visual recognition. The LBP operator transforms an image into an array or image of integer labels describing a micropattern, i.e., a pattern formed by a pixel and its immediate neighbors [32]. More specifically, LBP encodes the signs of the pixel differences between a pixel and its neighboring pixels to a binary code. The histogram of such codes in an image block is commonly used for further analysis. The popularity of this method is due to the following advantages. First, the exact intensities are discarded, and only the relative intensities with respect to the center are preserved; thus, LBP is less sensitive to illumination variations. Second, by extracting the histogram of micropatterns in a patch, the exact location information is discarded and only the patchwise location information is preserved. Thus, LBP is robust to alignment error. Lastly, LBP features can be extracted efficiently, which enables real-time image analysis.

Despite its success, the sensitivity to image noise limits the performance of LBP features [40]. Typically in a smooth image region, a small image variation may change an LBP bit from 0 to 1, or vice versa, and hence alter the LBP code significantly. In [31], uniform LBP was proposed to reduce the noise in the LBP histogram. Most LBPs in natural images are uniform patterns [1, 31]. Nonuniform patterns are statistically insignificant, and hence noise-prone. By grouping the nonuniform patterns into one label, the noise in nonuniform patterns is suppressed. In [5, 25, 28, 43, 50], information in nonuniform patterns is extracted and used for classification. "Soft histogram" [2, 16, 39] is another approach to improve robustness to noise. Instead of hard-coding the pixel difference, a probability measure is used to represent its likelihood as 0 or 1. However, the probability is closely related to the magnitude of the pixel difference, thus, it is still sensitive to noise. Local ternary pattern (LTP) was proposed in [40] to tackle the image noise in uniform regions. Instead of binary code, the pixel difference is encoded as a 3-valued code according to a threshold t. Then, the ternary code is split into a positive LBP and a negative LBP in order to reduce the dimensionality. LTP showed to be less sensitive to noise, especially in uniform regions [40]. Subsequently, many LTP variants [3, 10, 13, 21, 22, 27] were proposed in the literature. LBP and its variants partially solve the noise-sensitive problem; however, they lack the mechanism to recover corrupted image patterns. In this chapter, we propose a noise-resistant LBP (NRLBP) and an extended noise-resistant LBP (ENRLBP) to address this issue.

The signs of pixel differences used to compute LBP and its variants are vulnerable to noise when they are small. Thus, we propose to encode small pixel difference as an *uncertain* bit first and then determine its value based on the other bits of the LBP code. Uniform patterns are more likely to occur as against nonuniform patterns in natural images [1, 31]. Most image structures are represented by uniform patterns, while nonuniform patterns are most likely caused by noise. Thus, in NRLBP, the values of *uncertain* bits are assigned to form uniform patterns. A nonuniform pattern is generated only if no uniform pattern can be formed. As noise may change a uniform pattern into an unstable nonuniform pattern, NRLBP corrects many distorted nonuniform patterns to uniform patterns.

For LBP and LTP, line patterns are treated as nonuniform patterns and grouped into the nonuniform bin. Uniform patterns mainly represent spot, flat region, edge, edge end, and corner. A local image is a line pattern if it is a line against the background, as shown in Fig. 1.6. Line patterns may appear less frequently than uniform patterns, but they represent an important group of local primitives for pattern recognition. Thus, we propose an extended set of uniform patterns corresponding to line patterns. Then, we propose extended noise-resistant LBP (ENRLBP). During the encoding process, we assign the values of *uncertain* bits so as to form extended uniform patterns.

To evaluate NRLBP, we first inject Gaussian noise and uniform noise of different levels on the AR database [24] for face recognition and facial expression recognition. NRLBP and ENRLBP demonstrate strong resistance to noise compared with LBP/LTP and its variants. They are further compared with LBP/LTP variants for face recognition on the extended Yale database [8, 18] and the O2FN database [33]. NRLBP and ENRLBP consistently achieve better performance.

1.2 Literature Review

LBP and its variants have been widely used in many recognition applications, e.g., facial analysis [1, 34, 37, 40], texture classification [9, 20, 25, 31], dynamic texture recognition [35, 47, 49], human detection [26, 42], scene classification [36, 43, 44] and others [14, 22, 38]. LBP encodes the relative pixel difference of the neighboring pixels to the central pixels, e.g., $LBP_{P,R}$ denotes the LBP code of P neighbors at a distance of R. Denote the gray level of the center pixel by i_c, and the gray level of the circular neighbors by i_p, where $p = 0, 1, \ldots, P - 1$. The LBP code for pixel (x, y)

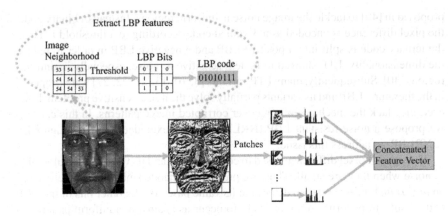

Fig. 1.1 Block diagram of LBP encoding process

is obtained as

$$LBP_{P,R}(x, y) = \sum_{p=0}^{P-1} s(i_p - i_c)2^p,$$ (1.1)

where $s(z)$ is the threshold function

$$s(z) = \begin{cases} 1 & \text{if } z \geq 0, \\ 0 & \text{if } z < 0. \end{cases}$$ (1.2)

The histogram of these codes is then used for further analysis. The block diagram of LBP encoding process is shown in Fig. 1.1. The image is first encoded as an LBP image that is divided into patches, and one LBP histogram is extracted from each patch. Finally, the LBP histograms of all patches are concatenated to form the final feature vector.

Despite its wide applications, the LBP feature still has some limitations, i.e., it is sensitive to image noise. A small image variation will alter the LBP bit from 0 to 1 or vice versa, and hence alter the code significantly. Many approaches have been proposed to address this issue, which are grouped into the following four categories.

1.2.1 Uniform LBP

It is shown in [1, 31] that most LBP codes in a natural image are uniform codes. An LBP code is defined as a uniform pattern if it has at most two circularly bit-wise transitions from 0 to 1 or vice versa, and nonuniform patterns if otherwise. For example, "11000000" is a uniform code, while "11001100" is a nonuniform code.

For $LBP_{8,2}$, there are 58 uniform codes and 198 nonuniform codes. Uniform patterns are statistically more significant and their occurrence probabilities can be more reliably estimated. By contrast, nonuniform patterns are statistically less insignificant, and hence noise-prone and unreliable. In uniform LBP mapping [31], one separate histogram bin is used for each uniform pattern and all nonuniform patterns are accumulated in a single bin. By grouping the nonuniform patterns into one label, the noise in nonuniform patterns is suppressed, while at the same time the number of patterns is reduced significantly.

In [5, 25, 28, 43, 50], information in nonuniform patterns is extracted and also used for classification. Liao et al. proposed a dominant LBP (DLBP) that considers the most frequently occurred patterns in a texture image [25]. This is based on the observation that some nonuniform codes may have higher occurrence frequency than uniform codes. Instead of being based on image microstructures [31], DLBP chooses LBP codes based on occurrence frequency directly. Zhou et al. [50] and Fathi et al. [5] proposed to extract information from nonuniform patterns based on pattern uniformity measure and the number of 1 s in the LBP codes. Principal component analysis [43] and random subspace approach [28] were used to extract information from the whole LBP histogram, including both uniform and nonuniform patterns. These approaches can extract discriminant information from the nonuniform codes. However, as the nonuniform codes may contain noise, these approaches tend to be sensitive to noise.

1.2.2 Fuzzy LBP

"Soft histogram" is another approach to improve the robustness to noise. Instead of hard-coding the pixel difference as shown in Eq. (1.2), a probability measure is used to represent its likelihood as 0 or 1. In [2, 16], a fuzzy LBP (FLBP) using piecewise linear fuzzy membership function was proposed that replaces $s(z)$ with two fuzzy membership functions:

$$f^1(z, d) = \begin{cases} 0 & \text{if } z < -d, \\ 0.5 + 0.5z/d & \text{if } -d \leq z \leq d, \\ 1 & \text{if } z > d. \end{cases} \tag{1.3}$$

$$f^0(z, d) = 1 - f^1(z, d). \tag{1.4}$$

The parameter d controls the amount of fuzzfication. $f^1(z, d)$ and $f^0(z, d)$ represent the probability that the pixel difference z is encoded as 1 and 0, respectively. When constructing the LBP histogram, we calculate the probabilities of all patterns as

$$P_j = \prod_{i=0}^{P-1} c_i f_i^1(z, d) + (1 - c_i) f_i^0(z, d), \tag{1.5}$$

where $j = \sum_{i=0}^{P-1} c_i \times 2^i$ and c_i is ith bit of the code. For example, the probability of "11001100" is calculated as $P_{11001100} = f_7^1 f_6^1 f_5^0 f_4^0 f_3^1 f_2^1 f_1^0 f_0^0$, where f_i^b is the probability of bit i to be encoded as $b \in \{0, 1\}$. The complete histogram is derived by summing the contributions of all pixels in an image patch.

Another fuzzy LBP uses Gaussian-like membership function [39], which is defined as

$$f^1(x, \sigma) = \begin{cases} 1 - 0.5e^{-x^2/\sigma^2} & \text{if } x \geq 0, \\ 0.5e^{-x^2/\sigma^2} & \text{if } x < 0, \end{cases} \tag{1.6}$$

$$f^0(x, \sigma) = 1 - f^1(x, \sigma), \tag{1.7}$$

where $x = (i_p - i_c)/i_c$ and σ controls the amount of fuzzfication. A comprehensive comparison between LBP and fuzzy LBP in classifying and segmenting textures can be found in [17].

When the original LBP operator is used, one pixel only contributes to one histogram bin. In fuzzy LBP, one pixel typically contributes to more than one bin. The contributions of a pixel to all bins always sum to 1. Using fuzzy LBP, a small change in the input image causes only a small change in the histogram. Thus, it is robust to image noise to a certain extent. However, the probability measures defined in Eqs. (1.3) and (1.6) are closely related to the magnitude of the pixel difference. Thus, it is still sensitive to noise.

1.2.3 LTP and Its Variants

The LBP code is sensitive to noise, especially in a near-constant image region. In LTP [40], the pixel difference z between a pixel and its neighbors is encoded by three values (1, 0 or -1) according to a threshold t, i.e.,

$$s_T(z) = \begin{cases} 1 & \text{if } z > t, \\ 0 & \text{if } -t \leq z \leq t, \\ -1 & \text{if } z < -t. \end{cases} \tag{1.8}$$

State "0" is used to handle the small image variations, i.e., if the difference is within the threshold t, it is encoded as state "0". These small variations are treated separately. Thus, LTP is less sensitive to noise. However, the LTP histogram is of high dimensionality, e.g., $LTP_{8,2}$ will exhibit a histogram of $3^8 = 6561$ bins. To reduce the dimensionality, the ternary pattern is split into a positive LBP code and a negative LBP code in [40].

Subsequently, many LTP variants were proposed in the literature. Nanni et al. proposed a quinary code of five values according to two thresholds [27]:

$$s_q(z) = \begin{cases} 2 & \text{if } z \geq t_2, \\ 1 & \text{if } t_1 \leq z < t_2, \\ 0 & \text{if } -t_1 \leq z < t_1, \\ -1 & \text{if } -t_2 \leq z < -t_1, \\ -2 & \text{if } z < -t_2, \end{cases} \tag{1.9}$$

where t_1, t_2 are two thresholds and $t_1 < t_2$. Then the quinary code is split into four binary codes, analogous to LTP. As LTP is not invariant under scaling of intensity values, Liao et al. proposed scale-invariant local ternary pattern (SILTP) to deal with the gray scale intensity changes in a complex background [22]. To reduce the high dimensionality of LTP, center-symmetric LTP (CSLTP) was proposed in [10]. Instead of using the pixel differences between the neighboring pixels and the central pixel, the pixel differences between diagonal neighbors are calculated. In local adaptive ternary patterns (LATP) [3] and extended LTP (ELTP) [21], instead of using a constant threshold, the threshold is calculated for each window using local statistics, which makes them less sensitive to illumination variations. In local triplet pattern [13], the equality is modeled as a separate state, and a tri-state pattern is formulated. It can be viewed as a special case of LTP [40].

To improve the robustness to noise, other thresholding and encoding techniques have been proposed. Instead of comparing with the center pixel, Hafiane et al. proposed median binary pattern (MBP) by thresholding the local pixel values against the median value within the local neighborhood [11]. In improved LBP [6], the neighboring pixels are thresholded against the mean intensity of the local neighborhood. Trefny and Matas [41] proposed two new encoding schemes: binary value transition coded LBP (tLBP) using the pixel differences of neighbors in clockwise direction and direction coded LBP (dLBP) encoding the second-order pixel differences. In centralized binary pattern (CBP) [7], the average intensity within the neighborhood is compared to the center pixel and added as an LBP bit. To reduce the sensitivity to noise, a Bayesian LBP (BLBP) was developed by He et al. [12]. It is formulated in a filtering, labeling, and statistic (FLS) framework, in which the labeling procedure is modeled as an optimization process.

1.2.4 Preprocessing

Image preprocessing techniques can also improve the robustness of LBP to image noise. Gabor filtering is often used before extracting LBP feature, as LBP captures image microstructures and Gabor filters encode image information on a large scale. Zhang et al. [46] proposed to extract LBP features from 40 Gabor-filtered images, known as local gabor binary patterns (LGBP). It has been used as a benchmark method in many recent face recognition studies, whose drawback however is its high dimensionality. Tan and Triggs [40] proposed an image preprocessing framework that consists of gamma correction, difference of Gaussian (DoG) filtering, masking (optional), and equalization of variations. Used with LTP, it has demonstrated superior performance in face recognition.

To tackle the small image variations in a near-constant region, Yao and Chen [45] proposed local edge patterns (LEP) for color texture retrieval, in which the Sobel edge detection is used to suppress the small image variations in the near-constant region, and LBP-like feature is extracted on the filtered image. Similar ideas have been used in [15] for shape localization and in [48] for facial image representation. Li et al. [19] proposed to extract LBP features from multiscale heat kernels, which capture the intrinsic topological structural information of face appearance. In [23], LBP features are extracted from curvelet-transformed images for medical image analysis.

1.2.5 Discussion

Although previous approaches partially solve the noise-sensitivity problem, they treat corrupted LBP patterns as they are, and lack the mechanism to recover the underlying patterns. In the following section, we present our noise-resistant LBP with an embedded error-correction mechanism that better handles image noise.

1.3 Noise-Resistant Local Binary Patterns

1.3.1 Problem Analysis of LBP and LTP

LBP encodes the pixel difference $z_p = i_p - i_c$ between the neighboring pixel i_p and the central pixel i_c. Let $C_{P,R}^B = \overrightarrow{b_{P-1}^B b_{P-2}^B \cdots b_1^B b_0^B}$ denote the LBP code of P neighbors at distance R to the center pixel. A code is also called a pattern. Let $LBP_{P,R}$ denote such a coding scheme for $C_{P,R}^B$. Each bit is obtained as in Eq. (1.2).

LBP is widely used in many applications because of its simplicity and robustness to illumination variations; its drawback is it is sensitive to image noise. In [31], uniform LBP was proposed to capture fundamental image structures and reduce the noise in an LBP histogram. The uniformity U is defined as the number of circularly bitwise transitions from 0 to 1 or vice versa. An LBP is $u2$-uniform or simply called uniform if $U \leq 2$. For example, "11110000" is a uniform pattern as $U = 2$, while "01010111" shown in Fig. 1.2a is a nonuniform pattern as $U = 6$. $LBP_{P,R}^{u2}$ indicates a coding and histogram mapping scheme in which $u2$-uniform LBP codes of P neighbors at the distance of R to the center pixel are used. Uniform patterns occur much more frequently than nonuniform patterns in natural images. It has been shown

Fig. 1.2 **a** An example of LBP encoding scheme for the smooth region with small image noise. LBP is sensitive to image noise. **b** An example of LTP encoding process. LTP doubles the number of patterns compared with LBP

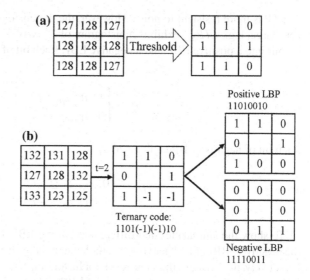

that $LBP_{8,1}^{u2}$ accounts for almost 90 % of all patterns for texture images [31] while $LBP_{8,2}^{u2}$ accounts for 90.6 % for facial images [1]. The occurrence probabilities of nonuniform patterns are so small that they cannot be reliably estimated [31]. Inclusion of such noisy estimates in the histogram would harm the classification performance. In addition, nonuniform patterns may be caused by the image noise. Therefore, when constructing the histogram, all nonuniform patterns are grouped into one bin. This not only reduces feature dimensionality, but more importantly, the noise due to unreliable estimates of nonuniform patterns is greatly suppressed. The number of patterns is reduced significantly from 2^P to $P(P-1)+3$. For example, $LBP_{8,2}$ consists of 256 patterns, while $LBP_{8,2}^{u2}$ has only 59 patterns.

Uniform LBP successfully reduces noise in the LBP histogram, though it is still sensitive to image noise. As shown in Fig. 1.2a, a small noise will cause the pixel difference to be encoded differently. Ideally such a smooth region should be encoded as "11111111," but owing to image noise it is encoded as "01010111" instead. LTP partially solves this problem by encoding the small pixel difference into a third state [40]. Instead of using binary code, each pixel difference is encoded as a 3-valued code. Let $C_{P,R}^T = \overrightarrow{b_{P-1}^T b_{P-2}^T \cdots b_1^T b_0^T}$ denote the LTP code of P neighbors at distance R to the center pixel and $LTP_{P,R}$ denote such a coding scheme for $C_{P,R}^T$. Each bit is obtained as

$$b_p^T = \begin{cases} 1 & \text{if } z_p \geq t, \\ 0 & \text{if } |z_p| < t, \\ -1 & \text{if } z_p \leq -t, \end{cases} \tag{1.10}$$

where t is a predefined threshold.

LTP is more resistant to noise. However, the dimensionality of LTP histogram is very large, e.g., $LTP_{8,2}$ exhibits a histogram of $3^8 = 6561$ bins. Thus, in [40], LTP is split into a positive LBP and a negative LBP. Each bit of positive LBP is obtained as

$$b_p^p = \begin{cases} 1 & \text{if } z_p \geq t, \\ 0 & \text{if } z_p < t. \end{cases} \tag{1.11}$$

Each bit of negative LBP is obtained as

$$b_p^n = \begin{cases} 0 & \text{if } z_p \leq -t, \\ 1 & \text{if } z_p > -t. \end{cases} \tag{1.12}$$

To show the similarities and differences among LBP, LTP, and NRLBP clearly, the negative LBP defined here is the complement of the negative LBP defined in [40]. Effectively, they achieve the same result for histogram-based comparison. Eventually, LTP is treated as two separate channels of LBP codes: one channel for positive LBP and the other for negative LBP. In general, uniform LTP is used in which both channels are uniform LBP. This coding scheme is denoted as $LTP_{P,R}^{u2}$. An example of LTP encoding process is shown in Fig. 1.2b. LTP doubles the number of patterns compared to LBP.

The small pixel difference may be easily distorted by noise. Both LBP and LTP lack the mechanism to correct the corrupted patterns. The corrupted image patterns are treated without any attempt to recover the underlining local structures. To address this issue, we propose a noise-resistant LBP and an extended noise-resistant LBP.

1.3.2 Noise-Resistant LBP

LBP is sensitive to noise. Even a small noise may change the LBP code significantly. Thus, we propose to encode the small pixel difference as an *uncertain* bit X first and then determine X based on other certain bits of the LBP code. As regards the pixel difference z_p between the neighboring pixel and the central pixel, we encode it into one of the three states b_p^N as

$$b_p^N = \begin{cases} 1 & \text{if } z_p \geq t, \\ X & \text{if } |z_p| < t, \\ 0 & \text{if } z_p \leq -t. \end{cases} \tag{1.13}$$

States *1* and *0* represent two strong states where the pixel difference is almost definitely positive and negative, respectively. Noise can unlikely change them from *0* to *1* or from *1* to *0*. State X represents an *uncertain* state where the pixel difference is small. A small pixel difference is vulnerable to noise if we only take its sign. More specifically, noise can easily change its LBP bit from *0* to *1* or vice versa. Therefore, we encode it as an *uncertain* state regardless of its sign.

Then, we constrain the value of the *uncertain* bit into either 0 or 1, represented by a variable x_i, $x_i \in \{0, 1\}$. Let $\mathbf{X} = (x_1, x_2, \ldots, x_n)$ denote the vector formed by n variables of a code. $\mathbf{X} \in \{0, 1\}^n$. The *uncertain* code can be represented by $C(\mathbf{X})$ as

$$\overrightarrow{b_{P-1}^N b_{P-2}^N \cdots b_1^N b_0^N} = C(\mathbf{X}). \tag{1.14}$$

Take the *uncertain* code "11X100X0" in Fig. 1.3a as illustration. The *uncertain* code $\overrightarrow{11x_2100x_10}$ can be viewed as a function of $\mathbf{X} = \{x_1, x_2\}$.

After we derive the *uncertain* code, we determine the *uncertain* bits based on the values of the other certain bits to form one or more codes of image local structures. Uniform patterns represent local primitives, including spot, flat, edge, edge end, and corner. They appear more often than nonuniform patterns in natural images. Since uniform patterns occur more likely than nonuniform ones, we assign the values of *uncertain* bits $\mathbf{X}$ so as to form possible uniform LBP codes. A nonuniform pattern is generated only if no uniform pattern can be formed. Take Fig. 1.3b as an example. We determine the *uncertain* bit of *uncertain* code "11X1X0X0" so as to form only uniform patterns, e.g., "11110000" and "11111000."

Mathematically, let Φ_u denote the collection of all uniform LBP codes. For $LBP_{8,2}^{u2}$, Φ_u consists of 58 uniform codes. Based on the *uncertain* code $C(\mathbf{X})$, a set of the NRLBP codes are obtained as

$$S_{NRLBP} = \{C(\mathbf{X})|\mathbf{X} \in \{0, 1\}^n, C(\mathbf{X}) \in \Phi_u\} \tag{1.15}$$

Now let us construct the histogram of NRLBP for a local image patch. Let m denote the number of elements in S_{NRLBP}. If $m > 0$, the bin corresponding to each element in S_{NRLBP} will be added by $1/m$. After all, all these patterns originate from one *uncertain* code. If $m = 0$, the nonuniform bin will be added by 1. This process is repeated for every pixel in the patch. Algorithm 1 summarizes the process.

Algorithm 1 Histogram construction for NRLBP

---

for Every pixel in a patch **do**
  1. Derive the *uncertain* code $C(\mathbf{X})$ as in Eqs. (1.13), (1.14).
  3. Search *uncertain* bits $\mathbf{X}$ in the space $\{0, 1\}^n$ so that $C(\mathbf{X})$ forms uniform LBP codes as in Eq. (1.15).
  4. Construct the histogram.
  if $m = 0$ **then**
    Accumulate the nonuniform bin with 1.
  else
    Accumulate the bin of each pattern in S_{NRLBP} with $1/m$.
  end if
end for

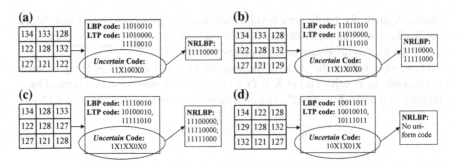

Fig. 1.3 Illustration of encoding process of NRLTP and comparison with LBP and LTP. **a–c** correspond to $m = 1, 2, 3$ resulting in NRLBP codes, respectively. **d** shows an example that no uniform code can be formed. NRLBP is significantly different from LBP and LTP. Threshold t is chosen as 2 for LTP and NRLBP in this figure. **a** $m = 1$, **b** $m = 2$, **c** $m = 3$, **d** $m = 0$

Now we compare NRLBP with LBP and LTP with examples. We consider the cases that different number of LBP codes are derived in S_{NRLBP}. Image patterns in Fig. 1.3a–c generate $m = 1, 2, 3$ NRLBP codes, respectively. Figure 1.3d shows an example where no uniform code can be formed for NRLBP. The corresponding LBP and LTP codes are also given. For LTP, the positive and negative LBPs are accumulated in two different histograms, while for LBP and NRLBP, the codes are accumulated in one histogram.

As noise may change a uniform image pattern into an unstable nonuniform pattern, NRLBP corrects such a code back to uniform code. As shown in Fig. 1.3a, the LBP code is "11010010," which may be distorted by noise. NRLBP first derives the *uncertain* code "11X100X0," and then determines its *uncertain* bits by forming the uniform code "11110000." This can be viewed as an error-correction mechanism. Note that we only attempt such an error correction on *uncertain* bits; we do not attempt to correct the nonuniform patterns that result from two strong states. Similarly, we can observe such an error-correction process in Fig. 1.3b, c. In these two cases, more than one NRLBP code is generated.

NRLBP corrects noisy nonuniform patterns back to uniform pattern. Figure 1.4 shows the histograms of LBP, LTP, and NRLBP for the image shown in Fig. 1.8g. The threshold t is chosen as 10 for LTP and NRLBP. The LTP histogram is the concatenation of the positive and negative LBP histograms. The last bin of each histogram corresponds to nonuniform patterns, while other bins correspond to uniform patterns. Clearly, compared with the LBP and LTP histograms, nonuniform patterns in the NRLBP histogram are reduced significantly from about 35 % to about 10 % only. NRLBP corrects a large amount of nonuniform patterns that are corrupted by noise back to uniform patterns.

NRLBP is different from LBP and LTP in many other aspects, besides the capability of noise resistance and error-correction. The LBP code is that of the NRLBP code set if it is uniform. The only exception is that the LBP code is nonuniform and is corrected back to uniform code in NRLBP. Compared with LTP, the treatment of *uncertain* state is totally different for NRLBP. For LTP, all *uncertain* bits are set to

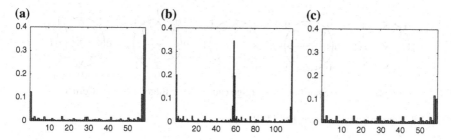

Fig. 1.4 The histograms of LBP, LTP, and NRLBP for the image shown in Fig. 1.8g. The LTP histogram is a concatenation of the positive and negative LBP histograms. The last bin of each histogram corresponds to nonuniform patterns. Compared with the LBP and LTP histograms, NRLBP significantly reduces nonuniform patterns from about 35 % to about 10 %. NRLBP corrects a large amount of noisy nonuniform patterns back to uniform patterns. **a** LBP histogram. **b** LTP histogram. **c** NRLBP histogram

0 for positive half and 1 for negative half as shown in Fig. 1.3, whereas for NRLBP, we do not hurry for a decision on the *uncertain* bits. We treat them as if they could be encoded as 1 and/or 0, and determine their values based on the other bits of code. Mathematically, for LTP, $\mathbf{X} \in \{0\}^n$ for positive half and $\mathbf{X} \in \{1\}^n$ for negative half, whereas $\mathbf{X} \in \{0, 1\}^n$ for NRLBP. The number of histogram bins is also different. The LTP histogram consists of 118 bins, while the NRLBP histogram has only 59 bins.

For implementation, a lookup table from the *uncertain* code to the feature vector of NRLBP histogram can be precomputed. Then, the feature vector of local image patch can be easily obtained by summing up the feature vector of each pixel in this image patch.

1.3.3 Extended Noise-Resistant LBP

The local primitives represented by uniform LBP mainly consist of spots, flat region, edges, edge ends, and corners [32], as shown in Fig. 1.5. However, a large group of local primitives are totally discarded, e.g., lines patterns, as shown in Fig. 1.6. Although these patterns may not appear as frequently as uniform patterns, they represent an important group of local primitives that may be crucial for recognition tasks. Grouping them with other nonuniform patterns into one bin may result in information loss. Therefore, we introduce an extended set of uniform patterns to preserve line patterns. Of all possible line patterns, diagonal lines appear less frequently. In order to keep the feature vector compact, we only choose nearly horizontal or vertical lines.

Let α denote the angle of the line away from the horizontal line. If $\alpha \in [0, 30°)$ or $\alpha \in (150°, 180°]$, it is considered a horizontal line. If $\alpha \in [60°, 120°]$, it is considered a vertical line. If $\alpha \in [30°, 60°)$ or $\alpha \in (120°, 150°]$, it is considered a

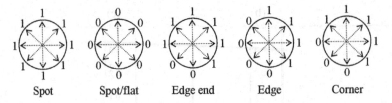

| Spot | Spot/flat | Edge end | Edge | Corner |

Fig. 1.5 Local primitives detected by $LBP_{8,2}^{u2}$

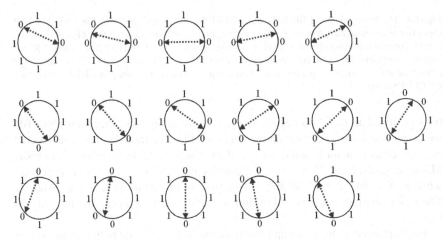

Fig. 1.6 Samples of line patterns. The three rows correspond to *horizontal*, *diagonal*, and *vertical lines*. The *diagonal lines* are rare patterns for natural images and hence are discarded. The remaining *horizontal* and *vertical lines* are the extended set of uniform patterns

diagonal line. Figure 1.6 shows some samples of horizontal, diagonal, and vertical lines.

The extended set of uniform patterns consist of 48 patterns. In addition to 58 uniform patterns, we derive the extended uniform patterns. Analogous to NRLBP, we can derive the extended NRLBP (ENRLBP). Instead of forming uniform patterns we form extended uniform patterns as our ENRLBP pattern. In such a way, line patterns are preserved during the encoding process. The number of bins of ENRLBP histogram is 107, which is smaller than the LTP histogram which has 118 bins.

1.3.4 Applications on Face and Facial Expression Recognition

NRLBP and ENRLBP can be used for many recognition tasks. Here, we focus on the applications on face and facial expression recognition. The block diagram for the face recognition system is shown in Fig. 1.7.

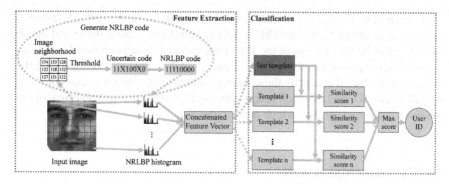

Fig. 1.7 Block diagram for face recognition system

The system consists of two parts: feature extraction and classification. Before feature extraction, we first geometrically normalize an image based on two eye locations so that the two eyes are in the same locations for all images. This typically involves rotation, scaling, and translation of the image. Then we divide the image into patches. One NRLBP histogram is extracted from each patch using Algorithm 1. The histograms of all patches are concatenated to form the final feature vector.

For classification, we use the nearest-neighbor (NN) classifier with three different distance measures: Chi-square distance, histogram intersection distance, and G-statistic as defined in Eqs. (1.16)–(1.18), respectively.

$$\chi^2(\mathbf{x}, \mathbf{y}) = \sum_{i,j} \frac{(x_{i,j} - y_{i,j})^2}{x_{i,j} + y_{i,j}}, \tag{1.16}$$

$$\mathbf{D}_{HI}(\mathbf{x}, \mathbf{y}) = -\sum_{i,j} min(x_{i,j}, y_{i,j}), \tag{1.17}$$

$$\mathbf{D}_G(\mathbf{x}, \mathbf{y}) = -\sum_{i,j} x_{i,j} \log y_{i,j}, \tag{1.18}$$

where $\mathbf{x}, \mathbf{y}$ are the concatenated LBP feature vectors of two image samples; $x_{i,j}$ and $y_{i,j}$ are jth dimension of ith patch. The G-statistic is numerically unstable, as many histogram bins may have zero elements, which easily causes $D_G \rightarrow inf$. Thus, we modify it into a numerically stable form

$$\mathbf{D}_G(\mathbf{x}, \mathbf{y}) = -\sum_{i,j} x_{i,j} \log(x_{i,j} + y_{i,j}), \tag{1.19}$$

Only when both $x_{i,j}$ and $y_{i,j}$ are zero, we set $0 \log(0) = 0$. We call this distance measure as modified G-statistic (MG). MG is numerically more stable and hence can better handle the problem of too few elements in the histogram than G-statistic.

For facial expression recognition, we use a similar approach, i.e., the NRLBP features are extracted in exactly the same way as face recognition. For classification, instead of user ID, we label each image with facial expressions. The objective of the classification is to determine which facial expression it is.

1.4 Experimental Results

We conducted extensive experiments to validate the advantages of NRLBP and ENRLBP. Table 1.1 summarizes the approaches compared with the classifiers used and the applications tested. NRLBP and ENRLBP are compared with uniform LBP and uniform LTP, i.e., $LBP_{8,2}^{u2}$ and $LTP_{8,2}^{u2}$ are used. Let $NRLBP_{P,R}$, $ENRLBP_{P,R}$ denote the coding schemes for NRLBP and ENRLBP using P neighbors at distance R to the center pixel, respectively. The number of features for each patch is 59 for $LBP_{8,2}^{u2}$, 118 for $LTP_{8,2}^{u2}$, 59 for $NRLBP_{8,2}$, and 107 for $ENRLBP_{8,2}$. Dominant LBP (DLBP) [25], novel extended LBP (NELBP) [50], and noise tolerant LBP (NTLBP) [5] are compared as they extract information from nonuniform bins, analogous to our approaches. We choose the dominant patterns that account for 80 % of the total pattern occurrences, same as in [25]. Fuzzy LBP (FLBP) [2, 16, 17] is also compared. We implement fuzzy LBP using piecewise linear fuzzy membership function in [2].

We conducted comparitive experiments for various applications. First, we injected Gaussian and uniform noise of various noise levels onto images of the AR database [24] for face recognition and the Outex-13 dataset [30] for texture recognition. NRLBP and ENRLBP are compared with various LBP/LTP variants in order to val-

Table 1.1 Summary of the approaches compared with the classifiers used and the application tested

The approaches	The classifier	The applications
LBP [29]	Nearest-neighbor classifier + Chi-square distance	Facial expression recognition on the AR database [24]
LTP [40]	Nearest-neighbor classifier + histogram intersection distance	Face recognition on the AR database [24]
Dominant LBP [25]	Nearest-neighbor classifier + modified G-statistic	Face recognition on the extended Yale B database [8, 18]
Fuzzy LBP [2, 16, 17]		Face recognition on the O2FN database [33]
Novel extended LBP [50]		
Noise tolerant LBP [5]		

idate their noise-resistance property. Then we apply them to real images that are noise-prone. Illumination variation is one of the challenges in face recognition. We conducted experiments on two challenging face databases with large illumination variations: the extended Yale B database [8, 18] and the O2FN database [33]. They are compared with LBP/LTP variants for protein cellular classification on the 2D Hela database [4] and image segmentation on the image of the Outex segmentation database [30] and one image from the Web. In order to reduce illumination variations, the images of the Outex-13 dataset, the extended Yale B database, and the O2FN database are preprocessed similarly as in [40]. We use the source codes provided by the authors of [40] to perform this photometric normalization.

1.4.1 Facial Expression Recognition on the AR Database

On the AR database [24], NRLBP and ENRLBP are compared with LBP/LTP variants on images injected with noise in order to demonstrate their noise-resistant property. The AR database is of high resolution and high image quality, and is considered as a face database with almost no image noise. We choose 75 subjects, where each subject contains images from two sections. Each section contains images of four different facial expressions: neutral, smile, anger, and scream, as shown in Fig. 1.8. We use the images of the first section as the gallery set and the images of the second section as the probe set. Gaussian noise is one of the most common types of noise. We normalize the images in the range of (0, 1), and then apply additive Gaussian noise with zero mean and standard derivation of σ. We conduct experiments for

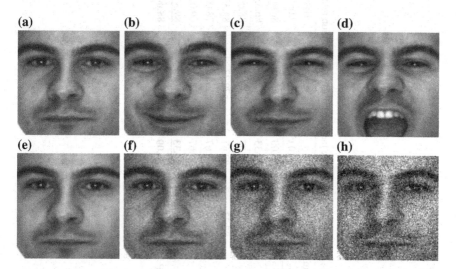

Fig. 1.8 *First row* shows images with different facial expressions. *Second row* shows images with additive Gaussian noise of $\sigma = 0, 0.05, 0.1, 0.15$, respectively. **a** Neutral. **b** Smile. **c** Anger. **d** Scream. **e** $\rho = 0$. **f** $\rho = 0.05$. **g** $\rho = 0.10$. **h** $\rho = 0.15$

Table 1.2 Summary of the average facial expression recognition rate of each approach at optimal setting on the AR database injected with Gaussian noise

Algorithm	χ^2 Distance, $\sigma =$			Histogram intersection, $\sigma =$			Modified G-statistic, $\sigma =$		
	0.05 (%)	0.10 (%)	0.15 (%)	0.05 (%)	0.10 (%)	0.15 (%)	0.05 (%)	0.10 (%)	0.15 (%)
LBP	85.33	76.00	63.67	86.00	74.00	58.00	83.33	69.00	50.67
LTP	87.33	79.33	72.00	86.33	78.00	69.00	86.67	74.00	62.67
DLBP	86.33	79.67	67.67	88.00	78.67	67.67	88.00	79.33	65.00
FLBP	87.33	83.67	79.33	86.33	83.67	**79.00**	87.00	84.00	79.67
NELBP	79.00	63.67	46.67	78.00	61.67	44.67	79.00	59.67	41.00
NTLBP	80.67	53.67	40.67	80.00	61.67	45.33	79.00	54.33	37.67
NRLBP	**88.67**	**86.33**	**81.00**	**89.33**	**85.67**	**79.67**	**88.67**	**86.33**	**80.67**
ENRLBP	**89.00**	86.00	80.33	88.00	85.67	78.67	**89.33**	**86.67**	**82.67**

$\sigma = 0.05, 0.10, 0.15$. The samples of noisy images are shown in Fig. 1.8. When the noise level is high, the images are barely recognizable and the recognition task becomes more challenging.

For LTP, NRLBP, and ENRLBP there is one free parameter: threshold $t \in [0, 255]$. Fuzzy LBP also has a free parameter: fuzzification d. We vary t for LTP, NRLBP, and ENRLBP and d for fuzzy LBP. Only the recognition rates at the optimal setting are reported. The experimental results are summarized in Table 1.2. It can be seen that for most settings, NRLBP and ENRLBP outperform other approaches. When the noise level increases, the performance gain becomes more significant. This clearly demonstrates that NRLBP and ENRLBP are more resistant to noise compared with other LBP variants. We also observe that the experimental results for NRLBP and ENRLBP are fairly consistent for three different distance measures.

To study the effect of threshold t (or fuzzification parameter d), we plot the recognition rates versus t (or d) for LTP, FLBP, NRLBP, ENRLBP using Chi-square distance, as shown in Fig. 1.9. LBP and DLBP are shown as dashed lines. For low noise level, $\sigma = 0.05$, NRLBP, and ENRLBP are slightly better than DLBP and visibly better than LBP, LTP, and FLBP. For the middle and high noise levels, NRLBP and ENRLBP slightly outperform FLBP and significantly outperform LBP, LTP, and

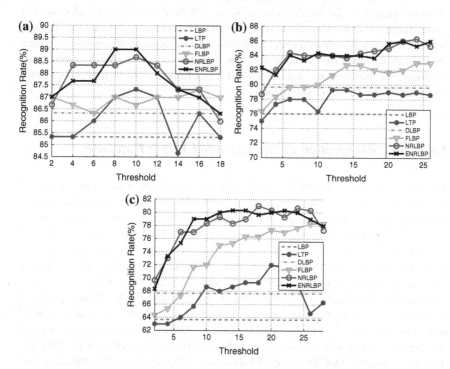

Fig. 1.9 The recognition rates of LBP, LTP, DLBP, FLBP, NRLBP, and ENRLBP using Chi-square distance versus threshold t on the AR database injected with Gaussian noise $\sigma = 0.05$ (**a**), $\sigma = 0.10$ (**b**), $\sigma = 0.15$ (**c**)

BLBP. Figure 1.9 shows that NRLBP, ENRLBP, and FLBP are the only ones that work well for all tested noise levels.

1.4.2 Face Recognition on the AR Database

For face recognition, we adopt a challenging experimental setting. Only one image per subject is used as the gallery (or training) set and all others are used as the probe set. In many real applications, we are not able to obtain multiple images per subject and we may have only one image per subject. 75 subjects are chosen from the AR database, each with 14 images. Each subject contains images from two sections. Each section contains 7 images: one neutral image, 3 images with different facial expressions, and 3 images in different illumination conditions. We repeat the experiments 6 times. For each trial, we use Image 1, 5, 6, 8, 12, 13 of each subject as the gallery set, respectively. The other 13 images of each subject are used as the probe set. It is a challenging experimental setting as face images with facial expression variations need to be identified based on a single face image.

Table 1.3 summarizes the average recognition rate and the standard derivation of each approach at the optimal setting on the AR database injected with Gaussian noise. Table 1.3 shows that NRLBP and ENRLBP achieve comparable or slightly better performance compared with FLBP, whereas they consistently outperform other approaches for all settings using different distance measures. As the noise level increases, the performance gain of NRLBP and ENRLBP over approaches other than FLBP becomes more significant.

1.4.3 Face Recognition on the Extended Yale B Database

The extended Yale B database [8, 18] contains 38 subjects under 9 poses and 64 illumination conditions. We follow the same database partition as in [40]. Images with the most neutral light source("A+000E+00") are used as gallery images and all other frontal images are used as probe images (in total 2414 images of 38 subjects). This dataset contains large illumination variations. The sample images are shown in the first row of Fig. 1.10. Some images are taken under extreme lighting conditions. Even after photometric normalization, as shown in the second row of Fig. 1.10, a large amount of image noise exists in the images. NRLBP and ENRLBP are compared with 6 LBP/LTP variants using nearest-neighbor classifier with Chi-square distance, histogram intersection, and modified G-statistic. Table 1.4 summarizes the highest recognition rates at the optimal threshold for various approaches using different distance measures. NRLBP and ENRLBP achieve slightly better performance than LBP, LTP, DLBP, and FLBP, and much better performance than NELBP and NTLBP.

Table 1.3 Summary of the average face recognition rate and the standard derivation of each approach at the optimal setting on the AR database injected with Gaussian noise

Algorithm	χ^2 distance, $\sigma =$			Histogram intersection, $\sigma =$			Modified G-statistic, $\sigma =$		
	0.05	0.10	0.15	0.05	0.10	0.15	0.05	0.10	0.15
LBP	83.44 % ± 1.44 %	64.65 % ± 2.92 %	40.91 % ± 6.52 %	81.64 % ± 1.58 %	55.18 % ± 7.37 %	34.34 % ± 4.38 %	79.04 % ± 1.71 %	56.63 % ± 3.02 %	34.56 % ± 5.93 %
LTP	83.91 % ± 1.03 %	65.09 % ± 5.88 %	43.78 % ± 9.96 %	81.85 % ± 2.08 %	55.26 % ± 12.07 %	37.69 % ± 10.77 %	80.26 % ± 0.90 %	62.58 % ± 2.44 %	42.74 % ± 3.74 %
DLBP	85.11 % ± 0.83 %	62.82 % ± 6.92 %	39.57 % ± 9.76 %	85.47 % ± 1.74 %	62.44 % ± 7.09 %	39.03 % ± 9.87 %	84.24 % ± 1.68 %	61.26 % ± 5.46 %	33.49 % ± 9.04 %
FLBP	83.95 % ± 1.32 %	78.19 % ± 1.08 %	**71.04 %** ± 1.70 %	84.17 % ± 1.42 %	74.26 % ± 2.01 %	59.86 % ± 3.06 %	81.44 % ± 1.41 %	74.97 % ± 1.45 %	68.77 % ± 2.14 %
NELBP	65.50 % ± 3.19 %	34.82 % ± 3.01 %	18.32 % ± 1.35 %	64.46 % ± 3.84 %	31.56 % ± 1.81 %	16.32 % ± 1.07 %	66.51 % ± 3.27 %	34.85 % ± 2.23 %	17.85 % ± 1.69 %
NTLBP	63.71 % ± 3.32 %	28.94 % ± 1.53 %	13.42 % ± 1.48 %	67.25 % ± 3.37 %	35.69 % ± 2.85 %	17.83 % ± 1.44 %	61.01 % ± 3.40 %	25.35 % ± 1.62 %	11.47 % ± 1.64 %
NRLBP	**85.33 %** ± 1.43 %	**79.93 %** ± 0.79 %	70.67 % ± 2.90 %	**85.88 %** ± 0.96 %	**78.65 %** ± 1.22 %	**67.62 %** ± 4.87 %	**84.92 %** ± 1.29 %	**79.08 %** ± 1.03 %	**70.55 %** ± 3.22 %
ENRLBP	<u>85.98 %</u> ± 1.35 %	<u>80.43 %</u> ± 0.97 %	<u>71.71 %</u> ± 1.79 %	<u>86.02 %</u> ± 1.09 %	<u>80.24 %</u> ± 1.55 %	<u>68.77 %</u> ± 3.05 %	<u>85.42 %</u> ± 1.03 %	<u>80.58 %</u> ± 0.72 %	<u>72.43 %</u> ± 1.50 %

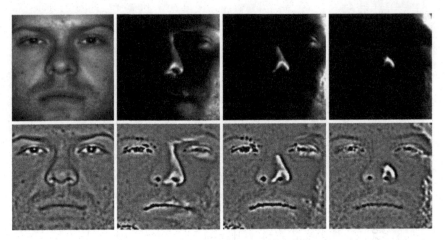

Fig. 1.10 The *1st row* and *2nd row* show the samples of geometrically normalized and photometrically normalized images for the extended Yale B database, respectively. The *leftmost image* is the gallery image, and the *other 3 images* taken under extreme lighting conditions are the probe images

Table 1.4 The face recognition rate and the optimal threshold on the extended Yale B database

Algorithm	Chi-square distance (%)	Histogram intersection (%)	Modified G-statistics (%)
LBP	96.07	93.32	96.12
LTP	98.25 (10)	97.99 (10)	98.29 (8)
DLBP	96.12	97.83	98.45
FLBP	98.45 (9)	98.16 (9)	98.54 (12)
NELBP	81.91	82.29	84.92
NTLBP	80.37	80.16	83.12
NRLBP	**98.71** (9)	**98.66** (8)	**98.66** (11)
ENRLBP	**<u>98.75</u>** (9)	**<u>98.66</u>** (8)	**98.62** (10)

1.4.4 Face Recognition on the O2FN Mobile Database

The O2FN mobile face database [33] is our in-house face database. It is designed to evaluate the face recognition algorithms on mobile face images, which are of low resolution and low image quality, and significantly corrupted by noise. It contains 2000 face images of size 144×176 pixels from 50 subjects. The images are self-taken by the users. The users are instructed to take about 20 indoor images and 20 outdoor images with minimum facial expression variations and out-plane rotations. Thus, the O2FN database mainly contains in-plane rotations and illumination variations. Figure 1.11 shows some samples of geometrically normalized and photometrically normalized images. The images are captured by an O2 XDA frontal camera with native phone settings and without postprocessing. The images are severely distorted

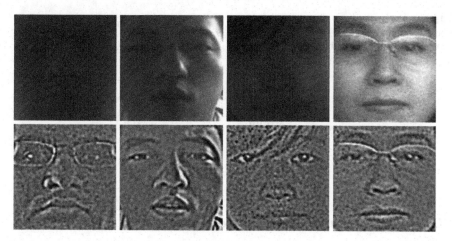

Fig. 1.11 The samples of geometrically normalized (*Row 1*) and photometrically normalized (*Row 2*) face images of the O2FN databases

Table 1.5 Performance comparison of face recognition on the O2FN database

Algorithm	Chi-square distance	Histogram intersection	Modified G-statistics
LBP	76.59 % ± 1.60 %	74.14 % ± 1.44 %	75.18 % ± 1.15 %
LTP	78.88 % ± 1.65 %	76.88 % ± 1.91 %	78.16 % ± 1.39 %
DLBP	78.07 % ± 1.69 %	79.88 % ± 2.10 %	79.01 % ± 2.04 %
FLBP	80.24 % ± 1.58 %	79.15 % ± 1.49 %	80.01 % ± 1.46 %
NELBP	56.74 % ± 1.75 %	58.25 % ± 2.16 %	59.12 % ± 1.73 %
NTLBP	56.96 % ± 1.82 %	58.40 % ± 1.65 %	58.63 % ± 2.18 %
NRLBP	**80.76 %** ± 1.56 %	**80.29 %** ± 1.63 %	**80.68 %** ± 1.57 %
ENRLBP	**81.66 %** ± 1.83 %	**81.28 %** ± 1.80 %	**81.44 %** ± 1.91 %

by noise, e.g., Gaussian noise, salt-and-pepper noise, and motion blur. To reduce the noise and illumination variations, the images are photometric normalized as in [40]. Even after photometric normalization, as shown in Fig. 1.11, the images still contain a large amount of noise.

NRLBP and ENRLBP are compared with 6 LBP/LTP variants using nearest-neighbor classifier with three different distance measures. The experiments are repeated five times. For each trial, we randomly choose one image of each subject as the gallery set and the rest as the probe set. We test LTP, NRLBP, and ENRLBP for different thresholds, and FLBP for different d. Only the performance at the optimal setting is reported. The average recognition rates and the standard derivation at the optimal setting on the O2FN database are summarized in Table 1.5. NRLBP and ENRLBP achieve a comparable or slightly better performance compared with LTP, DLBP, and FLBP, and significantly outperform LBP, NELBP, and NTLBP using all three distance measures.

Algorithm	Time (ms)
LBP	10.8
LTP	16.4
DLBP	21.5
FLBP	161.7
NELBP	21.2
NTLBP	21.2
NRLBP	17.0
ENRLBP	23.1

Table 1.6 The time consumption for feature extraction on the AR database

1.4.5 Comparison of Computational Complexity

NRLBP and ENRLBP can be implemented by a lookup table to compute the NRLBP/ENRLBP histogram from uncertain code. It is very fast to compute the contribution of an *uncertain* code to the histogram by the lookup table and hence derive the feature vector of NRLBP/ENRLBP during recognition. The average time per image of feature extraction on the AR database for various LBP/LTP variants is shown in Table 1.6. The image is of size 128×128 pixels. Features are extracted under the setting of $P = 8, R = 1$. We use Matlab 2012b on Intel Duo CPU @3.0 GHz with 4 Gb RAM. Compared with LBP, NRLBP and ENRLBP introduce only small overhead. By contrast, it takes much more time to compute FLBP features, e.g., 161.7 ms, which is about 9.5 times that of NRLBP.

1.5 Conclusion

Facial expression and face recognition are two important functionalities of the virtual human and the social robot in order to achieve autonomous behavior. LBP has been widely used for face and facial expression analysis; however, it is sensitive to noise. Even a small noise may change the LBP code significantly. Both LBP and its variants lack the mechanism to recover corrupted image local structures. In NRLBP, we assign the values of *uncertain* bits so as to form all possible uniform LBP codes. In this way we correct noisy nonuniform patterns back to uniform code. For LBP and LTP, a large group of local primitives, i.e., line patterns, is completely ignored. Thus, we proposed extended uniform patterns and formed them as our ENRLBP patterns when determining *uncertain* bits. NRLBP and ENRLBP show stronger noise-resistance than other approaches for face and facial expression recognition on various datasets.

References

1. Ahonen T, Hadid A, Pietikäinen M (2006) Face description with local binary patterns: application to face recognition. IEEE Trans Pattern Anal Mach Intell 28(12):2037–2041
2. Ahonen T, Pietikäinen M (2007) Soft histograms for local binary patterns. In: Proceedings of the finnish signal processing symposium (FINSIG 2007), pp 1–4
3. Akhloufi MA, Bendada A (2010) Locally adaptive texture features for multispectral face recognition. In: IEEE international conference on systems man and cybernetics (SMC), IEEE, pp 3308–3314
4. Boland MV, Murphy RF (2001) A neural network classifier capable of recognizing the patterns of all major subcellular structures in fluorescence microscope images of hela cells. Bioinformatics 17(12):1213–1223
5. Fathi A, Nilchi ARN (2012) Noise tolerant local binary pattern operator for efficient texture analysis. Pattern Recogn Lett 33:1093–1100
6. Froba B, Ernst A (2004) Face detection with the modified census transform. In: Proceedings of sixth IEEE international conference on automatic face and gesture recognition, IEEE, pp 91–96
7. Fu X, Wei W (2008) Centralized binary patterns embedded with image euclidean distance for facial expression recognition. In: International conference on natural computation, vol 4, IEEE, pp 115–119
8. Georghiades AS, Belhumeur PN, Kriegman DJ (2001) From few to many: illumination cone models for face recognition under variable lighting and pose. IEEE Trans Pattern Anal Mach Intell 23(6):643–660
9. Guo Z, Zhang L, Zhang D (2010) A completed modeling of local binary pattern operator for texture classification. IEEE Trans Image Process 19(6):1657–1663
10. Gupta R, Patil H, Mittal A (2010) Robust order-based methods for feature description. In: IEEE conference on computer vision and pattern recognition (CVPR), pp 334–341
11. Hafiane A, Seetharaman G, Zavidovique B (2007) Median binary pattern for textures classification. In: Image analysis and recognition, Springer, pp 387–398
12. He W, Ahonen T, Pietikäinen M (2008) A bayesian local binary pattern texture descriptor. In: International conference on pattern recognition, IEEE, pp 1–4
13. He D, Cercone N (2009) Local triplet pattern for content-based image retrieval. In: Image analysis and recognition, pp 229–238
14. Heikkilä M, Pietikäinen M, Schmid C (2009) Description of interest regions with local binary patterns. Pattern Recogn 42(3):425–436
15. Huang X, Li SZ, Wang Y (2004) Shape localization based on statistical method using extended local binary pattern. In: IEEE first symposium on multi-agent security and survivability, IEEE, pp 184–187
16. Iakovidis DK, Keramidas EG, Maroulis D (2008) Fuzzy local binary patterns for ultrasound texture characterization. In: Image analysis and recognition
17. Keramidas E, Iakovidis D, Maroulis D (2011) Fuzzy binary patterns for uncertainty-aware texture representation. Electron Lett Comput Vis Image Anal 10(1):63–78
18. Lee KC, Ho J, Kriegman DJ (2005) Acquiring linear subspaces for face recognition under variable lighting. IEEE Trans Pattern Anal Mach Intell 27(5):684–698
19. Li X, Weiming H, Zhang Z, Wang H (2010) Heat kernel based local binary pattern for face representation. IEEE Signal Process Lett 17(3):308–311
20. Li Z, Liu G, Yang Y, You J (2012) Scale-and rotation-invariant local binary pattern using scale-adaptive texton and subuniform-based circular shift. IEEE Trans Image Process 21(4):2130–2140
21. Liao W-H, Young T-J (2010) Texture classification using uniform extended local ternary patterns. In: 2010 IEEE international symposium on multimedia (ISM), IEEE, pp 191–195
22. Liao S, Zhao G, Kellokumpu V, Pietikäinen M, Li SZ (2010) Modeling pixel process with scale invariant local patterns for background subtraction in complex scenes. In: IEEE conference on computer vision and pattern recognition (CVPR), IEEE, pp 1301–1306

23. Li B, Meng MQ-H (2009) Texture analysis for ulcer detection in capsule endoscopy images. Image Vis comput 27(9):1336–1342
24. Martinez AM, Benavente R (1998) The AR face database. CVC Tech. Report #24
25. Max LS, Law WK, Chung ACS (2009) Dominant local binary patterns for texture classification. IEEE Trans Image Process 18(5):1107–1118
26. Mu Y, Yan S, Liu Y, Huang T, Zhou B (2008) Discriminative local binary patterns for human detection in personal album. In: Proceeding of IEEE conference on computer vision and pattern recognition, pp 1–8
27. Nanni L, Lumini A, Brahnam S (2010) Local binary patterns variants as texture descriptors for medical image analysis. Artif Intell Med 49(2):117–125
28. Nanni L, Brahnam S, Lumini A (2012) A simple method for improving local binary patterns by considering non-uniform patterns. Pattern Recogn 45(10):3844–3852
29. Ojala T, Pietikäinen M, Harwood D (1996) A comparative study of texture measures with classification based on featured distributions. Pattern Recogn 29(1):51–59
30. Ojala T, Maenpaa T, Pietikainen M, Viertola J, Kyllonen J, Huovinen S (2002) Outex-new framework for empirical evaluation of texture analysis algorithms. Proc Int Conf Pattern Recogn 1:701–706
31. Ojala T, Pietikäinen M, Maenpaa T (2002) Multiresolution gray-scale and rotation invariant texture classification with local binary patterns. IEEE Trans Pattern Anal Mach Intell 24(7):971–987
32. Pietikäinen M, Hadid A, Zhao G, Ahonen T (2011) Computer vision using local binary patterns, vol 40. Springer, Berlin
33. Ren J, Jiang X, Yuan J (2013) A complete and fully automated face verification system on mobile devices. Pattern Recogn 46(1):45–56
34. Ren J, Jiang X, Yuan J (2013) Noise-resistant local binary pattern with an embedded error-correction mechanism. IEEE Trans Image Process 22(10):4049–4060
35. Ren J, Jiang X, Yuan J (2013) Dynamic texture recognition using enhanced lbp features. In: IEEE international conference on acoustics, speech and signal processing (ICASSP), pp 2400–2404
36. Ren J, Jiang X, Yuan J (2013) Learning binarized pixel-difference pattern for scene recognition. In: IEEE international conference on image processing (ICIP), pp 2494–2498
37. Ren J, Jiang X, Yuan J (2013) Relaxed local ternary pattern for face recognition. In: IEEE international conference on image processing (ICIP), pp 3680–3684
38. Satpathy A, Jiang X, Eng H-L (2014) LBP based edge-texture features for object recognition. IEEE Trans Image Process 23(5):1953–1964
39. Tan N, Huang L, Liu C (2009) A new probabilistic local binary pattern for face verification. In: Proceeding of IEEE international conference on image processing, pp 1237–1240
40. Tan X, Triggs B (2010) Enhanced local texture feature sets for face recognition under difficult lighting conditions. IEEE Trans Image Process 19(6):1635–1650
41. Trefný J, Matas J (2010) Extended set of local binary patterns for rapid object detection. In: Proceedings of the computer vision winter workshop, vol 2010
42. Wang X, Han TX, Yan S (2009) An HOG-LBP human detector with partial occlusion handling. In: Proceeding of IEEE international conference on computer vision, pp 32–39
43. Wu J, Rehg JM (2011) CENTRIST: a visual descriptor for scene categorization. IEEE Trans Pattern Anal Mach Intell 33(8):1489–1501
44. Xiao Y, Jianxin W, Yuan J (2014) mCENTRIST: a multi-channel feature generation mechanism for scene categorization. IEEE Trans Image Process 23(2):823–836
45. Yao C-H, Chen S-Y (2003) Retrieval of translated, rotated and scaled color textures. Pattern Recogn 36(4):913–929
46. Zhang W, Shan S, Gao W, Chen X, Zhang H (2005) Local gabor binary pattern histogram sequence (lgbphs): a novel non-statistical model for face representation and recognition. In: IEEE international conference on computer vision, vol 1, IEEE, pp 786–791
47. Zhao G, Ahonen T, Matas J, Pietikäinen M (2012) Rotation-invariant image and video description with local binary pattern features. IEEE Trans Image Process 21(4):1465–1477

48. Zhao S, Gao Y, Zhang B (2008) Sobel-LBP. In: IEEE international conference on image processing, IEEE, pp 2144–2147
49. Zhao G, Pietikäinen M (2007) Dynamic texture recognition using local binary patterns with an application to facial expressions. IEEE Trans Pattern Anal Mach Intell 29(6):915–928
50. Zhou H, Wang R, Wang C (2008) A novel extended local-binary-pattern operator for texture analysis. Inf Sci 178(22):4314–4325

Chapter 2
Body Movement Analysis and Recognition

Yang Xiao, Hui Liang, Junsong Yuan and Daniel Thalmann

Abstract In this chapter, a nonverbal way of communication for human–robot interaction by understanding human upper body gestures will be addressed. The human–robot interaction system based on a novel combination of sensors is proposed. It allows one person to interact with a humanoid social robot with natural body language. The robot can understand the meaning of human upper body gestures and express itself by using a combination of body movements, facial expressions, and verbal language. A set of 12 upper body gestures is involved for communication. Human–object interactions are also included in these gestures. The gestures can be characterized by the head, arm, and hand posture information. CyberGlove II is employed to capture the hand posture. This feature is combined with the head and arm posture information captured from Microsoft Kinect. This is a new sensor solution for human-gesture capture. Based on the body posture data, an effective and real-time human gesture recognition method is proposed. For experiments, a human body gesture dataset was built. The experimental results demonstrate the effectiveness and efficiency of the proposed approach.

2.1 Introduction

Recently, human–robot interaction (HRI) has drawn the attention of the academic and industrial communities. Regarded as the sister community of human–computer interaction (HCI), HRI is still a relatively young field that began to emerge in the

Y. Xiao (✉)
School of Automation, Huazhong University of Science and Technology, Wuhan, China
e-mail: Yang_Xiao@hust.edu.cn

H. Liang · J. Yuan · D. Thalmann
BeingThere Centre, Nanyang Technological University, Singapore, Singapore

J. Yuan
e-mail: JSYUAN@ntu.edu.sg

D. Thalmann
e-mail: danielthalmann@ntu.edu.sg

© Springer International Publishing Switzerland 2016
N. Magnenat-Thalmann et al. (eds.), *Context Aware Human-Robot and Human-Agent Interaction*, Human–Computer Interaction Series,
DOI 10.1007/978-3-319-19947-4_2

Fig. 2.1 Human–robot social interaction, with human on the *right* and robot on the *left*

1990s [10, 14]. It is an interdisciplinary research field that requires contributions from mathematics, psychology, mechanical engineering, biology, computer science, etc. [14].

HRI aims to understand and shape the interactions between humans and robots. Unlike early interactions, more social dimensions must be considered in HRI, especially when interactive social robots are involved [10, 13]. In this case, robots should be believable. Moreover, humans prefer to interact with robots as they do with other people [10, 13]. Therefore, one way to increase believability would be to make the robot interact with humans using the same modalities as human–human interaction. This includes verbal and body language as well as facial expressions; i.e., the robots should be able to use these modalities for both perception and expression. Some social robots have already been proposed toward this goal. For instance, the Leonardo robot expresses itself using a combination of voice, facial, and body expressions [25]. Another example is the Nao humanoid robot[1] that can use vision along with gestures and body expression of emotions [2]. Different from these two robots, the Nadine robot is a highly realistic humanoid robot (Fig. 2.1). This robot presents some different social challenges. In this chapter, a human–robot interaction system that addresses some of these challenges is proposed. As shown in Fig. 2.1, it supports a person to communicate and interact with a humanoid robot. In the proposed system, the human can naturally communicate with the Nadine robot using body language. The Nadine robot is able to express herself by using a combination of speech, body language, and facial expressions. In this chapter, the main research concern addressed is how to establish communication between human and robot using body language.

Verbal and nonverbal language are two means of communication for human–human interaction. Verbal language has been used in many HRI systems

---

[1]http://www.aldebaran-robotics.com/

Fig. 2.2 Human–human
interaction accompanied
with nonverbal language

[11, 21, 23, 26–28]; however, it still has some constraints. That is, speech recognition accuracy is likely to be affected by the background noise, human accents, and device performance. Moreover, learning and interpreting the subtle rules of syntax and grammar in speech is a difficult task. These factors limit the practical use of verbal language to a certain degree. On the other hand, nonverbal clues can convey rich communication messages [7, 19]. Evidently, they play an important role in human–human interaction to reinforce the communication performance as shown in Fig. 2.2. Thus, one of our research motivations is *to apply nonverbal language to human–robot social interaction*. More specifically, upper body gesture language is employed. Currently, 12 human upper body gestures are involved in the proposed system, which are all natural gestures with intuitive semantics. They are characterized by head, arm, and hand posture information simultaneously. It is worth noting that *human–object* interactions are involved in these gestures. *Human–object* interaction events manifest frequently during human–human interaction in daily life. However, to our knowledge, they were largely ignored by previous HRI systems.

The main challenge to apply upper body gesture language to human–robot interaction is how to enable the Nadine robot to understand and react to human gestures accurately and in real-time. To achieve this goal, two crucial issues need to be solved:

- First, an appropriate human gesture-capture sensor solution is required. To recognize the 12 upper body gestures, head, arm, and hand posture information is needed simultaneously. As robustly obtaining hand posture based on vision-based sensors (such as the RGB camera) is still a difficult task [18, 29], the wearable Cyber-Glove II [15] (shown in Fig. 2.3) is used. Using this device, high-accuracy hand

Fig. 2.3 CyberGlove II

Fig. 2.4 The microsoft
kinect RGB and depth sensor

posture data can be acquired stably. Meanwhile, Microsoft Kinect [24] (shown in
Fig. 2.4) is an effective and efficient low-cost depth sensor applied successfully to
human body tracking. The skeletal joints can be extracted from the Kinect depth
images [24] in real-time (30 fps). In our work, Kinect is applied to capture the
upper body (head and arm) posture information. Recently, Kinect 2 that supports
tracking multiple people with better depth imaging quality was released. Since our
work investigates the HRI scenario involving only one person, Kinect is sufficient
to handle the human body tracking task;

- Second, an effective and real-time gesture recognition method should be developed. Based on the CyberGlove II and Kinect posture data, descriptive upper body
gesture feature is proposed. To leverage the gesture understanding performance,
LMNN distance metric learning method [33] is applied. Then, the energy-based
LMNN classifier is used to recognize the gestures.

To evaluate the proposed gesture recognition method, a human upper body gesture dataset is constructed. This dataset contains gesture samples from 25 people
of different genders, body sizes, and culture backgrounds. The experimental results
demonstrate the effectiveness and efficiency of our method.

Overall, the main contributions of this chapter include:

- A novel human gesture-capture sensor solution is proposed. That is, the Cyber-
Glove II and Kinect are integrated to capture head, arm, and hand posture information simultaneously;
- An effective and real-time upper body gesture recognition approach is proposed;
- To support humans to communicate and interact with robots using body language,
a gesture understanding and human–robot interaction (GUHRI) system is built.

The remainder of this chapter is organized as follows. Problematic issues are
discussed in Sect. 2.2. Section 2.3 gives an overview of the related state-of-the-art
works. The recent approaches are described in Sect. 2.4. Section 2.5 introduces the
future avenues. The conclusions are drawn in Sect. 2.6.

2.2 Problematic

To successfully apply nonverbal language to HRI by understanding human upper body gestures, some critical problematic issues and challenges need to be addressed. A brief discussion of this point has been made in Sect. 2.1. In this section, we extend the discussion from the perspectives of the HRI system in detail.

- As our research aims to promote social interaction between humans and robot, the semantics of natural human body language need to be analyzed. To fully understand the human upper body gestures, head, arm, and hand posture information should be captured simultaneously in an effective way. This proposition is effectively demonstrated by Figs. 2.1 and 2.2. However, to our knowledge, very few previous body gesture recognition works take hand and rough body posture information into consideration together. Thus, appropriate human gesture-capture devices are the essential components to construct a successful HRI system. For human gesture capture, vision-based sensors are the trend as they exert no burden on the users and lead to better user experience. Some successful examples have already emerged recently, such as Microsoft Kinect, which is applied to human body parsing and tracking. However, under unconstrained conditions, it is still difficult to capture the hand posture robustly because of drastic hand rotation and serious occlusion as shown in Fig. 2.5. Meanwhile, it is not feasible to restrict the user's hand position and orientation during the phase of natural HRI. As a consequence, according to the current capacity of vision-based sensors, they are not the optimal choice to capture the hand posture for the HRI system. Thus, a more applicable human gesture-capture sensor solution should be proposed. In addition to effectiveness,

Fig. 2.5 The different hand gestures with drastic rotation and serious occlusion

another important factor for human gesture capture is efficiency. As HRI is in high real-time demand, the data acquisition stage must be finished as soon as possible.

- Based on the reliable hand and body posture feature, how to recognize the upper body gestures effectively in real-time is the latest concern that needs to be addressed. Since the hand and rough body posture information is captured from different sensors, i.e., they are multimodular data, how to fuse them to form a unified body gesture description is the first point we focus on. Second, for HRI application an adequate classification scheme should be proposed to leverage the performance, including the distance metric learning method and the choice of classifier. Last but not least, enough training samples are required to drive the supervised body gesture recognition approach. However, there is no existing body gesture dataset that can be applied to our work directly. Thus, building a novel upper body gesture dataset with sufficient available samples is another crucial task.

- Whether robots can naturally react to human body language will largely affect the user experience. Since the Nadine robot has the capacity to express herself using a combination of speech, body language, and facial expressions, a suitable interaction scenario is required for robot control to make her more humanlike and vivid. Indeed, the interaction scenario should be designed according to the human habits during human–human interaction.

2.3 State of the Art

HRI systems are constructed mainly based on verbal, nonverbal, or multimodal communication modalities. As mentioned in Sect. 2.1, verbal language still faces constraints in practical applications. Our work focuses on studying how to apply nonverbal language to human–robot social interaction, especially using upper body gesture language. Some HRI systems have already employed body gesture language for human–robot communication. In [30], an arm gesture-based interface for HRI was proposed. The user could control a mobile robot using static or dynamic arm gestures. Hand gesture was used as the communication modality for HRI in [5]. The HRI systems addressed in [27, 28] could recognize the human pointing gesture using the 3D head and hand position information, and head orientation was further appended to leverage the performance. In [11], the social robot could understand the human body language characterized by arm and head posture. Our proposition on nonverbal human–robot communication is different from previous works mainly in two aspects. First, head, arm, and hand posture are jointly captured to describe the 12 upper body gestures involved in the GUHRI system. Second, the gestures accompanied with human–object interaction can be understood by the robot. These gestures were always ignored by previous HRI systems, although they manifest frequently in daily life as shown in Fig. 2.6.

Fig. 2.6 Human–object interactions in daily life

Body gesture recognition plays an important role in the GUHRI system. According to the gesture-capture sensor type, gesture recognition systems can be categorized as encumbered and unencumbered [4]. Encumbered systems require the user to wear physical assistive devices such as infrared responders, hand markers, or data gloves. These systems have high precision and fast response, and are robust to environmental changes. Many encumbered systems have been proposed. For instance, two education systems [1] were built for the deaf using data gloves and optical motion capture devices; Lu et al. [18] proposed an immersive virtual object manipulation system based on two data gloves and a hybrid ultrasonic tracking system. Although most commercialized gesture-capture devices are currently encumbered, unencumbered systems are expected to be the future choice, especially vision-based systems. With the emergence of low-cost 3D vision sensors, the application of such devices becomes a hot topic in both the research and commercial fields. One of the most famous examples is Microsoft Kinect, which has been successfully employed in human body tracking [24], activity analysis [31], and gesture understanding [37, 38]. Even for other vision applications (such as scene categorization [36] and image segmentation [34, 35]), Kinect holds the potential to boost the performance. However, accurate and robust hand posture capture is still a difficult task for vision-based sensors.

As discussed above, both encumbered and unencumbered sensors possess intrinsic advantages and drawbacks. For specific applications, they can be complementary. In the GUHRI system a tradeoff between the two kinds of sensors is made, that is, the fine hand posture is captured by the encumbered device (CyberGlove II), while the rough upper body posture is handled by the unencumbered sensor (Kinect).

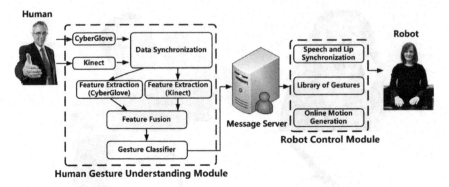

Fig. 2.7 The GUHRI system architecture

2.4 Recent Approaches

In this section, we give an overview of the GURHI system. The human upper body gesture understanding method is then illustrated. Next, the scenario for HRI is introduced. Experiment and discussion are finally given.

2.4.1 System Overview

The proposed GUHRI system is able to capture and understand human upper body gestures and trigger the robot's reaction in real-time accordingly. The GUHRI system is implemented using a framework called Integrated Integration Platform (I2P) specifically developed for integration. I2P was developed by the Institute for Media Innovation.[2] This framework allows for the link and integration of perception, decision, and action modules within a unified and modular framework. The platform uses client–server communications between the different components. Each component has an I2P interface and communication between the client and servers is implemented using thrift.[3] It should be noted that the framework is highly modular and components can be added to make the GUHRI system extendable. As shown in Fig. 2.7, the current GUHRI system is mainly composed of two modules. One, the *human gesture understanding module* that serves as the communication interface between human and robot, and the other is the *robot control module* proposed to control the robot's behaviors for interaction. At this stage, our system supports the interaction between one person and one robot.

One right-handed CyberGlove II and one Microsoft Kinect are employed to capture the human hand and body posture information simultaneously for gesture

---

[2]http://imi.ntu.edu.sg/Pages/Home.aspx

[3]http://thrift.apache.org/

understanding. This is a new gesture capturing sensor solution, different from all the approaches introduced in Sect. 2.3. Specifically, CyberGlove is used to capture the hand posture, and Kinect is applied to acquire the 3D position information of the human skeletal joints (including head, shoulder, limb, and hand). At this stage, the GUHRI system relies on the upper body gestures triggered by the human right hand and right arm.

Apart from the CyberGlove, the user does not need to wear any other device. Thus, the proposed sensor solution does not exert a heavy burden to make the user uncomfortable. Meanwhile, as the CyberGlove II is involved in the system using Bluetooth, the user can move freely. In addition, the GUHRI system is able to recognize gestures with human–object interaction, such as "*call*", "*drink*", "*read*" and "*write*" by fusing the hand and body posture information. These gestures were often ignored by previous systems. However, they manifest frequently during the daily interaction between humans. These affect the interaction state abruptly and should be considered as essential elements of the natural HRI. In our system, the robot is able to recognize and give meaningful responses to these gestures (Fig. 2.8).

The first step of the gesture understanding phase is to synchronize the original data from CyberGlove and Kinect. The descriptive features are then extracted from them respectively. The multimodal features are then fused to generate the unified input for the gesture classifier. Lastly, the gesture recognition and understanding results are sent to the robot control module via message server to trigger the robot's reaction.

The robot control module enables the robot to respond to the human's body gesture language. In our system, the robot's behavior is composed of three parts: body movement, facial expression, and verbal language. Combining these modalities makes the robot more lifelike, and should enhance the users' interest during interaction.

Fig. 2.8 The GUHRI system deployment

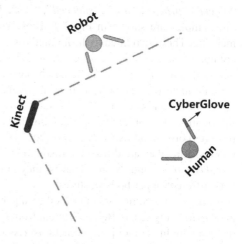

2.4.2 Human Upper Body Gesture Understanding

As an essential part of the GUHRI system, the human upper body gesture understanding module plays an important role during interaction. Its performance will highly affect the interaction experience. In this section, our upper body gesture understanding method by fusing the gesture information from CyberGlove and Kinect is illustrated in detail. First, the body gestures included in the GUHRI system are introduced. The feature extraction pipelines for both CyberGlove and Kinect are then presented. To generate an integral gesture description, the multimodal features from different sensors are fused as the input for classifier. Aiming to enhance the gesture recognition accuracy, LMNN distance metric learning approach [33] is applied for mining the optimal distance measures, and the energy-based classifier [33] is applied for decision making.

2.4.2.1 Gestures in the GUHRI System

At the current stage, 12 static upper body gestures are included in the GUHRI system. As we only have one right-hand CyberGlove, to obtain accurate hand posture information all the gestures are mainly triggered by the human right hand and right arm. The involved gestures can be partitioned into two categories, according to whether human–object interaction happens:

- *Category 1*: body gestures *without* human–object interaction;
- *Category 2*: body gestures *with* human–object interaction.

Category 1 contains 8 upper body gestures: *"be confident"*, *"have question"*, *"object"*, *"praise"*, *"stop"*, *"succeed"*, *"shake hand"* and *"weakly agree."* Some gesture samples are shown in Fig. 2.9. These gestures are natural and have intuitive meaning. They are related to the human's emotional state and behavior intention and are not ad hoc for specific applications. Therefore, gesture-to-meaning mapping is not needed in our system. As human behavior habits are not all the same, recognizing natural gestures is more challenging than ad hoc ones. However, natural gestures are more meaningful for HRI. As shown in Fig. 2.9, both hand and body posture information are required for recognizing these gestures. For instance, the upper body postures corresponding to *"have question"* and *"object"* are very similar. Without the hand posture, they are difficult to distinguish. The same happens to *"have question,"* *"weakly agree,"* and *"stop."* That is, they correspond to similar hand gestures but very different upper body postures.

Category 2 is composed of four other upper body gestures: *"call,"* *"drink,"* *"read,"* and *"write"* (Fig. 2.10). Being different from *Category 1* gestures, these four gestures happen with human–object interactions. Existing systems do not consider such gestures (see Sect. 2.3). One main reason is that objects often cause body occlusion, especially to the hand. In this case, vision-based hand gesture recognition methods are impaired. Hence, the CyberGlove is employed to capture the hand posture. In the

be confident   have question   object   praise

stop   succeed   shake hand   weekly agree

Fig. 2.9 The *Category 1 upper body* gestures. These gestures can be characterized by the body and hand posture information simultaneously

call   drink   read   write

Fig. 2.10 The *Category 2 upper body* gestures. These gestures can be characterized by the body and hand posture information simultaneously

GUHRI system, *Category 2* gestures are recognized and affect the interaction in a realistic way. These gestures are also recognized based on the hand and upper body posture information.

Fig. 2.11 CyberGlove II
data joints [15]

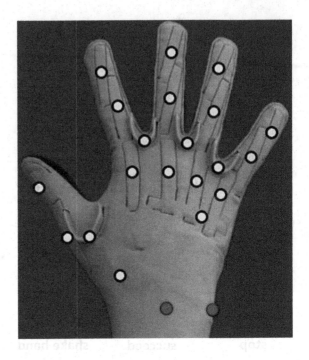

2.4.2.2 Feature Extraction and Fusion

In this section, we introduce the feature extraction methods for both human hand and upper body posture description. The multimodal feature fusion approach is also illustrated.

(a) Hand Posture Feature
As discussed above, the description of the human hand and upper body posture is key to recognize and understand the 12 upper body gestures.

The immersion wireless CyberGlove II is used as the hand posture capture device in the GUHRI system. As one of the most sophisticated and accurate data gloves, CyberGlove II provides 22 high-accuracy joint-angle measurements in real-time. These measurements reflect the bending degree of the fingers and wrist. The 22 data joints (marked as big white or black dots) are located on the CyberGlove as shown in Fig. 2.11. However, not all the joints are used. For the hand gestures in our application, we found that the wrist posture does not provide stable descriptive information. The wrist bending degrees of different people vary to a large extent even for the same gesture. This phenomenon is related to different behavior habits. This is the reason that the two wrist data joints (marked as black) are discarded. A 20-dimensional feature vector F_{hand} is extracted from the 20 white data joints to describe the human hand posture as

$$F_{hand} = (h_1, h_2, h_3 \ldots h_{19}, h_{20}), \qquad (2.1)$$

Fig. 2.12 The selected body skeletal joints

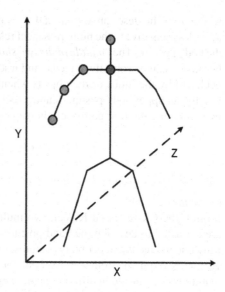

where h_i is the bending degree corresponding to the white data joint i.

(b) Upper Body Posture Feature
Using the Kinect sensor, we shape the human upper body posture intermediately using the 3D skeletal joint positions. For a full human subject, 20 body joint positions can be detected and tracked by the real-time skeleton tracker [24] based on the Kinect depth frame. This is invariant to posture, body shape, clothing, etc. Each joint J_i is represented by three coordinates at the frame t as

$$J_i = (x_i(t), y_i(t), z_i(t)). \tag{2.2}$$

However, not all the 20 joints are necessary for upper body gesture recognition. As aforementioned, head and right arm are highly correlated with the 12 upper body gestures (Figs. 2.9 and 2.10). For efficiency, only four upper body joints are chosen as the descriptive joints for gesture understanding. These are *"head," "right shoulder," "right elbow,"* and *"right hand"* that are shown as gray dots in Fig. 2.12.

Directly using the original 3D joint information for body posture description is not stable, because it is sensitive to the relative position between human and Kinect. Solving this problem by restricting the human's position is not appropriate for interaction. In [31], human action is recognized by using the pairwise relative positions between all joints, which is robust to the human–Kinect relative position. Inspired by this work, a simplified solution is proposed. First, the *"middle of the two shoulders"* joint (black dot in Fig. 2.12) is selected as the reference joint. The pairwise relative positions between the four descriptive joints and the reference joint are then computed for body posture description as

$$J_{sr} = J_s - J_r, \tag{2.3}$$

where J_s is the descriptive joint and J_r is the reference joint. With this processing, J_{sr} is less sensitive to the human–Kinect relative position. It is mainly determined by the body posture. The "*middle of the two shoulders*" was chosen as the reference joint because it can be robustly detected and tracked in most cases. Moreover, it is rarely occluded by the limbs or the objects when the gestures in GUHRI system happen. Finally, an upper body posture feature vector F_{body} of 12 dimensions is constructed by combining the four pairwise relative positions as

$$F_{body} = (J_{1r}, J_{2r}, J_{3r}, J_{4r}), \tag{2.4}$$

where J_{1r}, J_{2r}, J_{3r} and J_{4r} are the pairwise relative positions.

(c) Feature Fusion

From CyberGlove II and Kinect, two multimodal feature vectors: F_{hand} and F_{body} are extracted to describe the hand posture and upper body posture respectively. To fully understand the upper body gestures, the joint information about the two feature vectors is required. Both are essential for the recognition task. However, the two feature vectors locate in different value ranges. Simply combining them as the input for classifier will yield performance bias on the feature vector of low values. To overcome this difficulty, we scale them into similar ranges before feature fusion. Suppose F_i is one dimension of F_{hand} or F_{body}, F_i^{max} and F_i^{min} are the corresponding maximum and minimum value in the training set. Then F_i can be normalized as

$$\hat{F}_i = \frac{F_i - F_i^{min}}{F_i^{max} - F_i^{min}}, \tag{2.5}$$

for both training and test.

After normalization, the effectiveness of the two feature vectors for gesture recognition will be balanced. Finally, they are fused to generate an integral feature vector by concatenation as

$$\mathbf{F} = (\hat{F}_{hand}, \hat{F}_{body}). \tag{2.6}$$

This process results in a 32-dimensional feature vector $\mathbf{F}$ used for upper body gesture recognition.

2.4.2.3 Classification Method

Using $\mathbf{F}$ as the input feature, the upper body gestures will be recognized by template matching based on the *energy-based LMNN classifier* proposed in [33].[4] It is derived from the energy-based model [8] and the LMNN distance metric learning method [33]. The latter part is the key to constructing this classifier. LMNN distance metric learning approach is proposed to seek the best distance measure for the

---

[4]The source code is available at http://www.cse.wustl.edu/~kilian/code/lmnn/lmnn.html

k-nearest neighbor (KNN) classification rule [9]. As one of the oldest methods for pattern recognition, KNN classifier is simple to implement and use. Nevertheless, it can still yield comparative results in certain domains such as object recognition and shape matching [3], it has also been applied to action recognition [20].

The KNN rule classifies each testing sample by the majority label voting among its k-nearest training samples. Its performance crucially depends on how to compute the distances between different samples for the k nearest neighbors search. Euclidean distance is the most widely used distance measure, although it ignores any statistical regularities that may be estimated from the training set. Ideally, the distance measure should be adjusted according to the specific task being solved. To achieve better classification performance, LMNN distance metric learning method is proposed to mine the best distance measure for the KNN classification.

Let $\{(\mathbf{x}_i, y_i)\}_{i=n}^n$ be a training set of n labeled samples with inputs $\mathbf{x}_i \in \mathbb{R}^d$ and class labels y_i. The main goal of LMNN distance metric learning is to learn a linear transformation $\mathbf{L} : \mathbb{R}^d \to \mathbb{R}^d$ that is used to compute the square sample distances as

$$\mathcal{D}(\mathbf{x}_i, \mathbf{x}_j) = \|\mathbf{L}(\mathbf{x}_i - \mathbf{x}_j)\|^2. \tag{2.7}$$

Using $\mathcal{D}(\mathbf{x}_i, \mathbf{x}_j)$ as the distance measure tends to optimize the KNN classification by making each input $\mathbf{x}_i$ have k nearest neighbors that share the same class label y_i to the greatest possibility. Figure 2.13 gives an intuitive illustration on LMNN distance metric learning. Compared with Euclidean distance, LMNN distance tries to pull the nearest neighbors of class y_i closer to $\mathbf{x}_i$, while pushing the neighbors from different classes away. On the assumption that the training set and the test set keep the similar feature distribution, LMNN distance metric learning can help to improve the KNN classification result.

The energy-based LMNN classifier makes use of both the $\mathcal{D}(\mathbf{x}_i, \mathbf{x}_j)$ distance measure and the loss function defined for LMNN distance metric learning. It constructs an energy-based criterion function, and the testing sample is assigned to the class that yields the minimum loss value. As the related theory is sophisticated, we do not give a detailed definition of the energy-based LMNN classifier here; readers can turn to [33] for reference.

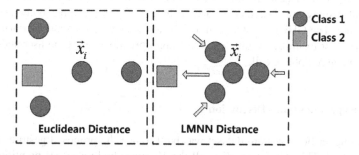

Fig. 2.13 Illustration of the LMNN distance metric learning

happy   **moderate**   **sad**

Fig. 2.14 Examples of body movements and facial expressions from the library of gestures

2.4.2.4 Human–Robot Interaction

As a case study for the GUHRI system, a scenario was defined in which a user
and the robot interact in a classroom. The robot is the lecturer, and the user is the
student. The robot is a female named "Nadine." Nadine can understand the 12 upper
body gestures described in Sect. 2.4.2.1 and react to the users' gestures accordingly.
In our system, Nadine is humanlike and capable of reacting by combining body
movement, facial expression, and verbal language. In this way, Nadine's reactions
provide the user with vivid feedback. Figure 2.14 shows some examples of Nadine's
body movements along with corresponding facial expressions. Nonverbal behaviors
can help to structure the processing of verbal information as well as giving affective
feedback during the interaction [6, 17]. Thus, body movements and facial expressions
are expected to enhance the quality of the interaction with Nadine.

In this scenario, Nadine's behaviors are triggered by the users' body language. Her
reactions are consistent with the defined scenario (see Table 2.1). Note that because
it is difficult to fully describe the robot's body actions, the robot's movements and
emotional display are described at a high level. All the 12 upper body gestures
are involved. The GHURI system can also handle unexpected situations during the
interaction. For example, Nadine can react appropriately even if the user suddenly
answers a coming phone call.

2.4.2.5 Experiment and Discussion

A human upper body gesture dataset was built to test the proposed gesture recognition method. This dataset involves all the 12 upper body gestures mentioned in
Sect. 2.4.2.1. The samples are captured from 25 volunteers of different genders,

Table 2.1 The scenario for human–robot interaction

Human gestures	Nadine's response	
	Nonverbal	Verbal
"be confident"	Happy	It is great to see you so confident
"have question"	Moderate	What is your question?
"object"	Sad	Why do you disagree?
"praise"	Happy	Thank you for your praise
"stop"	Moderate	Why do you stop me?
"succeed"	Happy	Well done. You are successful
"shake hand"	Happy	Nice to meet you
"weakly agree"	Head nod	OK, we finally reach an agreement
"call"	Head shake	Please turn off your phone
"drink"	Moderate	You can have a drink. No problem
"read"	Moderate	Please, take your time and read it carefully
"write"	Moderate	If you need time for taking notes, I can slow my presentation

body sizes, and races. During the sample collection, no strict constraint was imposed on the people. They carried out the gestures based on their own habits. The user–Kinect relative position was also not strictly limited. For convenience, CyberGlove II was precalibrated for all the people with a standard calibration. Due to the dataset collection setup, large diversities may exist among the gesture samples from different people. This will yield challenges on body gesture recognition. Figure 2.15 exhibits parts of the *Category 1* and *Category 2* gesture samples (*"have question,"* *"succeed,"* *"call,"* and *"drink"*) captured from five people for comparison. For the sake of brevity, not all the gestures are shown. The five descriptive and reference skeletal joints proposed in Sect. 2.4.2.2 are marked as big dots in Fig. 2.15, and they are connected by the straight segments to shape the upper body posture intuitively. From the exhibited samples, we can observe that:

- For the different people, the listed body gestures can indeed be differentiated from the hand and upper body posture information, and the people execute the gestures differently to a certain degree. As aforementioned, this phenomenon leads to challenges on upper body gesture recognition;
- For different people and gestures, the five skeletal joints employed for gesture recognition can be tracked robustly, even when human–object interaction occurs. Generally, their resulting positions are accurate for gesture recognition. Meanwhile, CyberGlove II is a human-touch device that can capture the hand posture

Fig. 2.15 Some gesture samples captured from different volunteers. These people are of different genders, body sizes, and races. They executed the gestures based on their own habits

robustly to yield high-accuracy data. Thus, the proposed human gesture-capture sensor solution can stably acquire available data for gesture recognition.

For each gesture, one key snapshot is picked up to build the dataset among all the 25 people. As a consequence, the resulting dataset contains $25 \times 12 = 300$ gesture samples in all. During experiment, the samples are randomly split into the training and testing set five times, and the average classification accuracy and standard deviation are reported.

The KNN classifier is used as the baseline to make comparison with the energy-based LMNN classifier. They are compared both on the items of classification accuracy and on time consumption. The KNN classifier runs with different kinds of distance measures. Following the experimental setup in [33],"k" is set as 3 in all cases. As the training sample number is a crucial factor that affects the classification accuracy, the results of two classifiers are compared corresponding to different amounts of training samples. For each class, the training sample number will increase from 4 to 14 with step size 2.

Table 2.2 Classification result (%) of the constructed *upper* body gesture dataset

Classifiers	Training sample number per class		
	4	6	8
KNN (Euclidean)	86.51(±2.89)	89.56(±2.43)	91.47(±2.21)
KNN (PCA)	73.81(±4.78)	84.04(±5.41)	79.31(±3.09)
KNN (LDA)	79.68(±5.33)	90.44(±2.56)	92.35(±2.44)
KNN (LMNN)	86.67(±2.18)	90.35(±2.56)	92.16(±1.80)
Energy (LMNN)	**90.00**(±**3.40**)	**92.28**(±**0.85**)	**94.31**(±**2.04**)
	10	12	14
KNN (Euclidean)	93.00(±1.15)	93.33(±0.73)	92.27(±2.30)
KNN (PCA)	86.11(±2.75)	88.21(±4.17)	86.67(±3.70)
KNN (LDA)	92.44(±1.34)	94.74(±0.84)	93.48(±1.38)
KNN (LMNN)	93.67(±1.34)	93.85(±1.48)	93.48(±1.15)
Energy (LMNN)	**95.22**(±**1.50**)	**95.64**(±**1.39**)	**96.52**(±**2.37**)

The best performance is shown in boldface. Standard deviations are in parentheses

Other two well-known distance metric learning methods, PCA [16] and LDA [12], are used for comparison with the LMNN distance metric learning approach. For PCA, the first 10 eigenvectors are used to capture roughly 90 % of the sum of eigenvalues, while the first 6 eigenvectors are used for LDA. The distance measures yielded by PCA and LDA are applied to the KNN classifier.

Table 2.2 lists the classification results yielded by the different classifier and distance measure combinations. It can be observed that:

- The 12 upper body gestures in the dataset can be well recognized by the proposed gesture recognition method. More than 95.00 % classification accuracy can be achieved if enough training samples are used. With the increase in training sample amount, the performance is generally enhanced consistently;
- Corresponding to all the training sample numbers, the energy-based LMNN classifier can yield the highest classification accuracy. Even with a small number (such as 4) of training samples it can still achieve relative good performance (90.00 %). When the training sample number reaches 14, the classification accuracy (96.52 %) is nearly satisfied for practical use, and its standard deviations are relatively low in most cases, which means that the energy-based LMNN classifier is robust to the gesture diversities among people;
- KNN classifier can also yield good results on this dataset. However, it is inferior to the energy-based LMNN classifier. Compared to Euclidean distance, LMNN distance metric learning method can improve the performance of KNN classifier consistently in most cases. However, it works much better on the energy-based model;
- PCA does not work well on this dataset. Its performance is worse than the basic Euclidean distance. The reason may be that PCA needs a large number of training

Table 2.3 Average testing time consumption (ms) per sample

Classifiers	Training sample number per class		
	4	6	8
KNN (LDA)	0.0317	0.0398	0.0414
KNN (LMNN)	0.0239	0.0282	0.0328
Energy (LMNN)	0.0959	0.1074	0.1273
	10	12	14
KNN (LDA)	0.0469	0.0498	0.0649
KNN (LMNN)	0.0342	0.0418	0.0525
Energy (LMNN)	0.1359	0.1610	0.1943

The program is run on the computer with Intel (R) Core (TM) i5-2430M @ 2.4 GHz (only using one core)

samples to obtain the satisfied distance measures [22]. This is the limitation for practical applications.

- LDA also achieves good performance for upper body gesture recognition. However, it is still consistently inferior to energy-based LMNN, especially when the training sample number is small. For example, when the training sample number is only 4, energy-based LMNN's accuracy (90.00 %) is significantly better than that of LDA (79.68 %) by a large margin (10.32 %).

Besides the classification accuracy, the testing time consumption is also what we are concerned about. The reason is that the GUHRI system should run in real-time for good HRI experience. According to the classification results in Table 2.2, the energy-based LMNN classifier, LMNN KNN classifier, and LDA KNN classifier are the three strongest ones for gesture recognition. Here, comparison on their testing time is also made. Table 2.3 lists the average running time per testing sample of the three classifiers, corresponding to different amounts of training samples. We can see that the three classifiers are extremely fast under our experimental conditions, and the time consumption mainly depends on the number of training samples. Frankly, the LDA KNN classifier and LMNN KNN classifier are much faster than the energy-based LMNN classifier. If a huge number of training samples were used (such as tens of thousands), the LDA KNN classifier and LMNN KNN classifier would be a better choice to achieve the balance between classification accuracy and computational efficiency.

2.5 Future Avenues

Our current research mainly pays attention to understanding the static upper body gestures. However, the dynamic ones are also the essential components of body language in daily life. For human–human interaction, they provide additional communication clues to boost the interaction performance. To make human–robot interaction more natural and lifelike, the robot should be capable of understanding both static and dynamic gestures. Being different from static gestures, motion information is required to recognize the dynamic gestures. From Microsoft Kinect SDK, human body 3D joint information can be achieved in real-time (30 fps). Motion information can be intuitively extracted from the position change in body joints along the temporal axis. The body joint motion information has earlier been applied to activity recognition [31, 32]. Nevertheless, these works still ignore hand gestures, which may lead to ambiguity on gesture understanding. Thus, one of our future research avenues is to recognize the dynamic human upper body gestures (such as "*wave hand*," "*say no*," and "*clap*," etc.) by combing both body motion and hand gesture information.

Another future research topic is to recognize human gestures from the egocentric perspectives of the robot. In the proposed GUHRI system, Kinect is employed as the vision sensor with fixed position. This system setup has some limits for real applications under challenging conditions. That is, the robot cannot change her viewpoint due to the fixed position of Kinect. In this case, the robot is not able to always acquire the optimal viewpoint to capture human body gesture information. Actually, due to this viewpoint reason, body occlusion may happen that will seriously confuse the accurate body joint position extraction. One feasible solution for this problem is to capture the human body gesture information from the robot's egocentric perspectives. In this way, the robot can change her viewpoint accordingly. However, to achieve good results, some new challenges need to be solved; one main problem is how to distinguish camera motion and real body motion.

In addition, how to integrate the verbal clues in the GURHI system to further enhance the human–robot interaction performance is also what we are concerned about in the future work. Making the robot "see" and "listen" will let her become more autonomous and humanlike.

2.6 Conclusion

The GUHRI system, a novel body gesture understanding and human–robot interaction system, is proposed in this paper. A set of 12 human upper body gestures with and without human–object interactions can be understood by the robot. Meanwhile, the robot can express herself by using a combination of body movements, facial expressions, and verbal language simultaneously, aiming to give the users a natural and vivid experience.

A new combination of sensors is proposed. That is, CyberGlove II and Kinect are combined to capture the head, arm, and hand posture simultaneously. An effective and real-time gesture recognition method is also proposed. In the experiment, a human upper body gesture dataset is built. The experimental results demonstrate the effectiveness and efficiency of our gesture recognition method.

So far, the gestures involved in GUHRI system have been static ones, e.g., *"have question," "praise," "call," "drink,"* etc. As the future work, we plan to enable the robot to understand dynamic gestures such as *"wave hand," "say no," "clap,"* etc. Speech recognition can be further added to make the interaction more natural.

References

1. Adamo-Villani N, Heisler J, Arns L (2007) Two gesture recognition systems for immersive math education of the deaf. In: Proceedings of the first international conference on immersive telecommunications (ICIT 2007). ICST (Institute for Computer Sciences, Social-Informatics and Telecommunications Engineering), p 9
2. Beck A, Cañamero L, Hiolle A, Damiano L, Cosi P, Tesser F, Sommavilla G (2013) Interpretation of emotional body language displayed by a humanoid robot: a case study with children. Int J Soc Robot: 1–10
3. Belongies S, Malik J, Puzicha J (2002) Shape matching and object recognition using shape contexts. IEEE Trans Pattern Anal Mach Int 24(4):509–522
4. Berman S, Stern H (2012) Sensors for gesture recognition systems. IEEE Trans Syst Man Cybern: Appl Rev 42(3):277–290
5. Brethes L, Menezes P, Lerasle F, Hayet J (2004) Face tracking and hand gesture recognition for human-robot interaction. In: Proceedings of IEEE conference on robotics and automation (ICRA 2004), IEEE, vol 2. pp 1901–1906
6. Cañamero L, Fredslund J (2001) I show you how i like you—can you read it in my face? [robotics]. IEEE Trans Syst Man Cybern: Syst Hum 31(5):454–459
7. Cassell J et al. (2000) Nudge nudge wink wink: elements of face-to-face conversation for embodied conversational agents. Embodied conversational agents, pp 1–27
8. Chopra S, Hadsell R, LeCun Y (2005) Learning a similarity metric discriminatively, with application to face verification. In: Proceedings of IEEE conference on computer vision and pattern recognition (CVPR 2005), vol 1. pp 539–546
9. Cover T, Hart P (1967) Nearest neighbor pattern classification. IEEE Trans Inf Theory 13(1):21–27
10. Dautenhahn K (2007) Socially intelligent robots: dimensions of human-robot interaction. Philos Trans Royal Soc B: Biol Sci 362(1480):679–704
11. Faber F, Bennewitz M, Eppner C, Gorog A, Gonsior C, Joho D, Schreiber M, Behnke S (2009) The humanoid museum tour guide robotinho. In: Proceedings of IEEE symposium on robot and human interactive communication (RO-MAN 2009), IEEE, pp 891–896
12. Fisher RA (1936) The use of multiple measures in taxonomic problems. Ann Eugenics 7:179–188
13. Fong T, Nourbakhsh I, Dautenhahn K (2003) A survey of socially interactive robots. Robot Auton Syst 42(3):143–166
14. Goodrich MA, Schultz AC (2007) Human-robot interaction: a survey. Found Trends Hum-Comput Interact 1(3):203–275
15. Immersion (2010) Cyberglove II specfications
16. Jolliffe IT (1986) Principal component analysis. Springer, London
17. Krämer NC, Tietz B, Bente G (2003) Effects of embodied interface agents and their gestural activity. In: Intelligent virtual agents. Springer, London, pp 292–300
18. Lu G, Shark L-K, Hall G, Zeshan U (2012) Immersive manipulation of virtual objects through glove-based hand gesture interaction. Virtual Reality 16(3):243–252
19. Mehrabian A (1971) Silent messages
20. Müller M, Röder T (2006) Motion templates for automatic classification and retrieval of motion capture data. In: Proceedings of the 2006 ACM SIGGRAPH/Eurographics symposium on computer animation (SCA 2006), Eurographics Association, pp 137–146

21. Nickel K, Stiefelhagen R (2007) Visual recognition of pointing gestures for human-robot interaction. Image Vis Comput 25(12):1875–1884
22. Osborne JW, Costello AB (2004) Sample size and subject to item ratio in principal components analysis. Pract Assess, Res Eval 9(11):8
23. Perzanowski D, Schultz AC, Adams W, Marsh E, Bugajska M (2001) Building a multimodal human-robot interface. IEEE Intell Syst 16(1):16–21
24. Shotton J, Fitzgibbon A, Cook M, Sharp T, Finocchio M, Moore R, Kipman A, Blake A (2011) Real-time human pose recognition in parts from single depth images. In: Proceedings of IEEE conference on computer vision and pattern recognition (CVPR 2011), pp 1297–1304
25. Smith LB, Breazeal C (2007) The dynamic lift of developmental process. Dev Sci 10(1):61–68
26. Spiliotopoulos D, Androutsopoulos I, Spyropoulos CD (2001) Human-robot interaction based on spoken natural language dialogue. In: Proceedings of the European workshop on service and humanoid robots, pp 25–27
27. Stiefelhagen R, Ekenel HK, Fugen C, Gieselmann P, Holzapfel H, Kraft F, Nickel K, Voit M, Waibel A (2007) Enabling multimodal human-robot interaction for the karlsruhe humanoid robot. IEEE Trans Robot 23(5):840–851
28. Stiefelhagen R, Fugen C, Gieselmann R, Holzapfel H, Nickel K, Waibel A (2004) Natural human-robot interaction using speech, head pose and gestures. In: Proceedings of IEEE conference on intelligent robots and systems (IROS 2004), IEEE, vol 3, pp 2422–2427
29. Teleb H, Chang G (2012) Data glove integration with 3d virtual environments. In: Proceeedings of international conference on systems and informatics (ICSAI 2012), IEEE, pp 107–112
30. Waldherr S, Romero R, Thrun S (2000) A gesture based interface for human-robot interaction. Auton Robots 9(2):151–173
31. Wang J, Liu Z, Wu Y, Yuan J (2012) Mining actionlet ensemble for action recognition with depth cameras. In: Proceedings of IEEE conference on computer vision and pattern recognition (CVPR 2012), pp 1290–1297
32. Wang J, Liu Z, Chorowski J, Chen Z, Wu Y (2012) Robust 3d action recognition with random occupancy patterns. In: Proceedings of European conference on computer vision (ECCV). Springer, London, pp 872–885
33. Weinberger KQ, Saul LK (2009) Distance metric learning for large margin nearest neighbor classification. J Mach Learn Res 10:207–244
34. Xiao Y, Cao Z, Zhuo W (2011) Type-2 fuzzy thresholding using glsc histogram of human visual nonlinearity characteristics. Opt. Express 19(11):10656–10672
35. Xiao Y, Cao Z, Yuan J (2014) Entropic image thresholding based on GLGM histogram. Pattern Recogn Lett 40:47–55
36. Xiao Y, Wu J, Yuan J (2014) mCENTRIST: a multi-channel feature generation mechanism for scene categorization. IEEE Trans Image Process 23(2):823–836
37. Xiao Y, Yuan J, Thalmann D (2013) Human-virtual human interaction by upper body gesture understanding. In: Proceedings of the 19th ACM symposium on virtual reality software and technology (VRST 2013), pp 133–142. ACM, Las Vegas
38. Xiao Y, Zhang Z, Beck A, Yuan J, Thalmann D (2014) Human-robot interaction by understanding upper body gestures. Presence: teleoperators and virtual environments (Accepted)

Chapter 3
Sound Source Localization and Tracking

Kai Wu and Andy W.H. Khong

Abstract Sound source localization and tracking plays an important role in a tele-conferencing system and social robot applications. Given the location of a sound, the social robot can be endowed with the capability of sound event awareness, which results in enhanced interaction with human beings. This chapter presents the problem of sound source localization and tracking, highlights their challenges, and reviews several existing techniques. In addition, a speech source tracking algorithm is proposed in order to achieve robust speaker tracking in the presence of sound interferers. Simulation is conducted and shows the effectiveness of the proposed method in a typical room environment.

3.1 Introduction

Sound source localization and tracking (SSLT) refers to the problem of estimating the location from which a sound signal originates with respect to the microphone array geometry. It plays an important role in a teleconferencing system and in social robot applications. In a teleconference scenario, a camera that is capable of automatic steering can be deployed to focus on the speaker given the estimated speaker position [22, 29]. In addition, source localization is often required and regarded as a preprocessing step before the enhancement of an acoustic signal from a particular location [20]. In the domain of social robotics, the localization technique is applied so that the robot can concentrate on a subject of interest or be made aware of where other sound events are coming from.

Multiple microphones are, in general, required in order to achieve SSLT. Different microphone array configurations have been used in the recent literature, e.g., binaural microphones [5], linear array [39], circular array [9] and distributed microphone

K. Wu (✉) · A.W.H. Khong
BeingThere Centre, Nanyang Technological University, Singapore, Singapore
e-mail: WU0001AI@e.ntu.edu.sg

A.W.H. Khong
e-mail: AndyKhong@ntu.edu.sg

© Springer International Publishing Switzerland 2016
N. Magnenat-Thalmann et al. (eds.), *Context Aware Human-Robot and Human-Agent Interaction*, Human–Computer Interaction Series,
DOI 10.1007/978-3-319-19947-4_3

arrays [13, 25]. The source position is estimated by exploiting the range differences from the source to the microphones. Although various algorithms have been developed in recent decades for SSLT applications, room reverberation, background noise, and sound interference are some of the key challenges that need to be addressed in a realistic environment. In the context of room acoustics, the microphones capture not only the direct-path propagation component of the source signal but also the multipath propagation component due to the reflections at the room boundaries. The multipath component, together with the background noise, distorts the time delay information contained in the microphone received signals and degrades the localization performance. In addition, one is often interested in localizing and tracking a desired source (e.g., human speech source) in the presence of certain sound interferers (e.g., fan noise, air-conditioner noise) which often exist in a room environment. These interferers may distract the system which, as a result, localizes the interferers rather than the desired source.

The organization of this chapter is as follows: in Sect. 3.2, mathematical formulation of the SSLT problem is introduced. Conventional localization and tracking methods are then reviewed. In Sect. 3.3, a proposed method that deals with the problem of speech source tracking in the presence of sound interference is discussed. The proposed method exploits the speech harmonicity feature so as ensure that only speech signals are used for tracking. The integration of SSLT for social robot application is discussed in Sect. 3.4. Finally, the future possible research directions and conclusions are presented in Sects. 3.5 and 3.6, respectively.

3.2 Overview of Sound Source Localization and Tracking Algorithms

SSLT algorithms can be classified into two categories: localization approach and tracking approach. The localization approach assumes independence between successive audio frames and estimates the source location independently across each data frame. The tracking approach exploits consistency between successive frames by assuming that the source is stationary or moving at a slow rate. In this section, the mathematical formulation for these two approaches is discussed.

3.2.1 Mathematical Formulation of Sound Source Localization

The SSLT problem is illustrated in Fig. 3.1. The speech signal $s(n)$ radiates away from the source position and propagates to the microphones. The received signals contains not only direct-path but also multipath components caused by reflection from

Fig. 3.1 Signal propagation model

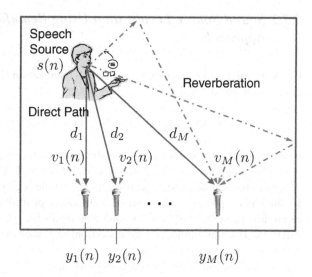

the room boundaries. Within a short time frame, the channel from the source to the ith microphone can be considered as a linear time-invariant system and is represented by a channel impulse response $h_i(n)$. The ith microphone received signal can thus be formulated as [3]

$$y_i(n) = s(n) * h_i(n) + v_i(n), \quad i = 1, 2, \ldots, M, \tag{3.1}$$

where $*$ is the convolution operator, $v_i(n)$ is the additive noise, and M is the number of microphones. In order to infer the signal delay information, the impulse response $h_i(n)$ can be further decomposed into a direct-path component and a multipath component. The microphone received signal can thus be rewritten as

$$y_i(n) = a_i s(n - \tau_i) + s(n) * h_i'(n) + v_i(n), \quad i = 1, 2, \ldots, M, \tag{3.2}$$

where $0 \leq a_i \leq 1$ is the attenuation factor due to propagation, τ_i is the direct-path time delay from the source to the ith microphone, and $h_i'(n)$ denotes the remaining impulse response which is defined as the difference between the original response and the direct-path component. In (3.2), the time delay τ_i is dependent on the source position with respect to the microphone array. However, direct estimation of τ_i is not achievable since SSLT is a passive localization problem. Most of the algorithms exploit the relative time delay information among microphones and one such algorithm is introduced in the following section.

3.2.2 Sound Source Localization Using Beamforming-Based Approach

Given the microphone received signal $y_i(n)$, localization is usually performed using each data frame defined as

$$\mathbf{y}_i(k) = [y_i(kN) \; y_i(kN+1) \; \ldots \; y_i(kN+N-1)], \tag{3.3}$$

where N is the frame length and k is the frame index. Beamforming is one of the widely used approaches for sound source localization. In principle, the beamformer computes the spatial power spectrum for the whole region of interest and searches for the highest power corresponding to the source position estimate (see Fig. 3.2 for example). The family of beamforming techniques includes steered response power (SRP) [8, 10], minimum variance distortionless response [34], linearly constrained minimum variance [11, 34], etc.

The SRP beamformer gained popularity due to its simplicity. Considering M microphones, the SRP function defines the power

$$\mathcal{P}_k(\mathbf{r}') = \sum_{\omega_l \in \Omega} \left| \sum_{i=1}^{M} W_i(k, \omega_l) Y_i(k, \omega_l) e^{j\omega_l \|\mathbf{r}' - \mathbf{r}_i^m\|_2/c} \right|^2 \tag{3.4}$$

corresponding to the current steered location $\mathbf{r}'$ at time frame k, where $\mathbf{r}' = [x' \; y']^T$ is the steered location in the region of interest, $W_i(k, \omega_l)$ is a weighting function, $Y_i(k, \omega_l)$ is the short-time Fourier transform of the ith microphone received signal defined as $Y_i(k, \omega_l) = \mathcal{F}(\mathbf{y}_i(k))$, ω_l is the angular frequency of the lth bin index, c is the speed of sound, $\mathbf{r}_i^m$ is the position of the ith microphone, $\|\mathbf{r}' - \mathbf{r}_i^m\|_2$ is the distance from the steered location to the ith microphone position, and Ω is the interested frequency range over which the computation is carried out. In (3.4), the

Fig. 3.2 The power spectrum when $SNR = 20\,dB$, $T_{60} = 150\,ms$. The ground truth of the source position is denoted by the *circle dot* which is plotted on *top* of the spectrum for clarity of presentation

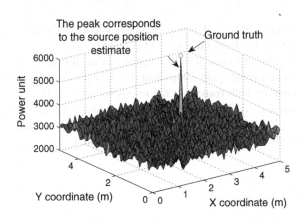

SRP is performed by computing the time delay from the steered location $\mathbf{r}'$ to each microphone in the first step. The corresponding power is then calculated by time aligning the signals in the frequency domain according to the signal delays and summing over all the microphones. The weighting function $W_i(k, \omega_l)$ is important in power calculation. While different weighting functions can be used [24], the phase transform (PHAT) given as

$$W_i^{\text{PHAT}}(k, \omega_l) = \frac{1}{|Y_i(k, \omega_l)|} \tag{3.5}$$

remains one of the most commonly used weighting schemes. The corresponding beamformer is therefore named as SRP-PHAT. By substituting (3.5) into (3.4), it can be seen that the PHAT weighting is independent of the source energy and the computed SRP response is only dependent on the phase delay.

Furthermore, by steering the beamformer across the whole region of interest, one can obtain the power spectrum as shown in Fig. 3.2. Estimating the source position is therefore achieved by searching for the location that corresponds to the maximum power, i.e.,

$$\widehat{\mathbf{r}}_k = \arg\max_{\mathbf{r}' \in \mathcal{D}} \mathcal{P}_k(\mathbf{r}'), \tag{3.6}$$

where $\mathcal{D} = \{x, y | x_{\min} \leq x \leq x_{\max}, y_{\min} \leq y \leq y_{\max}\}$ is the considered searching domain.

It has been shown in [7] that the beamforming method achieves higher spatial resolution than other localization methods such as those based on time-difference-of-arrival method [3]. However, one drawback is the high computation complexity required for scanning the region of interest. Some researchers choose different resolution grids to reduce the computation burden [12]. In addition, a recently proposed work integrates the energy in each discrete grid to achieve better performance [4].

3.2.3 Sound Source Tracking Using Particle Filter-Based Approach

The localization algorithm discussed in Sect. 3.2.2 estimates the source position using each microphone data frame $\mathbf{y}_i(k)$ independently. The performance reduces when the background noise and reverberation increase since under these conditions, some of the data frames suffer from signal distortion and are therefore unable to provide reliable location estimates. However, if we assume that the source is stationary or moving at a low rate with respect to the convergence of the tracking algorithm, one possible approach to improve the performance is to exploit the temporal consistency of location measurements across successive frames.

We now consider successive data frames $\{\mathbf{y}_i(k) | k = 1, 2, \ldots, K\}$ where k is the frame index, and K is the total number of audio frames. The aim is to estimate the source positions over all the time frames, leading to a source tracking problem. We first define the state variable as $\boldsymbol{\alpha}_k = [x_k \ y_k \ \dot{x}_k \ \dot{y}_k]^T$ at frame index k, where x_k and y_k correspond to the source position while $\dot{x}_k$ and $\dot{y}_k$ are the source velocities in x and y direction, respectively. Similarly, the measurement variable $\mathbf{z}_k = [\widehat{x}_k \ \widehat{y}_k]^T$ is defined. This measurement vector can be obtained from the SRP location estimate by evaluating (3.4)–(3.6) for the kth time frame data. Therefore, the state-space model can be written as

$$\boldsymbol{\alpha}_k = \mathcal{G}(\boldsymbol{\alpha}_{k-1}, \mathbf{u}_k), \tag{3.7a}$$

$$\mathbf{z}_k = \mathcal{H}(\boldsymbol{\alpha}_k, \mathbf{w}_k), \tag{3.7b}$$

where $\mathcal{G}(\cdot)$ is the process function defining the time evolution of the state, $\mathbf{u}_k$ is the process noise, $\mathcal{H}(\cdot)$ is the measurement equation defining the mapping from $\boldsymbol{\alpha}_k$ to $\mathbf{z}_k$, and $\mathbf{w}_k$ is the measurement noise.

To formulate $\mathcal{G}(\cdot)$ in (3.7a), the *Langevin* process model has been widely used as it provides a realistic model to simulate human source motion [13, 25, 31, 35, 37]. This model can be described using

$$\boldsymbol{\alpha}_k = \begin{bmatrix} 1 & 0 & aT & 0 \\ 0 & 1 & 0 & aT \\ 0 & 0 & a & 0 \\ 0 & 0 & 0 & a \end{bmatrix} \boldsymbol{\alpha}_{k-1} + \begin{bmatrix} bT & 0 \\ 0 & bT \\ b & 0 \\ 0 & b \end{bmatrix} \mathbf{u}_k, \tag{3.8}$$

where $\mathbf{u}_k \sim \mathcal{N}(\boldsymbol{\mu}, \boldsymbol{\Sigma})$ is the noise vector following Gaussian distribution, T is the time interval between consecutive frames, and $\boldsymbol{\mu} = [0 \ 0]^T$ and $\boldsymbol{\Sigma} = \mathbf{I}_{2\times 2}$ correspond to the mean vector and covariance matrix, respectively. In addition, the model parameters are defined as $a = \exp(-\beta T), b = \bar{v}\sqrt{1 - a^2}$, where $\bar{v} = 0.8\,\text{m/s}$ is the steady-state velocity and $\beta = 10\,\text{Hz}$ is the rate constant [25]. To formulate $\mathcal{H}(\cdot)$ in (3.7b), we note that $\mathbf{z}_k$ is defined as the two-dimensional location estimate obtained from SRP and hence, we can express

$$\mathbf{z}_k = \begin{bmatrix} 1 & 0 & 0 & 0 \\ 0 & 1 & 0 & 0 \end{bmatrix} \boldsymbol{\alpha}_k + \mathbf{w}_k, \tag{3.9}$$

where $\mathbf{w}_k$ represents the measurement error.

The process of sound source tracking is performed in a probabilistic manner. Statistically, the posterior probability density function (pdf) $\Pr(\boldsymbol{\alpha}_k | \mathbf{z}_{1:k})$ is used to denote the probability of state $\boldsymbol{\alpha}_k$ conditioned on the measurements up to time k and the measurement likelihood $\Pr(\mathbf{z}_k | \boldsymbol{\alpha}_k^{(p)})$ represents the probability of attaining measurement $\mathbf{z}_k$ conditioned on the state. Considering continuous data frames, the sound source tracking problem can therefore be formulated as follows: for each frame index k, given $\Pr(\boldsymbol{\alpha}_{k-1} | \mathbf{z}_{1:k-1})$ at the previous time frame, the objective is to estimate $\Pr(\boldsymbol{\alpha}_k | \mathbf{z}_{1:k})$ using the source motion model $\mathcal{G}(\cdot)$ and the new measurement $\mathbf{z}_k$.

While Kalman filtering has been proposed for source tracking [15, 18], the particle filter (PF) framework [1, 17] is deemed to be a better approach for the SSLT problem due to the absence of linearity and Gaussian distribution requirement in the state-space formulation. The PF was first introduced in SSLT in [35] and has gained great popularity [13, 14, 25, 27, 31, 37].

In the PF framework, the posterior density $\Pr(\boldsymbol{\alpha}_k | \mathbf{z}_{1:k})$ is approximated by a set of particles of the state space with associated weights $\{(\boldsymbol{\alpha}_k^{(p)}, w_k^{(p)})\}_{p=1}^{N_p}$, i.e.,

$$\Pr(\boldsymbol{\alpha}_k | \mathbf{z}_{1:k}) = \sum_{p=1}^{N_p} w_k^{(p)} \delta(\boldsymbol{\alpha}_k - \boldsymbol{\alpha}_k^{(p)}), \tag{3.10}$$

where $p = 1, \ldots, N_p$ denotes the particle index, $\boldsymbol{\alpha}_k^{(p)}$ is the pth particle of state space, $w_k^{(p)}$ is its associated weight, and $\delta(\cdot)$ is the Dirac delta function. The bootstrap PF-based sound source tracking is performed as follows: suppose at time $k - 1$, the set $\{(\boldsymbol{\alpha}_{k-1}^{(p)}, w_{k-1}^{(p)})\}_{p=1}^{N_p}$ is an approximation of the posterior density $\Pr(\boldsymbol{\alpha}_{k-1} | \mathbf{z}_{1:k-1})$, the set $\{(\boldsymbol{\alpha}_k^{(p)}, w_k^{(p)})\}_{p=1}^{N_p}$ at time index k corresponding to $\Pr(\boldsymbol{\alpha}_k | \mathbf{z}_{1:k})$ is then obtained by a propagation step

$$\boldsymbol{\alpha}_k^{(p)} = \mathcal{G}(\boldsymbol{\alpha}_{k-1}^{(p)}, \mathbf{u}_k), \tag{3.11}$$

followed by an update step,

$$w_k^{(p)} \propto w_{k-1}^{(p)} \Pr(\mathbf{z}_k | \boldsymbol{\alpha}_k^{(p)}). \tag{3.12}$$

Computation of $\Pr(\mathbf{z}_k | \boldsymbol{\alpha}_k^{(p)})$ is required in (3.12) and a *pseudo* likelihood approach has been proposed [25, 37] to reduce the computational load involved in the process of determining the SRP maximum corresponding to the source location measurement. In this formulation, the SRP map itself is used as an approximation of $\Pr(\mathbf{z}_k | \boldsymbol{\alpha}_k^{(p)})$. To some extent the SRP can define the probability of the source being located in the steered positions within the room as it corresponds to the energy originating from those positions. The pseudo likelihood approach defines the likelihood as

$$\Pr(\mathbf{z}_k | \boldsymbol{\alpha}_k) = \begin{cases} \mathcal{P}_k^{\gamma}(\boldsymbol{\ell}_k), & \text{for voiced frame} \\ \mathcal{U}_{\mathcal{D}}(\boldsymbol{\ell}_k), & \text{for unvoiced frame} \end{cases}, \tag{3.13}$$

where $\gamma = 2$ is a control parameter to regulate the SRP function for source tracking [25], $\mathcal{U}_{\mathcal{D}}(\cdot)$ is the uniform pdf over the considered enclosure domain $\mathcal{D}$, and $\boldsymbol{\ell}_k$ denotes the first two elements of $\boldsymbol{\alpha}_k$.

In practice, due to the proportionality in (3.12), the normalization process is always computed using

$$w_k^{(p)} \Leftarrow \frac{w_k^{(p)}}{\sum_{i=1}^{N_p} w_k^{(i)}}, \tag{3.14}$$

Table 3.1 Summary of the bootstrap PF

At time $k-1$, a set of particles $\{\boldsymbol{\alpha}_{k-1}^{(p)}, w_{k-1}^{(p)}\}_{p=1}^{N_p}$ is a discrete representation of posterior $\Pr(\boldsymbol{\alpha}_{k-1}|\mathbf{z}_{k-1})$.

For the kth frame:

1. *Particles propagation*: propagate each particle through the source dynamic model (3.7a),

$$\boldsymbol{\alpha}_k^{(p)} = \mathcal{G}(\boldsymbol{\alpha}_{k-1}^{(p)}, \mathbf{u}_k).$$

2. *Update*: the weight corresponding to each particle is updated according to the likelihood,

$$w_k^{(p)} = w_{k-1}^{(p)} \Pr(\mathbf{z}_k|\boldsymbol{\alpha}_k^{(p)}),$$

followed by a normalization step $w_k^{(p)} \Leftarrow w_k^{(p)} (\sum_{i=1}^{N_p} w_k^{(i)})^{-1}$.

3. *Resampling*: resample the particles if the effective sample size is below a threshold, $N_{\text{eff}} < N_{\text{thr}}$, where $N_{\text{eff}} = (\sum_{p=1}^{N_p} (w_k^{(p)})^2)^{-1}$.

4. *Result*: the particle set $\{\boldsymbol{\alpha}_k^{(p)}, w_k^{(p)}\}_{p=1}^{N_p}$ is obtained for approximation of $\Pr(\boldsymbol{\alpha}_k|\mathbf{z}_k)$. The state estimate at the kth frame is $\widehat{\boldsymbol{\alpha}}_k = \sum_{p=1}^{N_p} w_k^{(p)} \boldsymbol{\alpha}_k^{(p)}$.

where $\Leftarrow$ denotes the assignment of a new value to the variable. In addition, the PF usually consists of a resampling stage which prevents the degeneration phenomenon where, after a few iterations, a majority of the particles would possess small weights incurring a waste of computation [1]. Finally the state estimate, at time frame index k, is given as

$$\widehat{\boldsymbol{\alpha}}_k = \sum_{p=1}^{N_p} w_k^{(p)} \boldsymbol{\alpha}_k^{(p)}, \tag{3.15}$$

and the first two elements of $\widehat{\boldsymbol{\alpha}}_k$ represent the position estimate from the tracking framework. A summary of the bootstrap PF-based sound source tracking algorithm can be found in Table 3.1.

3.3 Proposed Robust Speech Source Tracking

In Sect. 3.2, several approaches have been discussed for localizing and tracking a stationary or moving source. Significant progress has been made in recent decades for robust SSLT in different adverse environments. However, localizing or tracking a speech source in the presence of sound interferences is still an open problem. This is particularly important in robotic applications since the robots are expected to continue interacting with a human user in a noisy environment. It is also important to note that sound interferences may be nonstationary and unpredictable in nature. Take an office room for instance, the fan noise, air-conditioner noise, or a telephone ring may be located at different positions. Existing methods, in general, are unable to distinguish between the desired speech source and interferers. The performance may be degraded when these interferers are present.

In this section, a speech source tracking method that is robust to interferers is introduced [38]. The proposed method incorporates a well-known speech feature in the frequency domain known as harmonicity. We first compare the speech spectrogram with some typical sound interference in Sect. 3.3.1 and illustrate the speech harmonic feature. Details of the proposed method will be introduced in Sect. 3.3.2. In Sect. 3.3.3, simulations are conducted to evaluate the performance of the proposed method in the presence of interference, noise, and reverberation.

3.3.1 The Harmonic Structure in the Speech Spectrogram

Figure 3.3 shows the spectrogram of a typical speech signal obtained from the TIMIT database [16] and that corresponding to different sound interferers obtained from the NOISEX-92 database [33]. The speech spectrogram, as shown in Fig. 3.3a, indicates that several harmonics (dark curves) corresponding to multiple integers of a pitch frequency are present. The pitch frequency represents the frequency of the vocal cord vibration, which normally ranges from 100 to 300 Hz , depending on whether

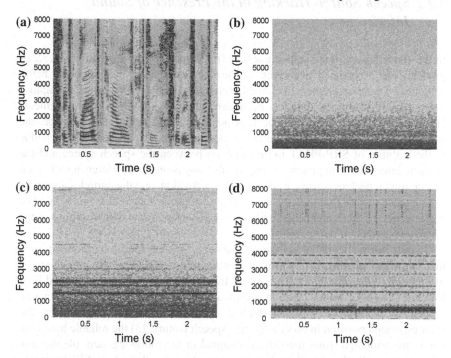

Fig. 3.3 Spectrograms of different signals. **a** Speech signal spectrogram. **b** Fan noise spectrogram. **c** Power drill noise spectrogram. **d** Telephone ring noise spectrogram

it is a male or a female voice [6]. This spectrogram indicates that speech energy is dominant on these harmonics. Figure 3.3b shows the spectrogram of a recorded fan noise where the energy is concentrated below 2 kHz. The spectrogram of a recorded power drill noise, shown in Fig. 3.3c, indicates a similar energy distribution in the low frequency range although high energy spectral lines appear at approximately 1.5, 2, and 2.2 kHz. These dominant frequencies may be caused by mechanical rotation or vibration. It is useful to note that no regular harmonic structure is exhibited in these two types of sound. In terms of the telephone ring sound, shown in Fig. 3.3d, a regular harmonic structure is caused by the presence of a single tone. However, the harmonics differ from that of the speech signal due to a difference in pitch frequency.

In the following, we therefore assume that the sound interference does not share the same harmonic bands as speech due to different pitch frequency, or that the interference does not possess any harmonic structure. The key objective of the proposed method is to estimate these harmonic bands corresponding to the speech components and to emphasize on the harmonic bands as they provide high signal-to-interference ratio (SIR). Other frequency regions are not used for tracking as these frequencies are contaminated by the sound interferers.

3.3.2 Speech Source Tracking in the Presence of Sound Interference

In the conventional sound source tracking framework, as introduced in Sect. 3.2.3, particles are propagated according to the source dynamic model before being weighted by the measurement likelihood. It computes the particle weights by employing a pseudo-likelihood that has been derived from SRP-PHAT measurements [13, 25, 37]. While this technique may achieve good tracking performance, the performance may significantly reduce in the presence of interference. This is due to the inability of SRP-PHAT to discriminate between the speech source and the acoustic interference in general. It implies that any acoustic interference will result in a dominant peak occurring at the interferer's position, and the particles are likely to propagate toward that location away from the speech source (see Fig. 3.7a). The performance of these algorithms reduces significantly in low SIR, resulting in the SSLT losing track of the speech source.

To mitigate the degradation in performance, we exploit speech harmonicity such that the measurement likelihood is predominantly weighted by the speech signal as opposed to the interferers. The overall framework of the proposed method is as follows: (1) a prior source position is estimated using the assumed source dynamic model, (2) a beamformer is then applied to enhance the source signal from the prior estimated position in order to extract speech feature, (3) the reliable harmonic bands are estimated using the enhanced signal in the following step, (4) the new measurement likelihood is then derived by emphasizing these high SIR harmonic bands while discarding the other frequency regions.

3.3.2.1 Prior Prediction

In general, a clear source signal is often required in order to extract the corresponding speech features. However, due to the presence of interference and background noise, obtaining such a clear source signal is challenging. To improve the feature extraction performance, we propose a speech signal enhancement stage consisting of prior source position prediction and a beamformer. Considering the Langevin source dynamic model introduced in Sect. 3.2.3, for time frame index k, the prior source state can be estimated using (3.7a) and (3.8) as

$$\widehat{\alpha}_k^- = \mathcal{G}(\widehat{\alpha}_{k-1}^+, \mathbf{u}_k), \tag{3.16}$$

given the state estimate at the previous frame. Here, $\widehat{\alpha}_{k-1}^+$ is the posterior state estimate at time frame index $k - 1$. The prior source location estimate

$$\widehat{\mathbf{r}}_k^- = [\widehat{x}_k^- \quad \widehat{y}_k^-]^T, \tag{3.17}$$

corresponds to the first two elements in $\widehat{\alpha}_k^-$. Note that this prior estimate is based only on the assumed source motion. Its objective is to allow the beamformer to enhance the signal from this preliminary estimated source position. The feature-directed measurements, as will be described in the subsequent sections, will further refine the state estimate.

3.3.2.2 Feature Extraction

After obtaining a prior estimate of source position at each iteration, a beamformer can be employed to enhance the signal from that particular position. Note that the beamformer was used as a localization technique in Sect. 3.2.2. However, beamforming was initially used for enhancing the signal from a known source position and suppressing the interference and noise [34]. Various beamformers can be applied after a prior source location has been estimated. We consider, for example, the delay-and-sum beamformer [23] due to its simplicity although other forms of beamformers such as presented in [21, 32] may be used to enhance the speech signal. The delay-and-sum beamformer output for the prior estimated source location $\widehat{\mathbf{r}}_k^-$ is given as

$$S(\omega_l, \widehat{\mathbf{r}}_k^-) = \sum_{i=1}^{M} \Phi\left(D_i(\widehat{\mathbf{r}}_k^-)\right) Y_i(k, \omega_l) e^{j\omega_l D_i(\widehat{\mathbf{r}}_k^-)/c}, \tag{3.18}$$

where i is the microphone index, M is the number of microphones, and $Y_i(k, \omega_l)$ is the frequency-domain received signal from the ith microphone at kth frame. The variable ω_l is the angular frequency of lth frequency bin, c is the speed of sound, $D_i(\widehat{\mathbf{r}}_k^-) = \|\widehat{\mathbf{r}}_k^- - \mathbf{r}_i^m\|_2$ is the distance from the prior estimated source position to the ith microphone, and $\Phi(\cdot)$ is a monotonic function that weighs the ith microphone signal according to the source-sensor distance. In our simulations, we found that $\Phi\left(D_i(\widehat{\mathbf{r}_k})\right) = 1/D_i(\widehat{\mathbf{r}_k})$ performs well as it emphasizes the signal from the microphone that is closer to the source.

Figure 3.4 shows the signal enhancement result for a 6 s speech signal when a power drill interference is present at SIR = 5 dB and white Gaussian noise with signal-to-noise (SNR) ratio of 15 dB. These results were generated using the method of images [26] with $T_{60} = 200$ ms and eight microphones are placed 0.5 m away from the room perimeter (see Fig. 3.7). Figure 3.4a shows the spectrogram of the original speech signal where a clear harmonic structure can be found. Figure 3.4b shows the power drill interference spectrogram where no harmonic structure is present. In general, the source signal received by a single reference microphone is often distorted, especially when the interferer is close to the microphone, as shown in Fig. 3.4c. Extraction of speech harmonics from this received signal is therefore challenging. The beamformer enhanced signal, as shown in Fig. 3.4d, is indeed clearer than the microphone received signal. The speech harmonics are dominant across the whole spectrogram although certain interference energy leakage is visible. The beamformer enhanced signal will be used for feature extraction in the next step.

To extract the speech harmonics from a noisy spectrum, we use the multi-band excitation (MBE) fit method [2, 19]. As indicated in Fig. 3.5, the MBE model defines a voiced frame in the frequency domain as the product of spectrum envelop $H(\omega)$ and excitation spectrum $E(\omega, \omega_p)$ given by [19]

$$S_{\text{spch}}(\omega) = H(\omega)E(\omega, \omega_p), \tag{3.19}$$

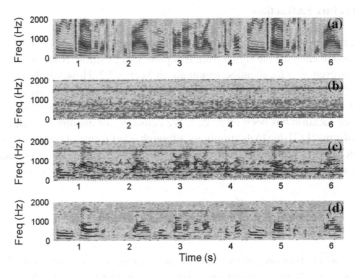

Fig. 3.4 Spectrogram and selected harmonic bands indicated in *blue lines*. **a** Clean speech. **b** Power-drill interference. **c** Reference microphone received signal and its selected harmonic bands (in *blue*). **d** Beamformer enhanced signal and its selected harmonic bands (in *blue*)

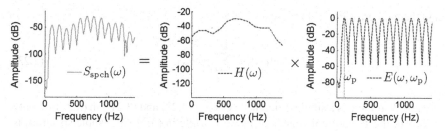

Fig. 3.5 MBE model for a speech signal. The voice frame can be modeled as a product of spectrum envelop $H(\omega)$ and excitation spectrum $E(\omega, \omega_{\mathrm{p}})$ in the frequency domain

where ω_{p} is the pitch frequency, such that

$$E(\omega, \omega_{\mathrm{p}}) = \sum_{q=1}^{Q} \Psi(\omega - q\omega_{\mathrm{p}}), \tag{3.20}$$

where q is the harmonic index, Q is the number of harmonics, ω_{p} is the pitch frequency, and $\Psi(\omega)$ is the Fourier transform of the Hamming window.

We now consider extracting the harmonic information from the beamformer enhanced signal $S(\omega, \widehat{\mathbf{r}_k^-})$ via MBE model fitting. The harmonic information ω_{p} and $H(\omega)$ can be estimated via minimization of the fitting error between $S(\omega, \widehat{\mathbf{r}_k^-})$ and the MBE modeled signal

$$\varepsilon(\omega_{\mathrm{p}}) = \int_0^{2\pi} |S(\omega, \widehat{\mathbf{r}_k^-}) - S_{\mathrm{spch}}(\omega)|^2 d\omega$$

$$= \int_0^{2\pi} |S(\omega, \widehat{\mathbf{r}_k^-}) - H(\omega)E(\omega, \omega_{\mathrm{p}})|^2 d\omega, \tag{3.21}$$

where $S(\omega, \widehat{\mathbf{r}_k^-})$ has been defined in (3.18).

In practice, the above process is computed in discrete frequency domain where $\omega_l = 2\pi l/L$ denotes the angular frequency of lth frequency bins, L is the number of frequency bins, and ω_{p} is now computed from the discrete angular frequencies. In order to solve the nonlinear minimization problem in (3.21), the whole spectrum is further decomposed into several harmonic bands. The qth harmonic band ranges in the interval $[a_q, b_q]$, where the lower and upper limits are defined as $a_q = \lceil (q - 0.5)\omega_{\mathrm{p}} \rfloor$ and $b_q = \lceil (q + 0.5)\omega_{\mathrm{p}} \rfloor$, respectively, and $\lceil \cdot \rfloor$ denotes the selection of the nearest frequency bin. The variable $H(\omega)$ is also decoupled into complex amplitude H_q for each harmonic band q, so that the fitting error for each harmonic band is

$$\varepsilon_q(\omega_{\mathrm{p}}) = \sum_{\omega_l=a_q}^{b_q} |S(\omega_l, \widehat{\mathbf{r}_k^-}) - H_q E(\omega_l, \omega_{\mathrm{p}})|, \tag{3.22}$$

and the total error in (3.21) becomes

$$\varepsilon(\omega_p) = \sum_{q=1}^{Q} \varepsilon_q(\omega_p). \tag{3.23}$$

We note that there is a subtle difference between (3.23) and (3.21); in (3.23) we only sum over the Q harmonic bands of interest, while in (3.21) the whole spectrum is integrated.

The harmonic information is thus represented by two parameters, the pitch frequency ω_p and complex amplitude H_q for all harmonic bands. The variable H_q can be obtained by considering the derivative of (3.22) to be zero giving

$$H_q = \frac{\displaystyle\sum_{\omega_l=a_q}^{b_q} S(\omega_l, \widehat{\mathbf{r}_k}) E^*(\omega_l, \omega_p)}{\displaystyle\sum_{\omega_l=a_q}^{b_q} |E(\omega_l, \omega_p)|^2}, \tag{3.24}$$

where $*$ denotes conjugate operation. The pitch frequency ω_p can be estimated by the following steps: each fitting error $\varepsilon_q(\omega_p)$ is evaluated using the optimal value of H_q obtained in (3.24). The error function in (3.23) is then computed with respect to all pitch frequencies ω_p of interest. Finally, the global minimum of $\varepsilon(\omega_p)$ is determined and the corresponding ω_p is selected as the estimated $\widehat{\omega}_p$ due to speech.

3.3.2.3 Feature-Directed Particle Weight Update

To obtain the feature-directed particle weight update, it is required to determine the most reliable harmonic bands and select them for computation of the likelihood. Two criteria are proposed to determine the reliability of the harmonic bands: (1) the normalized fitting error and (2) the normalized harmonic energy.

First, the normalized fitting error [2] is defined, for each harmonic, as the effectiveness of a given frequency band to be fitted with the speech harmonic model. It is computed as

$$\bar{\varepsilon}_q = \frac{\varepsilon_q(\widehat{\omega}_p)}{\displaystyle\sum_{\omega_l=a_q}^{b_q} |S(\omega_l, \widehat{\mathbf{r}_k})|^2}, \tag{3.25}$$

where the fitting error $\varepsilon_q(\widehat{\omega}_p)$ is computed by substituting the estimated pitch frequency $\widehat{\omega}_p$ into (3.22). The fitting error is normalized by the energy of each corresponding harmonic band.

In the second step, the normalized harmonic energy, defined by the ratio of energy distributed on that harmonic over the total energy, i.e.,

$$P_q = \frac{\displaystyle\sum_{\omega_l=a_q}^{b_q} H_q E(\omega_l, \widehat{\omega}_p)}{\displaystyle\sum_{q=1}^{Q} \sum_{\omega_l=a_q}^{b_q} H_q E(\omega_l, \widehat{\omega}_p)}. \tag{3.26}$$

is computed. As the energy of the speech signal is expected to be concentrated in a harmonic structure, those harmonic bands with low $\bar{\varepsilon}_q$ and high P_q are more likely to retain most of the speech components, while other regions are expected to contain the interference signal. We therefore set two harmonic-band thresholds ζ and η for selecting the reliable (speech) harmonic bands such that

$$G_q(\omega_l) = \begin{cases} \Psi(\omega_l - q\widehat{\omega}_p), & \text{if } \bar{\varepsilon}_q \leq \zeta \ \& \ P_q \geq \eta, \ \omega_l \in [a_q, b_q] \\ 0, & \text{otherwise} \end{cases}, \tag{3.27a}$$

$$G(\omega_l) = \sum_{q=1}^{Q} G_q(\omega_l). \tag{3.27b}$$

Equation (3.27a) indicates that only harmonic bands that satisfy the thresholds are selected; the other frequency bands are discarded. Equation (3.27b) indicates that the selection process is carried out over all frequency bands of interest. The sum of the selected harmonic bands are denoted as $G(\omega_l)$.

Figure 3.6 shows extraction results of the speech harmonics using a frame of 32 ms. Figure 3.6a shows the MBE fitting result, computed using (3.22)–(3.24), for the case of clean speech where no interferer is present. We note that the MBE approximation, shown by the dotted line, is capable of estimating the harmonics of clean speech. Figure 3.6b shows the result for the case where a power-drill signal is added to the speech signal at an SIR $= 5$ dB. The beamformer output $S(\omega_l, \widehat{\ell_k})$, shown by the solid line, therefore consists of spectral components corresponding to the power drill at 400 and 1500 Hz and the speech signal. Comparing Fig. 3.6a, b, we note that the MBE fit shown in Fig. 3.6b is able to estimate the speech harmonics with reasonable accuracy, albeit with some distortion. The estimated reliable speech harmonic bands are shown with $G(\omega_l)$ and are denoted by the bold lines (which has been normalized to 0 dB for clarity).

The extraction discussed above considers a single data frame. By iterating the procedure over all the frames, $G(\omega_l)$ in (3.27b) can be extended to $G(k, \omega_l)$ which denotes the selected harmonic bands at the kth frame. The selected harmonics over all the frames are shown in Fig. 3.4d where a 6 s speech in the presence of power-drill interference is considered. We note that using the beamformer and MBE fit, speech harmonic bands can be estimated as indicated by the dark lines in the spectrogram.

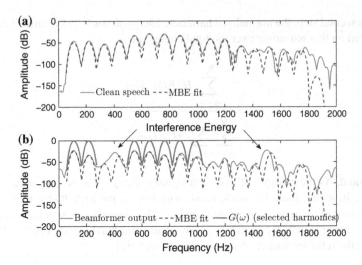

Fig. 3.6 MBE fitting result. **a** Clean speech and MBE fit. **b** Beamformer output, MBE fit, and $G(\omega)$ in the presence of a power drill signal

With $G(k, \omega_l)$, the new SRP function $\mathcal{P}_k(\boldsymbol{\ell})$ with weight $W_i(k, \omega_l)$ is given as

$$\mathcal{P}_k(\boldsymbol{\ell}) = \sum_{\omega_l \in \Omega} \left| \sum_{i=1}^{M} W_i(k, \omega_l) Y_i(k, \omega_l) e^{j\omega D_i(\boldsymbol{\ell})/c} \right|^2, \qquad (3.28a)$$

$$W_i(k, \omega_l) = \frac{G(k, \omega_l)}{|Y_i(k, \omega_l)|}, \qquad (3.28b)$$

where Ω is the frequency over which the SRP function is evaluated. Similar to the pseudo likelihood method [25, 37], the SRP function is used to define the measurement likelihood in the PF framework,

$$\Pr(\mathbf{z}_k | \boldsymbol{\alpha}_k) = \begin{cases} \mathcal{P}_k^{\gamma}(\boldsymbol{\ell}), & \text{for voiced frame} \\ \mathcal{U}_D(\boldsymbol{\ell}), & \text{for unvoiced frame} \end{cases}, \qquad (3.29)$$

where $\gamma = 2$ is a control parameter to regulate the SRP function for source tracking [25], and $\mathcal{U}_D(\cdot)$ is the uniform pdf over the considered enclosure domain $D = \{x_k, y_k | x_{\min} \le x_k \le x_{\max}, y_{\min} \le y_k \le y_{\max}\}$. The likelihood function is then used to update the particle weights of the particles. The proposed SSLT framework is summarized in Table 3.2.

3.3.3 Simulation Results

Simulations were conducted using synthetic impulse responses generated by the method of images [26]. The dimension of the room was $5\,m \times 5\,m \times 2.5\,m$, and the reverberation time T_{60} were 200–300 ms. Eight microphones were distributed $0.5\,m$ away from the perimeter of the room (see Fig. 3.7). An 8 s male speech signal sampled at 16 kHz from the TIMIT database [16] was used as the source signal. A power drill (PD) signal and a recorded telephone ring (TR) signal obtained from the NOISEX-92 database [33] were used as interferers. White Gaussian noise of 15 dB SNR was added to the microphone signals. The speed of source was approximately set at 0.6 m/s. The positions of speech source were estimated using a frame size of 512 samples with $N_p = 100$ particles. We also used an effective sample size threshold $N_{\text{thr}} = 37.5$, harmonic-band thresholds $\zeta = 0.6$ and $\eta = 0.03$. A total of 12 harmonic bands ($Q = 12$) were considered. The proposed method is compared with the conventional tracking method using SRP-PHAT as pseudo likelihood [25]. Both methods were evaluated using $0 \leq \Omega \leq 2\,kHz$ from which, for the proposed algorithm, speech pitch frequency was estimated from 100 to 300 Hz using (3.22)–(3.24). In this chapter, we quantify the performance using the average tracking error across all audio frames, i.e.,

Table 3.2 Summary of the proposed algorithm

At time $k - 1$, given that a set of particles $\{\alpha_{k-1}^{(p)}, w_{k-1}^{(p)}\}_{p=1}^{N_p}$ is a discrete representation of posterior $\Pr(\alpha_{k-1}|\mathbf{z}_{k-1})$, the posterior state estimate is $\widehat{\alpha}_{k-1}^{+} = \sum_{p=1}^{N_p} w_{k-1}^{(p)} \alpha_{k-1}^{(p)}$.

For the kth frame:

1. *Prior prediction*: Propagate the previous state estimate through (3.16) to obtain prior estimate of the current state $\widehat{\alpha}_k^{-}$.

2. *Feature extraction*: Apply beamformer according to (3.17), (3.18) to enhance the signal from the prior estimated position $\widehat{\mathbf{r}}_k^{-}$, and extract speech features using (3.22)–(3.24).

3. *Particles propagation*: Propagate each particle through the source dynamic model (3.7a),

$$\alpha_k^{(p)} = \mathcal{G}(\alpha_{k-1}^{(p)}, \mathbf{u}_k).$$

4. *Posterior weights update*: Obtain the feature directed particle likelihood using (3.25)–(3.29) and each particle is then assigned a weight according to its likelihood

$$w_k^{(p)} = w_{k-1}^{(p)} \Pr(\mathbf{z}_k|\alpha_k^{(p)}),$$

followed by normalization $w_k^{(p)} \Leftarrow w_k^{(p)} (\sum_{i=1}^{N_p} w_k^{(i)})^{-1}$. The posterior state estimate is $\widehat{\mathbf{x}}_k^{+} = \sum_{p=1}^{N_p} w_k^{(p)} \alpha_k^{(p)}$

5. *Resampling*: Resample the particles if the effective sample size is below a threshold, $N_{\text{eff}} < N_{\text{thr}}$, where $N_{\text{eff}} = (\sum_{p=1}^{N_p} (w_k^{(p)})^2)^{-1}$.

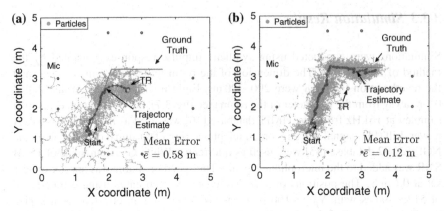

Fig. 3.7 Comparison of tracking results when TR is present at SIR = −3 dB, T_{60} = 250 ms.
a Conventional SRP-PHAT tracking method. b Proposed tracking method

$$\bar{e} = \frac{1}{K} \sum_{k=1}^{K} ||\widehat{\mathbf{r}}_k^+ - \mathbf{r}_k||_2, \tag{3.30}$$

where $\widehat{\mathbf{r}}_k^+$ is the posterior estimated position at kth frame, $\mathbf{r}_k$ is the true source position,
$|| \cdot ||_2$ is the L-2 norm, and K is the number of frames.

Figure 3.7 compares the tracking result for T_{60} = 250 ms in the presence of
telephone ring at −3 dB SIR. Figure 3.7a shows that the tracking performance of the
conventional SRP-PHAT approach is adversely affected by the interferer. Due to the
high measurement likelihood of SRP-PHAT for the interferer region, the particles are
"trapped" once they are propagated there, in this case the region near the telephone
ring. The SRP-PHAT method has an average error of 0.58 m indicating that it does
not converge to the speech source trajectory. On the other hand, Fig. 3.7b shows the
tracking performance of the proposed method. This result shows that the proposed
method is less significantly affected by the presence of the telephone ring achieving
an average error of 0.12 m.

Figure 3.8 shows the tracking result when both power drill and telephone ring
are present at 3 and 0 dB SIRs, respectively, with T_{60} = 250 ms. Again, Fig. 3.8a
shows the conventional SRP-PHAT approach losing track of the speech source. The
particles are "trapped" at the region near the power drill, leading to the average error
of 0.61 m. On the other hand, the proposed method, shown in Fig. 3.8b, retains its
robustness with an average error of 0.13 m.

Table 3.3 shows the average tracking error for various test conditions. The source
trajectory and interference positions remain the same as the previous setup. These
results show that the proposed algorithm can achieve better accuracy than the SRP-
PHAT method. For instance, in the presence of power drill at 3 dB SIR, the SRP-PHAT
method exhibits a large tracking error of 0.56 m when T_{60} = 0.2 s. The proposed
method achieves an error of 0.11 m, which translates to an 80 % reduction of error over

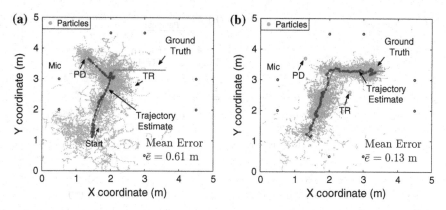

Fig. 3.8 Comparison of tracking results when both PD and TR are present at SIR = 3 dB, 0 dB, respectively, T_{60} = 250 ms. **a** Conventional SRP-PHAT tracking method. **b** Proposed tracking method

the SRP-PHAT method. Furthermore, the proposed method maintains its robustness in localization and tracking in the presence of two interferers, while the SRP-PHAT approach suffers from large tracking error under low SIR condition. However, it is also observed that the performance of the proposed algorithm degrades modestly when reverberation time is increased. The proposed method may fail under adverse environments as indicated when T_{60} = 0.3 s, PD and PR are present at SIR of 3 and −6 dB.

Different source trajectory and interference configurations were also examined in Figs. 3.9 and 3.10. As before, these results show that the conventional SRP-PHAT approach is likely to be affected by interferers, while the proposed approach retains its robustness; the particles are propagated closely along the source trajectory.

Figure 3.11 shows the performance of both algorithms under different reverberation conditions. Figure 3.11a shows the results when power drill is present at an SIR = 0 dB. The SRP-PHAT tracking method, indicated by the dashed line, results in consistently high tracking errors of more than 1 m. The SRP-MBE tracking method, shown by the solid line, results in errors of less than 0.3 m when T_{60} is below 0.35 s.

Table 3.3 Comparison of mean tracking error $\bar{e}$ between the SRP-PHAT tracking method and the proposed tracking method

	SRP-PHAT tracking method		Proposed tracking method	
	$T_{60} = 0.2$ s	$T_{60} = 0.3$ s	$T_{60} = 0.2$ s	$T_{60} = 0.3$ s
PD (SIR = 3 dB)	0.56 m	0.59 m	0.11 m	0.15 m
TR (SIR = 0 dB)	0.51 m	0.59 m	0.09 m	0.13 m
TR (SIR = −3 dB)	0.53 m	0.64 m	0.10 m	0.15 m
PD+TR (SIR = 3, 0 dB)	0.57 m	0.68 m	0.12 m	0.16 m
PD+TR (SIR = 3, −3 dB)	0.65 m	0.69 m	0.15 m	0.18 m
PD+TR (SIR = 3, −6 dB)	1.08 m	1.01 m	0.20 m	0.75 m

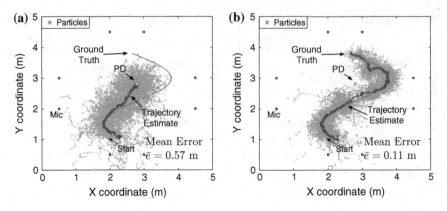

Fig. 3.9 Comparison of tracking results when PD is present at SIR = 3 dB, T_{60} = 200 ms. **a** Conventional SRP-PHAT tracking method. **b** Proposed tracking method

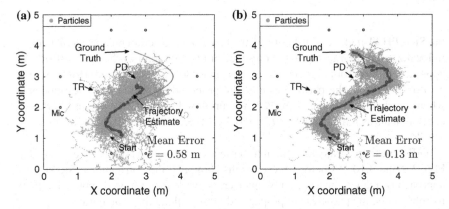

Fig. 3.10 Comparison of tracking results when both PD and TR are present at SIR = 3 dB, 0 dB, respectively, T_{60} = 200 ms. **a** Conventional SRP-PHAT tracking method. **b** Proposed tracking method

However, the performance deteriorates rather significantly when T_{60} is beyond 0.4 s. A similar conclusion can be drawn from Fig. 3.11b where the telephone ring is present at SIR = −5 dB. The SRP-PHAT tracking method consistently results in high tracking errors of more than 0.5 m, while the SRP-MBE deteriorates when T_{60} is higher than 0.3 s.

3.4 Integration with Social Robot

Sound source localization and tracking have been investigated in the previous sections. In this section, we describe a system where the SSLT module has been inte-

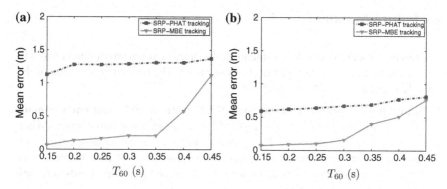

Fig. 3.11 Comparison of mean tracking error versus different reverberation time T_{60}. **a** Power drill is present at SIR $= 0$ dB. **b** Telephone ring is present at SIR $= -5$ dB

grated to the social robot and to the virtual human. Figure 3.12 shows the demo setup of a social robot system in the BeingThere Center, Nanyang Technological University. Microphones are employed linearly with known positions. The SSLT module estimates the position of a speaker within the room and delivers the position information through I2P connections to the server. The other modules (e.g., the head controller module) would therefore have access to the sound position information. Either the virtual human or the social robot is able to turn its head to a person who is speaking in the room. By focusing on the speaker, the interaction between robot and users is improved. The sound position information can also be combined with the face detection module, which allows the robot to be aware of all the users while focusing on the active speaking person.

Fig. 3.12 Integration setup with the social robot system

3.5 Future Avenues

This research focuses on SSLT problems in the meeting room environment and will continue to be the research focus in the near future. The following are some of the possible suggestions for future research:

1. **Improving the performance of SRP-MBE in the reverberant environment.** The performance of the proposed SRP-MBE tracking algorithm degrades when reverberation time increases. This is due to the fact that the harmonic bands are disturbed by a high amount of reverberation. The issue of how to recover or extract the time delay information from the degraded harmonic bands certainly requires future investigation.

2. **Tracking time-varying number of sources.** In recent years, tracking time-varying number of sources has gained much interest in the research community [14, 28, 30]. In a typical environment, there might be multiple speakers speaking at the same time, which results in speech signals overlapping. In addition, some speakers may become quiet after talking for a while. This practical situation requires an advanced probabilistic model such as random finite set [28, 36] to be incorporated in the particle filter framework to achieve multiple speaker tracking. In addition, it requires a mechanism to detect and initialize a newborn target and remove certain inactive targets from the state at a certain time instant [14].

3.6 Conclusions

In this chapter, we first reviewed the SSLT problem in a meeting room environment for teleconference purposes. The challenges include room reverberation, background noise, and sound interference. After reviewing some of the existing methods, a proposed SSLT framework was discussed for tracking a speech source in the presence of sound interference. This method is capable of estimating the speech harmonic bands for localizing and tracking. By only emphasizing the harmonic bands, better speech-sensitive measurement likelihood can be achieved resulting in better weight update for the particles. Simulation results show that the proposed method can achieve lower tracking error than the conventional SRP-PHAT method in the presence of multiple interferers.

References

1. Arulampalam MS, Maskell S, Gordon N, Clapp T (2002) A tutorial on particle filters for online nonlinear/non-Gaussian Bayesian tracking. IEEE Trans Signal Process 50(2):174–188
2. Brandstein MS (1999) Time-delay estimation of reverberated speech exploiting harmonic structure. J Acoust Soc Am 105:2914–2919

3. Chen J, Benesty J, Huang YA (2006) Time delay estimation in room acoustic environments: an overview. EURASIP J Adv Signal Process 2006:1–1

4. Cobos M, Marti A, Lopez JJ (2011) A modified SRP-PHAT functional for robust real-time sound source localization with scalable spatial sampling. IEEE Signal Process Lett 18(1):71–74

5. Deleforge A, Horaud, R (2012) The cocktail party robot: sound source separation and localisation with an active binaural head. In: Proceedings 7th ACM/IEEE international conference human-Robot interaction (HRI), pp 431–438

6. Deller JR, Proakis JG, Hansen JHL (2000) Discrete-time processing of speech signals. Wiley-IEEE Press, New York

7. DiBiase JH (2000) A high accuracy, low-latency technique for talker localization in reverberant environments using microphone arrays. PhD thesis, Brown University

8. DiBiase JH, Silverman HF, Brandstein MS (2001) Robust localization in reverberant rooms. Microphone arrays: signal processing techniques and applications, pp 157–180

9. Dmochowski J, Benesty J, Affes S (2007) Direction of arrival estimation using the parameterized spatial correlation matrix. IEEE Trans Audio, Speech, Lang Process 15(4):1327–1339

10. Dmochowski J, Benesty J, Affes S (2007) A generalized steered response power method for computationally viable source localization. IEEE Trans Audio, Speech, Lang Process 15(8):2510–2526

11. Dmochowski J, Benesty J, Affes S (2008) Linearly constrained minimum variance source localization and spectral estimation. IEEE Trans Audio, Speech, Lang Process 16(8):1490–1502

12. Do H, Silverman HF, Yu Y (2007) A real-time SRP-PHAT source location implementation using stochastic region contraction (SRC) on a large-aperture microphone array. In: Proceedings IEEE international conference on acoustics, speech and signal processing (ICASSP'07), vol 1, pp I–121–I–124

13. Fallon MF, Godsill S (2010) Acoustic source localization and tracking using track before detect. IEEE Trans Audio, Speech, Lang Process 18(6):1228–1242

14. Fallon MF, Godsill S (2012) Acoustic source localization and tracking of a time-varying number of speakers. IEEE Trans Audio, Speech, Lang Process 20(4):1409–1415

15. Gannot S, Dvorkind TG (2006) Microphone array speaker localizers using spatial-temporal information. EURASIP J Appl Signal Process (special issue on microphone arrays) 2006:1–17

16. Garofolo J, Lamel L, Fisher W, Fiscus J, Pallett D, Dahlgren N, Zue V (1993) TIMIT acoustic-phonetic continuous speech corpus. Philadelphia

17. Gordon NJ, Salmond DJ, Smith AFM (1993) Novel approach to nonlinear/non-Gaussian Bayesian state estimation. In: Proceedings of IEE -F, radar and signal processing, vol 140, pp 107–113. IET

18. Grewal MS, Andrews AP (2011) Kalman filtering: theory and practice using MATLAB. Wiley, New York

19. Griffin DW, Lim JS (1988) Multiband excitation vocoder. IEEE Trans Acoust Speech Signal Process 36(8):1223–1235

20. Habets EAP, Benesty J (2012) A perspective on frequency-domain beamformers in room acoustics. IEEE Trans Audio, Speech, Lang Process 20(3):947–960

21. Habets EAP, Benesty J, Naylor PA (2012) A speech distortion and interference rejection constraint beamformer. IEEE Trans Audio, Speech, Lang Process 20(3):854–867

22. Huang Y, Benesty J, Elko GW, Mersereau RM (2001) Real-time passive source localization: a practical linear-correction least-squares approach. IEEE Trans Speech, Audio Process 9(8):943–956

23. Johnson DH, Dudgeon DE (1992) Array signal processing: concepts and techniques. Simon & Schuster

24. Knapp CH, Carter GC (1976) The generalized correlation method for estimation of time delay. IEEE Trans Acoust Speech Signal Process 24(4):320–327

25. Lehmann EA, Johansson AM (2007) Particle filter with integrated voice activity detection for acoustic source tracking. EURASIP J Adv Signal Process 2007

26. Lehmann EA, Johansson AM (2008) Prediction of energy decay in room impulse responses simulated with an image-source model. J Acoust Soc Am 124(1):269–277

27. Levy A, Gannot S, Habets EAP (2011) Multiple-hypothesis extended particle filter for acoustic source localization in reverberant environments. IEEE Trans Audio, Speech, Lang Process 19(6):1540–1555

28. Ma W-K, Vo B-N, Singh SS, Baddeley A (2006) Tracking an unknown time-varying number of speakers using TDOA measurements: a random finite set approach. IEEE Trans Signal Process 54(9):3291–3304

29. Marti A, Cobos M, Lopez JJ (2011) Real time speaker localization and detection system for camera steering in multiparticipant videoconferencing environments. In: Proceedings of IEEE international conference on acoustics, speech, signal processing (ICASSP'11), pp 2592–2595

30. Morelande MR, Kreucher CM, Kastella K (2007) A bayesian approach to multiple target detection and tracking. IEEE Trans Signal Process 55(5):1589–1604

31. Talantzis F (2010) An acoustic source localization and tracking framework using particle filtering and information theory. IEEE Trans Audio, Speech, Lang Process 18(7):1806–1817

32. Timofeev S, Bahai ARS, Varaiya P (2008) Adaptive acoustic beamformer with source tracking capabilities. IEEE Trans Signal Process 56(7):2812–2820

33. Varga A, Steeneken HJM (1993) Assessment for automatic speech recognition: II. NOISEX-92: a database and an experiment to study the effect of additive noise on speech recognition systems. Speech Commun 12(3):247–251

34. Van Veen BD, Buckley KM (1988) Beamforming: a versatile approach to spatial filtering. IEEE ASSP Magazine 5(2):4–24

35. Vermaak J, Blake A (2001) Nonlinear filtering for speaker tracking in noisy and reverberant environments. In: Proceedings of IEEE International Conference on Acoustics, Speech, Signal Processing (ICASSP'01), pp 3021–3024

36. Vo B-T, Vo B-N, Antonio C (2008) Bayesian filtering with random finite set observations. IEEE Trans Signal Process 56(4):1313–1326

37. Ward DB, Lehmann EA, Williamson RC (2003) Particle filtering algorithms for tracking an acoustic source in a reverberant environment. IEEE Trans Speech Audio Process 11(6):826–836

38. Wu K, Goh ST, Khong AWH (2013) Speaker localization and tracking in the presence of sound interference by exploiting speech harmonicity. In: Proceedings of IEEE international conference on acoustics, speech, signal processing (ICASSP'13), pp 365–369

39. Zeng W-J, Li X-L (2010) High-resolution multiple wideband and nonstationary source localization with unknown number of sources. IEEE Trans Signal Process 58(6):3125–3136

Part II
Facial and Body Modelling Animation

Chapter 4
Modelling Conversation

Martin Constable, Justin Dauwels, Shoko Dauwels, Rasheed Umer, Mengyu Zhou and Yasir Tahir

Abstract Conversation is clearly important in our daily lives. Functionally, it serves to deliver and exchange information. However, there is much of a conversation that lays outside of its verbal content, yet impacts directly on those involved and in a manner that might be to their detriment or benefit. For example, in an interview (which is a special class of conversation) the interviewee might needlessly interrupt the interviewer or be too silent, both of which are detrimental to the health of the conversation. This is the non-verbal component of conversation, which is to say it lays outside of the conversation's spoken content. By and large it also lays outside the sphere of what we are consciously aware of. The unsolved problem is how the non-verbal component of a conversation might be visualised in a concise, yet effective manner that would be suitable for use in a communication skill training scenario.

4.1 Learning Conversation Skills

Consciously or unconsciously, we adjust our voice and body movement while communicating with others. These are skills we acquire through everyday social engagement. In other words we learn communication skills through experience.

Experience is a powerful source of learning, especially in the acquisition of soft skills such as human-to-human communication. In such communication, especially

M. Constable (✉) · J. Dauwels · S. Dauwels · R. Umer · M. Zhou · Y. Tahir
BeingThere Centre, Nanyang Technological University, Singapore, Singapore
e-mail: MConstable@ntu.edu.sg

J. Dauwels
e-mail: JDAUWELS@ntu.edu.sg

S. Dauwels
e-mail: SDauwels@ntu.edu.sg

R. Umer
e-mail: UMER1@e.ntu.edu.sg

Y. Tahir
e-mail: YASIR001@e.ntu.edu.sg

© Springer International Publishing Switzerland 2016
N. Magnenat-Thalmann et al. (eds.), *Context Aware Human-Robot and Human-Agent Interaction*, Human–Computer Interaction Series,
DOI 10.1007/978-3-319-19947-4_4

in that which takes place face-to-face, we focus not only on what we say but also on how we say it. The manner in which we speak could change the meaning of what we are saying. For example, if someone smiles and say 'OK', it gives a positive impression and most probably means 'yes'. On the other hand, if they frown, roll their eyes and say 'Oooo-Kay', they can come across as displeased. We gather such subtle information about the mental state of others while they are speaking.

These skills are informed by one's past experience and may not work as intended in all situations. We learn these skills as children within a small group of culturally homogeneous people, but as we develop and mature it is likely that we will be required to communicate with a far wider variety of people. These people will be of diverse language, culture and religion and will also be diverse in their personality. We, therefore, need to maintain and upgrade our communication skill set as we grow, to ensure that it is suitable for a wide range of needs.

Since communication skill is practice-oriented, we need real-world experience in order to acquire such skills. However, just by engaging in an activity does not mean that we are necessarily learning from it. How can we knowingly develop such skills? What do we need for such learning/training? We discuss in this section some of the problems associated with learning within this domain, and we propose that a fusion of technology and new generation media provides an effective platform for serving these needs.

Communication skills are quite personal and occur through an invisible cognitive process. Although recent advances in brain science and neuroscience reveal some of the mechanisms underpinning this practice, the brain is still effectively a 'black box' and we cannot fully assess how we use non-verbal behaviours while speaking. This type of highly embedded intelligence is known as 'tacit knowledge'. As tacit knowledge is difficult to articulate, we cannot learn by textbook-based learning. Instead, we need direct experience.

The experiential learning model was proposed by Kolb et al. [11]. This was based on earlier work by scholars engaged in professional learning [3, 15]. In the experiential learning framework (Fig. 4.1), the student follows the four steps of continuing

Fig. 4.1 The experiential learning framework

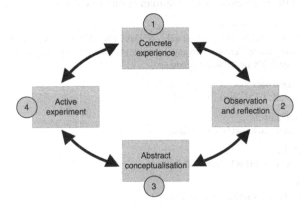

process: 1 concrete experience, 2 observation and reflection, 3 abstract conceptuali-
sation and 4 active experiment.

Without the students knowing their current performance, it is difficult for them to
modify their communication behaviour within a conversation. Therein lies the need
for feedback in the training process. Such feedback would require that a visualisation
of a conversation be available.

4.2 The State of the Art

Every time we look at a traditional Internet chat log or an SMS exchange (Fig. 4.2), we
are seeing a visualisation of a conversation from which we can derive a significant
amount of information. In the latter, the direction from which the speech bubbles
originate clearly indicates to whom a remark should be attributed, and the nested
response boxes of the former show us the nested sub-topics within a conversation.

Within an SMS exchange there might also be emojis that visualise the emotional
subtext of the conversation. Though an emoji is a visualisation of a participant's
emotional condition, it is a self-elected one and therefore vulnerable to misrepresen-

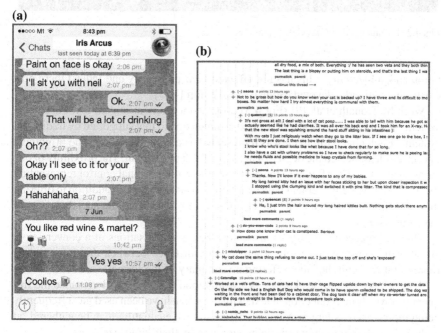

Fig. 4.2 Traditional forms of text-based exchange. **a** An SMS chat exchange showing emojis
integrated into the chat. **b** A chat log showing nested conversation

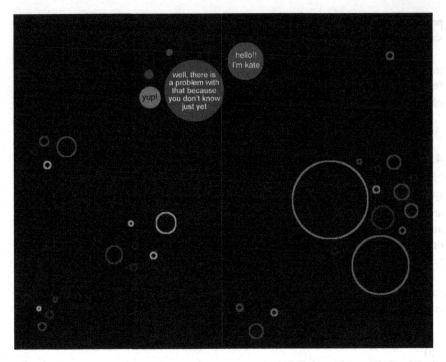

Fig. 4.3 Donath et al's. '*Chat Circle*' interface

tation and subjectivity. This has not affected their popularity and indeed there now exists chat networks devoted exclusively to emoji [4, 5].

Work by Donath et al. [9] (Fig. 4.3) proposed a multiparticipant text-based chat system ('Chat Circles') that added an extra dimension to that supported by traditional systems. Each chat participant was represented as a coloured circle. The brightness of each circle indicated the degree of activity of that participant. The proximity of one circle to another was offered to the participant as a dimensional control representing the degree of their engagement with a particular co-participant. In addition to offering this extra dimension to a chat conversation, it also visualised the social aspects of that conversation.

This and preceding examples, as well as being visualisations of a conversation, are also the conversation itself. There is little distance between the thing and its representation, with the latter offering no summary of the former.

A tag cloud, sometimes known as a word cloud (Fig. 4.4), will visualise the frequency of words in a collection of text, with those that have been used most frequently being represented as larger. A degree of summative evaluation may be gathered 'at a glance', with important words being signified by their large size.

Tat and Carpendale [23] propose a complex and evaluative approach: 'Bubba Talk'. This analysed a multiparticipant text-based conversation for such things as the frequency of exclamation marks, the number of words and the number of characters.

Fig. 4.4 An example of a tag cloud

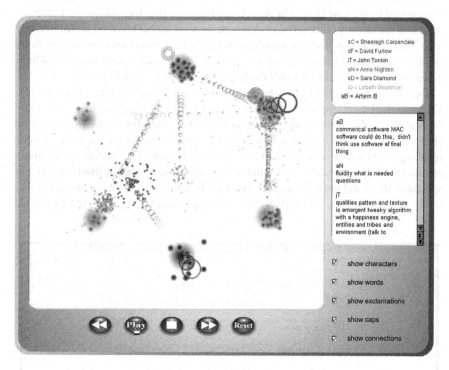

Fig. 4.5 Tat and Carpendale's visualisation of a text chat ('Bubba Talk')

It expressed the entirety of a conversation as a single complex circular-form abstract from which the social dynamics of the conversation may be inferred.

A range of further approaches for visualising text-based chat are reviewed by Uthus and Aha in 'Multiparticipant chat analysis: A survey' [26] (Fig. 4.5).

Visualising spoken dialogue presents a different challenge from that posed by text, being more dimensionally complex. While communicating with others, humans exchange messages verbally and non-verbally [16]. Non-verbal cues are from communication channels that lie outside of speech (sometimes known as 'paralanguage').

Examples include: eye movement, facial expression, gesture, posture, etc. It is the non-verbal aspects of a conversation that signify its 'health'. For example, what you are saying may be perfectly reasonable and polite, but if you have interrupted someone as you are speaking (which is a non-verbal cue) then you may come across as rude. It should also be noted that although we can easily manipulate what we say in order to create a particular impression, it is far harder to do so using the non-verbal aspects of how we speak. In this sense it is harder to 'lie' non-verbally. However, non-verbal cues do not lend themselves to easy visualisation, and therein lies one of the challenges of our research.

Campbell proposed an approach whereby a spoken conversation was synchronised with a text-based transcription of its content. The length of each spoken utterance was represented by the length of a simple coloured bar on a timeline; the colour of the bar indicated the identity of the speaker. A mouse-over on the bar revealed the transcribed text. Non-verbal cues such as simultaneous speech, interruptions and interjections could be inferred from the relative position of the bars to each other upon the timeline, however, this information was not explicitly processed or visualised (Fig. 4.6).

Bergstrom et al. visualised conversations between small groups of people [1]. The output of their approach resembled that of Tat and Carpendale's: a circular-form abstract, this form having a degree of natural suitability to the expression of group conversations. The parameters from which this visualisation was derived were speaking activity (active/not active) and speaking volume. The secondary (inferred) parameters were turn-taking and simultaneous speaking. Different from Campbell's approach, theirs did not address the content of the conversation, being instead exclusively concerned with non-verbal cues. Although fascinating, and even beautiful,

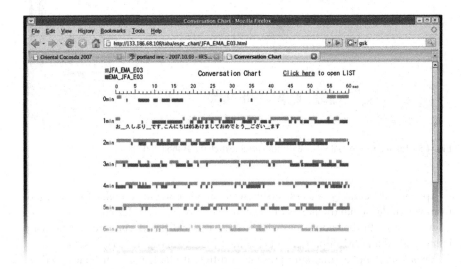

Fig. 4.6 Campbell's transcription interface showing a two-party conversation with the transcribed text (in Japanese) visible in the *top row*

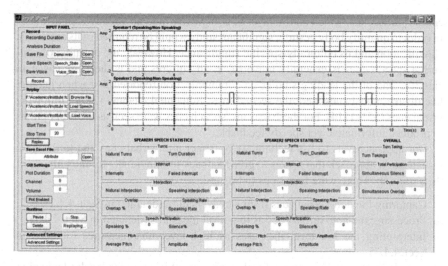

Fig. 4.7 Sarda's et al's. visualisation of non-verbal speech cues

their approach does not of its own offer any high-level evaluation of the health of a conversation. This point will be elaborated upon later in this chapter in Sect. 4.4.3.

Research in the fields of psychology and cognitive science, in which human behaviour within social interaction is studied, has examined these cues. [17, 19] and Gatica-Perez [6] describe ways in which non-verbal cues may be automatically gathered. Referencing such work, Sarda et al. [20] visualised a large number of non-verbal speech cues as a plot along a timeline (Fig. 4.7). They did this using recent advances in recording equipment and signal processing in order to automatically detect these conversation dynamics.

Sarda's approach was not primarily designed for use in a training scenario, being limited for use by researchers wishing to review their data. Additionally, the data it records is low level, being concerned only with statistics and would therefore have to be interpreted by an expert to have any value in a training scenario.

In sum, a conversation is a dimensionally complex phenomenon involving at least two streams of time-varying data that interact in meaningful and complex ways. There are many ways to visualise a conversation, depending on the form of the conversation and what is required of the visualisation. For purposes of aiding in the training of conversation skills, we exclusively focused on visualising its non-verbal cues.

4.3 Summary of Our Approach

We focused on cues derived from non-verbal speech. There are several reasons for choosing speech cues as opposed to visual cues. First, speech data can be processed quicker than visual data. In a learning situation, it would be of clear advantage to have feedback that is available at short notice. Second, body gesture strongly reflects cultural difference, which adds a layer of complexity onto an already complex task. In order to quantify body gesture, significant study would be required of its automatic classification and its culturally-specific significance. However, the meaning of non-verbal speech cues is generally universal to all cultures and is therefore easier to classify. One of the leading studies on communication reported that when judging like/dislike, vocal cues were the second most influential channel (38 %) following visual cues (55 %) [14]. For these reasons, speech cues were seen as the best options to produce informative yet speedy feedback.

Our approach was to use technology to detect non-verbal cues and to design a visualisation approach that serves to give feedback to individuals for the purpose of their training. There were four steps to this task:

1. Capturing the non-verbal cues from a conversation (detailed in Sect. 4.4.1)
2. Processing the non-verbal cues as low-level measures (detailed in Sect. 4.4.2)
3. Interpreting the low-level measures as high-level metameasures (detailed in Sect. 4.4.3)
4. Visualising the metameasures for the purposes of training feedback (detailed in Sect. 4.5).

Additionally, the results of a user study are presented in Sect. 4.6.

4.4 The Capture, Processing and Interpreting of Non-verbal Speech Cues

For our purposes the conversation size was restricted to the dyadic. This made our visualisation approach easier to test bed and was also more suitable for a training scenario, which would typically consist of a single trainer/trainee pair. The process required that the raw conversation data was gathered in a manner that did not impact upon its quality. From this data, non-verbal speech cues were automatically gathered and then classified using a number of measures. These measures were the statistical low-level features of the conversation. Using machine learning 3 metameasures were extrapolated from these measures: dominance, interest and discord. These metameasures quantify the high-level 'health' of a conversation.

4.4.1 Protocols for Capturing of Speech Data

The following section outlines the step-by-step procedure that constituted our protocol for capturing the speech data from face-to-face dyadic conversations. It was designed to gather data in a controlled manner and without distracting the participants too much.

1. In order to ensure effective communication the recording environment was set up so as to be as non-invasive as possible. Therefore, minimal apparatus was used. For audio recording, we used easy-to-use portable equipment for recording conversations. It simply consisted of lapel microphones for each of the two speakers and an audio H4N recorder that allowed multiple microphones to be interfaced with the computer. The speech from each speaker was saved simultaneously in a 2-channel audio .wav file.
2. In order to ensure smooth conversation throughout the recording we kept one of the participants constant in the experiment. They acted as a control and facilitated different social scenarios in conversation with their co-participant.
3. In order to obtain a high-quality recording the microphones were attached directly onto the participant's collar. Directional microphones were used so that one speaker's voice did not impede the other speaker's channel.
4. Both speakers were seated about 1.5 m apart so that each microphone only recorded the voice of the respective participant, and there was no interference from the other participant.
5. The two participants remained in a noise-free environment without any interruptions.
6. The participants were briefed about the experiment and were asked to act naturally. They were also asked to agree on a topic of mutual interest. The topics of discussion ranged from small talk to heated debates on sports, politics, etc. The topics were selected carefully in order to evoke a variety of behaviours.
7. The recording was initiated via a laptop remotely connected to a server.
8. The conversation was monitored remotely via a wireless live feed. Each conversation was about 2.5–3 min in duration and was without any interruptions.

The final speech database consisted of about 100 two-person conversations, each about 1–1.5 min long: a combined total of 200 individual audio recordings. The topics of conversation varied from discussion of assignments, student projects, social and political views, etc. The dataset encompassed many distinct social scenarios such as conflicts and disagreements, periods of boredom, aggressive behaviour, story-trading between speakers, speaker-to-speaker exploration, lecturing, etc. This wide range of sociometric samples provided an effective and flexible database.

4.4.2 Processing the Speech Data as Measures

We took from the literature [6] seven conversational measures (Table 4.1) which together broadly describe the social dynamic of a dyadic conversation and which could also be automatically processed from the speech data.

In Fig. 4.8 the process of deriving a measure from the speech data is visually summarised for the two measures: 'interruption' and 'failed interruption'. The peaks in the plots represent the duration of a participant's speaking. It can be seen that in the second example the speaking duration of speaker A lies inside of speaker B's speaking duration. This is classified as a failed interruption.

Table 4.1 The conversation measures derived from the speech data

Measure	Significance
Speaking percentage	The amount of speaking that person A or B has done is expressed as a percentage of the entire conversation
Natural turn taking	The number of times person A speaks in the conversation without interrupting person B
Turn duration	The average speaker turn duration. The turns of speaker A and B are both considered
Interjection	The number of times person A speaks simultaneous to person B but for a period of 1 s or less. This is to indicate short utterances like 'no', 'ok', 'yeah', etc.
Interruption	The number of times person A, interrupts person B while speaking and takes over the conversation, causing person B to stop speaking
Failed interruption	The number of instances when person A interrupts person B while speaking but stops speaking before person B does
Mutual silence	A and B are both silent

Fig. 4.8 An interruption and a failed interruption evident in the speech data. See how in the second example the speaking duration of speaker A lies inside of speaker B's speaking duration. This is classified as a failed interruption

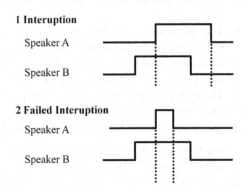

4.4.3 Interpreting the Measures as Metameasures

The measures themselves are statistical low-level features of the conversation and do not by themselves signify any high-level qualitative value. In order for these measures to be of use in a training scenario we summarised them as three high-level values: dominance, interest and discord [6]. These are described in Table 4.2. For this a training procedure was developed. This required that a ground truth be established, for which a manual classification was required. Each audio recording in the dataset was classified manually by at least five people. For each recording, they completed a questionnaire relating to their qualitative impression of the speaking mannerisms and behavioural aspects of each participant. The responses ranged from 1 (low) to 5 (high). For example, if a participant seemed bored, their interest level was classified as 'low'. In contrast, if they seemed excited, then the interest level was classified as 'high'. From these five votes the majority view was taken as the final score.

Table 4.2 The three metameasures described in terms of the speech data measures

Metameasure	Significance
Dominance	Dominance indicates the extent of a speaker's influence on their partner as measured by the difference in their **speaking percentage** and the difference in **natural turns**
Interest	Interest indicates the extent of a speaker's engagement with the conversation as measured by the **speaking percentage, turn duration** and **interjections**. The more they are involved in the conversation, the stronger the interest they have
Discord	Discord indicates the speaker's lack of agreement with their partner as measured by **interruptions, failed interruptions** and **mutual silence**

With the manual classification established as a ground truth, machine learning was applied and we were then in a position to perform automatic classification. Using this approach as our basis, a conversation can be automatically classified according to the three metameasures. Each metameasure was expressed in the final output as an intensity value between 0 and 3.

In addition to presenting the complex measures in a summarised and clear form, our approach also normalised the data. For each of the metameasures a long conversation would be subject to the same n out of 3 score as a short conversation. The advantage of this is that the length of a conversation is of no significance to the quantification of its quality. This makes comparative evaluation of two or more conversations easier to perform.

4.5 The Visualisation of the Data

The task of visualising the data required that its dimensional complexity be recognised. A conversation varies across time and is composed of emotional attributes which are abstract in nature. Visualising such data is therefore not an easy task.

Additionally, the intended application of our approach is within a training scenario. The exactitude of the visualisation is not as important as its form: it should be clear yet enticing. The metameasures should not only be presented as values but also as *experiences* that the trainee can relate to.

4.5.1 Metaphor and Data Visualisation

The task required that an appropriate model of visualisation be found: one that addresses the fundamentally abstract nature of non-verbal speech cues.

The heights of a group of people may be visualised as different points on the Y-axis in a graph. Here, the dots would be operating in a graphical manner and their successful interpretation would depend on the assumption that the reader is familiar with the convention of how such graphs function. This problem becomes more acute in the case of specialised forms of visualisation such as box plots, histograms and so on.

Some things are not suitable to being pictorially visualised in a straightforward manner. For example, how might a volatile political situation be represented? In the preceding examples, there was a clear *indexical* relationship between the heights of the pictograms and the heights of the people. However, given the inherently abstract nature of a political situation, this approach is not feasible. It might be that in such a case a metaphor may be a more effective strategy to employ.

Metaphors rely on our ability to transfer an understanding from one subject to another [12]. In the preceding example, a pictogram of a volcano might effectively signify a volatile political situation. The volcano does not and cannot *visually resemble* a volatile political situation, but it is nonetheless possible to read it as such. The disadvantage of a metaphor is that it is inherently ambiguous and therefore its correct interpretation depends upon the reader being privy to the correct way to read it. Thus we find that a metaphoric device, such as the inversion of a sign, might variously indicate the opposite of the signified (e.g. an upside-down cross signifying satanism), the death of the signified (in *The Book of Signs* Rudolph Koch describes a pictogram of an upside-down man as signifying a dead man [10]) or a 'special condition' of the signified (e.g. The figure of the upside-down man in Tarot cards can variously mean: acceptance, a new point of view or surrender). We may therefore conclude that a metaphoric visualisation can be subject to multiple interpretations and that the context is important in order that a specific reading may be pinned down.

4.5.2 Time and Data Visualisation

A conversation is time-varying in nature. For a human, time is a fundamentally experience-based phenomenon [18] that again presents challenges in its visualisation. Any data that is time-varying requires that time is accommodated as a navigational dimension that is extra to the data. A single value that varies in intensity over time can be presented as a graph on a timeline, as in Sarda et al's. work [20]. However, this is not suitable if the data is more complex such as in the case of several values varying over time. Some existing solutions utilise 3D as this extra navigational space [8, 24]; an example of 3D in everyday use is the depth dimension employed in Apple's Time Machine (their propriety data backup service).

However, what is missed in such approaches is an *experienced* sense of the difference between the beginning and the end. To the user, such an experience may allow them to effectively *live* the data and, by proxy, empathise more effectively with the conversation from which the data was derived. We are reminded here that a key need of information visualisation is not just to visualise data but also to communicate effectively, and empathy is a key component of communication.

A possible alternative to a timeline and 3D visualisation is to present the time-varying data as a narrative. There is much previous research on storytelling as an effective means of imparting information and much of it addresses storytelling as an effective way in which to present complex information in a simple and summarised manner [2, 7].

4.5.3 Game Engines and Data Visualisation

It was decided that the most suitable way of presenting the time-varying data was in the form of an animation of two characters engaged in a social exchange in a manner reminiscent of a narrative. Here, time was used to visualise itself, thereby preserving the experience of time, and narrative was employed to signify change. These characters were interacting with each other, similar to the way characters interact in games. The form of these interactions was chosen to metaphorically signify the three metameasures by which the conversation has been classified.

Visualisations of data can be easily generated using Microsoft's Excel or the open source Web app Raw. Using an application like Adobe's Flash or the open source Pure Data it is possible to parse time-varying data into forms that might be animated. However, these approaches are not equal to the task of producing a sophisticated animation. Normally, animation, especially that of the human figure, is an arduous task requiring expert input from experienced professionals. This would preclude against their use in a training situation where on-demand feedback would be a key requirement. A simple alternative is to use a game engine. A game engine is a layer of software that supports a digital game. Its job is to manage the physics and appearance of the game world and oversee the rules of the game. It also presents to the game designer the means to author and edit the game.

Game engines have been used before in the visualisation of information [22, 27]. However, the assumption that these approaches make is that the function of a game engine is to make a game. However, game engines have also been used to make stand-alone animations that permit no player interaction. Such animations are commonly known as Machinima, which are hybrids of gaming and film-making. More recently the game engine extension Source Filmmaker [21] has been developed to capture and edit game engine play into the form of an animation for post-capture editing. The advantage of these approaches is the ease with which animations may be made.

Using the Game engine Unity [25] as our development platform we built a visualisation application, whose purpose was to convert the metameasures into a simple animation. Unity was chosen for its flexibility, relative ease of use and the portability of its output.

The animation that a game engine produces is not the same as that an animator might produce using animation-specific software. It carries with it much of the 'language' of a game: apparent in its loop-form animations, low polygon count figures, sprite overlays (explosions, glows, etc.) and simplified camera moves. With these familiar cues come a particular set of expectations from the user: they would be primed to expect from the animation a degree of social engagement that is also likely to directly involve them (i.e. 'gameplay'). This was suitable to the particular demands of our task and provided the contextual underpinning by which the user may make sense of the metameasure metaphor.

4.5.4 Our Approach

The space that the animation is rendered within is of high importance to how the animation will psychologically impact upon the viewer. It was decided that the best option would be to use isometric projection. Different from the traditional 3-point perspectival rendering, objects in an isometric projection do not appear larger or smaller according to their distance from the camera. This form of spatial representation is employed in strategy games such as Starcraft and Age of Empires. It is suitable for eliciting in the viewer the 'gods eye' point of view, wherein all characters are of equal importance. This is unlike the 3-point perspective that is employed in first-person shooters and in which figures that lie nearest the camera are given psychological weightage over those that lie further away. We opted to use isometric projection as we felt it was suitable for the purpose of equalising the emphasis given to the two characters/participants.

In the course of the development of visualisation several dead ends were encountered. For example, before the development of the metameasures the collective dynamic of the conversation was expressed using a range of metaphors driven by the low-level measures. A floating platform was employed to reflect the global rate of the 'turn-taking' measure (Fig. 4.9). Should that measure fall below a threshold value (i.e. participants were not equal in the number of times they spoke) then, by the end of the animation the platform would have developed a wobble and the jets holding it up would be emitting black smoke. Here the notion of imbalance served two readings: the literal (the unbalanced state of the platform) and the metaphoric (the unbalanced state of the conversation).

Following the development of the metameasures as a means to summarise the entirety of the conversation, this approach was seen to be extraneous to our needs. Despite this, embodying a sense of collective health using a metaphorical environment remains an enticing idea that we feel is suitable for future exploitation.

We opted to use figures, environments, animations and effects that were similar to those of established gaming traditions. By doing so, we sought to build upon the association of this genre with social engagement and also with the notion of merit acquired through practice (a useful value in training). We purchased these figures, animations and visual effects from commercial resellers of gaming assets and customised them to our needs.

The figures were chosen for their broad similarity to existing 'steampunk' type game characters such as those found in the games Final Fantasy, Sudeki and Kirin. This we felt was suitably outside of any specific worldly context. They were placed within a natural environment which was not so noticeable as to be a distraction, and

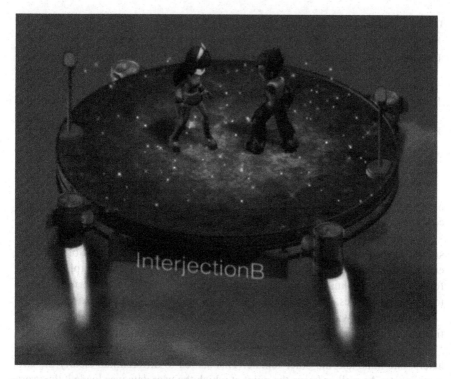

Fig. 4.9 The floating platform as an analogy

not so stark as to be disturbing. They were positioned so they were facing each other and were initially animated with a simple loop of an 'at rest' motion.

The figures were rigged to respond with predefined animations to each of the three metameasures (Table 4.4). 'Feeding' the timing of the animations was the metameasure values derived from the conversation data. This was presented in the form of a stream, wherein metameasure 'events' were delivered at random intervals. Table 4.3 represents such a stream, the values of which are as follows. Speaker A: Dominance = 3, Interest = 1, Discord 2. Speaker B: Dominance = 2, Interest = 2, Discord 1. Just as there was no one-to-one relationship between the length of the conversation and the length of the animation, as outlined in Sect. 4.4.3, so also there was no one-to-one relationship between the order of these events within the animation and the ordering

Table 4.3 Graphical presentation of an example data stream (key: Dom = dominance, Dis = discord, Int = interest)

Speaker A	Dom	0	Dis	Int	Dom	0	Dis	Dom	0
Speaker B	Dom	0	0	Int	Int	0	Dis	0	Dom

Table 4.4 The metameasures as metaphors

Metameasure	Give animation	Receive sequence	Sprite sequence
Dominance	Figure makes a punching gesture	Figure moves as if electrocuted	Energy ray, emanates from giver and hits the receiver
Interest	Figure makes a wide-arm gesture	Figure twirls	Bubbles and sparkles envelop the receiver
Discord	Figure makes a roaring gesture	Figure places their head in their hands	Rain envelopes the receiver

of the conversation. This served to ensure that the animation did not 'illustrate' the conversation, rather it 'symbolised' it.

The animations were augmented by use of animated sprites. These sprites were similar in form to those employed in games such as StarCraft, World of Warcraft, etc., where they are usually employed to signify such things as spells, explosions and forcefields. The animations and sprites were chosen for their metaphoric similarity to the metameasures. The animations are pictured in Figs. 4.10, 4.11 and 4.12.

The animation was available for viewing almost immediately after the conversation had finished. In a training scenario this is of clear advantage.

The startup screen of the application presented the two participants as two characters: one male and the other female. This served to differentiate clearly the two participants. As well as being the point at which the user data was loaded, the users also have the option to swap the gender assignment of their characters. As the training scenario was likely to consist of one trainer and one trainee, it was assumed that only the trainee would be concerned about the gender of their character.

Fig. 4.10 The dominance metameasure animation

Fig. 4.11 The interest
metameasure animation

Fig. 4.12 The discord
metameasure animation

The animation in play (Fig. 4.13) presented a running score of the metameasures in the traditional health bar format, which needs no explanation to most people under the age of 50.

As the metameasures did not relate directly to any particular event on the timeline, the animation was effectively functioning as a means by which the metameasure values could be slowly released to the trainee in as much time as the animation lasted (this was set at 1 min and 30 s). This was long enough to serve the purpose of allowing the trainer to discuss with the trainee the metameasures as they arose, yet also it was not so long as to risk being tedious to view.

The animation ended with a screen (Fig. 4.14) that summarised the score and gave a brief explanation of what each metameasure signified. The design and function of this followed the format of the traditional statistics screen (a.k.a 'stats'), which again is a familiar gaming device.

It was found that a surprising amount of information was available not only from the metameasures themselves, but also from how they combined. For example, high

Fig. 4.13 The animation in play, showing the health bars and a 'dominance' metameasure animation being employed

'interest' and moderate 'dominance' from both participants would indicate that the conversation was going smoothly. High 'dominance' and low 'discord' from one participant would indicate that they might be acting aggressively.

4.6 User Study and Discussion

To test the validity of our approach, we conducted a user study comprising four tasks. 34 students from Nanyang Technological University (Singapore) participated. 17 of these were from the school of Art, Design and Media (ADM), 17 were from the Schools of Computer Engineering and the School of Business. These two groups we term as the ADM and non-ADM (NADM) groups. 19 were male and 15 were female.

Evaluation of the results of the user study was done by a comparison of two modes of visualisation: our approach and a 2D graphic. The 2D graphic is shown in Fig. 4.15. These were also evaluated with respect to the two user groups.

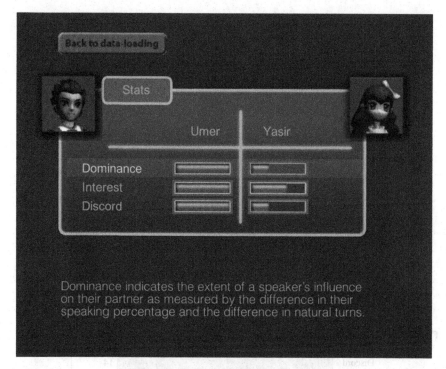

Fig. 4.14 The 'stats' screen, showing the final metameasure score and brief explanations of their significance

4.6.1 Task 1

The participants were shown the three animations depicting the three metameasures, each 10 s in length. They were then asked to match each animation with its respective metameasure.

The results are summarised in the bar charts Figs. 4.16, 4.17 and 4.18. Given the naturally non-indexical relationship of the metaphor device (i.e. animation) to the signified metameasure, a 100 % success rate in this task was not expected. However, there was nonetheless a high rate of successful pairings for all the metameasures and their respective animations.

Tellingly, the percentage of successful hits for the interest metameasure was slightly higher than that of dominance and discord. This can perhaps be accounted for by the fact that both dominance and discord are emotionally antagonist values and were therefore being confused with each other.

A comparison of the bar chart in Fig. 4.16 with Fig. 4.17 shows that there was no significant difference between the responses from the ADM and NADM groups.

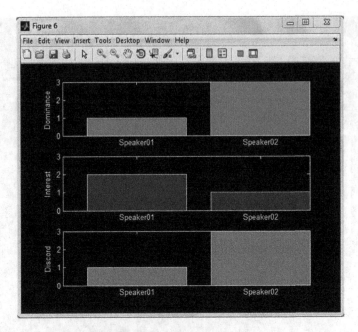

Fig. 4.15 The 2D graphic used in the user study

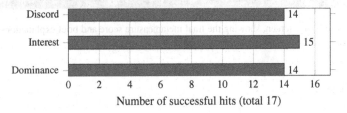

Fig. 4.16 Results for user study: task 1. *Bars* represent the number of successful hits for ADM group

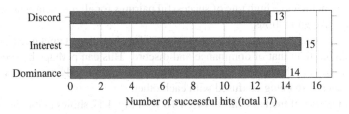

Fig. 4.17 Results for user study: task 1. *Bars* represent the number of successful hits for NADM group

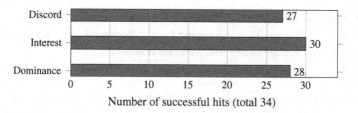

Fig. 4.18 Results for user study: task 1. *Bars* represent the number of successful hits for the ADM and NADM groups combined

4.6.2 Task 2

The participants were asked to listen to three audio recordings of dyadic conversations. Following this they were shown one animation that was generated from the metameasure values of one of these conversations. They were then tasked to match the animation with the correct audio recording.

The success rate for this task correlated strongly with that of task 1, with a correct count of 28/34. This suggests that most of the participants had no trouble extending the principle of the metaphor established in task 1.

Of the six incorrect responses, only two were from the ADM group. Narrative responses from participants in task 4 (Sect. 4.6.4) provide some illumination about the reasons for their response. One NADM participant declared that 'as they didn't play video games, the animations were not clear' (response ID 6, Table 4.11). Another from the same group believed that there was a direct one-to-one correlation between the timing of the events in the conversation with the timing of the metameasure animations (response ID 5). This was the only participant to have thought so. One ADM participant talked about the 'character's motivations and intentions' (response ID 13), clearly mistaking the visualisation for a traditional narrative animation.

4.6.3 Task 3

The participants listened to an audio recording of a dyadic conversation. Following this they were shown two visualisations of the metameasures: our animation and a simple graphic in the form of a bar chart. They were then asked to fill in a questionnaire. All responses were tabulated in the Likert style [13]. The questions and their response options are presented in Tables 4.5 and 4.6. The responses themselves are shown in the bar charts: Figs. 4.19, 4.20, 4.21, 4.22, 4.23, 4.24, 4.25, 4.26 and in the Tables 4.7 and 4.8. The results are also broken down into ADM and NADM responses. The average and standard deviation (SD) values are shown for all sets of results.

Table 4.5 Questions and response options for task 3: animation-related

Response 1	Response 2	Response 3	Response 4	Response 5
Question A: *Was the message clearly conveyed by the animation?*				
Not clear at all	Mostly not clear	Sometimes not clear	Mostly clear	Very clear
Question B: *Did you enjoy the communication training feedback in the form of an animation?*				
Didn't enjoy at all	Mostly didn't enjoy	Neutral feelings	Mostly enjoyed	Very much enjoyed
Question C: *In a communication-training scenario, would you like the feedback to be in the form of an animation?*				
Would not like at all	Mostly would not like	Neutral feelings	Mostly would like	Very much would like
Question D: *Was the length of the animation appropriate to a communication-training situation?*				
Far too short	Too short	Appropriate length	Too long	Far too long
Question E: *Was it helpful that the animation looked similar to a game?*				
Not helpful at all	Mostly not helpful	Neutral feelings	Mostly helpful	Very helpful

Table 4.6 Questions and response options for task 3: graph-related

Response 1	Response 2	Response 3	Response 4	Response 5
Question F: *Was the message clearly conveyed by the graph?*				
Not clear at all	Mostly not clear	Sometimes not clear	Mostly clear	Very clear
Question G: *Did you enjoy the communication training feedback in graphical form?*				
Didn't enjoy at all	Mostly didn't enjoy	Neutral feelings	Mostly enjoyed	Very much enjoyed
Question H: *In a communication-training scenario, would you like the feedback to be in a graphical form?*				
Didn't enjoy at all	Mostly didn't enjoy	Neutral feelings	Mostly enjoyed	Very much enjoyed

Questions A, B and C addressed the participants' response to the animation and were comparable to questions F, G, and H, which addressed the graph. To evaluate the differences between these question pairs, a paired t-test was performed. The results are presented in Table 4.9.

The low t-test result of the question pairs: A/F and B/G indicate that there was a significant difference of opinion about the perceived clarity of the animation and the degree to which it was enjoyed. However, this difference ran in different directions: a majority of the participants thought the graph was clearer than the animation (question pair: A/F), yet a majority also enjoyed the animation more than the graph (question pair: B/G). The B/G question pair elicited the lowest paired t-test result, indicating

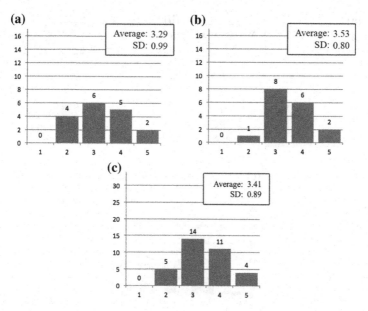

Fig. 4.19 Per-group response to question A: *Was the message clearly conveyed by the animation?* **a** Response from ADM group. **b** Response from NADM group. **c** Response from all participants

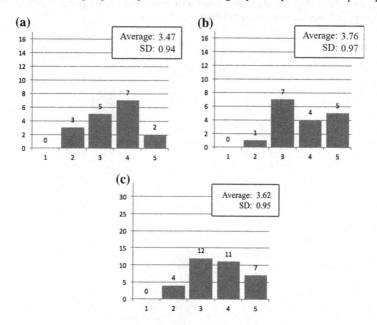

Fig. 4.20 Per-group response to question B: *Did you enjoy the communication training feedback in the form of an animation?* **a** Response from ADM group. **b** Response from NADM group. **c** Response from all participants

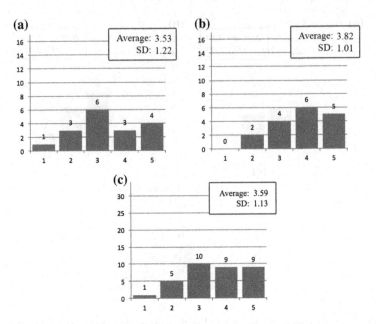

Fig. 4.21 Per-group response to question C: *In a communication-training scenario, would you like the feedback to be in the form of an animation?* **a** Response from ADM group. **b** Response from NADM group. **c** Response from all participants

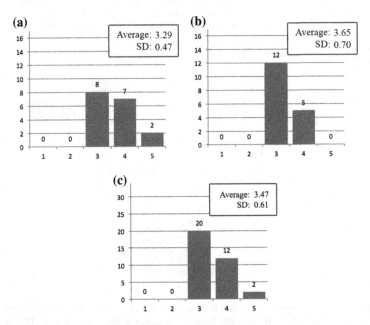

Fig. 4.22 Per-group response to question D: *Was the length of the animation appropriate to a communication-training situation?* **a** Response from ADM group. **b** Response from NADM group. **c** Response from all participants

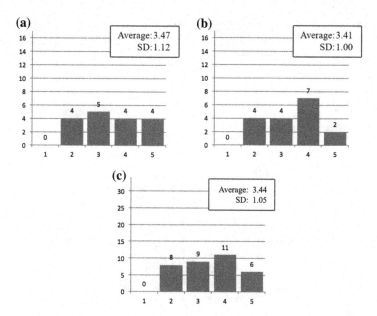

Fig. 4.23 Per-group response to question E: *Was it helpful that the animation looked similar to a game?* **a** Response from ADM group. **b** Response from NADM group. **c** Response from all participants

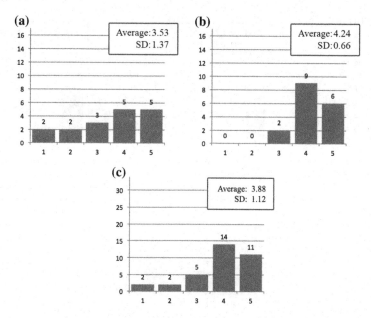

Fig. 4.24 Per-group response to question F: *Was the message clearly conveyed by the graph?* **a** Response from ADM group. **b** Response from NADM group. **c** Response from all participants

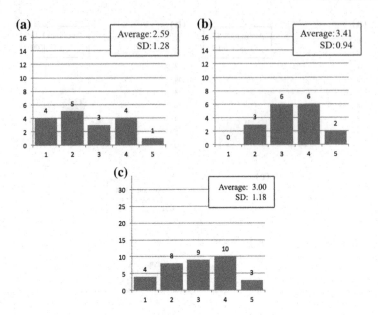

Fig. 4.25 Per-group response to question G: *Did you enjoy the communication training feedback in graphical form?* **a** Response from ADM group. **b** Response from NADM group. **c** Response from all participants

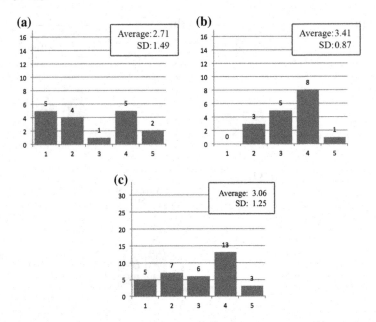

Fig. 4.26 Per-group response to question H: *In a communication-training scenario, would you like the feedback to be in a graphical form?* **a** Response from ADM group. **b** Response from NADM group. **c** Response from all participants

Table 4.7 Responses for task 3: animation-related

	Response count					Response percent				
	1	2	3	4	5	1	2	3	4	5
A	0	5	14	11	4	0	15	41	32	12
B	0	4	12	11	7	0	12	35	32	20
C	1	5	10	9	9	3	15	30	26	26
D	0	0	20	12	2	0	24	26	32	18
E	0	8	9	11	6	0	24	26	32	18

Table 4.8 Responses for task 3: graph-related

	Response count					Response percent				
	1	2	3	4	5	1	2	3	4	5
F	0	4	7	7	4	6	6	15	41	32
G	4	8	9	10	3	15	23	26	29	9
H	5	7	6	13	3	15	20	18	38	9

Table 4.9 Paired t-test results of question pairs (* significant at 0.05 level and below)

Question	Average	SD	Paired t-test result
A	3.41	0.89	0.05*
F	3.88	1.12	
B	3.62	0.95	0.03*
G	3.00	1.18	
C	3.59	1.13	0.11
H	3.06	1.25	

a strong difference with the majority favouring the animated feedback. The narrative responses in Sect. 4.6.4 shed some light on this, with some referring to its 'cuteness' and how it 'sparked their imagination'.

When asked which form of visualisation was clearer, the participants favoured the graph, though the near-borderline t-test result indicated that the difference was not extreme. This favouring was not a surprise, as the aim of our approach was never to present information in as clear a manner as possible, but in a form that was agreeable to the user and suitable for the needs of the training scenario.

There was no significant difference of opinion evident in the C/H question pair, indicating that participants were equally divided about whether they favoured the animation or the graph being used in a training scenario.

To test the difference in response between the ADM and NADM groups, a non-paired t-test was performed on the per-group responses. The results are shown in Table 4.10. The low non-paired t-test results of per-group question responses for F and G showed a significant per-group difference in the perceived clarity (F) and

Table 4.10 Per-group non-paired t-test results (* significant at 0.05 level and below)

Question	Average	SD	Non-paired t-test result
A ADM	3.29	0.99	0.45
A NADM	3.53	0.80	
B ADM	3.47	0.94	0.37
B NADM	3.76	0.97	
C ADM	3.53	1.22	0.23
C NADM	3.82	1.01	
D ADM	3.29	0.47	0.09
D NADM	3.65	0.70	
E ADM	3.47	1.12	0.87
E NADM	3.41	1.00	
F ADM	3.53	1.37	0.06*
F NADM	4.24	0.66	
G ADM	2.59	1.28	0.04*
G NADM	4.41	0.94	
H ADM	2.71	1.49	0.10
H NADM	3.41	0.87	

enjoyment (G) of the graph, with the ADM group more likely to favour the animation (although this difference was borderline in the case of its clarity). The low SD of the NADM group in response to question F indicated broad agreement of opinion, with most declaring the graph to be clear. However, amongst the ADM group the SD value was quite high, indicating a general disagreement.

Generally, the SD value of the ADM group in answer to all questions was higher than that of the NADM group, indicating less general agreement than the NADM group. This perhaps can be accounted for by the fact that visual art attracts both very technical students (as in the case of animation) and very visual ones (as in the case of graphics). The nature of their diversity of interests is likely to influence the form of visualisation that the participants favour.

Considering the natural interest and skill domains of these two groups of students, the differences in their responses come as no surprise. However, the low non-paired t-test value of the animation-related questions A to E indicates that both groups of participants were in broad agreement about its value.

The discipline the participants majored in should not be assumed to be the only factor at play in influencing their responses. How familiar they were with the gaming oeuvre would certainly have impacted on their ability to successfully interpret the results. This is borne out by the narrative responses presented in Sect. 4.6.4, particularly response IDs 1 and 6 (NADM and ADM participants respectfully). A few of these responses have been correlated to those of task 2, Sect. 4.6.2.

4.6.4 Task 4

The final task was of an open variety: inviting the participant to comment on any aspect of the user study. Most of the responses were perfunctory: reiterating preferences already stated in task 3. However, some were more informative and gave us unique information. Notable responses are given verbatim in Table 4.11. Some of these responses are discussed in the preceding sections.

Predictably, the ADM group was inclined to make suggestions about how the creative aspects of the approach might be improved. Response IDs 1 and 6 indicate correspondence between a participant's familiarity with gaming and their ability to interpret the animation successfully. Of the four from the NADM group that gave an incorrect response to task 2, one thought that there was a one-to-one correspondence

Table 4.11 Verbatim responses to user study: task 4

ID	Group	Response
1	NADM	Maybe you can define more choices like dominance, interest and discord. One scenario can be described with multiple tags. (note: this participant remarked verbally that he found the animation easy to read as he was an avid game player)
2	NADM	Characters should be the same gender
3	NADM	The people in the animation are cute
4	NADM	The animation was vivid and sparked my imagination
5	NADM	Interesting survey. The first part was a bit confusing and some clips could be categorised into two categories. In Task 3 I tried to match the activity in animation with that in the conversation
6	ADM	As I don't play video games, animation does not work well for me. Instead, I feel graph it is easier and direct to understand
7	ADM	There should be music for each animation in Task 1 also that will make it easier to match
8	ADM	I think there should be a balance between animation and graphical summary
9	ADM	Message is harder to convey using animation perhaps game characters are too distractive, simple and straightforward animated expression might help. Message from graph is clearer but less interesting than animation
10	ADM	The animation could include facial expressions to better express the character's feelings. The poses are also a little too subtle, can be made more dynamic for clarity
11	ADM	The background sound during the animation does not really suit well
12	ADM	Facial expressions on the animated characters will be even more helpful in explaining the sociometrics
13	ADM	While the content of the animation is clear on its own, they left me confused when they were played back to back, leaving me scratching my thoughts on the character's motives and intentions

between the animation and the conversation (ID 5). This was the only participant to have done so. This shows that the timing strategy of the metameasure animations, as outlined in Sect. 4.5.4, presented no problem for the majority of respondees.

4.7 Conclusion

An approach was developed that could deliver an animated metaphoric visualisation of the salient non-verbal speech cues of a dyadic conversion. We believe that it could serve as a suitable framework for the delivery of training feedback in a communication skill training scenario. From the analysis of the user studies we may conclude that the goals of our project were satisfactorily achieved.

Our approach was never intended to be better than a simple graphical approach as a means of precisely presenting information; however, the results show that it nonetheless presents information in a manner that is clear enough for the stated purposes: to serve as a means by which a trainer may deliver salient feedback about a trainee's conversational skills. Where it excels is in presenting the information in a manner that the trainee could enjoy and could experientially relate to.

Some user study participants gave suggestions on how our approach could be improved. These might be incorporated in further work.

In the selection of the animations and sprites it was required that there be a metaphoric correspondence between them and the metameasures. They were chosen by the authors, who used their experience in animation and not by any exact empirical method. Exactly on what terms this correspondence exists is a topic into which we did not delve in detail. It encompasses such diverse disciplines as cognitive linguistics, perception and neurology. Should our approach be expanded it is suspected that a more comprehensive involvement of such disciplines would be required.

References

1. Bergstrom T, Karahalios K (2007) Conversation clock: visualizing audio patterns in co-located groups. In: 2007 40th annual Hawaii international conference on system sciences (HICSS'07), pp 78–78
2. Denning S (2001) The springboard: how storytelling ignites action in knowledge-era organizations. Routledge
3. Dewey J (1962) The relation of theory to practice in education. University of Chicago, Chicago
4. Emojicate (2014) http://emojicate.com/. Accessed 29 Oct 2014
5. Emojli (2014) http://emoj.li/. Accessed 29 Oct 2014
6. Gatica-Perez D (2008) Automatic nonverbal analysis of social interaction in small groups: a review. Image Vis Comput 27(12):1775–1787
7. Gershon N, Page W (2001) What storytelling can do for information visualization. Commun ACM 44(8):31–37
8. Johansson J (2008) Efficient information visualization of multivariate and time-varying data
9. Judith D, Karrie K, Fernanda V (1999) Visualizing conversation. J Comput-Mediat Commun 4(4)

10. Koch R (2013) The book of signs. Courier Dover Publications, Dover
11. Kolb DA et al (1984) Experiential learning: experience as the source of learning and development, vol 1. Prentice-Hall, Englewood Cliffs
12. Kovecses Z (2002) Metaphor: a practical introduction. Oxford University Press, Oxford
13. Likert R (1932) A technique for the measurement of attitudes. Archives of psychology
14. Mehrabian A, Ferris SR (1967) Inference of attitudes from nonverbal communication in two channels. J Consult Psychol 31(3):248
15. Mezirow J (1997) Transformative learning: theory to practice. New Dir Adult Continuing Educ (74):5–12
16. Pentland AS (2010) Honest signals. MIT press, Cambridge
17. Poole MS, Hollingshead AB, McGrath JE, Moreland RL, Rohrbaugh J (2004) Interdisciplinary perspectives on small groups. Small Group Res 35(1):3–16
18. Pöppel E (1978) Time perception. In: Handbook of experimental psychology. Springer, London, pp 713–729
19. Salas E, Sims DE, Burke CS (2005) Is there a "big five" in teamwork? Small Group Res 36(5):555–599
20. Sarda S, Constable M, Dauwels J, Dauwels S, Elgendi M, Mengyu Z, Rasheed U, Tahir Y, Thalmann D, Magnenat-Thalmann N (2014) Real-time feedback system for monitoring and facilitating discussions. In: Natural interaction with robots, knowbots and smartphones. Springer, London, pp 375–387
21. Source filmmaker (2014) http://www.sourcefilmmaker.com. Accessed 29 Oct 2014
22. Stock C, Bishop ID, O'Connor A (2005) Generating virtual environments by linking spatial data processing with a gaming engine. In: Proceedings 6th international conference for information technologies in landscape architecture
23. Tat A, Carpendale MST (2002) Visualising human dialog. In: Sixth international conference on information visualisation, pp 16–21
24. Tominski C, Schulze-Wollgast P, Schumann H (2005) 3d information visualization for time dependent data on maps. In: Information visualisation, 2005. Proceedings, IEEE, pp 175–181
25. Unity (2014) https://unity3d.com. Accessed 29 Oct 2014
26. Uthus DC, Aha DW (2013) Multiparticipant chat analysis: a survey. Artif Intell 199:106–121
27. Wünsche BC, Kot B, Gits A, Amor R, Hosking J (2005) A framework for game engine based visualisations. In: Proceedings of image and vision computing. Citeseer, New Zealand

Chapter 5
Personalized Body Modeling

Hyewon Seo

Abstract In this chapter, we are concerned with the problem of modeling personalized body models from one or more 2D photos. One of the key tasks in this setting is the 3D shape recovery from the image, a yet-to-be-done task in computer vision which has traditionally been done using just geometric techniques. With our target objects limited to the human body, we try and make the problem easier and the solution more robust and efficient, by making use of high-quality shape data that has previously been acquired from 3D scanners. Based on a compact shape space, which has been built from a collection of range scans of real human body, we formulate the problem as an optimization one and search for the shape parameters that best matches the input silhouette. Texture coordinates are then generated by projecting the resulting shape onto the front and back images. In the presence of noise or missing views, our technique has a bias toward representing, as much as possible, the previously acquired collective knowledge on the body shape. As a result, efficiency is gained due to the fact that a model is generated by interpolating quality shapes from the body scans.

5.1 Introduction

Understanding and characterizing the shape and motion of a personalized body has numerous applications ranging from better ergonomic design of products (e.g., chairs, car compartments, and clothing) to easier modeling of realistic human characters for computer animation films.

- CAD: Personalized 3D virtual mannequin is practiced nowadays in the manufacturing or purchasing stages of many industrial goods. For instance, a cloth designer can be assisted to generate 3D mannequins of a specific individual on which garments under design are automatically dressed, modified, and simulated for test purposes. In addition, at the time of purchase, the customer can make de-

H. Seo (✉)
CNRS-University of Strasbourg, Strasbourg, France
e-mail: seohyewon@gmail.com

© Springer International Publishing Switzerland 2016
N. Magnenat-Thalmann et al. (eds.), *Context Aware Human-Robot and Human-Agent Interaction*, Human–Computer Interaction Series,
DOI 10.1007/978-3-319-19947-4_5

113

cisions about the size selection in a touchless manner, based on the body–garment relationship measured in a virtual simulation.

- Health: As it becomes more realizable to have human shape/motion simulators that are capable of dealing with complex anatomy and offer physical accuracy at the same time, recently the interest in adopting these simulators for preoperative study or augmented surgery has increased. Other possible applications include growth studies, aging, and the effects of nutrition and sports on body shape.
- Entertainment: Realistic human shape and motion modeling are one of the key tasks encountered by animators in the game and film industries. Data-driven modeling techniques offer powerful tools to them, as high-level control is provided while high realism exhibited in the captured data is retained.

Naturally, one of the oldest goals in virtual human modeling has been reconstruction of the body shape and appearance in order to faithfully depict an individual or a population in the digital world. Indeed, digitally modeling personalized human bodies from simple and easy-to-input data is now actively and successfully addressed by image-based and hybrid techniques. During its formative years, researchers focused on developing methods for modeling the appearance and movements of real people observed from 2D photographs or video sequences [14, 16, 20]. Most of these efforts use silhouette and color information from multiview images for determining the shape and, optionally, the texture of the model to be reconstructed. To simplify the problem of general reconstruction, a template or generic model has often been adopted and fitted to the observations of a particular subject.

Recently, whole body range scanners have become available and hence much of the focus of graphics research has been shifted to the acquisition of human body models from 3D range scans [1, 22]. The measurements acquired from such scanning devices provide a rich set of shape information, which otherwise requires a considerable amount of time and effort by experienced CG software users. Range scanners however remain by far more expensive, difficult to use, and offer limited accessibility compared to 2D imaging devices. Moreover, many whole body scanners today provide only geometric data without color or texture [12, 26, 27].

In this chapter, we show that combining 2D images and the range scanned measurement can lead to successful reconstruction results. The quality shape and collective knowledge from scanned datasets have been exploited to efficiently complement the geometric shape recovery from image inputs. More specifically, a set of 3D body scans that are put in correspondence have been used to parameterize the shape space, which we explore in order to find the optimizing parameters that best fit the given image data. With the target application as an online clothing store [7], where users can try on garment items on their 3D virtual human models, we limit our focus to the reconstruction of lightly clothed subjects.

5.2 State of the Art on Personalized Body Shape Reconstruction

The problem of modeling personalized body shapes is certainly not new, and there exist several ways to solve them. In Sect. 5.2.1, we review reconstructive approaches based on the direct use of measurement data, such as images and 3D scans. More recently, a trend of building and using the shape space has started, where multiple sets of previously reconstructed models are used. Section 5.2.2 provides a summary of these recent methods.

5.2.1 Shape Reconstruction from Measurement Data

There are numerous methods for acquiring shape and other visual properties from measurement data, such as range scans, photographs, and videos. For instance, in computer vision, registration of landmarks in multiple views is used to infer the object shape. Here, we limit our review to techniques devoted to human body modeling.

One way of creating detailed human models is the 3D scanning technology. Scanners based on photogrammetry (passive scanners) reconstruct the surface from single or multiple (stereo) images or from a video recording of the subject in relative motions. The 3D information of a point on the surface can be obtained by computing the binocular disparities between corresponding points from the images captured by several pairs of cameras, whose orientation and intrinsic parameters such as focus length and distortion parameters have been calibrated. More commonly used are laser range scanners. They illuminate the subject with a laser beam, and measure the distances using either triangulation, interference, or time-of-flight principles. An extensive survey of range imaging sensors can be found in [2]. Range scanning systems typically produce range images—rectangular grids of distances from the sensor to the object being scanned. If the positions of the sensor and the object are fixed, only objects that are "point viewable" can be fully digitized. More sophisticated systems such as those produced by Cyberware Laboratory, Inc. [8] are capable of digitizing cylindrical objects by rotating either the sensor or the object. Laser range scanners are promising because they can provide dense, accurate range data at high bandwidths.

However, to fully realize the potential of 3D scanning, it is essential to develop general, automatic, efficient, and robust surface reconstruction algorithms for converting the data points that 3D scanners produce into useful models. Substantial effort is needed to process the noisy and incomplete surface from a range scan into a model suitable for further use. The problem of surface reconstruction can be made easier if assumptions are made or additional knowledge can be exploited on the shape or the structure of the object being represented. A common restriction of surface reconstruction methods is that they assume the topological type of the surface is known a priori. Function reconstruction techniques that calculate the best approximating function to fit the surface data fall into this category. The goal of function reconstruction can be stated as follows: Given a surface D, a set $\{x_i \in D\}$ and a set $\{y_i \in R\}$, determine a function $\{f : D \rightarrow R\}$, such that $\{f(x_i) \approx y_i\}$. The radial basis function (RBF) approach [18] introduces a set of basis functions where the function is taken as a linear combination of the basis functions

$$f(x) = \sum \omega \cdot \Phi(\|x - x_i\|) \tag{5.1}$$

Carr et al. [5] demonstrated the use of RBF to solve the problem of interpolating incomplete meshes (hole-filling) from dense point clouds acquired from 3D range scanners. More recently, they have shown in [4] the use of implicit function with RBF for representation of object surfaces as a unified framework for the problem of interpolating incomplete meshes and smoothing/remeshing noisy surfaces (Fig. 5.1). They also propose a basis function optimization method for fast fitting and efficient evaluation to make it feasible to use RBF for large datasets and complicated objects.

As whole body scanners became available on the market [9], methods devoted to modeling the personalized human body focused on the extraction of semantic information from the scan data. In particular, the goal of many has been to convert the scan data into complete, readily animatable models. Apart from solving classical problems, such as hole filling and noise reduction, the internal skeleton hierarchy should be appropriately estimated in order to make them move. Accordingly, several approaches have been under active development to endow a semantic structure to the scan data. Dekker et al. [11] used a set of anatomical assumptions to optimize, clean, and segment data from a Hamamatsu whole body range scanner; [12] used it to generate quad mesh representations of human bodies and build applications for the clothing industry, while Ju and others [15] introduced methods to automatically segment the scan model to conform it to an animatable model.

Another approach in body shape reconstruction is to use image data. A number of model-based approaches have been introduced with their aim limited to the construction of human body models. The work of Hilton et al. [13] involves the extraction of body silhouettes from a number of 2D views (front, side, and back) and the subsequent deformation of a 3D template to fit the silhouettes. The 3D views are then mapped as texture onto the deformed model to enhance realism (Fig. 5.2). Similarly, Lee et al. [16] proposed a feature-based approach where silhouette information from

Fig. 5.1 Surface fitting by function reconstruction [4]

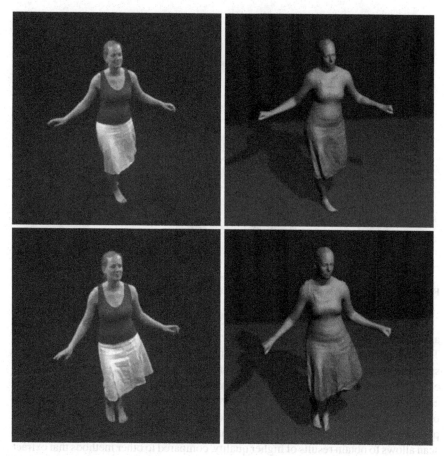

Fig. 5.2 de Aguiar et al. [10] started with a laser scan and found its deformation from eight video recordings

three orthogonal images is used to deform a generic model to produce a personalized animatable model (Fig. 5.3).

More recently, reconstruction techniques devoted to the modeling of both shape and motion of personalized human body from videos have become active. To recover the degrees of freedom associated with the shape and motion of a moving human body, many of the existing approaches introduce simplifications by using a model-based approach. Plankers et al. [17] used video cameras with a stereo pair for the model acquisition of a body part. A person's movements such as walking or raising arms are recorded on several video sequences and the program automatically extracts range information and tracks the outline of the body. The problem to be solved is twofold: First, robustly extract silhouette information from the images; second, fit the reference models to the extracted information. The data were used to instantiate the models, and the models, augmented by our knowledge about the human body

Fig. 5.3 A sequence of poses captured from eight videos by Starck and Hilton [25]

and its possible range of motions, are in turn used to constrain the feature extraction. They focus, however, more on the tracking of movement and the extraction of a subject's model is considered as the initial part of a tracking process. de Aguiar et al. [10] show impressive results of time-varying surface details they obtained from eight video recordings (Fig. 5.2). They start with the detailed shape of the laser scan of a body and combine it with the recorded performance by casting the problem of performance capture as deformation capture. The use of the detailed shape of laser scan allows to obtain results of higher quality, compared to other methods that extract shape data from video recordings, such as that by Starck and Hilton [25] (Fig. 5.3).

Based on adding details or features to an existing generic model, these approaches concern mainly the individualized shape and visual realism using high-quality textures. While they are effective and visually convincing in the cloning aspect, these approaches hardly give any control to the user; i.e., it is difficult to modify these meshes to a different shape as the user intends. These approaches have the drawback that they must deal with special cases using ad hoc techniques.

5.2.2 Building and Searching in a Shape Space

More recently, a time-saving generation of realistic, controllable body model has been made possible by building a shape space, which can be built from a collection of individual models that are placed in correspondence. Such shape space allows not only to systematically observe the diversity and individuality of shapes, but also to generate a new, plausible individual shape in an easier and simpler manner.

The facial shape space. Blanz and Vetter's morphable face model [3] was to our knowledge the first who introduced parameterization of a population model to the computer graphics community. They use the term morphable model to present the idea of manipulating a single surface representation that can be deformed to express all other faces. Using a polygon mesh representation, each vertex's position and color varies between examples, but its semantic identity remains the same—if a vertex is located at the tip of the nose in one face, it should be located at the tip of the nose in all faces. Thus, the main challenge in constructing the morphable model is to reparameterize the example surfaces so that they have a consistent representation. Using the cylindrical parameterization of head scans, they find the correspondence among vertices using a modified version of 2D optical flow.

After the parameterization, a face is represented with a shape vector

$$\mathbf{S} = (x_1, y_1, z_1, x_2 \ldots, y_n, z_n) \in R^{3n} \tag{5.2}$$

and a texture vector

$$\mathbf{T} = (r_1, g_1, b_1, r_2, \ldots, y_n, z_n) \in R^{3n}, \tag{5.3}$$

which contains coordinates and color values of its n vertices, respectively. From the m exemplar faces that are put in correspondence, principal component analysis (PCA) is applied to m shape vectors and m texture vectors. PCA performs a basis transformation to an orthogonal coordinate system (often called eigenspace) formed by the eigenvectors of the covariance matrices. A face shape is then described as a weighted sum of the orthogonal basis of 3D shapes called principal components:

$$\mathbf{S}(\vec{\alpha}) = \bar{\mathbf{S}} + \sum_{i=1}^{m-1} \alpha_i \cdot \mathbf{s_i} \tag{5.4}$$

$$\mathbf{T}(\vec{\beta}) = \bar{\mathbf{T}} + \sum_{i=1}^{m-1} \beta_i \cdot \mathbf{t_i}, \tag{5.5}$$

where $\mathbf{s}_i$ and $\mathbf{t}_i$ are eigenvectors of the covariance matrices in descending order according to their eigenvalues. Thus, the morphable model is parameterized by the coefficients; i.e., arbitrary new faces can be generated by varying the parameters $\vec{\alpha}$ and $\vec{\beta}$ that control the shape and texture.

Mapping high-level facial attributes (femaleness, concave or hooked nose, thickness of eyebrow, etc.) to the parameters of the morphable model is done by forming shape and texture vectors which, when added to or subtracted from a face, will change a specific attribute while keeping all other attributes as constant as possible. Hand-labeled facial attributes of a set of examples have been used to define such attribute-manipulating vectors.

The body shape space. Sheldon et al. [24] characterizes the physique using three parameters: endomorphy, the presence of soft roundness in the body; mesomorphy, the predominance of hardness and muscularity; and ectomorphy, the presence of linearity and skinniness. The field of anthropometry, the study of human measurement, uses dozens to hundreds of one-dimensional measurements taken on the body surface (body lengths and perimeters) to analyze body shape in a numerical way. The shortcoming of Sheldon's somatotype parameters and anthropometric measurements, particularly for body modeling, is that they do not capture the detailed shape variations that are exhibited in the population.

In Seo and Magnenat-Thalmann [22], one of the first methods for creating a whole body morphable model based on 3D scanned examples is proposed. We begin with a set of about 100 scans of different body types taken from European female and male subjects, in the framework of the EU project E-Tailor. These scans, each having different topology and posture, are not directly usable for the shape transformation. By bringing these scans into full correspondence with each other, we are able to morph between individuals, and begin to characterize and explore the space of probable body shapes. To establish the geometric correspondence among these data, an optimization-based fitting method is proposed, which finds the error and energy minimizing transformation of a template model onto each scan geometry in the database. Similar to the morphable face model, we assume that any body geometry can be obtained by deforming the template model. The deformation has two distinct entities, namely the skeleton and displacement components of the deformation (see Fig. 5.4). The skeleton component is the linear approximation of the physique, which is determined by the joint transformations (scale and translation; rotation remains constant throughout the manipulation as we assume that the pose is determined by

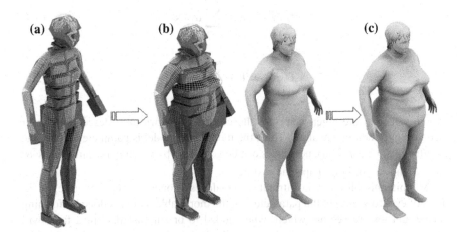

Fig. 5.4 The two phases of the deformation [21]. **a** Template model. **b** Skeleton adjustment. **c** Fine refinement

the front-end application afterwards) through the skinning. The displacement component is essentially vertex displacements, which, when added to the skin surface resulting from the skeletal deformation, depicts the detailed shape of the body.

We denote the skeleton component as

$$\mathbf{J} = (t_x^1, t_y^1, t_z^1, s_x^1, s_y^1, s_z^1, t_t^2, \ldots, t_y^m, t_z^m, s_x^m, s_y^m, s_z^m) \in R^{6m}, \qquad (5.6)$$

where t_x^j and s_x^j are the translation and scale of joint j ($j = 1, 2, \ldots, m$) along the x-axis, and the displacement component as

$$\mathbf{D} = (d_x^1, d_y^1, d_z^1, d_x^2, \ldots, d_y^m, d_z^m) \in R^{3n}, \qquad (5.7)$$

where d_x^v is the displacement of vertex v ($v = 1, 2, \ldots,$ n) along x-axis on the skin mesh. We therefore represent the geometry by combining the joint vector $\mathbf{J}$ and the vertex displacement vector $\mathbf{D}$, which respectively encode the skeleton-driven deformation and vertex displacement of a template model that is necessary to reproduce its shape.

Given a set of example body shapes represented as vectors, we apply PCA to both joint and displacement vectors. The result is two linear models for the two components:

$$\mathbf{J}(\vec{\gamma}) = \bar{\mathbf{J}} + \sum_{i=1}^{m-1} \gamma_i \cdot \mathbf{j_i} \qquad (5.8)$$

$$\mathbf{D}(\vec{\delta}) = \bar{\mathbf{D}} + \sum_{i=1}^{m-1} \delta_i \cdot \mathbf{d_i}, \qquad (5.9)$$

where $\bar{\mathbf{J}}$ and $\bar{\mathbf{D}}$ are the mean vectors, $\mathbf{j_i}$ and $\mathbf{d_i}$ are orthogonal modes of variation, and γ_i and δ_i are the ith PC weights of the joint and displacement vectors. The appearance of any body models can thus be represented by the coefficients set $\vec{\gamma}$ and $\vec{\delta}$. Note that the PCA has the additional benefit that the dimension of the vectors can be drastically reduced without losing the quality of shape. On finding the orthogonal basis, the original data vector $\mathbf{v}$ of dimension n can be represented by the projection of itself onto the first M ($\ll n$) eigenvectors that correspond to the M largest eigenvalues. In our work, we have used 30 bases both for the $\mathbf{J}$ and $\mathbf{D}$. Thus, each body is represented as a set of parameter vectors consisting of 30 PCs for the joints and 30 for displacement, giving a total of 60 parameters for the body shape space.

5.2.3 Dynamic data

In the late 1990s, commercial 3D whole body scanners started to appear but the subjects of the scan had to remain motionless during each scanning pass, which takes about several seconds, i.e., it was not feasible to scan objects under movement. With the significant advances in the 3D scanning device, it became more and more feasible to scan small objects undergoing some motion or deformation, such as hands with finger bending motion. Enabling techniques are under intense investigation, which allow for the estimation of inter-frame kinematic properties and inter-frame spatial correspondence. The increasing availability of such dynamic shape capture data will lead to a new mainstream in parametrization and statistic methods on population data. Recent investigations on the surface registration using dynamic data [6, 28, 30] are examples of such efforts.

5.3 2D-3D Registration of a Morphable Model

While image-based model reconstruction has been at the center of digital human modeling across several research groups, the majority of research progress in this avenue falls into the category of facial modeling. This is perhaps primarily due to the complex articulated structure and the high degree of self-occlusion exhibited in our bodies.

One approach that has been extensively investigated is model-based techniques. Hilton et al. [14] gathered silhouette observations from multiview images, so that they can be used to transform a template humanoid model. Affine transformation has been followed with geometric deformation of the prior surface model. They use feature point locations along the silhouette to find the correspondence among different views and to generate consistent texture coordinates. Sand et al. [20] used multiview recordings to derive the skeleton configuration of a moving subject, which subsequently derives the skin surface shape. These works show how a prior knowledge can be used to avoid difficulties of general reconstruction. However, they do not accumulate observations that can efficiently be used to handle uncertainties.

The strength of gathering information from collective observation has been illustrated in face model acquisition by Blanz and Vetter [3]. In their modeler, highly detailed 3D face shape and texture spaces have been obtained by transforming about two hundred laser-scanned faces into vector representation. Given a single photograph of a face, its 3D shape, orientation in space, and the illumination conditions are estimated. Starting from a rough initial estimate of shape, surface color, and lighting parameters, an optimization algorithm iteratively finds the best matching parameters to the input image. Shape and texture constraints derived from the statistics of our example faces are used to guide automated matching. While these methods are quite powerful, they have not been applied to image-based reconstruction of an entire human body. These considerations led us to look for a more robust approach to image-based human body modeling. The key idea is to complement the image-based reconstruction method by leveraging the quality shape and statistic information accumulated from multiple shapes of range-scanned people [23]. We use a sparse set of feature points and silhouette data extracted both from the input images and the deformable model to optimize the deformation parameters, such that the resulting geometry model best matches the silhouette on the image. In the presence of ambiguity either from the noise or from missing views, our technique has a bias toward representing as much as possible the previously acquired 'knowledge' on the shape geometry. The proposed technique has been used to successfully reconstruct quality human body models from a minimum number images, even from a single image input. Additionally, it runs at an arguably interactive speed.

An overview of our approach is illustrated in Fig. 5.5. We first take a minimum number of photographs of a subject (Fig. 5.5a), and extract silhouettes and feature points on the images (Fig. 5.5b, c). We then use a deformable model for the shape recovery. Using the silhouette data extracted from the input images, we explore the body space (a range of coefficient parameters that have been spanned by the database of the deformable model) and find the best fitting deformation parameters on a template model (Fig. 5.5d–g). Finally, we generate texture coordinate data by projecting the deformed template model onto the input images (Fig. 5.5h).

5.3.1 Dynamic data

Taking photographs. Our modeler in principle does not require any special camera arrangements, nor does it require a specific number of views. In practice, however, at least two views—one from the front and the other from the back—are preferred, as we want to generate a complete texture on the entire body. As our deformable model does not contain color data, we rely entirely on the input images for the texture. In our experiments, we generally take three photographs using a single camera, each from the front, the side, and the back of the subject, unless otherwise specified. Note that all our subjects are lightly clothed. To simplify the combinatorial complexity of the human shape and posture, we require the subject to stand in the specific posture; the limbs are straight and away from the torso as shown in Fig. 5.6.

Virtual camera setup for the template model projection. We now set up the virtual camera and projection matrix we use for projecting the deformable model onto the image space. The virtual camera is arranged as closely as possible to the physical setup, so that we can use input images directly for the silhouette comparison without additional processes such as image size normalization. We adopted Tsai's Pinhole camera model [29], which basically is a pinhole model taking the first-order radial lens distortion into account. It has five intrinsic parameters (focal length f, first-order radial lens distortion value Kappa, center of lens distortion C_x, C_y, scale factor S_x), and six extrinsic parameters (R_x, R_y, R_z, T_x, T_y, R_z). To calculate these intrinsic and extrinsic parameters, we have taken an image of a calibration frame, similar to the approach presented by Zhang [31].

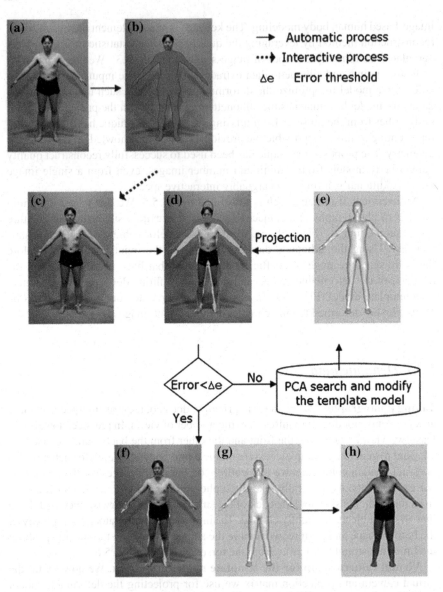

Fig. 5.5 Overview of the proposed body modeler. **a** Photograph. **b** Silhouette extraction. **c** Feature points. **d** Error calculation. **e** Generic model. **f** Final error. **g** Modified model. **h** Texture mapping

Silhouette extraction and feature point identification. Photographs have been taken in front of a uniformly colored screen so that simple methods such as using color key can be used for automatic silhouette detection. The method we use is a standard background subtraction to isolate silhouettes from images using a color key. We use the hue-saturation-value (HSV) color model. We first map each pixel in the image to

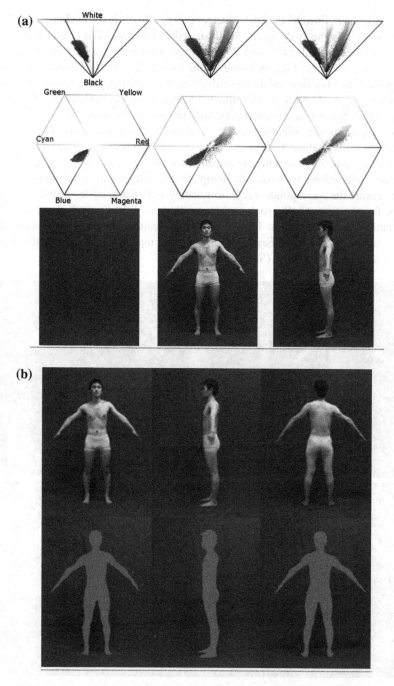

Fig. 5.6 Silhouette extraction from photographs. **a** Projection of images onto the HSV color space: Empty background (*left*), front (*middle*), and side (*right*) views. **b** Silhouette extraction results

the color space defined by the HSV hexagonal cone. Pixels in the background region form a cluster in the HSV space, as illustrated in Fig. 5.6a. The cluster is defined by the H value of 180–240°, and S value larger than a threshold, say, '0.3'. As a subject stands in front of the background, shadows appear and they contribute to the background clouds elongated downwards along the V-axis of the hexagon. Thus, we use color keys in H and S to determine the background pixel cluster. As illustrated in Fig. 5.6b, shadows have been successfully labeled as background.

Feature point identification. Next, we label 12–15 feature points on the silhouettes. In addition to the silhouette information, we make use of a number of feature points when matching the template model to the target subject in the image. Using features points allows to deform the template not only to match the silhouette but also to ensure the correspondence. Unfortunately, only a limited set of feature points can be found automatically, such as those on the top of the head, the bottom of the feet, and the tip of he hands. For the rest of the feature points, the user manually places them on the images. Feature points on the template model are identified in a similar way on the 3D mesh (See Fig. 5.7).

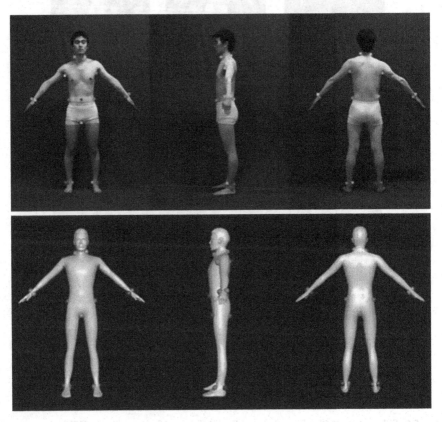

Fig. 5.7 The feature points we use for matching error are shown both on the images (*top*) and on the template model (*bottom*)

5.3.2 Shape Recovery by Searching Deformation Space

The extracted silhouette information is used to reconstruct the geometry by searching a body space and finding an optimum parameter set. Based on the previously developed body modeler, the body space comprises a range of coefficient parameters that are spanned by the database of the deformable model (Sect. 5.2.2). A set of coefficient parameters comprises an optimum solution if, when collectively applied to the template model, it produces silhouettes that best fit those of the given images. The key point is that instances of the models are deformed in ways that are found in the example set, guaranteeing a realistic, robust shape acquisition.

We find the solution in a coarse-to-fine manner. Since the deformation is parameterized with PCA space for each of the vector components, we first find the optimizing joint parameter γ_j, followed by the subsequent search for the displacement parameter δ_j. We use direction set method [19] for the optimization. The algorithm repeats 'search-deform-compare' loop until we obtain a sufficient degree of matching between the silhouette of the deformed model and that of the input image—it generates a body shape from the current coefficients, projects the body model onto 2D space, and updates the coefficients according to the silhouette difference. The first set of iterations is performed by optimizing only the first coefficients controlling the first few PCs. In subsequence iterations, more PCs are added to further deform the template. Figure 5.8 shows the female template model undergoing the progressive deformation.

Error metric. While searching for the error-minimizing deformation parameters, we consider two error terms: (1) the sum of distances between corresponding feature points (Ed) and (2) silhouette error E_a. By silhouette error we refer to the fraction of pixels for which the projected and observed silhouettes do not match, as shown in Fig. 5.9. The number of background pixels that lie inside the projected template model is summed up with that of foreground pixels that lie outside of it:

$$E_a = \frac{\sum(T(i,j) \cdot \bar{D}(i,j))}{\sum T(i,j)} + \frac{\sum(\bar{T}(i,j) \cdot D(i,j))}{\sum D(i,j)} \qquad (5.10)$$

$T(i,j)$, and $\bar{T}(i,j)$ are the Boolean values indicating if the pixel at location (i,j) is inside and outside of the template model, respectively. $D(i,j)$ and $\bar{D}(i,j)$ are 1 if the pixel located at (i,j) is foreground and background, respectively. This notion of nonoverlapping area is effectively equivalent to the silhouette error used by Sand et al. [20]. Note that the information about arms is taken only from the front/back view.

Weighted sum of the two error terms is used, as denoted by

$$E = \alpha E_d + (1 - \alpha)E_\alpha \qquad (5.11)$$

In the first iterations we need to quickly search for joint parameters, hence we set $\alpha = 1$. Feature points from both the frontal and side images are measured. Next,

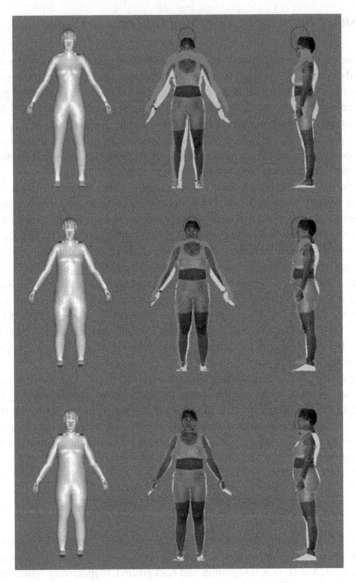

Fig. 5.8 The female template model undergoing the progressive deformation process: prior to fitting (*top*), joint parameter fitting using one PC (*middle*), and four PCs (*bottom*)

we further improve the fitting accuracy by setting $\alpha = 0.3$. The deformable model is first fit to the frontal image and then the side image error is added. Finally, the displacement map is explored with the same setting. At each iteration we combine the errors from the frontal and side images, so that the fitting of the template to frontal and side images can be simultaneously handled.

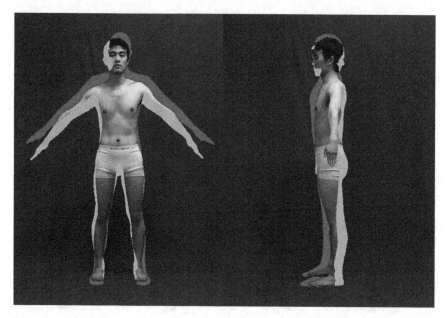

Fig. 5.9 Nonoverlapping area error calculated on the *front*, *side*, and *back* photographs of a male subject

5.3.3 Mapping Textures

Photo images are used to generate texture on the shape. Although we require the subject to keep consistent poses among different views, they may be slightly different from one view to another, as they are taken at distinct times. To handle such inconsistency, we use only the front and the side images for the shape recovery, and we handle the texture coordinate creation process for the front and the back parts separately.

Two separate texture coordinates are obtained by projecting the deformed template model onto the front and the back images; if the angle between the vertex normal and the view direction is between $-\pi/2$ and $\pi/2$, we project the vertex on the deformed template surface onto the front image. The other vertices are projected onto the back image. Prior to the second projection, we must adjust the posture of the model by matching the template with the silhouette data on the back image. This is due to the slight difference among postures seen from one view to another. Figure 5.10 shows the result of texture mapping on a reconstructed shape model.

5.3.4 Single Image Input

To demonstrate how our modeler can handle some uncertain situations robustly, we have reconstructed a 3D geometry using only a single image input. In Fig. 5.10a,

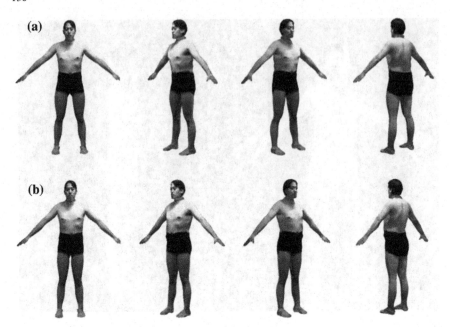

Fig. 5.10 Models obtained using a single image input. **a** Reconstructed model using only the *front* view. **b** Reconstructed model using only the *side* view

we used only the front image of the subject to reconstruct the shape of the template model. Analogously, only the side image of the subject was used to reconstruct the shape shown in Fig. 5.10b. In both cases, a back view image was used to complete the texture map.

5.4 Conclusion

We have presented a technique for reconstructing personalized human bodies from a few 2D images. Using the 3D body space that has been generated from processing range scans, we propose to reconstruct the 3D surface of a personalized body such that both the knowledge about the body shape and the photogrammetric information specific to the person of interest are exploited. For the shape recovery we start with a deformable template model whose deformation is parameterized with PCA of the scanned body shapes. Given a set of images, the optimizing shape is found by searching the shape space such that it minimizes the matching error measured between silhouettes. The idea is to start from a space consisting of a few PCs and to increase its size by progressively adding new PCs. This provides us powerful means of matching the template model to the image in a coarse-to-fine manner. In addition, a high level of detail and accuracy is acquired, since our modeler essentially blends multiple shapes of the human body acquired from 3D laser scanners. This constitutes a good complement to geometric methods, which cannot capture detailed shape solely from the image input.

References

1. Allen B, Curless B, Popović Z (2003) The space of human body shapes: reconstruction and parameterization from range scans. In: ACM SIGGRAPH 2003 papers, SIGGRAPH '03, New York, USA, ACM, pp 587–594
2. Besl PJ (1988) Active, optical range imaging sensors. Mach Vis Appl 1(2):127–152
3. Blanz V, Vetter T (1999) A morphable model for the synthesis of 3D faces. In: Proceedings of the 26th annual conference on computer graphics and interactive techniques, SIGGRAPH '99, New York, USA. ACM Press/Addison-Wesley Publishing Company, pp 187–194
4. Carr JC, Beatson RK, Cherrie JB, Mitchell TJ, Fright WR, McCallum BC, Evans TR (2001) Reconstruction and representation of 3D objects with radial basis functions. In: Proceedings of the 28th annual conference on computer graphics and interactive techniques, SIGGRAPH '01, New York, USA. ACM, pp 67–76
5. Carr JC, Fright WR, Beatson RK (1997) Surface interpolation with radial basis functions for medical imaging. IEEE Trans Med Imaging 16:96–107
6. Chang W, Zwicker M (2011) Global registration of dynamic range scans for articulated model reconstruction. ACM Trans Graph 30(3):26:1–26:15
7. Cordier F, Seo H, Magnenat-Thalmann N (2003) Made-to-measure technologies for an online clothing store. IEEE Comput Graph Appl 23(1):38–48
8. Cyberware. http://www.cyberware.com
9. Daanen HAM, van de Water GJ (1998) Whole body scanners. Displays 19(3):111–120
10. de Aguiar E, Stoll C, Theobalt C, Ahmed N, Seidel H-P, Thrun S (2008) Performance capture from sparse multi-view video. ACM Trans Graph 27(3):98:1–98:10
11. Dekker L, Douros I, Buxton BF, Treleaven PC (1999) Building symbolic information for 3D human body modeling from range data. In: Proceedings of the second international conference on 3-D digital imaging and modeling. IEEE Computer Society, pp 388–397
12. Hamamatsu BL scanner. http://www.hpk.co.jp
13. Hilton A, Beresford D, Gentils T, Smith RS, Sun W (1999) Virtual people: capturing human models to populate virtual worlds. In: Computer animation, pp 174–185
14. Hilton A, Beresford D, Gentils T, Smith R, Sun W, Illingworth J (2000) Whole-body modelling of people from multiview images to populate virtual worlds. Vis Comput 16(7):411–436
15. Ju X, Siebert JP (2001) Conforming generic animatable models to 3D scanned data. In: International conference of numberisation 3D—scanning 2001, pp 4–5
16. Lee W-S, Gu J, Magnenat-Thalmann N (2000) Generating animatable 3D virtual humans from photographs. Comput Graph Forum 19(3):1–10
17. Plänkers R, D'Apuzzo N, Fua P (1999) Automated body modeling from video sequences. In: Proceedings of the IEEE international workshop on modelling people, MPEOPLE '99, Washington, USA. IEEE Computer Society, pp 45–52
18. Powell MJD (1987) Algorithms for approximation. Radial basis functions for multivariable interpolation: a review. Clarendon Press, New York, pp 143–167
19. Press WH, Teukolsky SA, Vetterling WT, Flannery BP (1992) Numerical recipes in C (2Nd Ed.): the art of scientific computing. Cambridge University Press, New York
20. Sand P, McMillan L, Popović J (2003) Continuous capture of skin deformation. ACM Trans Graph 22(3):578–586
21. Seo H (2004) Parameterized human body modeling

22. Seo H, Magnenat-Thalmann N (2003) An automatic modeling of human bodies from sizing parameters. In: Proceedings of the 2003 symposium on interactive 3D graphics, I3D '03, New York, USA. ACM, pp 19–26

23. Seo H, Yeo YI, Wohn KY (2006) 3D body reconstruction from photos based on range scan. In: Technologies for E-learning and digital entertainment, first international conference, edutainment 2006, Hangzhou, China, 16–19 April 2006, Proceedings, pp 849–860

24. Sheldon WH, Stevens SS, Tucker WB (1940) The varieties of human physique: an introduction to constitutional psychology. Human constitution series. Harper, New York

25. Starck J, Hilton A (2007) Surface capture for performance based animation. IEEE Comput Graph Appl 27(3):21–31

26. Tecmath AG. http://www.tecmath.com

27. Telmat Industrie SA. http://www.telmat.com

28. Tevs A, Berner A, Wand M, Ihrke I, Bokeloh M, Kerber J, Seidel H-P (2012) Animation cartography—intrinsic reconstruction of shape and motion. ACM Trans Graph 31(2):12:1–12:15

29. Tsai RY (1986) An efficient and accurate camera calibration technique for 3D machine vision. In: Proceedings of IEEE conference on computer vision and pattern recognition, Miami Beach, FL, pp 364–374

30. Wand M, Adams B, Ovsjanikov M, Berner A, Bokeloh M, Jenke P, Guibas L, Seidel H-P, Schilling A (2009) Efficient reconstruction of nonrigid shape and motion from real-time 3D scanner data. ACM Trans Graph 28(2):15:1–15:15

31. Zhang Z (2000) A flexible new technique for camera calibration. IEEE Trans Pattern Anal Mach Intell 22(11):1330–1334

Chapter 6
Parameterized Facial Modelling and Animation

Junghyun Cho, Heeseung Choi, Sang Chul Ahn and Ig-Jae Kim

Abstract Facial modelling is a fundamental technique in a variety of applications in computer graphics, computer vision and pattern recognition areas. As 3D technologies evolved over the years, the quality of facial modelling greatly improved. To enhance the modelling quality and controllability of the model further, parametric methods, which represent or manipulate facial attributes (e.g. identity, expression, viseme) with a set of control parameters, have been proposed in recent years. The aim of this chapter is to give a comprehensive overview of current state-of-the-art parametric methods for realistic facial modelling and animation.

6.1 Introduction

The human face is the most important part of the human body, as the expressions and proportions of the human face are essential to represent identity, emotional status, health qualities and even some social characteristics. Wide availability of powerful and low-cost computing system and imaging devices has created great interest in automatic processing of digital facial images in a variety of applications, including huma–computer interaction, face recognition, multimedia management, virtual characters in film and in game industries. For example, in surveillance systems, face recognition is possible with analysis based on the intrinsic factors of a given face, such as appearance and shape, from a set of images or video. Moreover, in

J. Cho (✉) · H. Choi · S.C. Ahn · I.-J. Kim
Centre of Human-centred Interaction for Coexistence,
Korea Institute of Science and Technology, Seoul, Korea
e-mail: jhcho@kist.re.kr

S.C. Ahn
e-mail: asc@kist.re.kr

I.-J. Kim
e-mail: drjay@kist.re.kr

H. Choi
e-mail: hschoi@imrc.kist.re.kr

human–computer interaction, recognizing or understanding the emotional state of the user by facial analysis is crucial as it improves the interactivity of the user with the system. Thus, facial modelling and animation, core technologies of the facial image processing field, have attracted wide attention in the past few decades by researchers in computer graphics, computer vision and pattern recognition areas.

Conventionally, facial modelling and animation has required extensive human intervention due to the complex nature of the human facial anatomy and due to sensitivity to subtle changes in facial appearance. Beginning with Parke's pioneering work on animating faces [23], various computational methods for automatic face modelling and synthesis have been developed to handle such issues. These facial modelling techniques can be roughly divided into two categories depending on the source of facial models: facial modelling with active sensors and facial modelling from a set of images.

The active sensor-based approaches estimate 3D geometries of faces from several types of active sensors, including laser scanners and structured light systems. Recently, it has been advanced to capture the continuous motion of faces with various expressions so as to obtain ground-truth training data for face modelling and animation.

Image-based approaches reconstruct the facial geometry by analysing the illumination information about the projected image of a face or by supplementing more views of a face. They are based on computer vision algorithms, such as shape from shading, stereo vision (camera calibrated case) and structure from motion (camera uncalibrated case) techniques.

Various methods have been proposed to improve the quality of facial modelling by applying suitable illumination priors on the human face structure and removing outliers of the correspondences across different views.

Despite these improvements during the past decade, automatic facial modelling and animation remains a challenging problem. For instance, it is still difficult to obtain a high level of realism for various facial attributes (such as identity, expression) for performance-driven animation. Consequently, it requires complex data acquisition and tedious manual processing for high-quality animation.

To further enhance the realism and controllability of facial modelling and animation, parametric methods that represent or manipulate various face properties with several control parameters have been proposed in recent years. Many of these methods rely on the observation that variation in facial attributes can be approximated by a linear subspace on low dimension. These techniques estimate linear coefficients for known basis shapes, or both the coefficients and basis shape, simultaneously from images/videos or 3D point cloud data obtained from active sensors. One striking example is a morphable facial model [4] which combines 3D facial geometry with linear texture models. However, the morphable model is visually non-intuitive so it is difficult to reproduce or control facial expressions for animation. Currently, many alternatives including blendshape [21, 35], quasi-eigenface [17], multilinear models [7] and deformable models [31, 32] have been proposed to enhance the quality of facial modelling and animation. In Fig. 6.1, we briefly classify current parametric approaches for facial modelling and animation in terms of modelling and animation

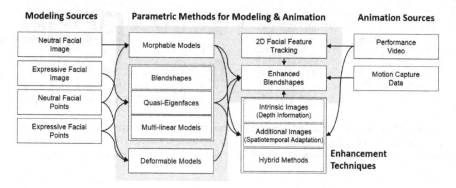

Fig. 6.1 Parametric methods for modelling and animation

sources, algorithms and enhancement techniques. This chapter provides detailed descriptions of the parametric approaches, algorithms and examples available for current facial modelling and animation technologies.

The remainder of this chapter is organized as follows. Section 6.2 explains the preliminaries and basic concept of parametric approaches. Section 6.3 presents the state-of-the-art techniques to model, animate and render faces. Section 6.4 describes the recent research done in our groups as an example of facial modelling and animation. Section 6.5 discuss the future avenues and conclusions are drawn in Sect. 6.6.

6.2 Parametric Representation of Facial Model

This section describes various types of representation of facial models commonly used in facial modelling and animation.

6.2.1 Linear/Multilinear Space of Facial Meshes

For representing geometrical facial shapes, polygonal mesh has been used. The polygonal mesh basically consists of a set of vertices, edges and polygons. Conventionally, the triangular mesh has been the most common choice among polygonal meshes. In recent years, the popularity of the quadrilateral mesh has grown mainly due to regularity and simplicity for parameterization, among others. Also, to manipulate the facial mesh, other properties such as texture coordinates and half-edge can be considered. Generating a facial mesh model manually is a difficult task since the facial shape is relatively complex and facial expressions can differ in each individual. Therefore, the facial mesh is usually obtained by active sensors with dense geometric details. For general facial shape modelling, linear space representation is widely used as people's faces have a similar topology; moreover, this significantly reduces the degree

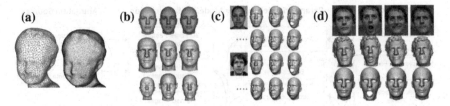

Fig. 6.2 Mesh representation and example of facial basis meshes: **a** triangular mesh (*left*) and quadrilateral mesh (*right*), **b** samples of eigenfaces and its appearances [18], **c** samples of blendshapes [6], **d** samples of bilinear models [7]: raw data (*middle*) and pre-processed data (*bottom*)

of freedom (i.e. dimensionality). In linear representation, the facial mesh can be represented as an element of the linear space spanned by a set of existing face meshes in the database, called basis meshes. Equation 6.1 denotes the linear representation of the facial model.

$$\mathbf{f} = \sum_{i=1}^{N} w_i \mathbf{b}_i, \tag{6.1}$$

where N is the total number of basis meshes, $\mathbf{f}$ is a facial model, w_i is an i-th weighting parameter and $\mathbf{b}_i$ is an i-th basis mesh, respectively.

Facial modelling can be considered as a parameter fitting problem. Hence, the modelling result depends on how well-defined basis meshes are. Figure 6.2 shows mesh representation and some examples of facial basis meshes. Basis meshes can be represented by statistical analysis such as principal component analysis (PCA). In this case, the basis meshes are called eigenshapes. The eigenshapes (or morphable model), however, are hard to interpret physical properties (visually non-intuitive) and have difficulties in reproducing or controlling facial expressions for facial animation. To solve the above issue, one of the most popular approaches used in facial animation production is the blendshape technique, which synthesizes expressions by taking a linear combination of a set of predefined expression bases. However, they may cover only a fraction of the expression space, resulting in large reproduction/animation error. To handle the above-mentioned problems, the method to combine the advantages of the eigenshape and blendshape approaches has been also developed [17]. Currently, multilinear facial models have been proposed for high-quality facial expression tracking and transferring, which decouple the facial attributes into several modes (e.g. identity, expression, viseme) and encode them consistently in mode spaces. One example of the facial mesh model in the multilinear space can be expressed as Eq. 6.2.

$$\mathbf{f} = \mathbf{C}_r \times_2 \mathbf{w}_{\text{id}}^T \times_3 \mathbf{w}_{\text{exp}}^T, \tag{6.2}$$

where $\mathbf{C}_r$ is the core tensor, $\mathbf{w}_{\text{id}}$, $\mathbf{w}_{\text{exp}}$ are identity and expression parameters, respectively, and the symbol $\times$ is the tensor product in multilinear space.

The linear or multilinear space representations of the facial model have the basic assumption that the topology of the basis meshes is consistent. Hence, finding point-to-point correspondences between different meshes from different people's faces or creating topologically consistent mesh is a critical issue in facial modelling.

6.2.2 Linear Space of Mesh Deformation

Alternatively, facial models can be obtained by deforming existing mesh directly. To make deformation easier, sparse control points on a facial mesh are usually adapted. Similar to linear space representation of the facial mesh model, mesh deformation can be represented in the linear space as Eq. 6.3.

$$\mathbf{f} = \mathbf{f}_0 + \sum_{i=1}^{M} w_i \mathbf{d}_i, \tag{6.3}$$

where $\mathbf{f}_0$ is the existing mesh, $\mathbf{d}_i$ is the deformation vector of an i-th control point and w_i is the corresponding weighting parameter, respectively.

In mesh deformation, the main concern is how to define deformation vectors, kernel functions or interpolation function on each control point. These deformation methods are especially important when we design non-rigid registration algorithms to find global and local correspondences between two different sets of points. The detailed description for this issue will be addressed in Sect. 6.3.

6.2.3 Optimization of Facial Parameters

The linear space representation reduces the number of unknowns substantially as the parameters are much smaller than the number of vertex coordinates in a mesh representation. If the basis meshes or the deformation vectors are predefined, a facial mesh model can be fitted to a facial image, image sequence (or video), motion capture data, or point cloud data obtained from 3D active sensors (i.e. Kinect system of Microsoft). Without loss of generality, image-based facial modelling is to solve the following optimization problem:

$$\underset{\mathbf{w}, \mathbf{w}_I}{\operatorname{argmin}} \left(\|\mathbf{I}_0 - \mathbf{I}_{\mathbf{w}_I}(\mathbf{f})\|^2 + c_1 \|\mathbf{w}\|^2 + c_2 \|\mathbf{w}_I\|^2 \right), \tag{6.4}$$

where $\mathbf{I}_0$ is a given facial image, $\mathbf{f}$ is a parameterized facial model, $\mathbf{I}$ is the projection image of the 3D facial model to the 2D screen space, c_1 and c_2 are the regularization factors, and $\mathbf{w}$ and $\mathbf{w}_I$ are parameters for the shape and appearance model, respectively.

In appearance modelling, we have to compute the colors of the facial model as well as the lighting condition as shown in Eq. 6.4. Therefore, the appearance of the facial model means not only its geometry but also the lighting environment and its reflectance property. The most common assumption on the reflectance property is the Lambertian reflectance [3], whose diffuse term only is considered.

$$i = i_L \rho \max(0, 1 \cdot n) \tag{6.5}$$

where i is the color on a point of the facial model, and i_L and l are the color intensity and the position of the point light source, respectively. ρ is the albedo and n is the surface normal. In Eq. 6.5, the diffuse reflectance on a surface point is described and the light position can be regarded as a parameter of the appearance model. However, in practice, the point light source gives unnatural illumination results, hence, the spherical harmonic basis is commonly used as Eq. 6.6.

$$i = \rho \sum_i^9 l_i h_i(n), \tag{6.6}$$

where l_i is the lighting parameter, h_i are the first nine spherical harmonic basis functions and n is the surface normal. The albedo ρ of the facial model can be parameterized statistically in linear color space similar to Eq. 6.1, and it is used in the image-based modelling methods.

On the other hand, point cloud-based facial modelling is to solve the following optimization problem:

$$\underset{w, w_R}{\operatorname{argmin}} \left(\| P_0 - R_{w_R}(f) \|^2 + d_1 \| w \|^2 + d_2 \| w_R \|^2 \right), \tag{6.7}$$

where P_0 is given 3D points, f is the parametrized facial model, R is the transformation function of the facial model, d_1 and d_2 are the regularization factors, and w and w_R are the parameters for the facial model and the transformation function, respectively.

After fitting the facial model, the details of the fitted model can be enhanced based on high-resolution photometry methods. Furthermore, the control of the fitted model is possible by using performance-driven approaches.

6.2.4 Possible Research Topics

In the parametric methods several issues should be considered to obtain high-quality facial modelling and animation.

- High-quality basis meshes that are large enough to cover possible facial shapes are required to use the parametric methods. The data acquisition and preprocessing technologies are critical to obtain the best results.

- The global shape of a face is captured from image-based facial modelling or point cloud-based facial modelling, but the local details are often lost. The details preserving fitting algorithms should be required.
- The optimization equation 6.4 is well known to have local minima, so that it is hard to solve and takes time for convergence; computation acceleration techniques are required.
- The mesh deformation causes inverted elements (bad polygons) if naive interpolation functions are applied. Fast and physically plausible interpolation methods are required.
- The facial feature tracking method plays a key role from the perspective of process automation and detail enhancement. Robust and highly efficient facial feature tracking methods are required.
- Complex and expensive set-ups would be inapplicable for some computing environments such as mobile devices. Methods towards more lightweight set-ups should be developed.

6.3 State of the Art

In this section, we introduce the state-of-the art works related to the issues described in the previous section.

6.3.1 Facial Data Acquisition

The parametric facial model requires a set of well-defined basis meshes which are topologically consistent. For example, in eigenshapes, the set has to contain sufficiently many facial shapes in order to span the entire range of possible shapes of different races, genders and ages. Owing to such demand, in the past few decades, 3D sensing technologies in both software and hardware have been greatly improved. Figure 6.3 shows various examples of the 3D facial data acquisition method. The data can be obtained from both active sensors and a set of images.

Fig. 6.3 Facial data acquisition methods: **a** data from a laser scanner [4]: raw data (*left*) and pre-processed data (*right*), **b** data from KinectFusion [15]: initial data (*left*) and accumulated data (*right*), **c** data from stereo images [14]: intrinsic images (*left*) and reconstructed model (*right*)

Pighin et al. [24] proposed a pioneering method to generate a set of blendshapes. They create blendshapes by fitting a generic facial mesh to multiview facial images in a semi-automatic way. Since the generic mesh is used, the resulting fitted meshes have the same mesh topology. On the other hand, Blanz and Vetter [4] use a laser scanner, *Cyberware*, to obtain a fair number of facial mesh data and then suggest a method to make them have the same mesh topology by optical flow techniques. Recently, Fyffe et al. [12] proposed a method to obtain high-resolution facial geometry using multiview stereo and gradient-based photometric stereo [14]. In order to span nearly the entire range of possible shapes for each part of the face, the set is created based on the Facial Action Coding System (FACS) [11]. Weise et al. [35], Li et al. [20, 21] and Cao et al. [6, 7] use *KinectFusion* [15] to obtain facial mesh data. Although the mesh quality is relatively low compared to the data from laser scanner and the stereo scanner, it computes the mesh interactively and hence it is widely used.

6.3.2 Mesh Correspondence and Deformation

In order to generate facial meshes with the same mesh topology, we first find the correspondences between two different meshes or point clouds. If the correspondences between meshes are found once, a large class of algorithms can be applied based on the correspondences, which include template matching, statistical analysis such as PCA and wavelet transforms, texture and deformation transfers between mesh models. The deformation transfer method suggested by Sumner et al. [31] is frequently used to create a new set of facial expression meshes from the previously well-defined mesh set based on FACS as shown in Fig. 6.4.

To establish correspondence, the consistent mesh parameterization method suggested by Praun et al. [25] can be used as shown in figure [25]. Optical flow method suggested by Blanz and Vetter [4] and non-rigid iterative closest point (ICP) method suggested by Amberg et al. [1] can also be good choices to find correspondence. The non-rigid point registration method suggested by Li et al. [19] can be a choice, as it considers various types of registration priors such as global rigidity, local rigidity

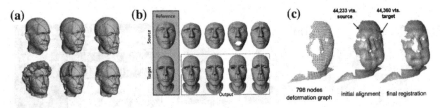

Fig. 6.4 Consistent mesh parameterization and deformation methods: **a** examples of consistent meshes [25], **b** example of deformation transfer [31], **c** example of the non-rigid registration [19]

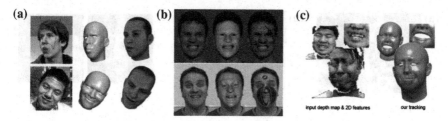

Fig. 6.5 Parametric facial model fitting methods: **a** example of the real-time bilinear model [6], **b** example of the detail enhanced method [13], **c** example of the real-time customized blend-shapes [21]

and the embedded deformation graph [32]; it shows robust performance even for largely differing facial meshes or point clouds.

On the other hand, in order to enhance the parametric facial model with local details and expressions, user controls or accurate 2D facial feature points are used as constraints to global shape deformation [7, 13, 21].

In order to deform the mesh efficiently, the methods suggested by Sorkine et al. [29, 30] can be used. The constrained deformation often causes the facial mesh to have inverted elements (triangles or quadilaterals) and to produce physically unplausible results. In order to prevent such inverted elements and unnatural results, locally injective mappings [28] and sparse localized deformation modes [22] can be applied (Fig. 6.5).

6.3.3 Parametric Facial Model Fitting

Based on the predefined sets of facial basis meshes, we can parameterize an arbitrary facial model in linear or multilinear spaces. As the parametric representation of the facial mesh model reduces the dimensionality, we can formulate image-based facial modelling and point cloud-based facial modelling.

6.3.3.1 Image-Based Methods

Pighin et al. [24] proposed the fitting method to obtain blendshapes. It finds the camera pose and rotation, focal length according to the manually given facial landmarks. By using blendshapes, animation of facial expression has been tractable. Blanz and Vetter [4] proposed the method to reconstruct 3D facial shape and appearance from an image. It solves the optimization problem as Eq. 6.4. Since the optimization is hard to solve and take times until convergence, the stochastic gradient descent algorithms are applied [5]. Alternatively, Knothe [18] applied multi-level optimization algorithms to the optimization problem in order to cope with the local convergence problems.

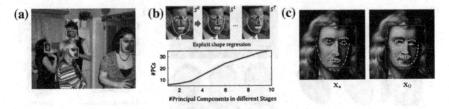

Fig. 6.6 The facial tracking methods: **a** the part-based facial tracker [26], **b** the real-time explicit shape regressor [8], which infers most probable PCA components in each optimization stage, **c** the real-time supervised descent method [36] in which the directions from the source feature (*right*) to the target feature (*left*) are trained

Vlasic et al. [34] and Cao et al. [6, 7] introduced the multilinear facial model to capture the facial expressions of a person as well as the facial shape of the person in the unified framework (Fig. 6.6).

6.3.3.2 Point-Based and Hybrid Methods

On the other hand, facial modelling and animation techniques using point cloud data obtained from active sensors such as Kinect have been introduced actively in recent years.

KinectFusion [15] is used basically to obtain the aligned and noise-removed facial mesh in interactive time. Weise et al. [35] proposed a method generating blendshapes and solving blendshape parameters based on the facial mesh obtained by Kinect in real-time. Li et al. [21] proposed the advanced method to customize and enhance blendshapes using the incremental PCA method. However, these methods gives a coarse control of virtual humans in real-time and do not yield a highly detailed face reconstruction.

Image-based approaches or multiview approaches help to overcome the limitations in shape detail and tracking accuracy that are purely geometric. Hence, in order to retain the facial details, hybrid methods have been introduced. Valgaerts et al. [33] proposed the method adapting passive stereo and Garrido et al. [13] proposed the method using sequence images and applying spatio-temporal enhancement techniques to the previous image-based method. Intrinsic image techniques such as [2, 16] can also be applied to increase the local quality of the facial mesh.

6.3.3.3 2D Facial Feature Tracking Methods

The 2D facial feature tracking methods developed in computer vision and pattern recognition areas play a key role from the perspective of process automation and detail enhancement. For instance, Cao et al. [6] proposed a fully automatic method tracking 3D facial shape based on a robust and efficient 2D facial feature tracking method. Garrido et al. [13] showed the high quality and detailed results of 3D facial shape using a 2D facial feature tracking method.

Active shape model (ASM) [10] and active appearance model (AAM) [9] are the most commonly used methods for facial feature tracking. ASM seeks to match a set of model points to an image, constrained by a statistical model of shape, while AAM seeks to match both the position of the model points and a representation of the texture of the object to an image. Hence, ASM is faster while AAM gives a better match to the texture. The constrained local model (CLM) [27] combines the power of the above two methods, the flexibility of AAM and the constraints of a full shape model (ASM). However, these methods have limitations to extract feature points from a facial image with large pose variations.

In order to increase the accuracy, Ramanan and Zhu [26] proposed the part-based facial feature detection method, but it is not efficient. Explicit shape regression (ESR) [8] and supervised descent method (SDM) [36] were introduced to increase both the accuracy and the efficiency. It is promising to adapt these methods to parametric facial modelling and animation as the acceleration techniques for solving the optimization problem by learning are effective.

6.4 Expression-Driven Facial Animation

In this section, we describe the recent approaches in our groups as an application of the parametric methods for facial modelling and animation.

6.4.1 Overview

We build an automatic image-based facial modelling system and a facial animation control method based on expression recognition technique. Figure 6.7 illustrates our modelling system and animation control system.

The image-based facial modelling methods usually demand the user's manual inputs and preprocessing stages while the animation controlling methods demand complex and expensive 3D motion capture devices for high-quality animation. For modelling automation, we adapt the robust facial feature tracker and the mesh correspondence solver. For the lightweight controlling system, we simply use a single off-the-shelf webcam as a control interface, which can easily combine with blendshape technique for 3D animation. We measure the user's emotional state by a robust facial feature tracker and facial expression classifier and then transfer the measured probabilities of facial expressions to the domain of blendshape basis. We demonstrate our method as one of the efficient interfaces for virtual human animation through our experiments.

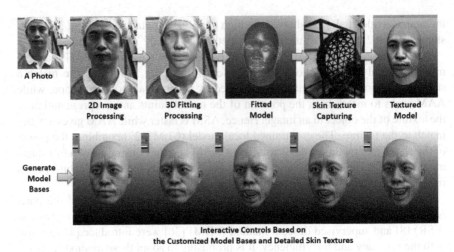

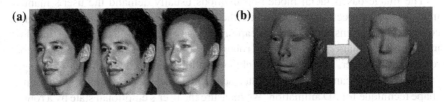

Fig. 6.7 Overview of the expression-driven facial animation system

6.4.2 Automatic Facial Modelling

An automatic facial modelling system needs to solve the following problems: detect faces in a cluttered scene of the given image, align an initial parametric facial mesh to a face in the image, and fit the facial parameters. Furthermore, for animation control, facial modelling should consider the blendshape generation. Hence, finding correspondences between two meshes for deformation transfer method is critical.

As the face in the image is taken from a lateral view, we developed a robust facial feature tracker and the perspective-n-points (PnP) solver for the initial alignment. The facial feature tracker for modelling is different from the facial feature tracker for the real-time animation control. Figure 6.8 demonstrates the robust facial feature tracker, the PnP solver and the mesh correspondence solver. Finally, we developed a modified version of the morphable model.

Fig. 6.8 Modules for automatic facial modelling: **a** example of the facial feature tracker (*center*) and the alignment solver (*right*). **b** Example of the mesh correspondence solver

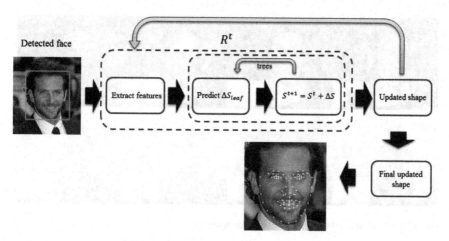

Fig. 6.9 Tree-based facial feature tracker

6.4.3 Facial Expression Recognition

An automatic facial expression recognition system needs to solve the following problems: detect faces in a cluttered scene of the given image in real-time, recognizing facial expressions.

Owing to the facial feature tracking methods described in Sect. 6.3.3.3, we developed a robust and fast algorithm to locate facial features based on the tree-regression concept, which is largely inspired from the explicit shape regression (ESR) method [8]. Figure 6.9 illustrates our tree-based facial feature tracker.

Based on the extracted facial features, we used a Gaussian mixture model (GMM) for facial expression recognition. Given training data and a GMM configuration, we estimate the parameters of the GMM using Maximum likelihood (ML) and solve the (nonlinear) optimization problem using a special case of the expectation-maximization (EM) algorithm.

6.4.4 Virtual Human Animation via Expression Transfer

Building appropriate key shape is an important part of shape decomposition. Each key shape adds flexibility and expressiveness to the model, suggesting that many key shapes should be used. However, the user must create a target model for each key shape. In order to reduce the user burden the number of key shapes should be kept small. An ideal method would balance these requirements to find the minimal set of key shapes that maintains the desired animation expressiveness. Here, we propose a simple but efficient way of building our expression basis. We select six representative

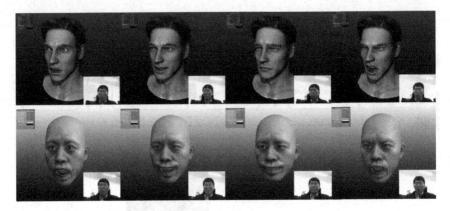

Fig. 6.10 Facial animation with expression recognition

expressions which our classifier can tell more separately and build the same number of expression bases with the shape of the corresponding expression of the subject.

Once each subject had trained his/her expressions, our classifier showed high performance of recognition overall, so we could get virtual humans natural expressive animation along with the performance of each subject.

Figure 6.10 shows two different characters that make the same expressions following the subjects' performance. This example also shows that our method can easily control any other different character without modifying interface. If there is a falling off in recognition quality due to some noise, abrupt expression changes may occur. As a consequence, we might have weird virtual human expressions. In such a case, we applied Kalman filter which enabled to get smooth transition. We could get realistic expressions of the virtual human even though we applied different virtual characters to the subject by simply transferring the basis weights. Through our test we could confirm that our proposed system can be an efficient and useful interface for controlling a virtual human.

6.5 Future Avenues

As the need for face modelling and animation continues to grow in a variety of applications, several issues for the future research may be placed either on full automatic modelling and animation, visual realism with a high level of user control, or computation acceleration. Some of these goals have been partially achieved, but many important issues still remain, especially in the field of real-time realistic facial modelling and animation.

Many conventional facial modelling techniques require the user to specify a set of landmarks on facial images. Hence, automating this process is essential for full automatic facial modelling. Various kinds of 2D face detection and facial feature tracking methods, including active shape model (ASM), active appearance model (AAM), constrained local model (CLM) and supervised descent method (SDM) have been proposed in the computer vision community. These techniques accurately localize and track the rigid and non-rigid motion of the user's face, and then enable to map the tracking parameters for suitable animation control. However, these approaches tend to fail when the face is under wide angular variation. Moreover, when obtaining overall 3D facial geometry using 3D scanners, the location of facial landmarks is often estimated incorrectly or imprecisely due to depth uncertainty. Therefore, developing reliable facial feature tracking and alignment methods in both 2D and 3D is still needed.

One of the difficulties in facial modelling remains creating or manipulating local details with a high level of usability in a short period of time. Typically, there is a tradeoff between the level of usability and the amount of manual input time. Therefore, one possible future direction in face modelling could be integrating different shaping techniques in a manner that maintains a high degree of user control while accelerating the user input time.

While early face animation methods, including shape interpolation and deformation-based methods, still lack physically based knowledge of facial anatomy, many advances have been made in terms of performance based on the use of training data of facial muscles and tongue. Especially for current approaches in parametric modelling, various facial attributes can be represented based on learned control parameters, but this is not sufficient to generate realistic virtual animation, such as eye gaze and lip motion. Therefore, the future research direction for realistic facial animation should consolidate the relation between face muscle behaviour and the corresponding facial motion.

6.6 Conclusion

Facial modelling and animation technologies have made impressive gains in a wide spectrum of applications. Although it is feasible to capture high-quality facial structure using 3D active sensors or high-resolution imaging devices, it is still difficult to obtain a high level of realism due to a lack of significant knowledge of facial anatomy and attributes. Based on the consideration of both high level of usability and visual realism, various kinds of parametric approaches have been proposed in recent years. In this chapter, current state-of-the-art methods for realistic facial modelling and animation, mainly focusing on parametric approaches that represent various facial attributes with a set of control parameters, have been described. We hope that this chapter will serve as a good reference and guidance for researchers, practitioners and students who are interested in facial modelling and animation.

References

1. Amberg B (2007) Optimal step nonrigid ICP algorithms for surface registration. In CVPR07
2. Barron JT, Malik J (2013) Shape, illumination, and reflectance from shading. Technical Report UCB/EECS-2013-117, EECS, UC Berkeley, May 2013
3. Basri R, Jacobs DW (2003) Lambertian reflectance and linear subspaces. IEEE Trans Pattern Anal Mach Intell 25(2):218–233
4. Blanz V, Vetter T (1999) A morphable model for the synthesis of 3D faces. In: Proceedings of the 26th annual conference on computer graphics and interactive techniques, SIGGRAPH '99. ACM Press/Addison-Wesley Publishing Company, New York, USA, pp 187–194
5. Blanz V, Vetter T (2003) Face recognition based on fitting a 3d morphable model. IEEE Trans Pattern Anal Mach Intell 25(9):1063–1074
6. Cao C, Weng Y, Lin S, Zhou K (2013) 3d shape regression for real-time facial animation. ACM Trans Graph 32(4):41:1–41:10
7. Cao C, Weng Y, Zhou S, Tong Y, Zhou Kun (2014) Facewarehouse: a 3D facial expression database for visual computing. IEEE Trans Visual Comput Graphics 20(3):413–425
8. Cao X, Wei Y, Wen F, Sun J (2012) Face alignment by explicit shape regression. In: CVPR 2012
9. Cootes TF, Edwards GJ, Taylor CJ (1998) Active appearance models. In: Burkhardt H, Neumann B (eds) Computer vision ECCV 98. Lecture notes in computer science, vol 1407. Springer, Berlin, pp 484–498
10. Cootes TF, Taylor CJ, Cooper DH, Graham J (1995) Active shape models-their training and application. Comput Vision Image Underst 61(1):38–59
11. Ekman P, Friesen W (1978) Facial action coding system: a technique for the measurement of facial movement. Consulting Psychologists Press, Palo Alto
12. Fyffe G, Jones A, Alexander O, Ichikari R, Graham P, Nagano K, Busch J, Debevec P (2013) Driving high-resolution facial blendshapes with video performance capture. In: ACM SIGGRAPH 2013 Talks, SIGGRAPH '13. ACM, New York, NY, New York, pp 33:1–33:1
13. Garrido P, Valgaert L, Wu C, Theobalt C (2013) Reconstructing detailed dynamic face geometry from monocular video. ACM Trans Graph 32(6):158:1–158:10
14. Ghosh A, Fyffe G, Tunwattanapong B, Busch J, Yu X, Debevec P (2011) Multiview face capture using polarized spherical gradient illumination. In: Proceedings of the 2011 SIGGRAPH Asia conference, SA '11. ACM, New York, NY, USA, pp 129:1–129:10
15. Izadi S, Kim D, Hilliges O, Molyneaux D, Newcombe R, Kohli P, Shotton J, Hodges S, Freeman D, Davison A, Fitzgibbon A (2011) Kinectfusion: Real-time 3D reconstruction and interaction using a moving depth camera. In: Proceedings of the 24th annual ACM symposium on user interface software and technology
16. Kemelmacher-Shlizerman L, Seitz SM (2011) Face reconstruction in the wild. In: IEEE computer society proceedings of the 2011 international conference on computer vision, ICCV '11, Washington, DC, USA, pp 1746–1753
17. Kim IJ, Ko H-S (2007) Intuitive quasi-eigen faces. In: ACM international conference on computer graphics and interactive techniques in Australasia and Southeast Asia, December 2007
18. Knothe R (2009) A Global-to-local model for the representation of human faces. PhD thesis, University of Basel, June 2009
19. Li H, Sumner RW, Pauly M (2008) Global correspondence optimization for non-rigid registration of depth scans. In: proceedings of the symposium on geometry processing SGP '08, Aire-la-Ville, Switzerland, Eurographics Association, pp 1421–1430
20. Li H, Weise T, Pauly M (2010) Example-based facial rigging. In: ACM SIGGRAPH 2010 Papers, SIGGRAPH '10. ACM, New York, NY, USA, pp 32:1–32:6
21. Li H, Yu J, Ye Y, Bregler C (2013) Realtime facial animation with on-the-fly correctives. ACM Trans Graph 32(4):42:1–42:10
22. Neumann T, Varanasi K, Wenger K, Wacker M, Magnor M, Theobalt C (2013) Sparse localized deformation components. ACM Trans Graph 32(6):179:1–179:10

23. Parke FI (1972) Computer generated animation of faces. In: Proceedings of the ACM annual conference, vol 1, ACM '72. ACM, New York, NY, USA, pp 451–457
24. Pighin F, Hecker J, Lischinski D, Szeliski R, Salesin DH (1998) Synthesizing realistic facial expressions from photographs. In: Proceedings of SIGGRAPH, pp 75–84
25. Praun E, Sweldens W, Schröder P (2001) Consistent mesh parameterizations. In: Proceedings of the 28th annual conference on computer graphics and interactive techniques, SIGGRAPH '01. ACM, New York, NY, USA, pp 179–184
26. Ramanan D, Zhu X (2012) Face detection, pose estimation, and landmark localization in the wild. In: 2013 IEEE conference on computer vision and pattern recognition, pp 0:2879–2886
27. Saragih JM, Lucey S, Cohn JF (2011) Deformable model fitting by regularized landmark mean-shift. Int J Comput Vision 91(2):200–215
28. Schüller C, Kavan L, Panozzo D, Sorkine-Hornung O (2013) Locally injective mappings. In: Computer Graphics forum proceedings of EUROGRAPHICS/ACM SIGGRAPH symposium on geometry processing 32(5):125–135
29. Sorkine O, Alexa M (2007) As-rigid-as-possible surface modeling. In: Proceedings of EURO-GRAPHICS/ACM SIGGRAPH symposium on geometry processing, pp 109–116
30. Sorkine O, Cohen-Or D, Lipman Y, Christian Rössl AM, Seidel HP (2004) Laplacian surface editing. In: Proceedings of the EUROGRAPHICS/ACM SIGGRAPH symposium on geometry processing. ACM Press, New York, pp 179–188
31. Sumner RW, Popović J (2009) Deformation transfer for triangle meshes. In: ACM SIGGRAPH 2004 papers, SIGGRAPH '04. ACM, New York, NY, USA, pp 399–405
32. Sumner RW, Schmid J, Pauly M (2007) Embedded deformation for shape manipulation. In: ACM SIGGRAPH 2007 Papers, SIGGRAPH '07. ACM, New York, NY, USA
33. Valgaerts L, Wu C, Bruhn A, Seidel H-P, Theobalt C (2012) Lightweight binocular facial performance capture under uncontrolled lighting. ACM Trans Graph 31(6):187:1–187:11
34. Vlasic D, Brand M, Pfister H, Popović J (2005) Face transfer with multilinear models. ACM Trans Graph 24(3):426–433
35. Weise T, Bouaziz S, Li H, Pauly M (2011) Realtime performance-based facial animation. In: ACM SIGGRAPH 2011 Papers, SIGGRAPH '11. ACM, New York, NY, USA, pp 77:1–77:10
36. Xiong X, De la Torre F (2013) Supervised descent method and its applications to face alignment. In: 2013 IEEE conference on computer vision and pattern recognition (CVPR), pp 532–539, June 2013

Chapter 7
Motion-Based Learning

Il Hong Suh and Sang Hyoung Lee

Abstract In this Chapter, we introduce several learning approaches to generate non-preprogrammed motions for a virtual human. Motion primitives and their causalities should first be learned from a task, which consists of a cascade of sub-tasks. Using programming by demonstration (PbD), it is now common for a virtual human to learn motion primitives and their causalities from a human demonstration. Typically, a virtual human can swiftly and effortlessly acquire a human demonstration from a PbD. To generate non-preprogrammed motions, a virtual human should possess the abilities to: (i) segment a whole movement into meaning segments; (ii) learn motion primitives for their adaptation in a changing environment; (iii) represent a combination of a motion primitive and its causalities (a motion tuple) by considering reusability; and finally, (iv) swiftly and reasonably select a dependable motion primitive in accordance with current and goal situations. In this chapter, we review the state of the art and several solution approaches including their limitations. We then discuss future avenues to target motion tuples in terms of the generation of non-preprogrammed motions for a virtual human.

7.1 Introduction

In the field of digital human study, it is a challenge for a virtual human to perform a task for which it has no experience using the information learned from previously performed tasks. Learning subtasks involved in an essential function is learning a task and developing a new, original task. Typically, a task consists of a cascade of subtasks [1]. To learn a subtask, it is important to identify a meaningful motion primitive and its causalities (i.e., pre-and post-conditions of a motion primitive) in the whole task. In this case, the set consisting of a motion primitive and its causalities

I.H. Suh (✉) · S.H. Lee
Hanyang University, Seoul, Korea
e-mail: ihsuh@hanyang.ac.kr

S.H. Lee
e-mail: zelog@hanyang.ac.kr

© Springer International Publishing Switzerland 2016
N. Magnenat-Thalmann et al. (eds.), *Context Aware Human-Robot and Human-Agent Interaction*, Human–Computer Interaction Series,
DOI 10.1007/978-3-319-19947-4_7

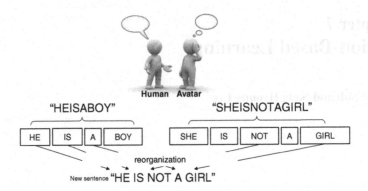

Fig. 7.1 Example of identifying meaningful words in a stream of linguistic sounds. In this example, a new, original sentence is created by recombining the words

is defined as a motion tuple. To reuse these learned motion tuples, they should be represented considering their reusability.

These can be determined in the process of learning a language [2]. In linguistics, an infant learns his/her language through the following three stages: first, the infant learns how to recognize and produce phonemes from a stream of sounds. Then, the infant learns morphemes of his/her language. It is important to recognize where a word begins and where it ends. These are called 'word boundaries'. Finally, the infant generates a sentence by combining meaningful words based on his/her experiences. To generate a sentence, it is important for an infant to possess how to locate, learn, and combine meaningful words from a stream of sounds. The infant can then create new, original sentences without directly learning the actual sentences, as depicted in Fig. 7.1.

A virtual human can learn motion tuples from a task similar to the process of learning a human language. A stream of movements (i.e., motion trajectories) is first divided by detecting the starting and ending points of the meaningful motion segments. Then, the motion segments of the virtual human are modeled as the motion primitives. To identify the motion primitives, their causalities are learned using the segments of task-relevant objects as a human learns the meaning of words for recombining the words. Finally, a task is achieved by sequentially selecting and/or reasonably recombining the motion primitives in accordance with its goal and its current situations. Therefore, it is possible for a virtual human to learn an extensive number of new, original tasks in the same manner as a human creates new, original sentences in linguistics.

To learn the motion tuples, programming by demonstration (PbD) is a useful technique. It is a well-known process where a naïve student effectively copies an expert [3]. Based on this technique, a virtual human can swiftly and effortlessly acquire motion tuples by user-friendly interaction, rather than by programming this knowledge. In computer science, the PbD technique appeared in the software development research as early as the mid-1980s to define operators without learning a programming language. It is now used in the industry as it can reduce the cost involved in the development and maintenance of programs. However, researchers now focus on reusing motion tuples [4–6]. In this chapter, we review the state of the technology and introduce several problems, solution approaches, and future avenues.

The remainder of this chapter is organized as follows: Sect. 7.2 presents several problems to be resolved in the PbD process. Section 7.3 reviews the state of the art and the limitations to learning and reusing the motion tuples. In Sect. 7.4, we introduce several solution approaches proposed to resolve the issues. Section 7.5 presents the future avenues to improve the generation of non-preprogrammed motion for a virtual human. Finally, in Sect. 7.6, we present our conclusions.

7.2 Problematic

As mentioned previously, the PbD technique continues to be used in direct repetition industries when conceiving an assembly line using exactly the same product components. A virtual human should also be able to learn a task by considering adaptability and reusability to generate non-preprogrammed motions using the PbD technique.

A virtual human should possess the ability to resolve the following problems. The movements of a virtual human and task-relevant objects should be first acquired from a human demonstration, as illustrated in Fig. 7.2a. Then, segmentation points should be autonomously estimated without the intervention of a human expert, as shown in Fig. 7.2b. All the movements are segmented using segmentation points, after which the segments of the virtual human's movements are represented as motion primitives, as indicated in Fig. 7.2c. The causalities should be learned from the segments of task-relevant objects, as shown in Fig. 7.2d. The causalities are used to activate their motion primitives. A motion tuple is represented by combining the motion primitives

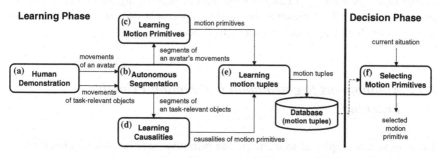

Fig. 7.2 Processes to learn and reuse motion primitives and their causalities. In the learning phase, there is *a* a process for acquiring movements of a virtual human and task-relevant objects, *b* a process for estimating segmentation points without the assistance of a human expert, *c* a process for learning motion primitives, *d* a process for learning causalities of motion primitives, and *e* a process for learning motion tuples. In the decision phase, there is *f* a process for achieving a task for selecting reasonable motion primitives based on the motion tuples

and their causalities, as illustrated in Fig. 7.2e. Finally, a task (i.e., the cascade of motion primitives) is achieved by selecting reasonable motion primitives based on the motion tuples, as shown in Fig. 7.2f.

During resolution of these problems, considerations are acquired as follows. In autonomous segmentation, it must be possible to find meaningful segments from various types of movements. The segmentation process should also be applied without requiring parameters to be manually predefined or pretuned according to the types of variables and tasks. The fineness and grossness of movements should be considered during the process of learning the motion tuples. The gross and fine movements are defined as follows; (i) gross movement: this movement involves simple patterns, though it may be varied over a large space during a short time interval. It allows flexible reproductions while repeating several trials and (ii) fine movement: this movement involves complex patterns (i.e., combinations of simple patterns), though it may be varied over smaller spaces during longer time intervals than gross movements. It also allows precise reproduction while repeating multiple trials. A virtual human should learn the motion primitives and their causalities to consider the grossness and fineness of movements because a task can succeed or fail based on these movement characteristics. Finally, the motion tuples should swiftly and reasonably select to perform a task under changing environments including perturbations.

7.3 State of the Art

To address the issues introduced in Sect. 7.2, in this section we review the state of the technology in two areas: (i) research on segment and model motion tuples (i.e., motion primitives and their causalities) from a human demonstration from the viewpoint of autonomous segmentation; (ii), approaches to select dependable motion primitives that allow a virtual human to achieve the goal of a task using these motion tuples. Section 7.3.1 describes the field of segmenting and learning motion primitives. Section 7.3.2 presents the existing approaches for selection of motion primitives, including approaches using affordances.

7.3.1 Autonomous Segmentation and Motion Primitive Learning

The approaches employed to learn motion primitives can be broadly classified as supervised (i.e., using known motion primitives) and unsupervised approaches. A qualitative comparison of these two methods is presented in Table 7.1.

Table 7.1 Qualitative comparison of related works from viewpoint segmenting and learning motion primitives

Category	Authors	Approach	Parameters that must be predefined or pretuned
Supervised methods	Billing et al.	Method for learning predictive sequence based on motion primitives	Presegmented or Predefined Primitives
	Cohen et al.	Method for heuristic search-based manipulation planner based on motion primitives	
	Bentivegna et al.	Method for increasing performance of motion primitives through repeated practice	
	Nicolescu et al.	Method for refining, learning, and generalizing primitives based on action networks and instructive demonstration	
	Nejati et al.	Method for learning and generalizing motion primitives based on hierarchical task networks	
Unsupervised methods	Drumwright et al.	Method using the velocities of the joint trajectories	Intervals, thresholds
	Kulic et al.	Method comparing density distributions with known or unknown models	Models, windows, thresholds
	Gribovskaya et al.	Method using the sum of the velocities with reference to the relative position in Cartesian coordinate	Smoothing factors, thresholds
	Mühlig et al.	Method using the relative distances and velocity between human's hand and objects	Thresholds, smoothing factors
	Asfour et al.	Method using the HMM based on the changing direction of trajectories and stopping the trajectories	Windows, thresholds
	Baby et al.	Method using the intersection of the transitions in the unified HMM which is merged by KL divergence	Threshold of K
	Kruger et al.	Method using indicator variable in Dirichlet process	Dirichlet prior

Several researchers have proposed the application of known motion primitives to achieve day-to-day tasks. Billing et al., Cohen et al., Bentivegna et al., Nicolescu et al., and Nejati et al. have proposed methods for learning and combining preseg-mented or predefined motion primitives. Billing et al. presented a predictive sequence learning method for recognizing and controlling the training data using known motion segments [7]. Cohen et al. proposed a heuristic search-based manipulation planner based on a set of predefined motion segments [8]. Bentivegna et al. presented a method for increasing the performance through repeated practices based on a set of predefined motion segments [9]. Nicolescu et al. proposed a method for refin-ing, learning, and generalizing motion segments using a predefined action network and an instructive demonstration [10]. Nejati et al. proposed a method for learning and generalizing known motion segments based on hierarchical task networks [11]. Each of these methods deals with predefined motion segments; they do not consider unknown motion segments.

For unsupervised approaches, Drumwright et al., Kulic et al., Gribovskaya et al., Mühlig et al., Asfour et al., Baby et al., and Kruger et al. have all proposed methods for obtaining unknown motion segments. Their methods focus on segmenting contin-uous motion trajectories to learn the motion primitives embedded in a task. Although most of these approaches are based on the learning of unknown motion primitives, they contain constraints that are predefined or tuned to obtain motion segments. These include manually predefined or pretuned parameters such as fixed intervals, window size, fixed time, smoothing factors, threshold values, and predefined mod-els according to the types of tasks or motion trajectories investigated (e.g., joints or human body parts). It is difficult to pretune and predefine these parameters according to the types of variables and tasks applied. Drumwright et al. proposed a method for segmenting joint motion trajectories [12]. The segmentation points are determined based on the points where the velocities of the joint trajectories maintain a fixed interval and the sum of the velocities is smaller than the threshold within this inter-val. The segmentation points are directly changed according to the threshold of the joint velocities and the interval. Kulic et al. proposed a method for obtaining motion segments using known or unknown models by comparing the probabilistic densities according to a fixed moving window [13]. The size of a moving window must be well defined to obtain reasonable motion segments. Gribovskaya et al. proposed a method for obtaining motion segments using the sum of velocities across a threshold with reference to the relative position in Cartesian coordinates [14]. In this method, the segmentation points are adjustable by tuning the parameters for the threshold. Mühlig et al. proposed a method for segmenting continuous motion trajectories using correlative features between a human hand and different objects [15]. The correlative features are acquired based on the relative distances between the hand and objects. The near and far degrees should be predefined or pretuned for estimating the motion segments. Asfour et al. proposed a method for obtaining motion segments by extract-ing the common states from several hidden Markov models (HMMs) [16]. In this method, an HMM is modeled using specific motion trajectory points. These points are selected based on two criteria: the change in direction of the motion trajectories and the termination of the motion trajectories within a sufficient period of time. These criteria (particularly, the sufficient time period) must be well defined to determine the motion segments. Baby et al. presented a method that uses the intersections of the transitions obtained from a unified HMM merged after the set of all training data are individually modeled using a left–right HMM [17]. All HMMs are merged into a unified HMM using Kullback-Leibler (KL) divergence. For the unified HMM, the authors refer to the set of states in the transitions to be split as motion segments. This method can be varied based on the threshold of the KL-divergence for constructing the unified HMM. That is, the segmentation points depend on adjusting the threshold value of the KL-divergence. Finally, Kruger et al. presented a method for determining segmentation points using a nonparametric approach [18]. The segmentation points are determined based on indicator variables included in the DP (Dirichlet process). The DP does not need to use priors (or weak priors) for estimating the segmentation points.

Although these approaches are based on the learning of unknown motion primitives, they include constraints that must be predefined or tuned. These include parameters such as the fixed intervals, window size, fixed time, smoothing factors, threshold values, and predefined models according to the type of tasks or motion trajectories (e.g., joint, human body parts). It is difficult to tune and predefine these parameters based on the type of variables and tasks. For example, velocity-based segmentation criteria require the tuning of several types of parameters (such as preprocessing smoothing factors and the velocity threshold). These may not be intuitive as the parameters may require tuning with respect to the type of variable being used. Moreover, humans may sometimes require intermediate pauses between two consecutive parts of a continuous motion trajectory that requires segmentation to exaggerate the segmentation process.

7.3.2 Selection of Motion Primitives

The motion-primitive selection mechanism of a robot has been studied using various approaches. Smith et al. [19] and Kunniawati et al. [20] proposed methods for decision making in approximate partially observable Markov decision processes (POMDPs). POMDPs constitute a powerful probabilistic method for modeling dynamic and stochastic sequences of events in the limited perceptions of a virtual human. However, the computation of exact optimal policies in the animation is intractable as this process has extensive computational complexity. To improve the computational efficiency, Smith et al. proposed a POMDP-based planning algorithm referred to as heuristic search value iteration (HSVI). Similarly, Kuniawati et al. proposed an algorithm referred to as successive approximations of the reachable space under optimal policies (SARSOP) that can select dependable motion primitives under various uncertainties. However, these algorithms cannot be used to generate various motion-primitive sequences that have never been previously experienced, or are 'unexperienced' because the dependable motion primitive is selected using a probabilistic method.

Lebeltel et al. [21] and Dearden et al. [22] presented methods for modeling a task using probabilistic approaches. Lebeltel et al. proposed a method for programming a robot based on Bayesian inference and learning with respect to incompleteness and uncertainty. They used predefined transition probabilities to manage temporal motion-primitive sequences. It is a challenge to predefine transition probabilities to solve all motion-primitive sequences. Dearden et al. proposed a method for using a Bayesian network as a learning technique to manage task execution in mobile robotics. Their research indicated that Bayesian networks are valuable learning mechanisms capable of dealing with uncertainty and variation.

Calinon et al. [4] and Lee et al. [23] presented methods for realizing a task by encoding probabilistic models. Calinon et al. encoded and generalized probabilistic models using Gaussian/Bernoulli mixture models and Gaussian mixture regression. Lee et al. encoded the probabilistic models using HMMs and reproduced a trajectory using a Viterbi algorithm. They focused on encoding probabilistic models of entire tasks and reproducing trajectories using demonstrated trajectories, i.e., they considered the reproduction of trajectories using encoded models and not the various motion-primitive sequences that can occur in a real environment. These probabilistic methods can be usefully applied under various uncertainties, especially limited perception, because they compute probabilities of motion primitives using a Bayesian inference algorithm. Although they can successfully achieve complete tasks based on experienced motion-primitive sequences, they have difficulty of achieving tasks in situations that require unexperienced motion-primitive sequences.

Pardowitz et al. [24] and Ekvall and Kragic [25] proposed hierarchical and incremental approaches for modeling a task based on many demonstrations. Pardowitz et al. hierarchically encoded motion primitives based on macro-operators and a task precedence graph. Ekvall and Kragic extracted and updated symbolic rules using demonstrations and achieved given tasks based on symbol-level methods. Although they dealt with motion primitive sequences of complex tasks, they were required to generate nodes of graphs or symbolic rules continually, whenever unexperienced motion-primitive sequences were necessary.

Brooks [26], Hoshino et al. [27], Jaafar et al. [28], Scheutz et al. [29], and Lee et al. [30] proposed behavior-based control methods to select a motion primitive to achieve a given task. Brooks proposed a robust layered control system where higher layers subsume the lower layers to control mobile robots. Hosino et al. explored a tree architecture to select or activate multiple behavior modules. Jaafar et al. proposed a motion-primitive selection mechanism using fuzzy logic, removing the need for a complex mathematical model. Scheutz et al. proposed an architecture for dynamic motion-primitive selection that can integrate existing motion-primitive selection mechanisms in a unified manner. Lee et al. proposed an ethology-based motion-primitive selection mechanism and a programming framework. These behavior-based control methods can generate various motion-primitive sequences based on rules/heuristics that are generated by prior knowledge or experiences without generating new rules/heuristics. However, it is difficult to achieve the given tasks under various uncertainties, especially limited perception. To resolve this, additional rules are generated by humans.

Table 7.2 Qualitative comparison for related works from viewpoint selecting motion primitives

Authors	Approach	Relationship between perceptions and motion primitives	Motion-primitive sequences	Possibility of selecting dependable motion primitive under limited perception	Possibility of generating unexperienced motion-primitive sequences
Smith et al. and Kunniawati et al.	Approximate POMDPs	Belief states and observation models	Probabilistic transition models	O	X
Lebeltel et al. and Dearden et al.	Bayesian network	Bayesian network	Probabilistic transition models	O	X
Calinon et al. and Lee et al.	Robot programming-by demonstration	GMM/BMM or HMM	Probabilistic transition models	O	X
Pardowitz et al. and Ekvall and Kragic	Robot programming-by demonstration	Rule and/or graphs	Rules and/or graphs	X	X
Brooks, Hoshino et al., Jaafar et al., Scheutz et al., and Lee et al.	Behavior-based control	Rules and/or heuristics	Rules and/or heuristics	X	O
Stoffregen, Chemero, Steedman, and Sahin et al.	Affordance	Rules	-(no consideration)	X	X

Stoffregen [31], Chemero [32], Steedman [3], and Sahin et al. [34] formalized an affordance using their own definitions. Sahin et al. defined an affordance with respect to equivalence classes that guarantee their own reusability. Their affordance acquired a relationship between the motion primitive and an object in the environment such that the application of the motion primitive on the object generated a certain effect [34]. However, they did not consider uncertainties regarding the objects, behaviors, and environments. Furthermore, they did not address the motion-primitive sequences for accomplishing a task. A qualitative comparison of the related works is presented in Table 7.2.

To resolve the limitations of the state-of-the art methods discussed, the autonomous segmentation framework for identifying the motion segments without tuning or predefining parameters is described in the following section. Further, a well-known method of modeling a motion primitive is introduced to represent the motion primitives using the segments. Finally, a dependable motion-primitive selection mechanism combining the advantages of the probabilistic method and the behavior-based control method is also described. The motion-primitive selection mechanism can select dependable motion primitives under various uncertainties, especially limited perception, using Bayesian inference, and can generate experienced as well as unexperienced the motion-primitive sequences based on motivation values.

7.4 Recent Approaches

7.4.1 Autonomous Segmentation for Learning Motion Primitives

To resolve the limitation of autonomous segmentation mentioned in Sect. 7.3, Lee et al. proposed an autonomous segmentation framework without using predefined or pretuned parameters [35]. The framework can estimate a set of segmentation points for learning motion primitives as presented in Fig. 7.3. In this process, the segmentation points are used to divide the continuous motion trajectories obtained from a whole demonstration by a human. In this context, the portions between two consecutive Gaussian components that are temporally adjacent in a Gaussian mixture model (GMM) are used to estimate the set of segmentation points. As noted by Ghahramani et al., a Gaussian component of the GMM competitively partitions the input space and learns a linear regression surface in each portion [36]. In the GMM therefore, each Gaussian distribution encodes a portion that indicates a quasi-linear segment in hyperspace. Representing continuous motion trajectories as a GMM provides a method for encoding the local directions and the local relations (i.e., covariances) among the variables involved in the trajectories. In the motion trajectories, a change of direction between two consecutive Gaussian components can be used to estimate a segmentation point for dividing two motion primitives representing the different subparts of the trajectories.

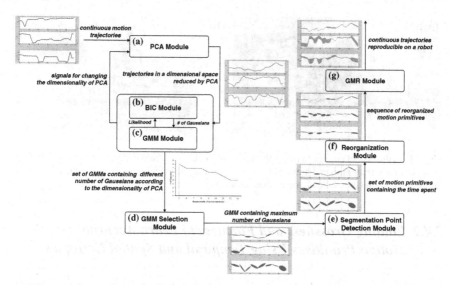

Fig. 7.3 Autonomous segmentation framework to estimate the segmentation points for obtaining motion segments from a complete demonstration *a* Principal component analysis (PCA) module, *b* Bayesian information criterion (BIC) module, *c* Gaussian mixture model (GMM) module, *d* GMM selection module, and *e* Segmentation point detection module

Although the GMM is modeled using the Bayesian information criterion (BIC) and expectation-maximization (EM) algorithms, it is important to obtain as many Gaussian components as possible to better characterize the nonlinear motion trajectories, which indicate quasi-linear segments. The number of Gaussian components that are well fitted by BIC depends on the dimensionality of the motion trajectories. In this context, therefore, the motion trajectories are projected into one of the PCA (principal component analysis)-reduced subspaces. This autonomous segmentation framework provides a clear physical interpretation for repartitioning the Gaussian components in the GMM. To date, information regarding the mean and covariance has been exploited to reconstruct motion trajectories [37, 38]. However, surprisingly little attention has been directed to the intersection between two consecutive Gaussian components in the GMM. The authors segment the continuous motion trajectories using these intersections in the learning process. This technique detects changes in the local trajectory shapes and in the local correlations among different variables. Figure 7.4 illustrates the result obtained using the autonomous segmentation framework in the task of cooking a rice dish. In this example, 26 motion segments were acquired by the segmentation method. These segments were then authenticated by evaluating the naturalness of a virtual human's motions in their different combinations.

Fig. 7.4 In the task of creating a rice dish, the illustrations of **a** a human demonstration, **b** a motion segment of a virtual human estimated by the autonomous segmentation method, and **c** a motion segment recombined to validate the motion segments

7.4.2 Finding Grossness and Fineness to Learn Accurate Motion Primitives Using Temporal and Spatial Entropies

Lee et al. presented a method to acquire accurate motion primitives using the spatial and temporal entropies calculated from a GMM [39]. A virtual human should be able to learn motion primitives using multiple demonstrations of a single task. In such a set, portions of the trajectories can be divided into four categories according to the spatial variations between the demonstrations and their duration. These portions are relatively long/short duration and relatively large/small spatial variation. Figure 7.5 illustrates these four categories with examples. Of these, those where a long time is required and the spatial variations are small (e.g., passing a thread through the eye of a needle) are typically modeled using a smaller number of parameters despite the fact that such portions represent a movement that is essential for achieving the task. The reason for this is that this portion changes only slightly in the task space

Fig. 7.5 Four categories according to spatial variations in multiple demonstrations and the time required in the demonstrations: **a** time spent—short, spatial variation—large; **b** time spent—long, spatial variation—large, **c** time spent—short, spatial variation—small; and **d** time spent—long, spatial variation—small. We focus on (**d**)

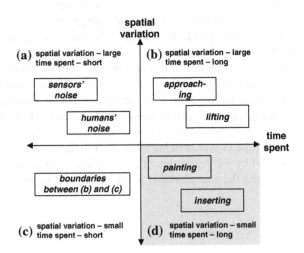

compared to the other portions. However, such portions should be densely modeled using more parameters (i.e., overfitting) to improve the performance of the GMM because the movements of these portions must be accurately executed to achieve the task. It is difficult for a virtual human to learn a daily task because mixtures of these properties are generally included in the task. Most PbD approaches focus not on the combinations of fine and gross movements but on totally fine (or totally gross) movements. Gross and fine movements are defined as follows; (i) gross movement: this movement involves simple patterns, though the movement may be varied over a large space during a short time interval. It allows flexible reproductions with several repeated trials and (ii) fine movement: this movement involves complex patterns (i.e., combinations of simple patterns), though the movement may be varied over smaller spaces during longer time intervals than gross movements. It also allows precise reproductions with several repeated trials.

To learn such tasks effectively, a virtual human should therefore be able to represent all its movements in accordance with grossness and fineness because a daily-life task usually includes gross and fine movements. However, it is challenging to represent gross and fine movements using a fixed criterion. It is possible to consider grossness and fineness by individually modeling segmented movements using segmentation approaches. Nevertheless, such segmentation approaches do not guarantee modeling gross and fine movements because grossness and fineness are not explicitly considered in these segmentation approaches. To resolve this problem, the authors proposed a new method for learning a motion primitive based on grossness and fineness acquired from the complexity and the repeatability of movements. To use spatial and temporal relationships between a virtual human and a task-relevant object, the grossness and fineness of movements are measured using following dataset; (i) change rate of relative distance between a virtual human and a task-relevant object and (ii) change rate of relative velocity between a virtual human and a task-relevant object. These are important data to analyze the spatial and temporal relationships between a virtual human and a task-relevant object.

The grossness and fineness depend on the degrees of complexity and repeatability of the movements, simultaneously. The rationale is as follows; if a movement is complex, it should be regarded as a fine movement even though variation is large between multiple trials (i.e., the movement is allowed to be flexibly reproduced during multiple trials). Conversely, a movement should be considered as a gross movement if it is simple (e.g., drawing a straight line) even if its variation is small between multiple trials. The complexity can be measured from correlations of Canonical Correlation Analysis (CCA) by determining linear combinations between basis vectors that maximize their correlations with datasets. In CCA, correlation tends to be low when there are complex patterns in the movements or otherwise [40]. Repeatability is also measured by variations (i.e., z-scores of the sum of eigenvalues) obtained from covariances between datasets acquired by multiple trials. The grossness and fineness are acquired by combining the correlations and variations.

Grossness and fineness should be applied to a motor skill. The k-means algorithm has been used to acquire initial parameters of a GMM [41]. The conventional k-means algorithm focuses on gross movements by a cost function (e.g., Euclidean distance).

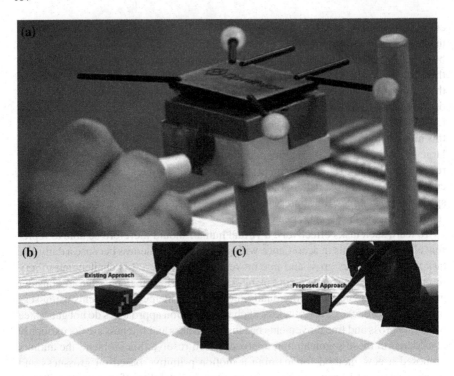

Fig. 7.6 In the task of painting a small assembly part, the illustrations of **a** a human demonstration, **b** a motion trajectory reproduced by a virtual human using standard GMM and GMR, and **c** a motion trajectory reproduced by a virtual human using GMM and GMR based on grossness and fineness. Although standard GMM cannot generate the painting trajectory, the GMM based on grossness and fineness can successfully replicate the task

To consider the characteristics of dataset, some researchers have proposed other cost functions for the k-means algorithm [42, 43]. However, grossness and fineness have not been considered, although this information is essential to achieve a daily-life task. Before learning a motor skill, the k-mean algorithm is first weighted by the grossness and fineness. Based on EM, a motor skill is then modeled as a GMM using the initial parameters acquired from the weighted k-means algorithm. Figure 7.6 presents the result obtained from two types of motion primitives. In this example, the motion primitive using standard GMM cannot reproduce the motion trajectories of painting a tiny assembly, as indicated in Fig. 7.6a. Conversely, the GMM based on grossness and fineness completes the painting task, as shown in Fig. 7.6b.

The proposed method was used for modeling GMMs. This learning method can also be used for applying well-known skill learning methods such as hidden Markov model (HMMs) and dynamic movement primitives (DMPs). In the learning process of HMMs, the grossness and fineness can be used to initialize the parameters for the Baum-Welch algorithm. For DMPs, the grossness and fineness can be used for adjusting the arrangements of the Gaussian basis functions because the forcing terms of the DMPs are fitted by the basis functions.

7.4.3 Learning Dynamic Motion Primitives

To achieve a task, the motion primitives should guarantee a certain performance including in a dynamic environment. However, it is not a trivial matter to guarantee the performance of motion primitives because of the various types of perturbation that exist in the real world, such as different initial and goal situations, human interference, and the uncertainties of sensors and motion primitives. To resolve this problem, a virtual human should pre-learn all possible motion primitives with respect to all situations that could change. However, it is impossible to pre-learn all motion primitives because there are an uncountable number of changing situations in the real world.

DMPs (dynamic movement primitives) are used to resolve this issue. The DMP method is a well-known formulation for representing motion primitives with non-linear differential equations whose time evolution creates smooth motion trajectories [6]. It was proposed by Ijspeert et al. and has been actively implemented by many researchers [44, 45]. DMPs are formulated in such a manner that convergence to a goal position is guaranteed. They are invariant with respect to scaling time and translating position. The DMP method was motivated from a simple mass-spring-damper system as

$$m\ddot{x} = -K(x - g) - D\dot{x} + F_{Ex}, \qquad (7.1)$$

where g, x, m, K, D, and F_{Ex} denote the goal position, current position, mass constant, spring constant, damping constant, and an external force term, respectively. Figure 7.7a illustrates a mass-spring-damper system regulated by an external force. The objective of the DMP method is to retrieve complex motion trajectories by learning the external force F_{Ex}, as illustrated in Fig. 7.7b.

DMPs are learned using a set of segmented motion trajectories. DMPs guarantee convergence to their goals because the external force term, F_{Ex}, depends on the phase

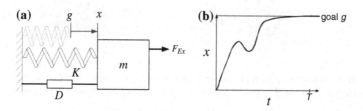

Fig. 7.7 Concept of DMPs: **a** Mass-spring-damper system regulated by an external force and, **b** nonlinear motion trajectory generated by the external force for achieving the goal position

variable $s(t)$ monotonically decreasing to zero. DMPs also generate goal-driven trajectories under dynamic environments. Without relearning the parameters, DMPs possess the following advantages: the motion trajectories achieve their goals despite changes in goal positions, initial positions, or both, and the motion trajectories can be temporally scaled by adjusting a variable. Consequently, the motion trajectories generated by DMPs are robust against various perturbations.

In spite of these advantages, DMPs have two weaknesses. The external force of a DMP is regulated by the number of Gaussian basis functions. Although the number of Gaussian basis functions can be increased, it is difficult to learn an external force when the motion trajectories that should be learned are excessively long. DMPs can retrieve motion trajectories according to the number of Gaussian basis functions. Although the number of Gaussian basis functions is increased sharply, a whole motion trajectory needed to achieve the entire task cannot be retrieved when learning the motion trajectories as a DMP. DMPs, therefore, should be learned using the segmented motion trajectories. Furthermore, although DMPs guarantee the achievement of their goals under dynamic environments, they do not consider intermediate trajectories. Depending on the type of task, the intermediate trajectories may be important. Indeed, all portions of trajectories should be guaranteed to enable the meaning of gestures to be recognized. Nevertheless, DMPs are useful in various tasks that require the motion primitives such as grasping, releasing, approaching, and delivering. Figure 7.8 displays the result of a DMP in the task of grasping a cup. The virtual human can complete the task in a changing environment using the DMP method.

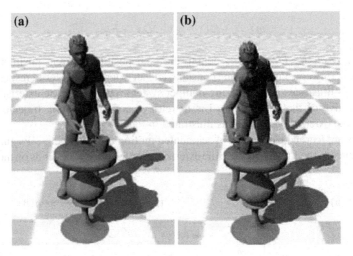

Fig. 7.8 In the task of grasping a cup, illustrations are captured in **a** the initial configuration and **b** the changed configuration. The virtual human can grasp the cup in the changing environment

7.4.4 Motivation-Based Dependable Motion-Primitive Selection Using Probabilistic Affordances

To select a motion primitive swiftly and reasonably, Lee et al. proposed a motivation-based dependable motion-primitive selection mechanism for generating their sequences [46]. This allows the achievement of given tasks by selecting dependable motion primitives under various uncertainties. The multiple training data are clustered based on a criterion known as effect equivalence. The affordances express the relationship between preconditions, motion primitives, and post-conditions. Furthermore, the affordances are arranged based on a sequential structure acquired from innate (i.e., nominal) sequences of the task.

As discussed previously, achieving a task requires several motion primitives to be performed in sequence [47]. As uncertainties and perturbations exist in the real world, a virtual human should perform motion primitives in various sequences to resolve current situations and accomplish a task. To resolve this problem, the virtual human should be able to learn and/or generate these motion-primitive sequences. However, it is difficult to learn and/or generate all these sequences in advance because there are an uncountable number of motion-primitive sequences in the real world. A virtual human must therefore be able to select a dependable motion primitive from a set to address the given task in the current situation.

To date, there has been a significant amount of research on the generation of various motion-primitive sequences using predefined reactive plans for achieving a given task [48–50]. Motivation has been used to recommend a motion primitive to the virtual human based on its current internal state [51, 52]. Figure 7.9 illustrates the causation between stimuli, internal states, motion primitives, and the transitions of internal states based on motivation. Internal states cannot be directly observed; however, they can be inferred by a selected motion primitive. Based on motivation, existing approaches have implicitly generated fully connected transitions of internal states by perceiving a current stimulus. Thus, these approaches can generate various motion-primitive sequences based on the transitions of internal states based

Fig. 7.9 Causation between stimuli, internal states and behaviors (i.e., motion primitives), and transitions between internal states to select a motion primitive based on motivation

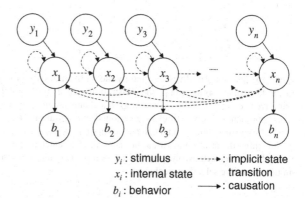

y_i : stimulus　　- - - ▸ : implicit state
x_i : internal state　　　　transition
b_i : behavior　　　—▸ : causation

on given situations. However, in these motivation-based motion-primitive selection approaches, it is difficult to select the goal-oriented motion primitive using the implicit transitions of internal states, as shown in Fig. 7.9. To select a dependable action, the motivation should be generated with respect to the goal orientedness of a given task. Furthermore, it is a challenge to select a dependable motion primitive using motivation in the real world because the environment includes various sensor, action noise, and limited perception. Motivation should therefore be designed such that it can be executed effectively despite various uncertainties in the sensors and/or motion primitives and human intentions.

To achieve this, the authors selected probabilistic affordance for considering various uncertainties and perturbations. Probabilistic affordances are designed as Bayesian networks to represent the relationships between preconditions, motion primitives, and post-conditions. Before modeling the probabilistic affordances, the segmented information about task-relevant entities is clustered based on the effects of the motion primitives. Then, the virtual human selects a dependable motion primitive based on the motivation values calculated from the probabilistic affordances after being arranged based on the sequential structure of given tasks. Figure 7.10 displays the result achieved by the motivation-based motion-primitive selection mechanism in the task of grasping a cup. The virtual human can achieve the task in a changing environment by swiftly and reasonably selecting the motion primitives according to the given situations.

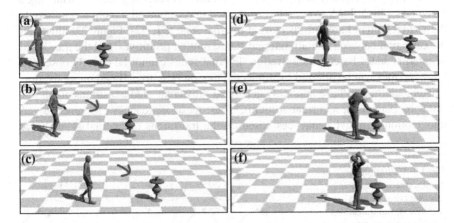

Fig. 7.10 Motion primitives selected by the motivation-based motion-primitive selection method in the task of grasping a cup; the illustrations are **a** initial configuration, **b** a selected motion primitive (i.e., approaching by walking) in a changed configuration, **c** a selected motion primitive (i.e., approaching by walking) in a changed configuration, **d** a selected motion primitive (i.e., approaching by walking) in a changed configuration, **e** a selected motion primitive (i.e., grasping by stretching the arm of the virtual human), and **f** a selected motion primitive (i.e., drinking). The virtual human can achieve the goal of the task in a changing environment using the motivation-based motion-primitive selection mechanism

7.5 Future Avenues

In the field of PbD, it is common for a virtual human to learn a daily task from a human. Despite using a human demonstration, however, it is still a challenge for a virtual human to learn a task without assistance from a human expert. To achieve autonomous learning, a virtual human should be able to determine both where and toward what attention should be directed in a human demonstration.

Let us consider why these two problems must be resolved for autonomous learning. Assume that a virtual human's task is to insert a (grasped) peg in a hole. This complete task can be divided into subtasks of various types. For example, the task can be divided into [Approaching]-[Inserting]-[Withdrawing] or [Approaching]-[Aligning]-[Inserting]-[Withdrawing]. In accordance with determining where the virtual human has to give attention in the demonstration, it focuses on different points in the demonstration based on the segmentation. This problem indicates the temporal segmentation of a demonstration.

To understand the problem of what a virtual human must focus in the demonstration, assume that the task is divided as follows; (1) approaching, (2) inserting, and (3) withdrawing. In these subtasks, the human demonstrator attempts to carefully consider both the peg and the hole to achieve the subtasks associated with (1) and (2). However, the demonstrator may not consider anything while executing the subtask associated with (3). Although this is a simple task, a human constantly chooses what he or she will focus on. The virtual human must choose what to give attention to in the subtasks; otherwise, the performance and reusability can be decreased by focusing on unnecessary information. This is because the virtual human attempts to satisfactorily handle this unnecessary information while executing the subtasks.

The two problems are closely related. Therefore, the problems should be resolved in a framework, simultaneously. Most researchers in this field have assumed that the two problems must be resolved by the prior knowledge of a human expert. Billing et al., Cohen et al., and Nejati et al. proposed approaches to learn tasks using the prior knowledge of a human [7, 8, 11]. On the other hand, Lee et al., Mühlig et al., and Kruger et al. presented several approaches to estimate segmentation points to resolve the problem of where the virtual human should direct its attention in a demonstration (i.e., autonomous segmentation) [15, 18, 35]. However, they did not address the problem of what a virtual human should focus on in the demonstration. Conversely, Montesano et al. and Abdo et al. proposed approaches to resolve the problem of what a virtual human should focus on in a demonstration without the consideration of where it should direct its attention in the demonstration [53, 54]. In this section, we propose a framework to resolve the two problems simultaneously.

To resolve these two problems, a framework must possess three abilities: (i) determine where to direct attention in a demonstration. To acquire motion primitives and their causalities (i.e., the pre- and post-conditions of motion primitives), it should be possible to divide the entire task using autonomous segmentation; (ii) determine on what attention should be directed in a demonstration. To achieve specific motion primitives, the causalties on which the virtual human should focus should be chosen without prior knowledge of the task; and (iii) represent motion tuples. It should be possible to represent the motion primitives and their causalities as motion tuples that can be executed by the virtual human. To achieve this, PbD researchers must propose a framework that possesses these three abilities.

7.6 Conclusion

To generate non-preprogrammed motions, abilities that a virtual human should possess were addressed:

- An autonomous segmentation method for learning motion primitives: In [35], the continuous motion trajectories were first segmented based on GMMs. Two alternative approaches were used: (1) using a geometrical interpretation of the Gaussian components contained in the GMMs and (2) using the weights estimated along the time component of the GMMs. The autonomous segmentation method was verified using experiments and public databases. In the verification, the performance was guaranteed with a correspondence of about 90 % compared to the results segmented by a human. Moreover, the motion primitives were modeled by re-estimating the portions that should be remodeled using temporal and spatial entropies obtained in the GMMs. Consequently, the motion primitives were accurately modeled by adopting an explicitly different model-fitting strategy. The segmented motion trajectories were formalized as DMPs. That is, each of the segmented motion trajectories was represented as a set of differential equations. The DMPs guaranteed the goal achievement in various dynamic environments such as changes in the initial and/or goal conditions. In particular, DMPs were executed for approaching, grasping, releasing, and avoiding the entities.
- Formalizing probabilistic affordance using a Bayesian network to learn the causalities of the motion primitives: In [46], probabilistic affordances were formalized to allow the selection of a dependable motion primitive under various uncertainties. In this context, the probabilistic affordances were represented as Bayesian networks after clustering the training data based on the effect equivalence.
- A dependable motion-primitive selection mechanism using probabilistic affordances: In [46], the probabilistic affordances were arranged based on a sequential task structure. The virtual human selected a dependable motion primitive based on the arranged affordances and the motivation value propagation algorithm. The virtual human was able to select a dependable motion primitive to achieve tasks under situations with different initial and goal positions and various perturbations without designing all motion-primitive sequences. Further, the virtual human was able to estimate the probabilities of motion primitives using the Bayesian inference algorithm, including with limited perception. Consequently, motion primitives were activated to select a dependable motion primitive in a dynamic environment.

Using the methods described in this chapter, PbD researchers can obtain a unified framework for a virtual human to learn and select suitable motion primitives to achieve the given tasks reliably under a dynamic environment. Thus, they can obtain a task-learning framework for increasing human trust. Considering the future avenues introduced in Sect. 7.4.4, PbD researchers can extract formal rules from the affordances to create motion-primitive sequences for achieving new, original tasks, as humans create a number of new, original sentences using words and grammar rules. Hence, we can obtain a method to generate non-preprogrammed motions by the motion grammar.

References

1. Tsutomu H, Takashi S, Kunikatsu T (1992) A model-based manipulation system with skill-based execution. IEEE Trans Robot Autom 8(5):535–544
2. Bainbridge C (2008) Characteristics of gifted children
3. Albert B, Dorothea R, Ross Sheila A (1963) Imitation of film-mediated aggressive models. J Abnorm Soc Psychol 66(1):3–11
4. Sylvain C, Florent G, Aude B (2007) On learning, representing, and generalizing a task in a humanoid robot. IEEE Trans SMC Part B: Cybern 37(2):286–298
5. Amor HB, Vogt D, Ewerton M, Berger E, Jung B, Peters J (2013) Learning responsive robot behavior by imitation. In: Proceedings of IEEE/RSJ international conference on intelligent robots and systems (IROS), Tokyo, Japan, pp 3257–3264
6. Schaal S (2006) Dynamic movement primitives—a framework for motor control in humans and humanoid robotics. In: Adaptive motion of animals and machines. Springer, Tokyo, pp 261–280
7. Billing EA, Hellstrom T, Janlert LE (2010) Behavior recognition for learning from demonstration. In: Proceedings of IEEE international conference on robotics and automation (ICRA), Anchorage, Alaska, USA, pp 866–872
8. Cohen BJ, Chitta S, Likhachev M (2010) Search-based planning for manipulation with motion primitives. In: Proceedings of IEEE international conference on robotics and automation (ICRA), Anchorage, Alaska, USA, pp 2902–2908
9. Bentivegna DC, Atkeson CG (2001) Learning from observation using primitives. In: Proceedings of IEEE international conference on robotics and automation (ICRA), Seoul, Korea, pp 1988–1993
10. Nicolescu MN, Mataric MJ (2003) Natural methods for robot task learning: instructive demonstrations, generalization and practice. In: Proceedings of the second international joint conference on autonomous agents and multiagent systems, Melbourne, Australia, pp 241–248
11. Nejati N, Langley P, Konik T (2006) Learning hierarchical task networks by observation. In: Proceedings of the 23rd international conference on machine learning, Pittsburgh, PA, USA, pp 665–672
12. Drumwright E, Jenkins OC, Mataric M (2004) Exemplar-based primitives for humanoid movement classification and control. In: Proceedings of IEEE international conference on robotics and automation (ICRA), New Orleans, LA, USA, pp 140–145
13. Dana K, Wataru T, Yoshihiko N (2009) Online segmentation and clustering from continuous observation of whole body motions. IEEE Trans Robot 25(5):1158–1166
14. Gribovskaya E, Billard A (2008) Combining dynamical systems control and programming by demonstration for teaching discrete bimanual coordination tasks to a humanoid robot. In: Proceedings of ACM/IEEE international conference on human-robot interaction (HRI), Amsterdam, Netherlands
15. Muhlig M, Gienger M, Steil JJ (2010) Human-robot interaction for learning and adaptation of object movements. In: Proceedings of IEEE/RSJ international conference on intelligent robots and systems (IROS), Taipei, Taiwan, pp 4901–4907

16. Asfour T, Azad P, Gyarfas F, Dillmann R (2006) Imitation learning of dual-arm manipulation tasks in humanoid robots. In: Proceedings of IEEE/RAS international conference on humanoid robots, Genoa, Italy, pp 40–47

17. Sanmohan, Kruger V, Kragic D, Kjellstrom H (2011) Primitive-based action representation and recognition. Adv Robot 25(6–7):871–891

18. Kruger V, Tikhanoff V, Natale L, Sandini G (2012) Imitation learning of non-linear point-to-point robot motions using Dirichlet processes. In: Proceedings of IEEE international conference on robotics and automation (ICRA), Saint Paul, Minnesota, USA, pp 2029–2034

19. Smith T, Simmons R (2004) Heuristic search value iteration for POMDPs. In: Proceedings of the 20th conference on uncertainty in artificial intelligence, Virginia, USA, pp 520–527

20. Kurniawati H, Hsu D, Lee WS (2008) SARSOP: efficient point-based POMDP planning by approximating optimally reachable belief spaces. In: Proceedings of robotics: science and systems

21. Olivier L, Pierre B, Julien D, Emmanuel M (2004) Bayesian robot programming. Auton Robot 16(1):49–79

22. Dearden A, Demiris Y (2005) Learning forward models for robots. In: Proceedings of international joint conference on artificial intelligence, Edinburgh, pp 1440–1445

23. Lee D, Nakamura Y (2006) Stochastic model of imitating a new observed motion based on the acquired motion primitives. In: Proceedings of IEEE/RSJ International conference on intelligent robots and systems (IROS), Beijing, China, pp 4994–5000

24. Michael P, Steffen K, Ruediger D, Raoul Z (2007) Incremental learning of tasks from user demonstrations, past experiences, and vocal comments. IEEE Trans SMC Part B: Cybern 37(2):322–332

25. Ekvall S, Kragic D (2006) Learning task models from multiple human demonstration. In: Proceedings of IEEE international symposium on robot and human interactive communication, Hatfield, UK, pp 358–363

26. Brooks Rodney A (1986) A robust layered control system for a mobile robot. IEEE J Robot Autom 2(1):14–23

27. Hoshino Y, Takagi T, Profio UD, Fujita M (2004) Behavior description and control using behavior module for personal robot. In: Proceedings of international conference on robotics and automation (ICRA), New Orleans, LA, USA, pp 4165–4171

28. Jafreezal J, Eric M (2008) A fuzzy action selection method for virtual agent navigation in unknown virtual environments. J Uncertainty Syst 2(2):144–154

29. Matthias S, Virgil A (2004) Architectural mechanisms for dynamic changes of behavior selection strategies in behavior-based systems. IEEE Trans SMC Part B: Cybern 34(6):2377–2395

30. Lee S, Suh LH (2006) A programming framework supporting and ethology-based behavior control architecture. In: Proceedings of IEEE/RSJ international conference on intelligent robots and systems (IROS), Beijing, China, pp 4138–4144

31. Stoffregen TA (2003) Affordances as properties of the animal-environment system. Ecol Psychol 15(2):115–134

32. Anthony C (2003) An outline of a theory of affordances. Ecol Psychol 15(2):181–195

33. Steedman M (2002) Formalizing affordance. In: Proceedings of the 24th annual meeting of the cognitive science society, pp 834–839

34. Erol S, Maya C, Dogar Mehmet R, Emre U, Gokturk Ucluk (2007) To afford or not to afford: a new formalization of affordances toward affordance-based robot control. Adapt Behav 15(4):447–472

35. Lee SH, Suh LH, Calinon S, Johansson R (2014) Autonomous framework for segmenting robot trajectories of manipulation task. Autonomous Robots. Springer, Berlin, pp 1–35

36. Zoubin G, Jordan Michael I (1994) Supervised learning from incomplete data via an EM approach. Adv Neural Inf Process Syst 6:120–127

37. Akgun B, Cakmak M, Yoo JW, Thomaz AL (2012) Trajectories and keyframes for kinesthetic teaching: a human-robot interaction perspective. In: Proceedings of ACM/IEEE international conference on human-robot interaction (HRI), Boston, Massachusetts, USA, pp 391–398

38. Argall BD, Sauser EL, Billard AG (2010) Tactile guidance for policy refinement and reuse. In: Proceedings of international conference on development and learning (ICDL), pp 7–12
39. Lee SH, Cho NJ, Suh LH (2013) Learning of motor skills based on grossness and fineness of movements in daily-life tasks. In: Proceedings of IEEE international conference on robotics and automation (ICRA), Hong Kong, China, pp 5260–5267
40. Hardoon DR, Sandor S, John S-T (2004) Canonical correlation analysis: an overview with application to learning methods. Neural Comput 16(12):2639–2664
41. Muhlig M, Gienger M, Hellbach S, Steil JJ, Goerick C (2009) Task-level imitation learning using variance-based movement optimization. In: Proceedings of IEEE international conference on robotics and automation (ICRA), Kobe, Japan, pp 1177–1184
42. Liping J, Ng MK, Huang ZJ (2007) An entropy weighting k-means algorithm for subspace clustering on high-dimensional sparse data. IEEE Trans Knowl Data Eng 19(8):1026–1041
43. Kerdprasop K, Kerdprasop N, Sattayatham P (2005) Weighted k-means for density-biased clustering. In: Data warehousing and knowledge discovery. Springer, Berlin, pp 488–497
44. Pastor P, Hoffmann H, Asfour T, Schaal S (2009) Learning and generalization of motor skills by learning from demonstration. In: Proceedings of IEEE international conference on robotics and automation (ICRA), Kobe, Japan, pp 763–768
45. Hoffmann H, Pastor P, Park DH, Schaal S (2009) Biologically-inspired dynamical systems for movement generation: automatic real-time goal adaptation and obstacle avoidance. In: Proceedings of IEEE international conference on robotics and automation (ICRA), Kobe, Japan, pp 2587–2592
46. Lee SH, Suh LH (2013) Skill learning and inference framework for skilligent robot. In: Proceedings of IEEE/RSJ international conference on intelligent robots and systems (IROS), Tokyo, Japan, pp 108–115
47. Gaver WW (1991) Technology affordances. In: Proceedings of the SIGCHI conference on human factors in computing systems: reaching through technology, New York, NY, USA, pp 79–84
48. Bryson JJ (2001) The study of sequential and hierarchical organisation of behaviour via artificial mechanisms of action selection. PhD thesis, University of Edinburgh
49. Blumberg BM (1996) Old tricks, new dogs: ethology and interactive creatures. PhD thesis, Massachusetts Institute of Technology
50. Suh LH, Kim MJ, Lee S, Yi BJ (2004) A novel dynamic priority-based action-selection-mechanism integrating a reinforcement learning. In: Proceedings of IEEE international conference on robotics and automation (ICRA), New Orleans, LA, USA, pp 2639–2646
51. Parker LE (1998) ALLIANCE: an architecture for fault tolerant multirobot cooperation. IEEE Trans Robot Autom 14(2):220–240
52. Kleinginna PR, Kleinginna AM (1981) A categorized list of emotion definitions, with suggestions for a consensual definition. Motiv Emot 5(4):345–379
53. Luis M, Manuel L, Alexandre B, Jose S-V (2008) Learning object affordance: from sensory-motor coordination to imitation. IEEE Trans Robot 24(1):15–26
54. Abdo N, Kretzschmar H, Spinello L, Stachniss C (2013) Learning manipulation actions from a few demonstrations. In: Proceedings of IEEE international conference on robotics and automation (ICRA), Karlsruhe, Germany, pp 1268–1275

Chapter 8
Responsive Motion Generation

Sukwon Lee and Sung-Hee Lee

Abstract In this chapter, we discuss the generation of natural behaviors of humanoids (virtual human characters in particular) responsive to the physical interaction with the user such as push and pull. These physical interactions play an important role for increasing the level of immersion of the user and lay foundations for more advanced level of interactions. One of the key components for physical interaction is the generation of suitable balancing behaviors of humanoids against user inputs. We review three major approaches for humanoid balancing, namely the ZMP-based methods, data-driven methods, and momentum-based methods. For each method, we discuss its basic ideas and principles, exemplar work, as well as important future research directions.

8.1 Introduction

A humanoid takes the form of a virtual human character in computer animation, and the form of a physical humanoid robot in robotics. In both fields of research the generation of humanoid motion remains a central problem, and the techniques developed in one field of research have been smoothly adopted in the other. In this chapter we focus on the motion generation problem for virtual human characters for computer animation, but many techniques discussed here originated from and can be applied to humanoid robots as well.

Rapid advancement of computing technologies allows more and more complex algorithms to be incorporated into real-time applications. In addition, natural user inputs based on gestures, gaze, and physiological signals of the users have been employed increasingly for human–computer interaction. These technical innovations trigger and require the development of computational methods to generate humanoid motions interacting with natural user inputs, which are characterized by their large degrees of freedom as opposed to a predefined set of inputs available from

S. Lee · S.-H. Lee (✉)
Korea Advanced Institute of Science and Technology, Daejon, Korea
e-mail: sunghee.lee@kaist.ac.kr

© Springer International Publishing Switzerland 2016   175
N. Magnenat-Thalmann et al. (eds.), *Context Aware Human-Robot
and Human-Agent Interaction*, Human–Computer Interaction Series,
DOI 10.1007/978-3-319-19947-4_8

conventional user input devices such as keyboards and joysticks. Increased level of interaction between humanoids and users widens the scope for VR content and enhances immersiveness of VR applications.

Among the broad possibilities of interaction between the user and the humanoids, in this chapter we discuss the generation of natural behaviors of humanoids responsive to physical interaction with the user through (virtual) contacts such as push and pull. These physical interactions play an important role in giving an impression to the users that humanoids share the same physical space with users and thus laying the foundations for more advanced level of interactions.

Specifically, in this chapter we present techniques regarding the balancing behaviors of the whole body. Among a number of behaviors that a human can employ to maintain balance, the two most representative strategies are postural balancing and reactive stepping as shown in Fig. 8.1. Postural balancing is usually chosen for relatively short and mild perturbations against which a human can maintain balance in place simply by rotating the ankles, hips, or the whole upper body. On long or strong perturbations, a human should take a reactive stepping, i.e., take one or more steps to prevent falling. Falling is a behavior taken when a human loses her balance. However, this is not a completely passive motion because during the fall a human takes action to protect her body or other valuable objects. Other interesting interactive motions such as those made through the hands (e.g., handshaking) are out of the scope of this chapter.

In this chapter, we review some important approaches for human balancing, namely the ZMP-based methods, data-driven methods, and momentum-based methods. In the ZMP-based methods, which have been used extensively in controlling humanoid robots, humanoids are controlled to move in such a way that the ZMP, an important feature point related with balance, is located in the desired position during standing and walking.

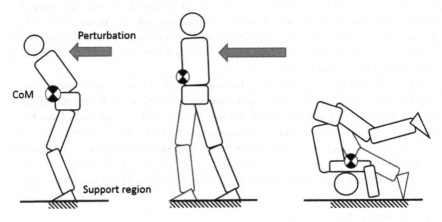

Fig. 8.1 Balance-related behaviors: *left* postural balancing, *middle* reactive stepping, and *right* falling

When only a physics-based controller (e.g., regular ZMP-based method) is used, the resulting motions typically look rather robotic and not humanlike. This would be fine for humanoid robots, but would be problematic for virtual humans that are expected to mimic the real human behavior. To overcome this limitation, data-driven approaches incorporate human motion capture data into the generation of humanoids motion. Usually the motion capture data provides the naturalness prior, while the motions are still generated by physics-based controllers to keep the responsiveness against the unpredictable inputs from the users.

Finally, we introduce the momentum-based approaches that are characterized by controlling both the linear and angular momenta of the whole body. By controlling not only the linear momentum (as typical ZMP-based methods do) but also the angular momentum, this approach enlarges the possible range of actions (i.e., the angular motion as well as the linear motion) for tracking the ZMP.

8.2 ZMP-Based Approaches

Let us first discuss ZMP-based methods. The *zero-moment point* (ZMP) [7, 16] is defined as a *center of pressure* (CoP) of the *ground reaction force* (GRF) and is a key concept regarding balance in humanoids. While ZMP has been used extensively for walking controllers, it has also been widely employed in postural balance controller as well. In fact, walking controller and balance controller are in many cases tightly bound and inseparable. We discuss the ZMP with respect to the postural balance, a main topic of this chapter.

Let us see the definition and computation of the ZMP first. Later, we discuss some methods using ZMP. The pressure on the foot in contact with the ground shows complex distribution over the contact surface. To express the force relationship between the foot and the ground compactly, the ground pressure is integrated into GRF applied to a point around which the horizontal components of the total moment vanish (Fig. 8.2). This point is referred to as ZMP. For simplicity, let us assume the ground is flat and all contact points lie in the XY-plane of the reference frame located on the ground. Suppose $\sigma_z(x, y)$ is the Z-component of the ground pressure at a point $p = [x, y, 0]^T$ as shown in Fig. 8.3. The sum of all vertical components of GRFs is thus

$$f_z = \int_S \sigma_z(x, y) dS, \tag{8.1}$$

where S is the area of contact between the foot and the ground. The moment $\tau_n(p)$ of GRF about a point p due to $\sigma_z(x, y)$ can be calculated as

$$\tau_n(p) = [\tau_{nx}, \tau_{ny}, \tau_{nz}]^T \tag{8.2}$$

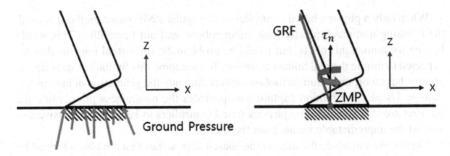

Fig. 8.2 Ground pressure on the base of the foot (*left*) can be equivalently expressed by the ground reaction force (*red arrow*) applied at the zero-moment point (ZMP) and a torque around the vertical axis

Fig. 8.3 *Left* The vertical components of the ground forces. *Right* The horizontal components of the ground forces

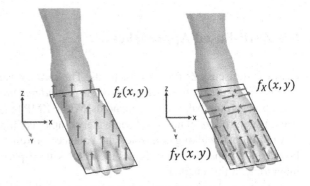

$$\tau_{nx} = \int_S (y - p_y) \times \sigma_z(x, y)dS \qquad (8.3)$$

$$\tau_{ny} = -\int_S (x - p_x) \times \sigma_z(x, y)dS \qquad (8.4)$$

$$\tau_{nz} = 0 \qquad (8.5)$$

Since $\tau_{nx} = \tau_{ny} = 0$ at ZMP, Eqs. 8.3 and 8.4 find the position of the ZMP:

$$p_x = \frac{\int_S x\sigma_z(x, y)dS}{\int_S \sigma_z(x, y)dS} \qquad (8.6)$$

$$p_y = \frac{\int_S y\sigma_z(x, y)dS}{\int_S \sigma_z(x, y)dS} \qquad (8.7)$$

The ZMP $p = [p_x, p_y, 0]^T$ is also called the *Center of Pressure* (CoP), and we use both terms interchangeably in this chapter. Second, let us consider the effect of the horizontal component of the ground forces. Integrating them over the contact surface gives the tangential components of the GRF:

$$f_x = \int_S \sigma_x(x, y) dS \qquad (8.8)$$

$$f_y = \int_S \sigma_y(x, y) dS \qquad (8.9)$$

The moment $\tau_t(p) = [\tau_{tx}, \tau_{ty}, \tau_{tz}]^T$ due to σ_x and σ_y is

$$\tau_{tx}(p) = 0 \qquad (8.10)$$

$$\tau_{ty}(p) = 0 \qquad (8.11)$$

$$\tau_{tz}(p) = \int_S \{(x - p_x)\sigma_y(x, y) - (y - p_y)\sigma_x(x, y)\} dS \qquad (8.12)$$

Note that $\tau_{tx}(p)$ and $\tau_{ty}(p)$ are zero because the horizontal components of the GRF cannot produce the moment about the horizontal axes. Nonzero $\tau_{tz}(p)$ means that the horizontal components of the GRF generate the normal component of the moment. Summing all components leads to the GRF and the moment about ZMP as

$$f = [f_x, f_y, f_z]^T \qquad (8.13)$$

$$\tau(p) = \tau_n(p) + \tau_t(p) = [0, 0, \tau_{tz}]^T \qquad (8.14)$$

Note that the ZMP is not a point where all components of the moment become zero: the vertical moment still exists.

ZMP is located inside the *support polygon*, a convex hull including all the contact points, and cannot get out of it. To see this, suppose the GRF consists of a finite number of forces $f_i := [f_{ix}, f_{iy}, f_{iz}]^T$ ($i = 1 \ldots N$) on contact points $p_i \in S$. Then the following relations hold:

$$f = \sum_{i=1}^{N} f_i \qquad (8.15)$$

$$\tau(p) = \sum_{i=1}^{N} (p_i - p) \times f_i. \qquad (8.16)$$

When p equals the ZMP, then $\tau_x(p) = \tau_y(p) = 0$, which leads to

$$p = \frac{\sum_{i=1}^{N} p_i f_{iz}}{\sum_{i=1}^{N} f_{iz}} \qquad (8.17)$$

Rearranging this term, we get

$$p = \sum_{i=1}^{N} \alpha_i p_i, \qquad \text{where,} \ \alpha_i = \frac{f_{iz}}{f_z} \tag{8.18}$$

Since the GRF is unilateral (the foot cannot pull the ground), $f_{iz} \geq 0$. Thus,

$$\begin{cases} \alpha_i \geq 0 \quad (i = 1 \dots N) \\ \sum_{i=1}^{N} \alpha_i = 1 \end{cases} \tag{8.19}$$

Equation (8.19) shows that p must lie in the convex hull of the contact point of the support polygon:

$$p = \left\{ \sum_{i=1}^{N} \alpha_i p_i \mid p_i \in S \ (i = 1 \dots N) \right\} \tag{8.20}$$

Figure 8.4 shows the ZMP for some cases of foot pressure distribution. When the pressure is evenly distributed over the contact surface, ZMP is located at the center of the foot indicating the posture is stably balanced and less likely to topple (Fig. 8.4, left). The quality of balance decreases as the pressure distribution is skewed, and a humanoid starts to topple when ZMP reaches an edge of the support polygon (Fig. 8.4, right).

Therefore, ZMP is regarded an important indicator for the balance of a humanoid, and researchers have put efforts in the development of efficient balance controllers using the ZMP. Most ZMP-based controllers are designed to move a subset of body parts (i.e., ankle or hip) or the whole body to make the ZMP located in the desired position, which is usually set at the center of the support polygon.

The simplest kind of ZMP-based methods would be the ankle control strategy [5, 17], which controls only the ankle torque to bring the ZMP toward the desired position inside the foot base; dorsiflexion of the ankle moves the ZMP backwards and plantar flexion moves it forward.

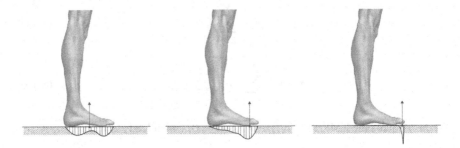

Fig. 8.4 Distributions of the pressure and the corresponding locations of ZMP

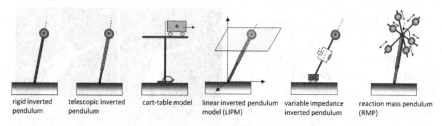

rigid inverted pendulum | telescopic inverted pendulum | cart-table model | linear inverted pendulum model (LIPM) | variable impedance inverted pendulum | reaction mass pendulum (RMP)

Fig. 8.5 Various reduced models for the dynamics of humanoid balance [14]

More advanced ZMP-based controllers operate to move the humanoid to follow the desired CoM position, which is appropriately set to achieve the desired ZMP position. For this, the relation between the CoM and the ZMP needs to be defined, and there are various models describing the core dynamics of the humanoid in terms of CoM and ZMP. Figure 8.5 shows some examples of such models. Note however that these reduced models only capture the important features of the humanoid dynamics, and there are always errors from the true dynamics of a humanoid caused by the simplification. For example, the 3D *linear inverted pendulum model* (LIPM) [9] relates the motion of CoM on a horizontal plane with respect to ZMP as follows:

$$\ddot{y} = \frac{g}{z_c}y, \quad \ddot{x} = \frac{g}{z_c}x, \tag{8.21}$$

where (x, y, z_c) is the position of CoM, and g denotes the acceleration of gravity. Therefore, the desired ZMP position is obtained by controlling the movement of the CoM. Different models provide different relations between the CoM and the ZMP.

Some methods [2, 6] take the strategies where the ground projection of the CoM moves to the support polygon. First, the desired acceleration of the CoM is determined from the desired CoM position.

$$\ddot{c}_d = k_s(c_d - c) - k_d\dot{c}, \tag{8.22}$$

where c_d is the desired CoM position. k_s and k_d are positional and damping gains, respectively, which control the influences of the positional and derivative terms on the desired acceleration. There are many choices on the desired CoM position for a stable configuration, but most opt for the center of the support polygon because in that case the humanoid can cope with perturbations from various directions.

Given the desired motion of the CoM, we need to determine the control input to achieve the goal. One method for this is the virtual force method [4, 6, 15]. The virtual force f_v is calculated from the desired acceleration of the CoM $\ddot{c}_d$

$$f_v = m\ddot{c}_d, \tag{8.23}$$

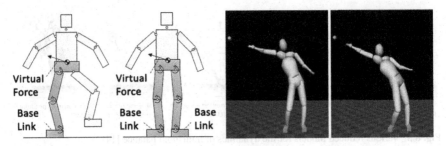

Fig. 8.6 *Left* Virtual forces applied to the CoM [4]. *Right* Reaching to the point while maintaining balance [2]

where m is mass of the humanoid. The virtual force is the imaginary force that would generate $\ddot{c}_d$. Then the virtual force is substituted by the joint torques τ from the relation:

$$\tau = J(p)^T f_v, \tag{8.24}$$

where $J(p)$ is the Jacobian matrix that maps the derivatives of the generalized coordinates to the velocity of the point p, the point on the foot that coincides with the ZMP. Equation (8.24) is a form of Jacobian transpose control that enables the operation space control by computing the corresponding joint torques (Fig. 8.6).

8.3 Data-Driven Approaches

Until now we have discussed ZMP-based approaches for maintaining balance of humanoids. They have shown good performance for maintaining balance, but the resulting motions may look rather robotic and do not closely look like human movements. This is a common downside of physics-based approaches that capture the physical aspect of human motions well but cannot account for other various factors related to human motion, such as aesthetic qualities and personal styles. These features are implicitly contained in motion capture data and thus the data-driven approaches that use recorded human motion data have great potential to generate natural looking motions. Thus, researchers have developed various methods that use recorded human motion data as a human motion prior to create humanoids motions.

Many data-driven approaches concern modifying recorded motion data to match different human figures and environments to increase reusability of the data through interpolating, blending, and rearranging motion clips. Some methods are effective for offline animation while others are good for interactive animation. Some pursue physical plausibility while others ignore it. Here we discuss only those data-driven approaches that generate physically plausible, interactive animation in real-time.

Naturally many methods of this kind employ physical controllers to generate motions or at least use physical principles to create movement kinematically.

A common framework of data-driven approaches for physical interaction is to generate reference motions using motion database and have a physical controller to track the reference motion. A basic tool for tracking is a PD controller, which is modeled as follows:

$$\tau = k_p(\theta_m - \theta_c) + k_d(\dot{\theta}_m - \dot{\theta}_c), \tag{8.25}$$

where θ_m and $\dot{\theta}_m$ denote the joint angles and velocities of the reference motion, and θ_c and $\dot{\theta}_c$ are the current joint angles and velocities of the humanoid. k_p and k_d are the proportional and derivative gains, respectively, which determine the magnitude of control force τ given the position and velocity differences.

The tracking controller is effective enough to follow simple motions such as upper body movement. Sometimes offline procedure for gain tuning achieves good tracking quality [4]. For more complex motions, simple tracking control may fail to achieve the goal. This is mainly because the human model (body dimensions and physical properties) and the environment (shape and contact configurations) at hand are different from those at the motion capture session. In this case motion data should also be modified. In order to create multi-contact motions such as walking and rolling, [11] developed a sampling-based optimization method, in which optimal reference motion is created through sampling so as to maximize the similarity to the original motion and the quality of balance. The latter is measured regardless of whether the CoM-ground projection is located inside the support polygon.

Nam et al. [13] divided the human model into dynamic and kinematic parts. Physical simulation is applied only to the dynamic parts, and the rest are moved kinematically. This approach eases the burden of physical controller while still being able to create responsive motions to user inputs interactively. To determine which part should be simulated, they compare each joint torque resisting the user disturbance with the predefined threshold value. If a joint torque exceeds the threshold, a chain of body parts from the joint to the terminal part that the user interacts with are treated as dynamic and a PD controller is applied to follow the reference motion. This approach provides rather simple means to creating responsive behaviors, but the resulting motions are generally limited to those not deviating much from the original motion.

Some methods create motions kinematically, but employ dynamic analysis or simulation as a tool to select suitable motion data to generate responsive motions against external perturbations. In general, motion data expresses human motions with high realism yet the range of expressible motion is limited by the size and content of the motion database. Therefore, motion data are usually interpolated and blended to make new motions. Yin et al. [19] (Fig. 8.7, left) used a set of motion data that captures responsive behaviors of humans under external push to create humanoid motions. By analyzing offline the momentum rate change of the motion data after push, the magnitude and direction of the external push are estimated and stored per each sample motion clip. Online, when a new external force is applied, the closest

Fig. 8.7 *Left* Parameterization of push response. *Color* represents the type of balancing strategy and the vector represents the direction and the magnitude of the push [19]. *Right* An example of making falling motion due to kicking. Before being hit, the character moves by motion data. Falling motion (*red*) is created by a PD controller that creates smooth transition to a suitable lying motion (*green*) [21]

sample to the given external force is found and the corresponding sample motion is scaled to account for the difference (magnitude and direction) in the input force and the force in the closest sample. The final motion is generated kinematically rather than created by a physics-based controller.

Data-driven approaches have the advantages that they provide rather straightforward methods to create complex motions, albeit of limited scope, which are often difficult to obtain through physics-based approaches. Zordan et al. [21] proposed a method to create natural falling motion using motion data (Fig. 8.7, right). In this method, when a humanoid starts to fall given a high impact, a falling motion is simulated first to approximate plausible falling motion. Then a motion clip that is mostly like to occur after falling is searched from a database. Specifically, a motion clip that has the least difference from the simulated motion for a certain time window is selected. After finding this target motion clip that should occur after falling, the humanoid is re-simulated with a PD-controller activated to make a smooth transition to the target motion.

We have reviewed several data-driven approaches for creating responsive motions. Thanks to the motion capture data, the resulting motions of these approaches are highly natural. By employing physics-based techniques, data-driven approaches can achieve responsiveness to the external inputs. However, the output motions are generally limited to the scope of the recorded motion data.

8.4 Momentum Control Approaches

In Sect. 8.2, we have seen that the GRF and CoP (or ZMP) are important features regarding balance. In fact, GRF and CoP are closely related with the linear and angular momenta of a human. Newton–Euler equations of motion state that the total external force and torque equal the rate of change of the linear and angular momenta, respectively. Consider a standing human with total mass of m, who gets external forces only from the ground f and the gravitational force mg. If we compute a torque generated by the external forces about the CoM r_g of the human, the rate of change of linear momentum $\dot{l}$ and angular momentum $\dot{k}$ is as follows:

$$\dot{l} = mg + f \tag{8.26}$$

$$\dot{k} = (p - r_g) \times f + \tau_n, \tag{8.27}$$

where p denotes the location of CoP and τ_n is the torque about the vertical axis generated by the tangential forces from the ground. The position of the CoP can be calculated by substituting (8.26) into (8.27) and using the conditions $p_z = 0$ and $\tau_{nx} = \tau_{ny} = 0$.

$$p_x = r_{gx} - \frac{1}{\dot{l}_z - mg}(f_x r_{gz} - \dot{k}_y) \tag{8.28}$$

$$p_y = r_{gy} - \frac{1}{\dot{l}_z - mg}(f_y r_{gz} - \dot{k}_x) \tag{8.29}$$

From the equations, one can easily verify that GRF and CoP are uniquely determined by the linear and angular momentum rate change. In particular, GRF has a one-to-one relation with the linear momentum rate change, and CoP is determined by both linear and angular momentum rate changes.

Since a human body can be modeled as an articulated system that consists of a set of rigid bodies connected by joints, the momentum of a human is calculated as the total sum of momentum of individual rigid bodies, i.e.,

$$h_g(q, \dot{q}) = \sum_i^n X_i^T h_i, \tag{8.30}$$

where $h = (k^T, l^T)^T$ is the spatial momentum, a combination of angular and linear momentum, and X_i^T transforms h_i (spatial momentum of part i, expressed in its local frame) to the CoM frame (a reference frame located at CoM with its orientation aligned to the world frame). Note that the momentum is uniquely defined by the generalized coordinates q and their time derivatives $\dot{q}$, which means the GRF and CoP are completely controlled by the joint motions of the humanoid.

The idea of momentum control approaches is that by controlling both the angular and linear momentum of a human, one can control the GRF and CoP. Comparing with the ZMP-based control that usually controls only the CoM motion (hence the linear momentum), the momentum control approaches take angular momentum into account for designing the controller; hence they have higher potential to control the position of the CoP more precisely.

For postural balance control problem, [8] introduced angular momentum control for the whole body control problem. Abdallah and Goswami [1] developed a postural balance controller that controls the rate of change of linear and angular momenta of

Fig. 8.8 *Left* The character responds to a disturbance [12]. *Right* A planar rimless wheel model (GFPE) [20]

a humanoid robot. More recently, [12] proposed a whole body postural balance controller that identifies the desired CoP as the high level input. (Figure 8.8, left) while [10] extended their method to present a balance controller for a nonlevel and nonstationary ground.

Recently, researchers have applied momentum control approaches to reactive stepping. Wu and Zordan [18] introduced a momentum-based stepping controller that generates parameterized curves for the swing foot and center of mass (CoM) trajectories according to the step position and duration. The method subsequently creates whole body motions to realize the trajectories via joint accelerations optimally calculated from the multiobjective function and joint torques computed by inverse dynamics. Yun and Goswami [20] presented a novel reactive stepping method based on a rimless wheel model. Specifically, they developed the *generalized foot placement estimator* (GFPE) to define the target stepping point. The proposed method is applicable to nonlevel ground (Fig. 8.8, right).

Here, we review a case of momentum control approach proposed in [10] for postural balance. In the work, the behavior of the momentum controller is determined by the set of inputs, the desired linear and angular momentum rate change ($\dot{l}_d$ and $\dot{k}_d$), as well as additional inputs such as the desired joint accelerations for the upper body (θ_d^u), and the desired position and velocity of the swing foot (T_d, v_d). Output is the appropriate joint torques for postural balance. Figure 8.9 shows the overall framework.

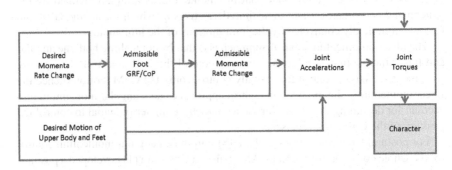

Fig. 8.9 Momentum control module [10]

The desired rate of change of the momenta is determined as

$$\dot{l}_d = \Gamma_{lp}\, m(r_{Gd} - r_G) + \Gamma_{ld}\, m(l_d - l) \tag{8.31}$$

$$\dot{k}_d = \Gamma_{kd}(k_d - k), \tag{8.32}$$

where Γ_{lp} and Γ_{ld} are proportional and derivative gains, respectively. Subscript d denotes the desired value of each property. Postural balance can be maintained if we set $l_d = 0$ and $k_d = 0$ to stabilize the momentum generated by the perturbation. r_{Gd} can be set such that the ground projection of CoM is located at the center of the support polygon.

Given the desired linear and angular momentum rate changes (which are not necessarily physically realizable by a humanoid), the admissible (physically realizable) GRF and CoP are determined such that they can create admissible momentum rate change that is as close as possible to its desired value. If both the desired linear and angular momentum rate changes are not admissible, one should choose either linear or angular momentum to satisfy and sacrifice the other. Here we will consider an easy case where both the desired momenta are admissible. This means that the admissible GRF and CoP can be calculated from (8.26) and (8.28)–(8.29) by substituting $\dot{l}$ and $\dot{k}$ with the desired values computed in (8.31) and (8.32).

After determining the admissible GRF, CoP, and momentum rate changes, the joint accelerations are determined to satisfy the desired values. As there are infinitely many solutions for the joint accelerations given the admissible momentum rate change, we can impose the preferred motion for the upper body and the swing foot as the secondary objective, so that the resulting joint accelerations will satisfy the given momentum rate change while generating the desired motion as close as possible. This is achieved by solving the following optimization problem:

$$\ddot{\theta}_a = \operatorname*{argmin}_{\ddot{\theta}} w_b \|\dot{h}_a - A\ddot{q} - \dot{A}\dot{q}\| + (1 - w_b)\|\ddot{\theta}_d^u - \ddot{\theta}^u\|$$

$$s.t. \quad J\ddot{q} + \dot{J}\dot{q} = a_d \quad \text{and} \quad \ddot{\theta}_l \le \ddot{\theta} \le \ddot{\theta}_u, \tag{8.33}$$

where the first term on the RHS concerns satisfying the admissible momentum rate change $\dot{h}_a$, which is related to the second derivative of the generalized coordinates from the differentiation of the momentum–velocity relation:

$$h(q, \dot{q}) = A(q)\dot{q}, \tag{8.34}$$

where $A(q)$ maps the derivative of the generalized coordinates to the momentum. Refer to [14] for calculation of the matrix. Note that the generalized coordinates include joint angles, i.e., $\theta \subset q$. $\ddot{\theta}_d^u$ denotes the desired joint accelerations for the upper body. The first constraint term enforces the support foot to be stationary. The Jacobian matrix J maps the derivative of generalized coordinates to the velocity of the foot. The inequality constraints bound the joint accelerations to a feasible region.

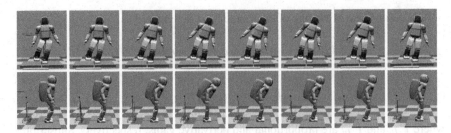

Fig. 8.10 Postural balancing using a momentum-control approach [10]

Given the admissible joint angles, one can use a PD-controller (8.22) to compute the necessary joint torques. A more advanced method is the inverse dynamics [3] that considers the physical properties of the humanoid model to compute the necessary joint torques. Figure 8.10 shows the balancing behavior of a standing humanoid when it is affected by external perturbation from the side and the back.

8.5 Conclusion

In this chapter, we discussed state-of-the-art technologies for generating responsive motions of humanoids in three categories: ZMP-based, data-driven, and momentum-based techniques.

The ZMP-based approach targets to control the position of ZMP by moving a subset of body parts or the whole body. To confront the complex humanoid dynamics, simplified reduced models that capture only the core dynamics of humanoids are used to determine suitable control inputs. Hence, ZMP-based methods are relatively simple and good for real-time applications that have a limited computational budget.

By referring to the motion capture data of real humans, the data-driven approach has great potential to create natural looking motions, which is particularly important for the visual quality of the virtual human characters. By combining with physics-based approaches, one can develop interactive humanoid animation. However, many factors related to the styles of human motions, such as gender, body dimensions, environment conditions, and personal styles, are all implicitly melted into the motion data, so it is challenging to extract such factors and control them at user's will. In general, the resulting motion is heavily dependent on the motion database. Generating diverse motions from a limited size of motion database remains an important future work.

Finally, the momentum-based approach attempts to control both the linear and angular momentum of the humanoids, thus it can control the movement of CoM and CoP more precisely. Postural controller and stepping controllers have been developed in this approach where it is rather straightforward to determine the desired linear and angular momenta. However, it remains an unsolved question as to how the desired momenta should be set for a wider range of human motions, e.g., running; an important topic for future work.

References

1. Abdallah M, Goswami A (2005) A biomechanically motivated two-phase strategy for biped upright balance control. In: Proceedings of the 2005 IEEE international conference on robotics and automation, ICRA '05, pp 1996–2001
2. Abe Y, da Silva M, Popović J (2007) Multiobjective control with frictional contacts. In: Proceedings of the ACM SIGGRAPH Eurographics symposium on computer animation 2007, Eurographics Association, pp 249–258
3. Featherstone R (1987) Robot dynamics algorithm. Kluwer Academic Publishers, Boston
4. Geijtenbeek T, Pronost N, van der Stappen F (2012) Simple data-driven control for simulated bipeds. In: Proceedings of the ACM SIGGRAPH/Eurographics symposium on computer animation 2012, Eurographics Association, pp 211–219
5. Golliday CL Jr, Hemami H (1976) Postural stability of the two-degree-of-freedom biped by general linear feedback. IEEE Trans Autom Control 21(1):74–79
6. Ha S, Ye Y, Liu CK (2012) Falling and landing motion control for character animation. ACM Trans Graph 31(6):155:1–155:9
7. Kajita S, Harada K, Hirukawa H, Yokoi K (2014) Introduction to humanoid robotics. Springer, New York
8. Kajita S, Kanehiro F, Kaneko K, Fujiwara K, Harada K, Yokoi K, Hirukawa H (2003) Resolved momentum control: humanoid motion planning based on the linear and angular momentum. In: Proceedings of 2003 IEEE/RSJ international conference on intelligent robots and systems, IROS '03, pp 1644–1650
9. Kajita S, Kanehiro F, Kaneko K, Yokoi K, Hirukawa H (2001) The 3D linear inverted pendulum mode: a simple modeling for a biped walking pattern generation. In: Proceedings of 2001 IEEE/RSJ international conference of intelligent robots and systems, IROS '01, pp 239–246
10. Lee S-H, Goswami A (2012) A momentum-based balance controller for humanoid robots on non-level and non-stationary ground. Auton Robots 33(4):399–414
11. Liu L, Yin K, van de Panne M, Shao T, Xu W (2010) Sampling-based contact-rich motion control. ACM Trans Graph 29(4):128:1–128:10
12. Macchietto A, Zordan VB, Shelton CR (2009) Momentum control for balance. ACM Trans Graph 28(3):80:1–80:8
13. Nam HN, Arista CR, Karen L, Victor BZ (2012) Adaptive dynamics with hybrid response. In: SIGGRAPH Asia technical briefs 5(1–5):4
14. Orin DE, Goswami A, Lee S-H (2013) Centroidal dynamics of a humanoid robot. Auton Robots 35(2–3):161–176
15. Pratt J, Chew C-M, Torres A, Dilworth P, Pratt G (2001) Virtual model control: an intuitive approach for bipedal locomotion. Int J Robot Res 20(2):129–143
16. Vukobratovic M (1990) Biped locomotion. Springer, New York
17. Vukobratovic M, Frank AA, Juricic D (1970) On the stability of biped locomotion. IEEE Trans Biomed Eng 17(1):25–36
18. Wu C-C, Zordan VB (2010) Goal-directed stepping with momentum control. In: Proceedings of the 2010 ACM SIGGRAPH/Eurographics symposium on computer animation, Eurographics Association, pp 113–118
19. Yin K, Pai DK, van de Panne M (2005) Data-driven interactive balancing behaviors. In: Proceedings of the 13th Pacific conference on computer graphics and applications, Pacific Graphics '05, pp 118–121
20. Yun S, Goswami A (2011) Momentum-based reactive stepping controller on level and non-level ground for humanoid robot push recovery. In: Proceedings of 2011 IEEE/RSJ international conference on intelligent robots and systems, IROS '11, pp 3943–3950
21. Zordan VB, Majkowska A, Chiu B, Fast M (2005) Dynamic response for motion capture animation. ACM Trans Graph, pp 697–701

Chapter 9
Shared Object Manipulation

Jun Lee, Nadia Magnenat-Thalmann and Daniel Thalmann

Abstract In this chapter, we introduce a concept of shared object manipulation between real and virtual humans. The shared object manipulation allows both real and virtual humans to collaborate in real-time. These can be applied to 3D telepresence applications such as computer-aided design and virtual simulation and training. However, it is still far from achieving the expected results from this area because it consists of three different and complex research domains. Firstly, we need to consider a virtual object grasping method for intuitive and convenient virtual object manipulation. Secondly, human-like animation is required for virtual object manipulation by virtual humans. Thirdly, consistency management of shared object manipulation is required to avoid conflicts from multiple simultaneous inputs. After review of state of the art, solution approaches and their limitations are introduced. We conclude with a discussion of future directions for the shared object manipulation between real and virtual humans.

9.1 Introduction

Virtual humans are increasingly being used for various virtual reality applications and virtual humans should react with natural reactions as similar to real humans. For example, we can consider virtual object manipulation between real and virtual humans. It can be applied to the collaborative designing, training, and simulation

J. Lee · N. Magnenat-Thalmann · D. Thalmann (✉)
BeingThere Centre, Nanyang Technological University, Singapore, Singapore
e-mail: danielthalmann@ntu.edu.sg

J. Lee
e-mail: jun.lee.mistra@gmail.com

N. Magnenat-Thalmann
e-mail: nadiathalmann@ntu.edu.sg

© Springer International Publishing Switzerland 2016
N. Magnenat-Thalmann et al. (eds.), *Context Aware Human-Robot
and Human-Agent Interaction*, Human–Computer Interaction Series,
DOI 10.1007/978-3-319-19947-4_9

191

process via the 3D telepresence environment. In the 3D telepresence environment, the virtual human can collaborate with real humans for supporting specific tasks. For example, a virtual trainer teaches real humans to improve behaviors of object manipulations in the best way. Virtual humans also replace the task of real participants who will be absent during collaboration. However, this area has received little attention because it consists of three different and complex research domains.

First, virtual object manipulation by a real human is important to decide the usability of the application. Grasping and manipulation with hands should be very intuitive. When a real human can grasp a virtual object with her hands and if she can feel realistic haptic feedback on her hands, the user can manipulate the object without the knowledge to manipulate it. Hence, conventional research generally focused on how to provide natural grasping with realistic haptic feedback [28]. Exoskeleton-based interfaces are attached to provide real human forces of the hand and fingers. However, it is still difficult to generalize direct hand manipulation for the end-user because conventional researches use expensive and cumbersome devices for manipulation and haptic feedback. Since the haptic interface uses wires to control devices, it also restricts the user's body movements. Computer vision-based direct hand manipulation method was proposed for less cumbersome grasping [13]. However, the working space is still limited and accuracy of grasping is lower than the glove-based approach.

Second, we need to consider virtual object manipulation by virtual humans. To do this, methods of creating grasping and manipulation motions of virtual human has been studied in the computer animation domain. In order to create real-time and natural-looking motion, motion synthesizing techniques with rule-based approach based on inverse kinematics are used [32]. Although IK-based synthesis creates grasping motion for various objects of different sizes and shapes, grasping posture of hand requires more realistic motions and it also should be combined with other motion of virtual humans such as reaching and locomotion to support a wide range of movement and manipulation tasks in real-time.

Third, consistency management of shared object manipulation is required to avoid conflicts from multiple simultaneous inputs. In order to avoid these conflicts, we need to keep the attributes of the shared data consistent. A concurrency control mechanism in a 3D telepresence system uses a basic rule that gives ownership or a lock on an object to eligible users. Other users that do not own the object have to wait until the lock is released [36]. In the shared object manipulation, the non-owners can only monitor the behavior of the owner. It restricts non-owners' behaviors even if the non-owners want to manipulate object. This mechanism does not fit realistic grasping and manipulation of virtual object. Dividing attributes of shared objects and handling ownership of each attribute can be an alternative to release restrictions on behavior [12]. However, another problem, called surprise, is a special behavior contrary to the expectations of participants. Especially, divided attributes have indirect relationships with each other.

In order to address these various requirements for virtual object manipulation and to apply shared object manipulation between real and virtual humans, we have been developing direct hand manipulation method using combinations of multiple devices and task-based concurrency control mechanism. In Sect. 9.2, we review and discuss in detail the virtual object manipulation by real human, virtual object manipulation by virtual human, and consistency management for shared object manipulation. Section 9.3 proposes current lines of work to allow real human grasping and manipulation of a virtual object and to provide concurrent control mechanism for shared object manipulation between real and virtual humans. Section 9.4 concludes the chapter.

9.2 State of the Art

9.2.1 Virtual Object Manipulation by the User

Virtual object manipulation is a key component of virtual reality applications because it determines natural and convenient interactions between real human and virtual environment. Thus, many studies have been done on 3D object manipulations using 3D devices. Early research proposed to use a pointing device with hands to manipulate 3D object [4, 8, 39]. With such 3D devices, 3D interaction methods proposed to increase usability of 3D object manipulation in immersive virtual environment, for example, Silk cursor [40], go–go interaction [31], ray-casting interaction [3], scaled manipulation [7]. Since the system only allows simple inputs from a user, the proposed interactions were simplified using specific metaphors different from real object manipulation. Another consideration is that a user generally holds a handheld device to manipulate a virtual object. Therefore, the user should learn how to operate the device and it is difficult to use hand gestures when the hand is holding a device.

Direct hand manipulation holds promise as a familiar, simple, and efficient method for novices because they may need less specialized knowledge and fewer technical skills than what may be necessary for more advanced types of interactions [26]. The important issues are how to recognize robust hands input with proper feedback and how to support simple and convenient manipulation using hands. Research generally falls into two categories: object manipulation with haptic feedback and object manipulation without haptic feedback.

When the user touches and grasps a virtual object, haptic feedback is created by the intended actions. If the feedback is consistent with contextual expectations, it can increase believability of virtual object manipulation by the user. During virtual object manipulation, the user may feel different kinds of haptic feedback on different areas of the hands. First, the sense of touch should be delivered to the palm and fingers. Second, force can control the angles of all fingers based on the shape and elasticity of the virtual object. Third, different forces may be triggered to the wrist when a user's hand collides with other objects. Thus, exoskeleton-based interfaces are required to support these kinds of haptic feedback. Thanks to CyberGloveSystems, three different haptic interfaces are provided: CyberTouch, CyberGrasp, and CyberForce.

Borst et al., proposed physical-based haptic feedback using CyberGrasp. They combined tracked hand information with calculated articulated hand model through linear and torsional spring-dampers [2]. Although the proposed spring model showed

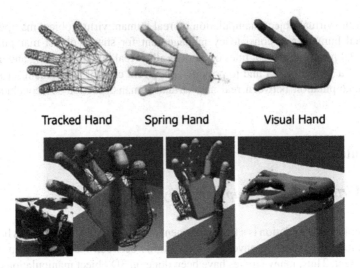

Tracked Hand   Spring Hand   Visual Hand

Fig. 9.1 Three hands with mass-spring model [29]

good simulation result to control fingers, more different kinds of haptic feedback are required for more natural feelings of grasping object. Ott et al., proposed a unified haptic feedback system that integrates the three different haptic feedback into one synchronised system [29]. It also optimized collision detection and collision response of hands. Thus, this system visualizes three different hands: tracked hands, mass-spring hands, and visual hands in Fig. 9.1. When the data glove recognizes tracked information from real hand, tracked hand is matched with the same posture. The tracked hand is converted into spring hand to detect collision and to calculate directions and forces from the collision. Finally, visual hand is shown to the real human. Furthermore, they concerned two handed manipulations for object grasping and manipulation [28] as shown in Fig. 9.2.

Although haptic feedback is important in virtual object manipulation, the devices are generally expensive and cumbersome to wear. Another concern is that working spaces are limited due to characteristics of devices which provide wired connections. In order to solve this issue, various virtual object manipulation methods were proposed without haptic interfaces.

First, data glove-based manipulation was widely used to manipulate object as highly accurate hand information could be achieved in real-time. Since data glove generally does not support tracking 3D position and rotation angles, conventional research used a combination involving other tracking devices. Park et al., showed that a combination of data gloves with magnetic-based trackers could successfully recognize twisting gestures by two hands for manipulation of 3D molecule models [30]. Gallo et al., combined a data glove with a WiiRemote to get accurate and fast hand input [9]. Their method was applied to manipulate 3D medical model from MRI images. Lu et al., used ultrasonic sensor-based data gloves and head trackers to manipulate 3D object using hand gestures [10]. Otsuki et al., proposed ungrouping

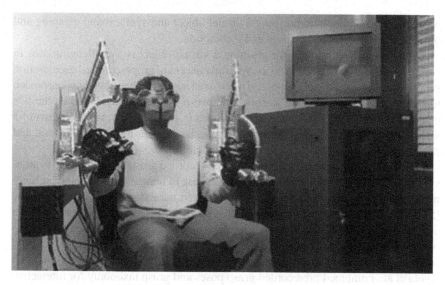

Fig. 9.2 Haptic workstation for two-handed manipulation [28]

interactions for complicated 3D object using a combination of a data glove and infrared-based tracking systems. The interaction visualizes elastic effects when a user grasps a small part and pulls it out of the object [27].

Second, computer vision-based hand manipulation uses a camera to capture hand information. Thus, the approach could offer convenient manipulation without wearing devices. As depth images can be easily captured by depth cameras, an interesting direct manipulation approach is proposed by Microsoft. HoloDesk [13] provides direct hand manipulation in a mixed reality environment using Kinect and optical see-through display. In HoloDesk, 3D virtual objects are shown through a half-silvered mirror, and user grasps and manipulates the object with a spatially aligned 3D virtual world. Although the possible working space is strictly limited, HoloDesk showed a new direction of virtual object manipulation.

9.2.2 Virtual Object Manipulation by Virtual Human

Generating realistic motion of a virtual human for a dynamic object manipulation is an interesting issue in interactive virtual reality applications. Many simulations and games require virtual humans to interact directly with dynamic objects such as reaching, grasping, touching, and moving. In order to manipulate 3D object, a virtual human may walk toward the object and reach out with his/her arm to grasp the object. However, it is difficult to get realistic enough result because research on character animation has generally focused on realistic motion generation using motion capture data. In order to address this issue, two classified research areas will be reviewed: animation on grasping a virtual object and synthesizing grasping and other animations such as reaching and locomotion.

Synthesis of hand motion for grasping a virtual object is a challenging area in computer animation. The early work by Rijpkema et al., proposed rule-based motion generation [32]. Sanso et al., proposed rule-based automatic hand synthesis approach to decide between one-handed grasping and two-handed grasping, based on the size of a virtual object [35]. Although this approach is available to grasp all or part of a virtual object, there is no guarantee that synthesized grasps motions are natural and consistent in comparison to a real grasping situation.

A feasible alternative approach is to use prerecorded grasps data for grasp synthesis [1, 5, 17, 22]. Elkoura et al., utilized a database of human grasps to process kinematically synthesized hand poses with persevered natural coupling between joints [5]. They applied this to playing musical instruments. Li et al., explored a data-driven approach to grasp synthesis by searching closet examples in a prerecorded grasp database to match the object shape [22]. Amor et al., proposed a probabilistic model to constrain the solution space of human grasp synthesis from prerecorded data [1]. Kyota et al., combined prerecorded grasp poses and grasp taxonomy for interactive grasp synthesis [17]. Zhao et al., proposed prerecorded grasp poses with physics-motion control to model interactive human grasping synthesis [41]. The physical model considered a wide variety of objects of different shapes, sizes, masses, frictions, and external perturbations. Finally, the synthesis model linked the real-time interaction module with Kinect.

We need to consider synthesis of other motions besides hand to create realistic motion of grasping and manipulation of virtual objects. Thus, the virtual human requires locomotion and reaching animations for a virtual object. In order to create dynamic animations, inverse kinematics approaches may be used. However, generated gestures of object grasping and manipulation are not the same as humanlike motion. Kallmann et al., proposed motion planning method to synthesize collision-free motions for both arms, with automatic column control and leg flexion [16]. They used a probabilistic inverse kinematics solver for matching predesigned grasps.

Recently, Huang et al., applied motor controllers with biomechanical rules to coordinate arm, spine, and leg movements to generate a full-body reaching motion including stepping [14]. Lv et al., proposed utilizing various reaching strategies based on biomechanics to optimize and reduce dimension [24]. Although biomechanical rules for synthesis enhance the result of animations, additional costs are involved in order to add the biomechanical rules to the synthesis model. Huang et al., proposed example-based motion synthesis method which combines prerecorded motions and IK-based upper body planner [14]. The method showed that a virtual human can grasp distinct objects using computation of whole planned motion to achieve real-time performance. Feng et al., showed the optimized synthesis approach to reduce computation costs using separation of the motion blending from path planning [6]. They also integrated synthesis of approximated grasp into the other motions. Thus, a virtual human can grasp and manipulate virtual object with synthesis of hand, arm, reaching, and gazing in real-time.

9.2.3 Consistency Management of Shared Object Manipulation

This section describes the recent state of the art on consistent management of shared object manipulation. When multiple humans are collaborating with each other on a shared object, the collaborative tasks are classified into two categories: one that always require concurrency control and one that does not [29]. Table 9.1 merges and summarizes these two classification aspects.

The example of moving a heavy object as in Table 9.1 generally does not need to use ownership management mechanism if the real humans are moving the object to their destination in the same direction. However, this example may also require some special adjustment of movement when multiple humans are manipulating the object in different ways. In their proposed scenario, two humans move a heavy piano together [34]. In this case, the movement of the object is adjusted according to the positions and directions.

Hence, the conventional research on collaborative systems allows only one human to manipulate a virtual object at a time. However, an inconsistent result, which is called a conflict, can occur if multiple humans try to access and manipulate the same object without proper concurrency control. Concurrency control is a well-studied problem in the field of distributed systems [15]. The concept of concurrency control has emerged in the 3D telepresence area to adjudicate simultaneous accesses and behaviors on a shared object among multiple real humans.

Conventional research on concurrency control in 3D telepresence is generally classified into two categories: optimistic approach and pessimistic approach. The optimistic approach allows every human to access and manipulate a shared object first until its real owner is determined. The system selects the first contacted human as the real owner of the shared object. After the determination, the approach updates the real owner's result. The intermediates of others are removed and then the inputs are ignored until the real owner releases the shared object. CIAO [37] used the optimistic method with a ghost image, which visualizes translucent images of humans' concurrent tasks. However, this mechanism can surprise non-owners, because their tasks are suddenly ignored. Ionescu et al., proposed an arbitrary phase mechanism that judges conflicting tasks among participants using a special event on a totally ordered channel in a distributed virtual environment [15]. Although ordering conflicts is a good approach to reduce restrictions of non-owner behaviors, when the arbitrary phase mechanism judges incorrect orders, the participants should solve the conflicts

Table 9.1 Requirement of concurrency control for task types

Needs concurrency control	Does not need concurrency control
Result of the tasks on the attributes in the shared object affects the other attributes (Eg: Transition, Rotation, Deletion of a shared object)	Participants can perform the same cooperative task on the attribute of the shared object together (Eg: They hold a single heavy object together)

manually. In addition, this approach also needs to solve the human-surprise problem. The CollFeature system described a similar optimistic approach performed on a modeling server by transposing and sorting conflicting operation sequences according to a predefined rule [38]. However, if humans try to access and use undefined tasks or break the rule, conflicts can still occur. Although the optimistic approaches are open to access the shared object at first glance, most participants may feel surprise because their works will disappear soon.

The pessimistic approach only allows human to manipulate a shared object with a proper ownership. When the owner releases the ownership of object, then others can access the ownership in order to manipulate the shared object [11]. Since this approach is easy to manage conflicts, the approach has been widely used in various applications such as online game and collaborative computer-aided designs. Li et al., suggested a token-based pessimistic approach in collaborative CAD. An owner must have a token to access a shared object. Non-owners can only watch the owner's tasks or chat with other humans. Although the pessimistic approach provides convenient ownership management, the others are restricted until the owner releases the ownership. To this end, fine-grained approaches are proposed in the collaborative CAD area. Tang et al., proposed a feature concept that can be divided into an atom of a shared object with a hierarchical structure [38]. The fine-grained concurrency control approach of shared features showed a high degree of parallelism among concurrent tasks and multiple participants [16, 22]. However, if an owner has exclusive authority of all features or parent features in the hierarchical structure, the behavior of non-owners is still restricted by the owner.

Another consideration of pessimistic approach is to use different attributes of a shared object using High Level Architecture(HLA). HLA is a standard framework for simulation and it supports interoperability in distributed virtual environments [12]. Since the attributes are linked with different tasks individually, the HLA approach provides more opportunities for the participants. Roberts et al., showed that concurrent manipulations of different attributes of a shared object are possible and the best performance is achieved when a human in immersive environment handles a difficult part of the shared object [33].

Well-known problems of the ownership management of HLA are delay times or synchronizations. Problems occur when the ownership of different attributes is transferred among participants. In order to solve these problems, various approaches have been considered. Implementation of advanced ownership transfer was proposed to minimize the transferring time of ownership [33]. A logical time approach was proposed for synchronization of transferring ownerships for multiple participants in the distributed environment [25]. Although the approaches provide more opportunities, "surprise" may occur when the results of tasks on the attributes affect the other attributes in this approach [23]. If participants want to manipulate a shared object concurrently with different tasks such as translation, rotation, and scaling, the result of manipulation leaves the object in a different state than what was expected even though each participant has the right permission of the attribute. The task of a participant can be interrupted by the task of another participant on the same object, which causes inefficient interaction and surprise among participants.

9.3 Recent Approaches

9.3.1 Manipulation of Virtual Objects Through Multiple Device Interfaces

Direct hand manipulation provides users with intuitive and convenient methods to manipulate virtual objects in the immersive virtual environment. However, it is still difficult to generalize direct hand manipulation for the end-user because conventional research used expensive and cumbersome devices for manipulation and its corresponding haptic feedback. Since the haptic interface uses wires to control devices, it also restricts the user's body movements. In this research, we present an interface framework that synchronizes different capabilities of multiple devices for fast and accurate direct hand manipulation. In our implementation, CyberGlove II and Data-Glove 16 are used to capture hand gestures. Wireless devices are used to recognize rotation angles and to provide tactile feedback. Microsoft Kinect takes charge of tracking hands' 3D position.

Figure 9.3 shows the overall system architecture of the proposed system. The proposed system recognizes input data from three different interfaces. The Sensor Manager integrates the given inputs into unified 3D coordinates. Then the coordinates are synchronized to the same update speed in order to avoid temporal mismatch issues among the three different interfaces. As the different interfaces have update rates, missing data can occur at a low speed device when the devices are stored according to temporal order as shown in Fig. 9.4, so that the proposed system fills the mission data using simplified linear extrapolation method.

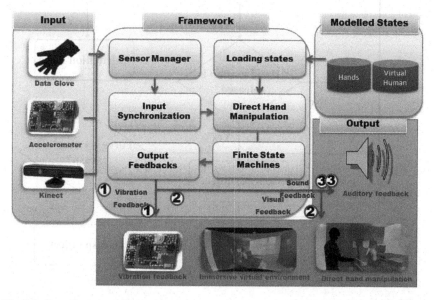

Fig. 9.3 Overall system architecture

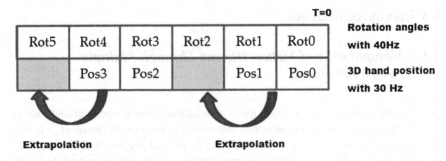

Fig. 9.4 Synchronization different data from different update rates

The unified and synchronized data is delivered to the direct hand manipulation module. As the proposed approach cannot provide haptic feedback to user, we combined modeling states of grasping with physics-based calculation.

The proposed system checks the states of grasping after tracking 3D position and angles as shown in Fig. 9.5. In case of non-grasping, the proposed system performs collision detection between hand and object. If collision occurs, the force of the

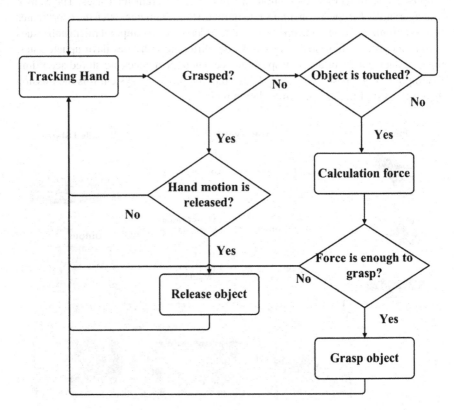

Fig. 9.5 Object grasping process

current hand is calculated to determine the grasping of an object. Determining the release of an object is slightly more difficult because the proposed system does not provide proper haptic feedback for grasping. Thus, we use a simplified method that detects release motions of hand and fingers. The original postures of hand and fingers are stored after grasping object. Release state is triggered if motions of hand and fingers are opening. During the grasping process, the proposed system provides the user proper visual, auditory, and tactile feedback.

9.3.2 Task-Based Concurrency Control for Shared Object Manipulation

As discussed in the previous section, one of the important issues in concurrency control mechanisms is to provide humans with more chances to access and manipulate shared objects with fewer conflicts in a 3D telepresence environment [18, 19]. The approach is to classify possible tasks of shared object and the model task types can be allowed to non-owners. Table 9.2 describes modeled collaborative tasks with their definitions.

A task can be regarded as one of the following five categories:

$TransformationAttributeSet = \{T, R, S\}$
$ExistenceAttributeSet = \{$ **N***, D, **C****$\}$
$GroupAttributeSet = \{F, M\}$
$SemanticDataAttributeSet = \{$**DC****$\}$
$PresentationAttributeSet = \{$**AP***, **AN*** $\}$
*: belongs to Accepted Task

Table 9.2 Collaborative tasks with relationship

Classifications	Definitions	Symbols
Transition	Transition of a shared object	T
Rotation	Rotation of a shared object	R
Scaling	Changed size of a shared object	S
Fission	One shared object is divided into two or more shared objects	F
Merge	Two or more shared objects are combined into one shared object	M
New	Add a shared object	N
Delete	Remove a shared object	D
Copy	Copy an instance of a shared object	C
Data calculation	Calculate specific conditions of a shared object (Ex: CAD simulation)	DC
Appearance	Change visual properties of a shared object	AP

**: belongs to Conditionally Accepted Task

TransformationAttributeSet is the 3D information of a shared object, and it consists of transition (T), rotation (R), and scaling (S). If a non-owner tries to execute a task in this set while an owner is also performing a task in the same set, these tasks interfere with each other because one task can be interrupted by the others.

In *ExistenceAttributeSet*, the proposed system provides several tasks relating to the existence of objects. An object can be deleted (D), added (N), or copied (C) in a public workspace. If a non-owner performs one of these tasks while an owner is manipulating a shared object with tasks in *ExistenceAttributeSet*, task D may break consistency between the owner and other users. However, the non-owner may execute a task C or N because these tasks can be done regardless of the owner's task.

In *GroupAttributeSet*, the proposed system provides tasks related to the grouping tasks. One object can be divided into two or more shared objects (F), or multiple objects can be merged into one object (M). These grouping tasks may break consistency between the owner and other users.

Tasks in *SemanticDataAttributeSet* change application-specific semantics. Task DC performs simulation and calculation of a shared object such as scientific calculation based on chemical equations for a molecular modeling system [20]. A task to handle the visual appearances of a shared object belongs to *PresentationAttributeSet*. Task AP presents several visual appearances of a shared object, such as color, texture. Task AN presents animations of a shared object.

The proposed approach can allow non-owners to access and exercise tasks of the *SemanticDataAttributeSet* and *PresentationAttributeSet* if their task does not conflict with the task of an owner of a shared object.

Based on the analysis of task classification, we created a task allowance strategy as described in Table 9.2. Tasks T, R, S, F, M, and D belong to the *Conflicting Task* type and only an owner is allowed to perform them. Tasks C, DC, AP, and AN are the *Conditionally Accepted Task* type, which means that they are allowed to be conducted by non-owners only if an owner is not working with the same task. Task N is the *Accepted Task* type because a new object can always be created regardless of its ownership.

Figure 9.6 illustrates an overall procedure of the proposed fine-grained concurrency control mechanism with personal workspace. When a user requests ownership of a shared object, the proposed system determines whether to allow this or not. If there is no owner of the shared object, the requested user will be an owner, and he/she will run any tasks of the shared object. Finally he/she can release the ownership. When the proposed system denies the request of ownership of the shared object, the user can request one of the tasks of the shared object. The requested task is analyzed and classified into one of the following four task types: *Conflicting Task*, *Conditionally Accepted Task*, *Accepted Task*, and *Personal Workspace Task*. If the requested task conflicts with the task of the owner, it determines the requested task as a *Conflicting Task* and denies the request. If the requested task is not identical to the owner's task and does not conflict with it, the system regards the requested task as a *Conditionally Accepted Task*. However, the requester's task can be canceled if the owner finishes the current task and starts a new task that happens to be the same

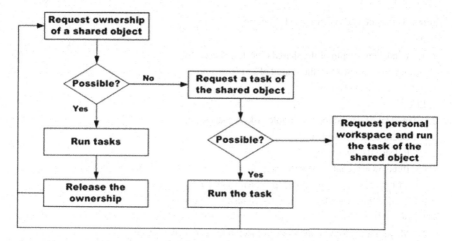

Fig. 9.6 Task-based concurrency control

as the requester's task. In this case, the requester's task is moved to his personal workspace and can be continued independently. If the requested task never affects the owner's task, it should be an *Accepted Task*. This task type is always allowed to be performed by non-owners. Finally, if the requester user wants to do a task privately, the requested task is defined as a Personal Workspace Task. Receiving a *Personal Workspace Task*, the system creates a personal workspace for the requester and duplicates the current state of the target object into the new workspace. Tasks in the personal workspace are isolated from the public workspace and are not shared by other users. The overall process of the proposed system is described in pseudo codes in Table 9.3. With the proposed concurrency control mechanism, we can release the behavior restrictions of non-owners by partially allowing the requested tasks.

The proposed concurrency control mechanism was applied to a collaborative game level design system [21]. Game level design is a collaborative work to create a virtual game world including maps, agents, monsters, objects, players, and events based on predefined game scenarios. General game design is executed by various participants including a game planner, an artist, a level designer, an asset designer, and so on. As different participants can create, modify, assemble, and simulate various versions of maps, buildings, monsters, and other objects it is difficult to maintain their consistencies among multiple participants.

9.4 Future Avenues

The proposed combination method for grasping a virtual object can be widely used in the near future. If robust computer vision-based hand tracking device and algorithms replace data gloves, usability of grasping may be increased. The proposed

Table 9.3 Pseudo code of proposed concurrency control

Requester
1. Try to take ownership of the shared object; if successful
1.1. Manipulate all tasks of the shared object
1.2. Release the ownership
2. Else
2.1. Try to take ownership of desirable task; if successful
2.1.1. Operate the allowed task
2.1.2. Release the ownership
2.1.3. If the owner wants to run the same task:
2.1.3.1. Copy current status into the personal workspace
2.1.3.2. Yield the ownership of the allowed task to the owner
2.2. Else
2.2.1. Manipulate a copy of the shared object in the personal workspace

Server
3. Receive a request of ownership
3.1. Try to give an ownership of the shared object to the requester
3.2. Reject if unsuccessful
4. Release an ownership
4.1. Try to give an ownership of the shared object to the requester
4.2. Reject if unsuccessful
5. Receive a request of a specific task
5.1. If the owner requests, allow any tasks
5.2. Else
5.3.1. If the task belongs to the conflicting task, reject
5.3.2. If the task belongs to the accepted task, accept
5.3.3. If the task belongs to the conditionally accepted task
5.3.3.1. If no one use the task, allow
5.3.3.2. Reject if the owner is using the requested task

approach will be adapted to support a combination of the new state of the art. The introduced synthesizing motions of a virtual human can be easily applied to various immersive virtual reality applications such as medical simulator and training system. The proposed concurrency control mechanism can be applied to shared manipulation between real and virtual humans. We may model specific sharing tasks between real and virtual humans on the task classification as described in Table 9.3. After discovering indirect relationships with the classified tasks, new concurrency control mechanisms can be modeled. With our approach, non-owners can be determined as a real human or virtual human from the given scenarios. While main owner is performing his own manipulation work, the non-owners can access a shared object and perform some tasks to support the owner's main task without conflicts or task surprises.

9.5 Conclusion

In order to perform virtual object manipulation between real and virtual humans, it is necessary take into account three different research domains: virtual object manipulation by real human, virtual object manipulation by virtual human, and consistency management mechanism of shared object manipulation. Although this requires a complicated process to achieve the goal, it will result in meaningful applications in the 3D telepresence environment. Below, we describe the possible approaches to undertake in order to perform virtual object manipulations in the 3D telepresence environment.

1. Combination of multiple devices for direct hand manipulation by real human.
2. Example-based motion synthesis for object manipulation by virtual human.
3. Task-based concurrency control for shared object manipulation.

The proposed combination of multiple devices for grasping virtual object can be generalized for general users without haptic feedback. Research on realistic or pseudo haptic feedback with such simple combination can be undertaken in the future work. The introduced example-based motion synthesis for object manipulation of virtual human can be applied to interactive applications. Finally, we proposed concurrency control mechanism for shared object manipulation between real and virtual humans. Since dynamic changes can occur during the shared object manipulation, we need to model collaborative tasks with proper concurrency control strategies. Although the proposed and introduced research ideas are not integrated together yet, research is and will integrate these research areas into one unified platform in the coming years. The proposed ideas also can be applied to various virtual reality applications in the interactive 3D telepresence environment.

References

1. Ben Amor H, Heumer G, Jung B, Vitzthum A (2008) Grasp synthesis from low-dimensional probabilistic grasp models. Comput Animation Virtual Worlds 19(3–4):445–454
2. Borst CW, Indugula AP (2005) Realistic virtual grasping. In: Proceedings of virtual reality 2005, VR 2005. IEEE, pp 91–98
3. Bowman DA, Hodges LF (1997) An evaluation of techniques for grabbing and manipulating remote objects in immersive virtual environments. In: Proceedings of the 1997 symposium on interactive 3D graphics. ACM, pp 35–ff
4. Conner BD, Snibbe SS, Herndon KP, Robbins DC, Zeleznik RC, Dam AV (1992) Three-dimensional widgets. In: Proceedings of the 1992 symposium on interactive 3D graphics. ACM, pp 183–188
5. ElKoura G, Singh K (2003) Handrix: animating the human hand. In: Proceedings of the 2003 ACM SIGGRAPH/Eurographics symposium on computer animation. Eurographics Association, pp 110–119
6. Feng AW, Xu Y, Shapiro A (2012) An example-based motion synthesis technique for locomotion and object manipulation. In: Proceedings of the ACM SIGGRAPH symposium on interactive 3D graphics and games. ACM, pp 95–102

7. Frees S, Kessler GD (2005) Precise and rapid interaction through scaled manipulation in immersive virtual environments. In: Proceedings of virtual reality 2005, VR 2005. IEEE, pp 99–106
8. Fröhlich B, Plate J (2000) The cubic mouse: a new device for three-dimensional input. In: Proceedings of the SIGCHI conference on human factors in computing systems. ACM, pp 526–531
9. Gallo L, Ciampi M (2009) Wii remote-enhanced hand-computer interaction for 3D medical image analysis. In: 2009 international conference on the current trends in information technology (CTIT). IEEE, pp 1–6
10. Gan L, Shark L-K, Hall G, Zeshan U (2012) Immersive manipulation of virtual objects through glove-based hand gesture interaction. Virtual Reality 16(3):243–252
11. Hagsand O (1996) Interactive multiuser ves in the dive system. IEEE MultiMedia 3(1):30–39
12. High level architecture (hla)—object model template (omt) specification
13. Hilliges O, Kim D, Izadi S, Weiss M, Wilson A (2012) Holodesk: direct 3D interactions with a situated see-through display. In: Proceedings of the SIGCHI conference on human factors in computing systems. ACM, pp 2421–2430
14. Huang Y, Kallmann M (2010) Motion parameterization with inverse blending. In: Motion in games. Springer, pp 242–253
15. Ionescu M, Marsic I (2003) Tree-based concurrency control in distributed groupware. Comput Support Coop Work 12(3):329–350
16. Kallmann M, Aubel A, Abaci T, Thalmann D (2003) Planning collision-free reaching motions for interactive object manipulation and grasping. In: Computer graphics forum, vol 22. Wiley Online Library, pp 313–322
17. Kyota F, Saito S (2012) Fast grasp synthesis for various shaped objects. In: Computer graphics forum, vol 31. Wiley Online Library, pp 765–774
18. Lee J (2012) Consistency management for synchronous and asynchronous collaborative design systems. PhD thesis, Konkuk University
19. Lee J, Lim M, Kim HS, Kim J-I (2012) Supporting fine-grained concurrent tasks and personal workspaces for a hybrid concurrency control mechanism in a networked virtual environment. Presence: Teleoperators Virtual Environ 21(4):452–469
20. Lee J, Kang L-W, Kim HS, Kim J-I (2011) Co-coot: a real-time collaborative tool for biomolecular modeling and visualization. In: 2011 IEEE international symposium on VR innovation (ISVRI). IEEE, pp 281–286
21. Lee J, Kim J-I, Lim M, Kim HS, Park SJ, Whitehead J (2014) Collaborative editing mechanisms based on concurrency control for efficient level design of a game map. Information Journal
22. Li M, Gao S, Fuh JYH, Zhang YF (2008) Replicated concurrency control for collaborative feature modelling: a fine granular approach. Comput Ind 59(9):873–881
23. Linebarger J, Kessler G (2004) Concurrency control mechanisms for closely coupled collaboration in multithreaded peer-to-peer virtual environments. Presence 13(3):296–314
24. Lv P, Zhang M, Mingliang X, Li H, Zhu P, Pan Z (2011) Biomechanics-based reaching optimization. Vis Comput 27(6–8):613–621
25. Minson R, Theodoropoulos GK (2008) Distributing repast agent-based simulations with HLA. Concurrency Comput Practice Experience 20(10):1225–1256
26. Osawa N (2006) Automatic adjustments for efficient and precise positioning and release of virtual objects. In: Proceedings of the 2006 ACM international conference on virtual reality continuum and its applications. ACM, pp 121–128
27. Otsuki M, Oshita T, Kimura A, Shibata F, Tamura H (2013) Touch and detach: ungrouping and observation methods for complex virtual objects using an elastic metaphor. In: 2013 IEEE symposium on 3D user interfaces (3DUI). IEEE, pp 99–106
28. Ott R, Vexo F, Thalmann D (2010) Two-handed haptic manipulation for cad and vr applications. Comput Aided Des Appl 7(1):125–138
29. Ott R, De Perrot V, Thalmann D, Vexo F (2007) Mhaptic: a haptic manipulation library for generic virtual environments. In: International conference on cyberworlds, 2007 (CW'07). IEEE, pp 338–345

30. Park S, Lee J, Kim J-I (2005) A molecular modeling system based on dynamic gestures. In: Computational science and its applications–ICCSA 2005. Springer, pp 886–895
31. Poupyrev I, Billinghurst M, Weghorst S, Ichikawa T (1996) The go-go interaction technique: non-linear mapping for direct manipulation in vr. In: Proceedings of the 9th annual ACM symposium on user interface software and technology. ACM, pp 79–80
32. Rijpkema H, Girard M (1991) Computer animation of knowledge-based human grasping. In: ACM Siggraph Computer Graphics, vol 25. ACM, pp 339–348
33. Roberts D, Wolff R, Otto O, Steed A (2003) Constructing a gazebo: supporting teamwork in a tightly coupled, distributed task in virtual reality. Presence: Teleoperators Virtual Environ 12(6):644–657
34. Ruddle RA, Savage JCD, Jones DM (2002) Symmetric and asymmetric action integration during cooperative object manipulation in virtual environments. ACM Trans Comput Hum Inter 9(4):285–308
35. Sanso RM, Thalmann D (1994) A hand control and automatic grasping system for synthetic actors. In: Computer Graphics Forum, vol 13. Wiley Online Library, pp 167–177
36. Steed A, Oliveira MF (2009) Networked graphics: building networked games and virtual environments. Elsevier
37. Sung UJ, Yang J-H, Wohn K-Y (1999) Concurrency control in ciao. In: Proceedings of IEEE virtual reality. IEEE, pp 22–28
38. Tang M, Chou S-C, Dong J-X (2004) Collaborative virtual environment for feature based modeling. In: Proceedings of the 2004 ACM SIGGRAPH international conference on virtual reality continuum and its applications in industry. ACM, pp 120–126
39. Thalmann NM, Thalmann D (1991) 3D devices and virtual reality in human animation. In: Proceedings of 2nd eurographics workshop on animation and simulation number VRLAB-CONF-2007-124. Wien
40. Zhai S, Buxton W, Milgram P (1994) The silk cursor: investigating transparency for 3D target acquisition. In: Proceedings of the SIGCHI conference on human factors in computing systems. ACM, pp 459–464
41. Zhao W, Chai J, Xu Y-Q (2012) Combining marker-based mocap and rgb-d camera for acquiring high-fidelity hand motion data. In: Proceedings of the ACM SIGGRAPH/Eurographics symposium on computer animation. Eurographics Association, pp 33–42

Part III
Modelling Human Behaviours

Chapter 10
Modeling Personality, Mood, and Emotions

Juzheng Zhang, Jianmin Zheng and Nadia Magnenat-Thalmann

Abstract This chapter considers affect dynamics which simulates the relation among the emotions, mood, and personality and updates emotional states for long-term human-agent interactions. Affect dynamics is an important component of the affective system which also contains affect detection, affect appraisal, and affect response and makes indispensable contributions to the personification, believability, and autonomy of autonomous virtual humans (AVH). We first examine basic psychological concepts and computational models for affect dynamics. Then, we present a psychologically plausible affect dynamics algorithm in which the personality influences the updating of emotional states during the whole interactions, rather than just at the beginning as in many previous works. This makes affect dynamics characterized by the personality, which is shown to be important for long-term interactions.

10.1 Introduction

Autonomous virtual humans (AVH) are intelligent virtual characters that make humanlike decisions automatically based on their perceptions of current environmental information, their current emotional states as a result of affective stimuli, and their memory of past experience. The affective system, which appraises, updates, and selects emotional states enables the virtual characters to think, express, and communicate with the user emotionally. The emotional states of the virtual characters are usually modeled in three hierarchies: emotions, mood, and personality, from the superficial surface to the deep nature. The affective system contains four

J. Zhang (✉) · J. Zheng · N. Magnenat-Thalmann
BeingThere Centre, Nanyang Technological University, Singapore, Singapore
e-mail: JZHANG19@e.ntu.edu.sg

J. Zheng
e-mail: ASJMZheng@ntu.edu.sg

N. Magnenat-Thalmann
e-mail: nadiathalmann@ntu.edu.sg

© Springer International Publishing Switzerland 2016
N. Magnenat-Thalmann et al. (eds.), *Context Aware Human-Robot and Human-Agent Interaction*, Human–Computer Interaction Series,
DOI 10.1007/978-3-319-19947-4_10

general components: affect detection, affect appraisal, affect dynamics, and affect response [9, 15, 26]. Both affect appraisal and affect detection deal with the input of affects; affect dynamics is responsible for the changes of affects in a long period of time, and affect response accounts for the output of affect. In particular, affect detection transfers physical, machine-detectable information from video [10, 47] or audio [13, 32] sensors to the abstract concepts in cognition. For multimodal systems, well-designed fusion techniques are needed to optimize the validity, reasonability, and robustness of the affect detection [44]. Then detected information is appraised to generate appropriate emotions with intensities [17, 30, 40, 45]. The appraised emotions update the affective states under the influence of current emotional context iteratively [5, 18, 53]. Finally, the artificial emotional intelligence rules enable the system to make appropriate responses to the user [15, 36, 43].

There are generally two kinds of behaviors of AVH: instant behaviors and longer term behaviors. Instant behaviors such as facial expressions or gestures are usually driven by emotions that are short-lived affects of AVH. Longer term behaviors such as dialogue are usually influenced by the mood and personality, which are longer lived affects of AVH [12]. Consequently, there is a fundamental difference between the affective characters focusing on problem solving and the affective characters focusing on human–agent interactions. The former characters aim at improving the behaviors by learning from emotional events as well as generating instant emotional behaviors such as facial expressions or emotional words. Hence, in this case emotions are important as they can drive instant behaviors and serve as a form of utility to improve agents' behaviors. As a result, a lot of attention has been paid to affect appraisal [15, 46]. The latter characters aim at interacting with the user in an autonomous and believable way. The behaviors of the virtual companion should change with the dynamics of affects in a long period of time. Hence, mood and personality play an important role because they influence the longer term behaviors, and affect dynamics is the main focus of these applications [18, 53].

In this chapter, we consider affect dynamics, which simulates the changes of emotional states in long-term interactions. It takes the result of emotion appraisal as input and sends the updated dominant emotion and mood as output to affect the response component. The relation among emotions, mood, and personality is the main focus of affect dynamics. In order to make the behaviors of AVH more believable in long-term interactions, there is a need to have psychologically plausible computational models and tractable algorithms for affect dynamics. We first review some basic psychological concepts and popular computational models of affect dynamics. Then we present a psychologically plausible affect dynamics algorithm in which the personality influences the updating of emotional states during the whole interactions, rather than just at the beginning. The development of the algorithm is motivated by the observations and facts that an individual usually has his own characteristics of behaviors and personality determines the frequently happened mood that reflects the affective tendency [8]. Thus, the algorithm can generate affect the dynamics that better reflects the personality of AVH.

10.2 State of the Art

The study of characteristics and rules of human affects has a long history in psychology. Many computational affect models are inspired by psychology. In this section we first introduce the psychological foundation of affect dynamics, including the definitions and principles of human emotions, moods, and personalities and the dimensional model that integrates these human affects. Then we review computational models for affect dynamics, which include deterministic models and nondeterministic models. We also show some evaluation methods for affect dynamics.

10.2.1 Psychological Foundation

Human affects are classified into emotions, mood, and personality. The emotions and mood are described by emotional states that change from time to time, and the personality is described by an emotional trait that represents the innate characteristics of the affect.

10.2.1.1 Emotion

Emotions can be defined as the subjective response of people to the confronted events during their interactions with the environment. Based on the work of [31] in neuropsychology, the thalamus, the limbic system, and the cortex are three important regions related to emotions. The thalamus collects and processes all the perception information from the external environment. The information is sent to the cortex and the limbic system for further processing. The limbic system generates corresponding emotions by analyzing the relationship of the needs and goals. The generated emotion both prepares the body for physiological response and biases cognitive processes such as attention in the cortex.

The event appraisal is a process to appraise the stimuli entering into the system and produce the resulting emotions with intensities. The advent of the OCC model [40], which defines emotions simply as classes of emotion eliciting conditions, throws light on establishing a cognitive event appraisal system in computer agents. The OCC model specifies 22 emotion types according to the positive or negative reactions to the three emotional aspects: events, actions, and objects based on the goals (desired states of the world), standards (ideas about how people should act) and preferences (likes and dislikes) of the agents. Later, Ortony simplifies the 22 distinct emotion types to 6 positive emotions and 6 negative emotions [39]. EMA [26] is a canonical example of affect appraisal using the OCC model that provides a general computational framework for emotional appraisal and coping for intelligent agents.

One of the most fundamental effects of emotion is to capture attention. Emotions that are generated by the appraisal of an event, based on the needs and goals of people, drive people to focus on the event. The degree of attention and the magnitude of arousal of the emotions are determined by the importance of the event [11]. Attention can further be influenced through a secondary process of emotion regulation. Once a triggered emotion is appraised as undesirable by higher cognitive processes, humans tend to shift the attention away from the appraised event [21]. Besides the effects on attention, emotions also influence the human memory. Thorson and Friestad [50] propose that stimuli with higher emotional intensity should be encoded in the episodic memory better. Moreover, the undesirable events are more intensively remembered than the desirable events [37]. What is more, emotions enhance the effect of remembering control content while reducing the performance of remembering background details [24].

There are three fundamental characteristics of emotions. First, emotions are object-directed. They are usually related to particular objects or situations [16]. Second, emotions are relatively short-lived. Third, emotions prepare people for instant actions, such as facial expressions [12].

10.2.1.2 Mood

Mood reflects a general, diffuse, and global emotional state over a period of time. Different from emotions, mood has no direct relation to objects or events, but is indirectly influenced by them. For example, "A person can be sad about something (an emotion) or generally depressed (a mood)" [8]. On the other hand, mood is a longer-lived emotional state and influences people on their cognitive strategies and processing [12]. Mood filters emotions in the affect appraisal. People tend to pay attention to mood-congruent information [8]. The relation between mood and emotions is bidirectional. Mood tends to strengthen those emotions that align well with mood; emotions, on the other hand, often cause or contribute to mood [8].

In the previous research on virtual humans, emotions seemed to get more attention. This may be because emotions are directly connected to some visual effects. Mood is in a supporting role for emotions by influencing the event appraisal process. By carefully studying the literature on psychology and neuroscience, we argue that the role of the mood should be at least no less important than that of emotions to build the virtual human. As mentioned above, emotions are short-lived affects that bias instant behaviors such as facial expressions, the rate and pitch of speech, etc., while mood is a longer-lived and stable affect that biases the strategy of behaviors. Below, we list some impacts of moods on attention, cognition, behavior, and memory, which are useful for the future development of the autonomous virtual human.

Rule 1 *Mood-congruent information is one of the important factors that determine people's attention.*

Rule 2 *Mood influences people's cognitive and behavior strategies.*

A human in a positive mood tends to be altruistic to an appropriate degree. According to [25], a positive mood decreases the possibility of making unreasonable choices with high risk, which helps to preserve the positive mood. Cognitive strategies such as style information processing are also influenced by mood. Positive affect biases broader/top-down processing, while negative affect biases narrower/bottom-up processing [4].

Rule 3 *Mood decreases the inconsistency of emotion-related behaviors.*

Mood, as emotional background, can modulate short-lived behaviors related to emotions. This kind of modulation largely reduces behavior discrepancy elicited by the rapid change of emotions.

Rule 4 *Memory encoding is influenced by mood-congruency effect.*

Mood congruence is a phenomenon that emotional material is remembered more reliably in the mood that matches the emotional contents of the memories [14]. The strength of the activities associated with the emotional contexts at encoding correlates with the probability of correct recall [48]. Information consistent with mood is more likely to be noticed and connected to other facts about the mood [22].

Rule 5 *Memory retrieval is influenced by mood-dependence effect.*

Mood dependence [14] is the phenomenon that memories are more reliably recalled given that the current mood is similar to the mood when the memories are encoded. An analogy is that our feelings are like a magnet that selects iron filings from a heap of dust [7].

10.2.1.3 Personality

Personality is defined as the predisposition of affects that determines the tendency of the moods [8]. Currently, one popular personality model is the "Big Five" theory or "Five Factor Model" (FFM) [20]. Based on the factor analytic studies using rating scales, self-reports, or peer-reports, five universal dimensions of personality are proposed: Extroversion, Agreeableness, Neuroticism, Openness, and Conscientiousness. The five traits of personality are shown in Table 10.1.

Temperament is "the characteristic phenomena of an individual's emotional nature" [2]. Temperament and personality are related and similar concepts. Significant similarities have been found between temperamental dispositions and the Big Five trait factors [1, 34]. Personality is believed to be developed on the basis of temperament. In the affective system for the virtual human, temperament and personality are regarded as the same.

Table 10.1 The dimensions of FFM model

Personality dimension	Descriptive words
Openness (O)	Imaginative, intelligent, and creative
Conscientiousness (C)	Responsible, reliable, and tidy
Extroversion (E)	Outgoing, sociable, and assertive
Agreeableness (A)	Trustworthy, kind, and cooperative
Neuroticism (N)	Anxious, nervous, and depressive

10.2.1.4 Dimensional Model

The PA (pleasure-arousal) space [29] and PAD (pleasure-arousal-dominance) space [34] are two-dimensional models to represent emotional states and traits. The PA space differentiates emotions by pleasure (valence) and arousal. The pleasure\unpleasure dimension represents the valence of affects and the arousal\calm dimension represents the physical excitedness of affects. Besides these two dimensions, the PAD space also considers an additional dominance\submission dimension that represents the initiative of affects. For example, "anger" and "fear" are both negative and intensive emotions. The difference between these two emotions is that "anger" is a dominant emotion that leads to initiative actions such as fighting, while "fear" is a submissive emotion that leads to passive actions such as fleeing.

The PAD space integrates emotions, mood, and personality in the same space (Fig. 10.1). Geometrically, the PAD space can be modeled as a 3D box, where each

Fig. 10.1 The relationship of the affects and the PAD space

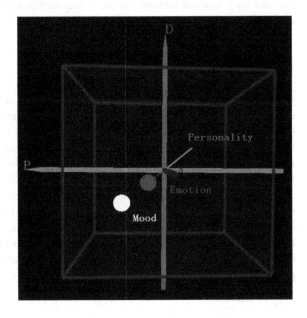

dimension is independent of each other and is between -1 and 1. The three orthogonal axes separate the whole space into eight octants, each of which corresponds to a general mood type [34] (see Table 10.2). An emotion can be represented as a moving point in the PAD space starting from the origin. Because a point can be viewed as a vector from the origin to the point itself, the length of the vector represents the intensity of the emotion and the direction of the vector represents the quality (type) of the emotion [42]. The mappings from the emotions to the PAD space are provided by [34] and complemented by [18] (see Table 10.3). The mood is also represented as a moving point in the PAD space. The big five personality traits are mapped into the PAD space by the mapping matrix given in Table 10.4 [34].

Table 10.2 Mehrabian mood types

PAD	Mood types	PAD	Mood types
P+, A+, D+	Exuberant	P+, A−, D+	Relaxed
P−, A−, D−	Bored	P−, A+, D−	Anxious
P+, A+, D−	Dependent	P+, A−, D−	Docile
P−, A−, D+	Disdainful	P−, A+, D+	Hostile

Table 10.3 Mappings from the 24 emotions to the PAD space

Emotion	P	A	D	Emotion	P	A	D
Admiration	0.5	0.3	−0.2	Hate	−0.6	0.6	0.3
Anger	−0.51	0.59	0.25	Hope	0.2	0.2	−0.1
Disliking	−0.4	0.2	0.1	Joy	0.4	0.2	0.1
Disappointment	−0.3	0.1	−0.4	Liking	0.40	0.16	−0.24
Distress	−0.4	−0.2	0.5	Love	0.3	0.1	0.2
Fear	−0.64	0.60	−0.43	Pity	−0.4	−0.2	−0.5
Fears-confirmed	−0.5	−0.3	−0.7	Pride	0.4	0.3	0.3
Gloating	0.3	−0.3	−0.1	Relief	0.2	−0.3	0.4
Gratification	0.6	0.5	0.4	Remorse	−0.3	0.1	−0.6
Gratitude	0.4	0.2	−0.3	Reproach	−0.3	−0.1	0.4
Happy for	0.4	0.2	0.2	Resentment	−0.2	−0.3	−0.2
Satisfaction	0.3	−0.2	0.4	Shame	−0.3	0.1	−0.6

Table 10.4 Mapping from the FFM to the PAD pace

Dimension	O	C	E	A	N
Pleasure	0	0	0.21	0.59	0.19
Arousal	0.15	0	0	0.30	−0.57
Dominance	0.25	0.17	0.60	−0.32	0

10.2.2 Computational Models

Inspired by psychological theories, researchers in human–agent interaction have developed many computational models for affect dynamics. Based on the characteristics of the models, we categorize the models into deterministic and nondeterministic models. Deterministic models simulate the general principles of human affect dynamics and give deterministic computational formula for the changes in emotional states. Nondeterministic models consider fuzzy states and rules to simulate unpredictable or random emotional changes. In general, while nondeterministic models simulate better the randomness of human affects, deterministic models are more concise and controllable to show the intention of the designers.

10.2.2.1 Deterministic Models

In event appraisal, the OCC model considers three aspects of events: consequence, action, and object from the viewpoint of both the agent itself and other agents or users. Moreover, the events are appraised in the past, current, or future development stages. Given one event as input, the OCC model outputs emotions.

Arjan et al. [5] present a basic framework for the simulation of emotions, mood, and personality. The Big Five Model of personality and the OCC emotion structure are used to implement the interaction and updating process of human affects.

Becker et al. [6] build a 3D space with the valence of emotion, the valence of mood, and boredom as three dimensions. Two springs are simulated for the first two dimensions to generate a reset force when the reference point is away from the origin. The coefficients of the two springs are set to be the personality. The changing rate of the mood valence is influenced by the emotion valence. Boredom serves as the result of absence of stimuli. In each time step, the reference point is mapped to the PAD space using a certain formula to determine the category of emotions, which depends on the emotion valence, mood valence, and personality. However, this method has no support from psychology theories. The mass-spring model is not very suitable to model the emotional state since with the model the reference point often oscillates and the motion cannot stop. Thus, the "damp" of the mass-spring model needs to be defined.

A well-known affect dynamics model is "A Layered Model of Affect" (ALMA) that combines the emotions, mood, and personality in the PAD space [18]. A pull and push method is proposed to simulate smooth and steady changes in mood. A virtual emotion center (VEC) is defined as the average of all active emotions. The strength of the emotion is determined by the length of VEC. If the mood position is between the origin of the PAD space and VEC, VEC attracts the mood; if the mood position is beyond VEC, the mood is pushed away from VEC. The mood starts from and finally decays to the personality position.

Zerrin et al. [53] design a long-term interaction by taking into account the human–agent relation including friendliness and dominance dimensions. Similar to the

ALMA model, the personality point in the PAD space is taken as the default mood position. The mood and emotions are then iteratively updated. The combination of the emotion engine with episodic memory enables emotions to be generated with consideration of the past interaction history.

10.2.2.2 Nondeterministic Models

Many nondeterministic approaches use fuzzy models. Some examples are given below.

Orozco et al. [38] propose a fuzzy model to update the affective states of emotions, mood, and personality. The personality is modeled as a ten-dimensional fuzzy vector, where each dimension represents a scale of the Minnesota Multiphasic Personality Inventory [49]. The emotion or mood is modeled as a fuzzy vector with each possible state as a dimension. The updating process involves several steps. First, the emotion is updated by personality, mood history, and the input event using predefined fuzzy rules. Then the mood is updated by personality, emotion history, and the input event. Finally, the emotion and mood are regulated by personality and the input event.

Van der Heide and Trivino [51] design a fuzzy finite state machine (FFSM) to simulate the temporal changes in emotional states. The Plutchik circumflex model [41] is used to specify emotions by labels that are differentiated by the activation (or arousal) and evaluation (or pleasure) values. By fuzzifying the two variables with linguistic labels (negative, zero, positive), the emotions are divided into nine fuzzy states. The inputs to the system are two environmental factors: temperature and luminosity. The temperature influences the evaluation and the luminosity influences the activation. By the Plutchik model, the inputs can be transferred into one of the fuzzy states with certain intensity. FFSM functions memorize the current fuzzy states. By designing sets of Takagi-Sugeno-Kang (TSK) fuzzy rules, the current fuzzy states are updated by the input fuzzy state and transferred into the other fuzzy states. The resulting evaluation and activation value is obtained by defuzzing the states in FFSM. Finally, the labels of the resulting emotions are obtained by the Plutchik model. The emotional states change with time as the above process iterates. The model is evaluated by designing three sets of fuzzy rules that represent the "reactive," "stable," and "active" personalities, respectively. Given a two-day record of temperature and luminosity, the trace of emotional state dynamics under the three personalities are compared. There are two flaws in this model: (1) The design of the set of fuzzy rules to simulate certain personality seems nonintuitive and time-consuming; (2) although we suppose each fuzzy rule to be reasonable, it is difficult to guarantee that the combination of these fuzzy rules leads to reasonable affect dynamics.

Karimi and Kangavari [27] design a fuzzy model to simulate the influence of anxiety on the action selection of social agents. Anxiety, as an aspect of the neuroticism dimension of the FFM personality, is modulated by the goal-setting mechanism and environmental stress. Anxiety and the ACT-R cognitive model [3] are combined to select an appropriate action for the current goal and environment. The model is validated by comparing with the "Inverted U" relationship between the stress and the performance proposed by psychology [52], and by analyzing the performance of a soccer simulation with or without the personality model.

Besides fuzzy models, Bayesian belief networks (BBN) are also used to simulate the uncertainty of human behaviors. Kshirsagar [28] proposes a layered personality model that adopts the "Big Five" model for personality simulation and considers the mood layer in addition. The personality and mood are modeled in a discrete form. The personality, current mood, changing threshold, interaction history, and the probabilities of response emotions produced by the OCC model determine mood transition. The changes in emotions are determined by the response emotions, current mood, and personality. A drawback of this approach is the inconvenience of setting the transition probabilities.

10.2.3 Evaluation

The evaluation of affect dynamics models is an important but nontrivial task. While there is lack of comprehensive evaluation mechanisms or benchmark for affect dynamics, some practices have been used to evaluate new models or algorithms. Roughly, they can be classified into three categories:

- **Component testing**: Experiments are designed to test emotions, mood, or personality in some responses, which are compared with psychology theories or commonsense of human affects.
- **Overall testing**: Virtual humans or agents are equipped with the proposed models. Dialogue scenarios between the virtual human/agents and users are designed. The overall responses of the virtual characters/agents are judged to evaluate the effectiveness of the affect dynamics model.
- **User study**: User study is more formal than the first two methods. Experiments are designed and people are invited to observe the experiments. Then participants are required to answer a carefully designed questionnaire. The answers of the participants are analyzed using statistical methods to evaluate the performance of the proposed models or algorithms.

10.2.3.1 Component Testing

Guoliang et al. [23] validate their affect dynamics model by observing the changes in emotions and mood under external stimuli in several examples. The changes are visualized using graph, based on which the performance against the psychological rules for human affects is analyzed. For example, given an input emotion "anger," an introvert has longer emotion duration, lower emotion intensity peak, and lower mood decay rate than an extrovert.

Liu [33] designs an example in which a hungry virtual character finds bread on a table. He tests the personality of the virtual character based on his facial expression as the response.

Orozco et al. [38] evaluate their fuzzy model by an example that compares the affect dynamics of a hysteric virtual human for a very negative event and that of a depressive virtual human for a negative event.

10.2.3.2 Overall Testing

Becker et al. [6] design human–agent interaction scenarios for evaluation. A virtual human is offended by the user using insulting words again and again. The emotion of the virtual human changes from "anger" to "annoyance" and the bad mood becomes increasingly intensive, which results in bad words and an angry face. If the user stops talking, the mood of the virtual human will return to calmness. The restoring time can be shortened or extended when the user compliments or insults him.

Kshirsagar [28] conducts interactions with the Alice chatbot that is equipped with the proposed multilayer personality model. The conversation is simulated between a manager and a virtual assistant whose personality is either agreeable or neurotic. The responsive words are selected by the personality and the mood-processing modules. The results show that the agreeable virtual assistant tends to be more pleasant and easier to keep pleasant than the neurotic one.

10.2.3.3 User Study

Gebhard and Kipp [19] employ user study to evaluate the plausibility of the emotions and mood generated by the ALMA model. Given the descriptions of conversational situations, participants are required to evaluate the affect plausibility for 24 types of emotions and 8 types of mood using a discrete ranking scale. Results show that the type of emotions is significantly more plausible than the type of mood. Most emotions and moods are significantly plausible above the neutral level, except for the emotion "fear" and "hate" as well as the mood "dependent" and "anxious."

10.3 A Psychologically Plausible Affect Dynamics Algorithm

This section presents a psychologically plausible affect dynamics algorithm for human–agent interactions [54]. The algorithm considers the relation among emotions, mood, and personality. The basic idea is to let personality influence the tendency of the mood, which is achieved by biasing the effects of personality-consistent emotions on the mood. As a result, the user can identify the personality of virtual humans from the changes in their affective behaviors during the interactions. This makes virtual humans more believable.

10.3.1 Definitions and Assumptions

Here we introduce some concepts and assumptions which have grounds in psychology. These concepts and assumptions guide the development of the psychologically plausible affect dynamics algorithm.

Definition 1 An emotion or mood is called **active** if its intensity is above the threshold.

Definition 2 An emotion is called **mood-consistent** if it has positive correlation with the mood. In contrast, an emotion is called **mood-inconsistent** if it has negative correlation with the mood.

Definition 3 An emotion is called **personality-consistent** if it has positive correlation with the personality. In contrast, an emotion is called **personality-inconsistent** if it has negative correlation with personality.

Definition 4 The effect that mood (or personality) biases mood-consistent (or personality-consistent) emotions in the appraisal process is called **mood-biasing** (or **personality-biasing**) effect.

While the concepts **"active emotion"** and **"mood-biasing"** or **"personality-biasing"** in Definitions 1 and 4 have already been considered in previous work [18, 35, 53], the concepts **"personality-consistent"** and **"mood-consistent"** in Definitions 3 and 2 are relatively new.

Assumption 1 (*Biasing effect to emotion*) The mood and personality bias the intensities of emotions in the appraisal process by enhancing the effect of mood-consistent or personality-consistent emotions while decreasing the effect of mood-inconsistent or personality-inconsistent emotions.

As mood and personality are background affective filters in the process of appraisal and bias emotions [8], we add the mood-biasing effect and personality-biasing effects to the process of emotion appraisal, similar to previous models [18, 35, 53].

Assumption 2 (*Personality consistency effect to emotions*) Personality-consistent emotions have more contributions to mood dynamics than to personality-inconsistent ones.

This hypothesis is supported by the psychological fact that personality determines the frequency of the mood, and emotions cause or contribute to the mood [8]. It is also suggested in [5] that the strength of emotions should be influenced by the personality of the virtual human.

Assumption 3 (*Mood-based emotion filtering*) If there are two or more active emotions, the dominant emotion is determined by their correlations with the current mood.

If there are two or more active emotions, a dominant emotion needs to be selected. The emotion that has the closest correlation with the current mood is chosen because a human tends to focus on mood-consistent emotions and neglect mood-inconsistent emotions [7].

10.3.2 Overview of the Algorithm

The affective dynamic algorithm simulates the change in emotional states during human–agent interaction. The process of affect dynamics is as follows. At the beginning, the variables and parameters in the system are initialized. Then in each iteration, the algorithm checks whether any new event is appraised. If yes, the intensities of the generated emotions are updated, followed by the updating of the velocity and the position of the mood. Active emotions, if any, decay with time. The mood decays if there is no active emotion. If there are multiple active emotions, a dominant emotion is selected. Finally, the system sends the dominant emotion and the current mood to the working memory. Figure 10.2 shows the workflow of the algorithm. The details are described in the following four subsections.

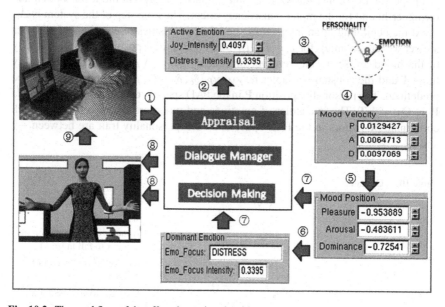

Fig. 10.2 The workflow of the affect dynamics algorithm

10.3.3 Initialization

To facilitate the description, we introduce some notation. The boldfaced letters represent column vectors or matrix and the other letters represent numbers. Some operators are given in Table 10.5.

The user can select a subset of emotions from the 22 emotions categorized by the OCC model. The specified emotions constitute an emotion-type list E whose index set is denoted by Π. For $i \in \Pi$, the intensity of emotion E_i is I_i, the direction of E_i is $\mathbf{D}_i$, and the coordinates of E_i in the PAD space are represented by $\mathbf{E}_i = (E_{ip}, E_{ia}, E_{id})^T$. The coordinates of the mood are represented by $\mathbf{M} = (M_p, M_a, M_d)^T$, and the velocity of the mood is represented by $\mathbf{V}_M = (V_p, V_a, V_d)^T$. The personality traits in the five-factor form are represented by $\mathbf{T}$, the coordinates of personality in the PAD space are represented by $\mathbf{P}$, and $\mathbf{Q}_{3 \times 5}$ denotes the matrix of the transformation that transforms the five-factor form into the PAD dimensions, as shown in Table 10.4. The coefficient that represents the "pull" or "push" effect from active emotions to the mood is denoted by α. The coefficients of the biasing effects from the mood and personality to emotions in event appraisal are denoted by γ_M and γ_P. The decay parameters of emotions and mood are represented by δ_e and δ_m, respectively. μ_a and μ_b represent the lower-bound and the upper-bound of the personality-consistency effect, and τ_a and τ_b represent the lower-bound and the upper-bound for the mood-consistency effect. The time step of the system is Δ_t.

At the beginning of an interaction, the initial intensities of emotions of all types are set to zero, namely for $i \in \Pi$, $I_{ei} = 0$. The initial position and the velocity of the mood are set to the zero vector, namely $\mathbf{M} = \mathbf{V}_M = \mathbf{0}$. The personality traits $\mathbf{T}$ and the constant variables $\alpha, \gamma_M, \gamma_P, \delta_e, \delta_m, \mu_a, \mu_b, \tau_a, \tau_b, \Delta_t$ need to be predefined. The personality position $\mathbf{P}$ in the PAD space is calculated by the formula $\mathbf{P} = \mathbf{Q}_{3 \times 5} \times \mathbf{T}$. The intensities of emotions and mood are between 0 and 1. Each coordinate of vectors in the PAD space and each personality trait are between -1 and 1.

Table 10.5 Operators

Operator	Meaning
$\langle \mathbf{x}, \mathbf{y} \rangle$	Dot product of two vectors $\mathbf{x}, \mathbf{y}$
$[\mathbf{x}]_a^b$	Truncate each dimension of vector $\mathbf{x}$ to fall in $[a, b]$
$[\mathbf{x}]^\circ$	The normalized vector of vector $\mathbf{x}$
$\mathbf{x}^T$	The transpose of vector $\mathbf{x}$
$\|\mathbf{x}\|_\infty$	The infinity norm of the vector $\mathbf{x}$

10.3.4 Mood Dynamics

For a new emotion generated by the event appraisal, its intensity will be influenced by the current mood and personality. In particular, assume the new emotion has index i, intensity I_{i0}, and direction $\mathbf{D}_i$ (see Table 10.3). Based on the biasing effect of mood and personality as described in Assumption 1, the following formula is used to update the intensity I_i:

$$I_i = (I_{i0} + \gamma_M \langle \mathbf{M}, \mathbf{D}_i \rangle + \gamma_P \langle \mathbf{P}, \mathbf{D}_i \rangle)_0^1, \qquad (10.1)$$

where dot product $\langle \mathbf{M}, \mathbf{D}_i \rangle$ measures the consistency between the mood and the new emotion, dot product $\langle \mathbf{P}, \mathbf{D}_i \rangle$ measures the consistency between the personality and the new emotion, and $(\cdot)_a^b$ defines the truncation by a and b. The emotion then becomes

$$\mathbf{E}_i = (E_{ip}, E_{ia}, E_{id}) = I_i \mathbf{D}_i, \, i \in \Pi. \qquad (10.2)$$

After the event appraisal, all active emotions contribute to the dynamics of the mood. However, the contribution of each emotion should be biased by the personality, which is different from the ALMA model. For this purpose, we introduce parameter μ_i for each $i \in \Pi$ to scale the contribution of emotion $\mathbf{E}_i$ to the mood based on certain consistency between the personality and emotion $\mathbf{E}_i$ (see Fig. 10.3). We call μ_i the *personality-consistency effect parameter*. The determination of μ_i is discussed in the following subsection. The velocity of the mood is computed as a weighted sum of the effects of all active emotions:

$$\mathbf{V}_M = \sum_{i \in \Pi} \alpha \mu_i \mathbf{E}_i, \qquad (10.3)$$

where α is the parameter reflecting the "pull" or "push" effect from active emotions to the mood.

The new mood position is then updated from the previous position by the mood change in this time step as

Fig. 10.3 Personality influences the emotion–mood interaction

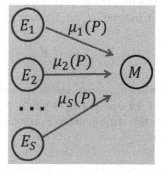

$$\mathbf{M}(t + \Delta_t) = [\mathbf{M}(t) + \mathbf{V}_M \Delta_t]_{-1}^1 . \qquad (10.4)$$

In each time step, active emotions decay at an exponential rate:

$$I_i = I_i e^{-\delta_e \Delta_t}, i \in \Pi. \qquad (10.5)$$

If there is no active emotion, the mood also decays at an exponential rate:

$$\mathbf{M}(t + \Delta_t) = \mathbf{M}(t)e^{-\delta_m \Delta_t}. \qquad (10.6)$$

10.3.5 Personality-Consistency Effect

While personality is used to initialize the mood position as in the ALMA model, here it is also used to determine the tendency of the mood. To achieve this, the personality-consistency effect parameter μ_i should be appropriately chosen. In particular, it should depend on the emotion direction and the personality, or it is a function of the emotion direction and the personality, i.e., $\mu_i = \mu_i (\mathbf{D}_i, \mathbf{P})$. Moreover, it should be positive and should change consistently with the emotion direction. Thus μ_i can be heuristically computed by

$$\mu_i = \| \mathbf{P} \|_\infty \cdot \frac{1}{2}(1 + \langle [\mathbf{P}]^\circ, \mathbf{D}_i \rangle), i \in \Pi. \qquad (10.7)$$

This formula implies two points:

- The more the direction of an emotion aligns with the personality, the more the emotion contributes.
- The more the intensity of the personality is, the more the personality-consistent emotions contribute (refer to Assumption 2).

If an emotion direction is just opposite to the personality, then the heuristic formula gives zero for the personality-consistency effect parameter, which implies that the emotion has no effect on the mood. To overcome this problem, we map further μ_i to an interval $[\mu_a, \mu_b]$, which gives

$$\mu_i = \| \mathbf{P} \|_\infty \cdot (\frac{\mu_b - \mu_a}{2}(1 + \langle [\mathbf{P}]^\circ, \mathbf{D}_i \rangle) + \mu_a), i \in \Pi, \qquad (10.8)$$

where μ_a and μ_b are the predefined lower-bound and upper-bound of μ_i, respectively. If the emotion E_i is totally personality-consistent, μ_i reaches its upper bound μ_b, while if the emotion E_i is totally personality-inconsistent, μ_i reaches its lower bound μ_a.

10.3.6 Dominant Emotions

When there exist multiple active emotions, the ALMA model chooses the dominant emotion based only on their intensities. According to psychology theories, people in different moods tend to focus on different events or emotions [7]. Therefore, the emotion–mood relationship should be taken into consideration while selecting the dominant emotion (refer to Assumption 3). Similar to computing the personality-consistency effect parameters, we can compute the mood-consistency effect values heuristically as

$$\tau_i = I_i(\frac{\tau_b - \tau_a}{2}(1 + \langle \mathbf{M}, \mathbf{D}_i \rangle) + \tau_a), i \in \Pi,$$

where τ_a, τ_b are the lower-bound and upper-bound of τ_i, respectively. For all the active emotions, the dominant emotion is the one that has the largest the mood-consistency effect value τ_i. If there is no active emotion, the dominant emotion is set to neutral. This strategy improves the consistency of emotion-related behaviors and makes virtual humans concentrate on mood-consistent information. For example, in Fig. 10.2, the virtual human in a very bad mood pays more attentions to the "distress" emotion, even though the intensity of the "distress" emotion is lower than that of the "joy" emotion. However, if the "joy" emotion is far more intensive than the "distress" emotion, the virtual human will concentrate on the positive event.

10.4 Experiments

This section presents four examples to evaluate the psychologically plausible affect dynamics algorithm (shortened to "*PPAD-algorithm*" for conciseness). Comparison with the ALMA model is also given. In each example, the dynamics of pleasure, arousal, and dominance of the mood are visualized by curves. In each subfigure, there are three curves representing the changes of the mood position under three types of personality: Optimistic, Neutral, and Pessimistic (see Table 10.6). The corresponding coordinates of the personality are shown in Table 10.7. While the mood in the ALMA model starts at the personality position, the mood in the PPAD-algorithm purposely starts at the origin of the PAD space to show that the initial position of the mood is not very important in the new model for long-time interaction.

Table 10.6 Three types of personalities

Personalities	O	C	E	A	N
Optimistic	0.4	−0.4	0.1	0.7	0.1
Neutral	0	0	0	0	0
Pessimistic	−0.2	0.4	−0.1	−0.5	−0.7

Table 10.7 The PAD coordinates of the personality

Personalities	P	A	D
Optimistic	0.45	0.21	−0.13
Neutral	0	0	0
Pessimistic	−0.45	0.22	0.12

The parameters used in the PPAD-algorithm are set as follows: $\lambda = 1/3, \alpha = 2, \delta = 1, \gamma_M = \gamma_P = 0$. The parameters used in the ALMA model are set as follows: Mooddecaytime = "1000000", Mooddecayperiod = "100", Personalitydecaytime = "50000", Personalitydecayperiod = "100" Personalitydecayfunction = "exponential", RealtimeOutputperiod = "100".

10.4.1 Example 1

A negative event generating an emotion "anger" with intensity 0.5 happens at the beginning. The dynamics of the mood position is shown in Fig. 10.4. In the PPAD-algorithm, the pessimistic virtual human has the biggest changes to the negative emotion "anger," while the optimistic virtual human has the smallest changes. In the ALMA model, the change rate of the mood position has no difference for different personalities.

10.4.2 Example 2

A positive event happens at the beginning, which generates an emotion "gratitude" with intensity 0.5. Figure 10.5 shows the dynamics of the mood position. In the PPAD-algorithm, the optimistic virtual human has the biggest changes to the positive emotion "gratitude," while the pessimistic virtual human has the smallest changes. In the ALMA model, the mood positions are different while the change rate of the mood position is the same for different personalities.

10.4.3 Example 3

A negative event generating an emotion "anger" with intensity 0.5 happens at the beginning, followed by a positive event generating an emotion "gratitude" with intensity 0.5. The dynamics of the mood position is shown in Fig. 10.6. In the PPAD-algorithm, the optimistic virtual human has the biggest changes to the positive

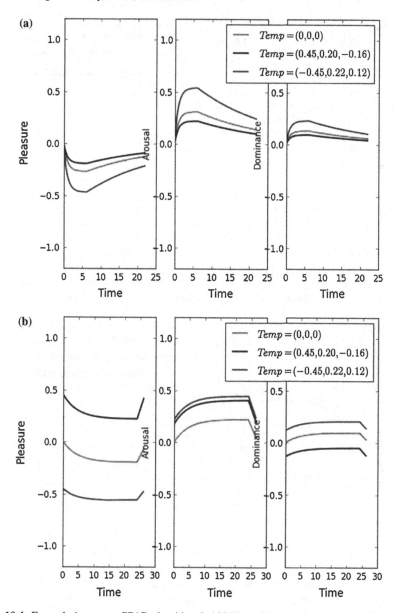

Fig. 10.4 Example 1: anger. **a** PPAD-algorithm. **b** ALMA model

emotion "gratitude" and the final mood position shares the same octant with the emotion "gratitude" in the PAD space, while the pessimistic virtual human has the biggest changes to the negative emotion "anger" and the final mood position shares the same octant with the emotion "anger." In the ALMA model, the tendency of the mood

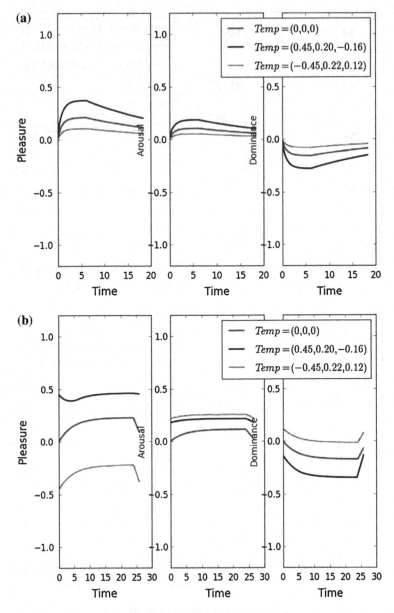

Fig. 10.5 Example 2: gratitude. **a** PPAD-algorithm. **b** ALMA model

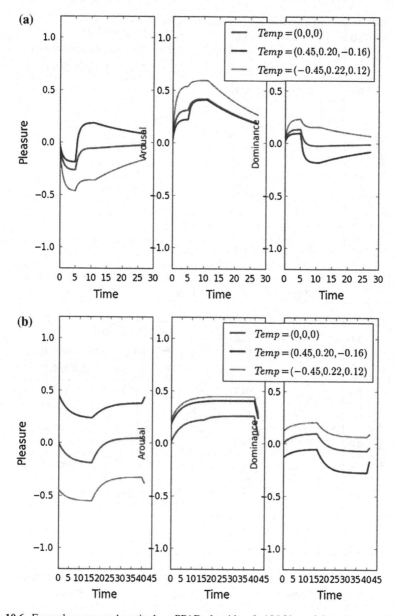

Fig. 10.6 Example: anger and gratitude. **a** PPAD-algorithm. **b** ALMA model

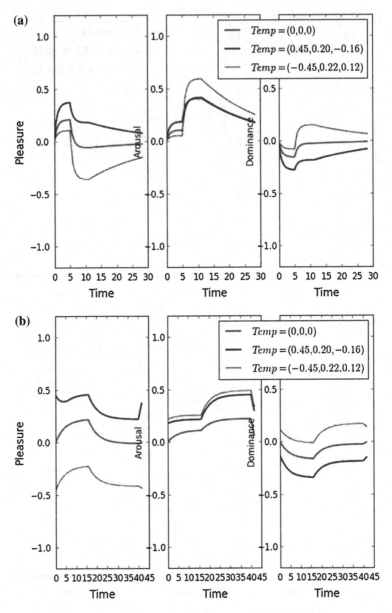

Fig. 10.7 Example: gratitude and anger. **a** PPAD-algorithm. **b** ALMA model

position is similar for different personalities. The mood of the pessimistic virtual human is always negative even though the positive event happens at the beginning.

10.4.4 Example 4

A positive event generating an emotion "gratitude" with intensity 0.5 happens at the beginning, followed by a negative event that generates an emotion "anger" with intensity 0.5. The dynamics of the mood position is shown in Fig. 10.7. In the PPAD-algorithm, the optimistic virtual human has the biggest changes to the positive emotion "gratitude" and the final mood position shares the same octant with the emotion "gratitude" in the PAD space. The pessimistic virtual human has the biggest changes to the negative emotion "anger" and the final mood position shares the same octant with the emotion "anger." In the ALMA model, the tendency of the mood positions is similar for different personalities. The mood of the optimistic virtual human is always positive though the negative event happens at the beginning.

10.4.5 Discussion

In the above four examples, the mood dynamics of optimistic, neutral, and pessimistic personalities are represented in blue, red, and green. The inflection point appears when a new emotion is processed. In the PPAD-algorithm, the initial mood starts at the neutral point because nothing has happened before. The optimistic virtual human is more sensitive to positive information while the pessimistic virtual human is more sensitive to negative information. The difference in personalities can be indicated by the change rate of the mood to different emotional stimuli during the interactions. In the ALMA model, the tendency of the mood position for different personalities keeps the same, although the initial mood positions are different. Hence, the difference in the personalities in the ALMA model is reflected by the mood position only at the very beginning, rather than by the tendency of the mood dynamics during the interactions. However, in long-term interaction, because the mood position can be arbitrary at any time during interaction, the tendency of the mood dynamics is more important to show the different influences of the personalities. Hence the incorporation of personality in affect dynamics is important for long-term interaction.

10.5 Conclusion

This chapter reviews some basic psychology concepts that are related to affect dynamics and a few computational models for affect dynamics. The chapter also presents a psychologically plausible affect dynamics algorithm, which incorporates personality into the process of updating the emotional states during the human–agent interaction. This is motivated by several psychological principles and observations. Experiments are conducted to demonstrate that the affect dynamics with the personality consistency effect is useful in long-time interaction.

In the research on AVH, most affect dynamics modules currently contain only emotions, mood, and personality. However, it is a trend to add other emotional factors such as stress and attitude into the modules. In particular, some efforts have been taken to combine the affective system with episodic memory due to the close relationship between affects and memory. Such a combination makes the emotional history play a role in human–agent interactions, which will enhance the believability of autonomous virtual humans.

References

1. Ahadi SA, Rothbart MK (1994) Temperament, development, and the big five. In: The developing structure of temperament and personality from infancy to adulthood, pp 189–207
2. Allport GW (1961) Pattern and growth in personality. Holt, Rinehart and Winston, New York
3. Anderson JR, Matessa M, Lebiere C (1997) ACT-R: a theory of higher level cognition and its relation to visual attention. Human-Comput Inter 12(4):439–462
4. Andrade EB (2005) Behavioral consequences of affect: combining evaluative and regulatory mechanisms. J Consum Res 32(3):355–362
5. Arjan E, Sumedha K, Nadia M-T (2004) Generic personality and emotion simulation for conversational agents. Comput Animation Virtual Worlds 15(1):1–13
6. Becker C, Kopp S, Wachsmuth I (2004) Simulating the emotion dynamics of a multimodal conversational agent. In: Affective dialogue systems. Springer, Heidelberg, pp 154–165
7. Bower GH (1981) Mood and memory. Am Psychol 36(2):129
8. Brave S, Nass C (2002) Emotion in human-computer interaction. In: The human-computer interaction handbook: fundamentals, evolving technologies and emerging applications, pp 81–96
9. Calvo RA, Mello SD (2010) Affect detection: an interdisciplinary review of models, methods, and their applications. IEEE Trans Affect Comput 1(1):18–37
10. Castellano G, Kessous L, Caridakis G (2008) Emotion recognition through multiple modalities: face, body gesture, speech. In: Affect and emotion in human-computer interaction. Springer, Berlin, pp 92–103
11. Clore GL, Gasper K (2000) Feeling is believing: some affective influences on belief. In: Emotions and beliefs: how feelings influence thoughts, pp 10–44
12. Davidson RJ (1994) On emotion, mood, and related affective constructs. In: The nature of emotion: fundamental questions, pp 51–55
13. Devillers L, Vidrascu L (2006) Real-life emotions detection with lexical and paralinguistic cues on human-human call center dialogs. In: International conference on spoken language processing
14. Ellis HC, Moore BA (1999) Mood and memory. In: Handbook of cognition and emotion, pp 193–210
15. El-Nasr MS, Yen J, Ioerger TR (2000) Flame-fuzzy logic adaptive model of emotions. Auton Agents Multi-Agent Syst 3(3):219–257
16. Frijda (1994) Varieties of affect: emotions and episodes, moods, and sentiments. In: The Nature of emotions: fundamental questions, pp 197–202
17. Frijda NH (1987) Emotion, cognitive structure, and action tendency. Cogn Emot 1(2):115–143
18. Gebhard P (2005) ALMA: a layered model of affect. In: Proceedings of the fourth international joint conference on autonomous agents and multiagent systems. ACM, pp 29–36
19. Gebhard P, Kipp KH (2006) Are computer-generated emotions and moods plausible to humans? In: Intelligent virtual agents. Springer, Heidelberg, pp 343–356
20. Goldberg LR (1990) An alternative "description of personality": the big-five factor structure. J Pers Soc Psychol 59(6):1216

21. Gross JJ (1998) Antecedent-and response-focused emotion regulation: divergent consequences for experience, expression, and physiology. J Pers Soc Psychol 74(1):224

22. Guenther RK (1988) Mood and memory. In: Davies GM, Thomson DM (eds) Memory in context: context in memory, pp 57–79

23. Guoliang Y, Zhiliang W, Guojiang W, Fengjun C (2006) Affective computing model based on emotional psychology. In: Advances in natural computation. Springer, Berlin, pp 251–260

24. Heuer F, Reisberg D (1992) Emotion, arousal, and memory for detail. In: The handbook of emotion and memory: research and theory, pp 151–180

25. Isen AM, Means B (1983) The influence of positive affect on decision-making strategy. Soc Cogn 2(1):18–31

26. Jonathan G, Stacy M (2004) A domain-independent framework for modeling emotion. Cogn Syst Res 5(4):269–306

27. Karimi S, Kangavari MR (2012) A computational model of personality. Procedia-Soc Behav Sci 32:184–196

28. Kshirsagar S (2002) A multilayer personality model. In: Proceedings of the 2nd international symposium on smart graphics. ACM, pp 107–115

29. Lang PJ (1995) The emotion probe: studies of motivation and attention. Am Psychol 50(5):372

30. Lazarus RS (1991) Emotion and adaptation. Oxford University Press, New York

31. LeDoux J, Bemporad JR (1997) The emotional brain. J Am Acad Psychoanal 25(3):525–528

32. Lee CM, Narayanan SS (2005) Toward detecting emotions in spoken dialogs. IEEE Trans Speech Audio Process 13(2):293–303

33. Liu Z (2008) A personality model of virtual characters. In: 7th world congress on intelligent control and automation. IEEE, pp 2497–2500

34. Mehrabian A (1996) Pleasure-arousal-dominance: a general framework for describing and measuring individual differences in temperament. Curr Psychol 14(4):261–292

35. Michael K, Thomas D, Patrick G (2011) Designing emotions. KI-Künstliche Intelligenz 25(3):205–211

36. Moussa MB, Magnenat-Thalmann N (2013) Toward socially responsible agents: integrating attachment and learning in emotional decision-making. Comput Animation Virtual Worlds 24(3-4):327–334

37. Newhagen JE, Reeves B (1992) The evening's bad news: effects of compelling negative television news images on memory. J Commun 42(2):25–41

38. Orozco H, Ramos F, Ramos M, Thalmann D (2010) A fuzzy model to update the affective state of virtual humans: an approach based on personality. In: International conference on cyberworlds (CW). IEEE, pp 406–413

39. Ortony A (2002) On making believable emotional agents believable. In: Trappl et al (eds), pp 189–211

40. Ortony A, Clore G, Collins A (1988) The cognitive structure of emotions. Cambridge University Press, New York

41. Plutchik R (1980) Emotion: a psychoevolutionary synthesis. Harper and Row, New York

42. Reisenzein R (1994) Pleasure-arousal theory and the intensity of emotions. J Pers Soc Psychol 67(3):525

43. Salichs MA, Malfaz M (2012) A new approach to modeling emotions and their use on a decision-making system for artificial agents. IEEE Trans Affect Comput 3(1):56–68

44. Scherer KR, Ellgring H (2007) Multimodal expression of emotion: affect programs or componential appraisal patterns? Emotion 7(1):158

45. Scherer KR (2001) Appraisal considered as a process of multilevel sequential checking. Appraisal Process Emot Theory Methods Res 92:120

46. Shu F, Tan A-H (2012) A biologically-inspired affective model based on cognitive situational appraisal. In: The 2012 international joint conference on neural networks (IJCNN). IEEE, pp 1–8

47. Sidney DM, Art G (2009) Automatic detection of learner's affect from gross body language. Appl Artif Intell 23(2):123–150

48. Susanne E, Markus K, Jo G, Wunderlich AP, Spitzer M, Walter H (2003) Emotional context modulates subsequent memory effect. Neuroimage 18(2):439–447
49. Tellegen A (2003) The MMPI-2 restructured clinical (RC) scales: development, validation, and interpretation. University of Minnesota Press, Minneapolis
50. Thorson E, Friestad M (1989) The effects of emotion on episodic memory for television commercials. cognitive and affective responses to advertising, pp 305–325
51. van der Heide A, Trivino G (2010) Simulating emotional personality in human computer interfaces. In: IEEE international conference on fuzzy systems (FUZZ). IEEE, pp. 1–7
52. Yerkes RM, Dodson JD (1908) The relation of strength of stimulus to rapidity of habit-formation. J Comp Neurol Psychol 18(5):459–482
53. Zerrin K, Moussa MB, Chaudhuri P, Thalmann NM (2009) Making them remember-emotional virtual characters with memory. IEEE Comput Graph Appl 29(2):20–29
54. Zhang J, Magnenat-Thalmann N, Zheng J (2012) Modeling emotions and moods in an affective system for virtual human and social robots. In: 25th international conference on computer animation and social agents

Chapter 11
Motion Control for Social Behaviors

Aryel Beck, Zhang Zhijun and Nadia Magnenat-Thalmann

Abstract Creating social robots that can interact with humans autonomously is a growing and promising field of research. Indeed, there has been a significant increase in the number of platforms and applications for social robots. However, robots are not yet able to interact with humans in a natural and believable way. This is especially true for physically realistic robot that can be affected by the Uncanny Valley. This chapter is looking at motion control for a physically realistic robot named Nadine. Robot controllers for such robot need to produce behaviours that match the physical realism of the robot. This chapter describes a robot controller that allows such a robot to fully use the same modalities as humans during interaction. These include speech, facial and bodily expressions.

11.1 Introduction

Creating social robots that can interact with humans autonomously is a growing and promising field of research. Humans prefer interacting with robots in the way they do with other people [19, 22]. Therefore, one way to increase the believability of such robots is to endow them with the capability to use the same modalities as in human–human interaction. These include verbal and body language as well as facial expressions. This chapter presents techniques to make the robot able to fully use these modalities during interaction. It should be noted that social robots that partially achieve this goal have already been proposed. For instance, the Leonardo robot expresses itself using a combination of voice, facial, and body expressions

A. Beck (✉) · Z. Zhijun · N. Magnenat-Thalmann
BeingThere Centre, Nanyang Technological University, Singapore, Singapore
e-mail: a.beck@ntu.edu.sg

Z. Zhijun
e-mail: zhangzhijun@ntu.edu.sg

N. Magnenat-Thalmann
e-mail: nadiathalmann@ntu.edu.sg

© Springer International Publishing Switzerland 2016
N. Magnenat-Thalmann et al. (eds.), *Context Aware Human-Robot and Human-Agent Interaction*, Human–Computer Interaction Series,
DOI 10.1007/978-3-319-19947-4_11

[48]. Another example is the Nao humanoid robot[1] that can use vision along with gestures and body expression of emotions [5]. In contrast with these two robots, the Nadine robot is a highly realistic humanoid robot. This robot presents some different challenges as it may be subject to the well-known Uncanny Valley [39]. In this paper, a robot controller that addresses some of these difficulties is proposed. Using this controller, the Nadine robot is able to express itself by using combinations of speech, body language, and facial expressions. The main research question addressed is how to control a humanlike robot so that it can sustain believable interaction with humans.

11.2 State of the Art

11.2.1 Overview of Social Robots

In the past decade, there has been a significant increase in the number of platforms and applications for social robots. The range of applications for which social robots have been deployed vary from supporting children in hospitals [10, 40] or affected by autism [54] to supporting the elderly living on their own [52].

- Kismet: Kismet is among the first social robots created [13]. Kismet expresses itself using vocal and facial expressions. The face of Kismet conveys emotions based on nine prototypical facial expressions that 'blend' together along three axes: Arousal, Valence, and Stance. Arousal defines the level of energy. Valence specifies how positive or negative the stimulus is. Stance defines how approachable the stimulus is. This method defines an Affect Space in which expressive behaviors span continuously across these three dimensions, creating a rich variety of expressions. The problem is that this method is difficult to extend to most other social robots which have very few or no degree of freedom for the face.
- Nao[2]: Nao is a humanoid robot with 25 degrees of freedom. It is nowadays a widely used research platform. In terms of expressive behaviors, Nao can use body movements and voice to express itself. Moreover, it has been shown that the Nao robot can successfully display emotion using its body [5, 6] highlighting the importance of body language for social robots. Interestingly, the Nao robot can also successfully use the LEDs in its eyes [9] as well as sounds [43] to express emotions. The Nao robot has been used for elderly support [52] as well as for investigating the building of long-term relationships with robotic companions [10].
- iCat[3]: In contrast with Nao, the iCat is not a humanoid robot and looks like a toy version of a cat [53]. The iCat has 13 degrees of freedom located in the face. This allows for the display of facial expressions. The iCat is not mobile and is solely designed as a research platform for human–robot interaction. The iCat can

---

[1] http://www.aldebaran-robotics.com/.

[2] http://www.aldebaran-robotics.com/.

[3] www.research.philips.com/technologies/projects/robotics.

Fig. 11.1 Examples of robots designed for social interaction. *From left to right* Kismet [13], Nao, Icat, Kaspar [20], ICub [37], Nadine [62]

also speak. Its vocal and facial expressions have been successfully used to convey empathy in child–robot interactions [31].

- Kaspar: The robot Kaspar, a child-sized humanoid robot [20], is anecdotally described as uncanny or scary (Fig. 11.1), suggesting that it falls in the Uncanny Valley. However, this does not stop users from interacting and engaging with it. The robot has been found to be socially engaging and has proven successful in evaluation studies [44], hence overcoming the issue raised by the Uncanny Valley. However, this success could be due to the population sampled as the robot was evaluated with children. This is supported by findings from Ho et al. [25] who reported that women were found more sensitive than men to the phenomenon [25]. Taken together, it suggests that individual differences, such as gender, age, etc., might affect the Uncanny Valley. Kaspar's success could also indicate that the Uncanny effect fades over time as users get used to the appearance of a character. Thus, existing studies do not seem to fully explore the full complexity of the problem, which may involve a complex combination of individual, contextual, cultural, and social factors among others [32].

- iCub: The iCub [37] is a humanoid robot developed at IIT[4] as part of the EU project RobotCub[5] and subsequently adopted by more than 20 laboratories worldwide. It has 53 motors that move the head, arms and hands, waist, and legs. It can see and hear and it has the sense of proprioception (body configuration) and movement (using accelerometers and gyroscopes).

- Realistic humanoids: These robots simulate the physical appearance of real humans. For instance, the geminoids[6] are highly realistic humanoid robots. Another example is the Nadine robot (Fig. 11.1) which is modeled after a Caucasian woman. Due to their highly realistic appearances these types of robots pose specific research problems. Indeed, they seem to be particularly affected by the Uncanny Valley theory and as such have been used to investigate it [46]. Robot controllers for such robots need to produce movements that match the physical

---

[4]http://www.iit.it/en/research/departments/icub-facility.html.

[5]http://www.robotcub.org/.

[6]http://www.geminoid.jp/en/index.html.

realism of the robot. To date, most of the robot controllers for these robots are designed for telepresence. In other words, they are controlled by remote operators. In contrast, this chapter introduces a motion controller for an autonomous robot.

11.2.2 Motion Generation

There are three approaches for motion generated: "hand animation", motion capture, and inverse kinematics. These three methods have different advantages and drawbacks.

- The first method, hand animation, is typically realized by professional artists. In this method, the joint values at each key frame are set manually. The blending between key frames is carefully generated using a mix of automatic tools and manual modifications. Typically, this method results in the most believable animations. However, it is a time-consuming method; more importantly, it is not adaptive. Indeed, solely using this approach, robots would be limited only to the set of available predefined animations. This would make it impossible to adapt to new situations or to display gestures like pointing toward an object or a person.
- The second approach, motion capture, includes two steps, i.e., recording human movements and mapping these data to a humanoid robot. In comparison to hand animation, this usually results in more realistic animations (not necessarily more believable). However, it presents the same drawbacks as hand animation in the sense that it is not adaptive.
- The third approach, inverse kinematics, is a precise mathematical modeling method. However, analytic solutions work for a few kinds of robots [41]. For redundant robots, the traditional solutions are pseudoinverse-based approaches [57]. These approaches need to compute matrix inverse, which may cost much time in real-time computation. In addition, pseudoinverse-based approaches have an inner limitation, i.e., they cannot solve inequality problems. In recent years, optimization methods are preferred and studied widely. Kim proposes an optimization method of a whole-body robot which performs a throwing task [27]. Zhang et al. propose quadratic program (QP) -based motion planning algorithms that can effectively solve redundancy resolution problems for industrial robots [60, 64, 66]. More importantly, the above QP-based optimization schemes can be used in the dual-arms situation [65]. This is useful for humanoid robots as it endows them with the capability to display gestures that are not realizable with the other two methods. Moreover, it is more adaptive to new situations as the gestures are generated on-the-fly according to the specificity of a situation.

11.2.3 Emotional Expression for Robots

This section focuses on the existing work on emotional body expressions that has been conducted in psychology, computer science, and robotics. Researchers have categorized the different types of human body language, depending on how it occurs. The following categorization separates body language into three different areas that should be considered for robots to express emotion during social interactions.

11.2.3.1 Postures

Postures are specific positions that the body takes during a time frame. Following the seminal work by Wallbott [55], a body of research endeavors to define distinctive features of postures that correspond to certain emotions [33]. An important source of information regarding the expression of emotion from static postures comes from automatic recognition of emotion. For instance, existing studies in this field show that collar joint angle and shoulder joint angles are elements that can be used to automatically recognize emotions [21, 29]. Moreover, Kleinsmith et al. [28] investigated cross-cultural recognition of four emotions (anger, fear, happiness, sadness) through interpretations of body postures [28]. They built a set using actors to perform emotional postures and showed that it was possible for participants to correctly identify the different emotions [28]. Specific features of body posture have been isolated, in particular collar and shoulder joint angles which have been found to be expressive for adults [8, 29] as well as for children [2, 5]. Roether and colleagues investigated the portraying of emotions through gait. They found that head inclination as well as the amplitude of the elbow joint angles is particularly salient to the expression of fear and anger [45]. Thus, a robot displaying emotions has to take up postures appropriate to the emotion. Previous results have shown that this is an effective medium to convey emotions as it was found that people correctly identify emotions displayed through postures displayed by a humanoid robot [5, 8]. Moreover, work on emotional behavior generation has shown that by blending key poses, it is possible to generate a continuous space of emotional expressions [7].

11.2.3.2 Movement

Research in psychology has shown that emotions affect the way movements are executed. For instance, Coombes et al. [18] show that exposure to unpleasant stimuli magnifies the force production of a sustained voluntary movement. Moreover, the quality of movements seem to be specific to emotion [30, 55]. Movements are effective clues for judging the emotional state of other people in conjunction with or in the absence of facial and vocal clues [3, 8]. Thus, a robot displaying emotions should also do so during, and via, motion. Body movements include the motion as well as the manner in which it is performed. Researchers in automatic recognition of emotions have focused on different aspect of movements that can be used to discriminate between emotions. These aspects are often based on Laban seminal work [30]. For instance, Camurri et al. [15] used, among others, *Quantity of Motion* (a measure of the amount of body motion), *Contraction Index* (a measure of contraction/expansion of the body) and *Fluidity* (a measure of the uniformity of movements' acceleration). Bernhardt [11] show that movement dynamics, including *speed* (velocity at which the limbs are moving), *acceleration* (change of speed), and *jerk* (rate change of acceleration) can be used to capture the emotion expressed through movements. Interestingly, some of these aspects have been captured by the traditional animation principles [51]. For instance , one of the principles used in animation is referred to as "timing" and emphasizes the importance of the speed at which movements occur [51]. The quality of movements has also been successfully used for virtual agents such as Greta, to express emotions [24]. Greta uses a set of five attributes to describe expressivity: *Overall Activation* (amount of activity, e.g., static versus animated), *Spatial Extent* (amplitude of movements, e.g., contracted versus expanded), *Fluidity* (smoothness and continuity of movements), *Repetition* (rhythmic repetition of the same movement) and *Power* (dynamics property of the movements, e.g., weak versus strong). In this system, these parameters act as filters on the character animation affecting the strength, fluidity, and tempo of the movements. Roether et al. [45] systematically investigated features of gait performed in different emotional states. Their findings highlight the importance of amplitude and speed of movements. These parameters were also successfully reused to modulate gait in order to make them expressive [45]. Changing the dynamics of movements to express emotions has also been used in robotics. For instance, Barakova [4] used Laban's movement theory to model a small set of emotions using an E-puck robot. They found reliable recognition of most of the behaviors. However, it is still necessary to build a library of expressive gestures that will be modified by this set of parameters. Saerbeck and Bartneck [47] investigated the effect of acceleration (change in speed) and curvature (change in direction) on the perception of emotions. They found that arousal was related to acceleration and that valence could be partly encoded in the interaction between these two parameters. They concluded that more research is still needed in this field [34]. It should also be noted that body movements can occur in conjunction with speech and facial expressions, which would also be affected by the emotional state of the character.

11.2.3.3 Proxemics

Proxemics is the distance between individuals during social interaction. Walters and colleagues [56] propose a framework for human–robot proxemics that takes into account a wide range of factors including the physical appearance of the robot and some of its functionalities. Although this framework did not take it into account,

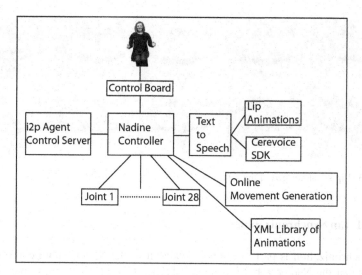

Fig. 11.2 Main components of the robot controller

proxemics is also indicative of emotional state. For example, angry individuals have a tendency to reduce distance during social interaction. This same reduction can also be observed between intimate individuals. Proxemics cannot therefore be considered as an emotional expression in itself but is required to complete a representation of realistic emotional behavior. The reader can refer to [1] for a psychological overview of proxemics and to [12] for examples of use in robotics. It should be noted that the Nadine robot used in this chapter does not have the possibility to directly act on proxemics as it is not mobile. However, proxemics, can still be used to assess the interaction and how comfortable users are while interacting.

11.2.4 System Overview

The Nadine robot is a realistic human-sized robot developed by Kokoro Company, Ltd.[7] It has 27 degrees of freedom and uses pneumatic motors to display natural looking movements. Motion planning and control are always an important issue for robots [38] and are becoming a necessary and promising research area [42, 50]. They allow the synchronization of animations (predefined and online animations), speech, and gaze. The following sections describe the core elements of the Nadine robot controller. These include lip synchronization, blending mechanisms, idle behaviors, signaling attention, and online motion generation (Fig. 11.2).

---

[7]http://www.kokoro-dreams.co.jp/english/.

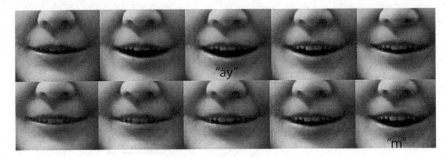

Fig. 11.3 Lip-synch for part of the sentence *"I am Nadine"*. *Picture* taken from [59]

11.2.4.1 Lip Synchronization

Lip synchronization is part of the core function of the Nadine robot controller. It ensures that the Nadine robot looks natural when talking. However, implementing this on a robot such as the Nadine is a challenging task. On one hand, the Nadine robot is physically realistic raising users' expectations, on the other hand, it has strong limitations in terms of the range and speed of movements that it can achieve. The Cerevoice text-to-speech library[8] is used to extract the phonemes as well as to synthesize the speech. Figure 11.3 illustrates the process for the beginning of the sentence "I am Nadine." First, the following phonemes are extracted: "sil", "ay", "ax", "m", "n", "ey", "d", "iy", "n" along with their durations. Due to the Nadine robot's velocity limits, it is not possible to generate lips movements for all the phonemes. This is why, to maintain the synchronization any phonemes that last less than 0.1 second is ignored and the duration of the next one is extended by the same amount. In Fig. 11.3 example "ax" is removed and "m" is extended, "n" is removed and "ey" is extended, and "d" is removed and "iy" is extended. The phonemes are then mapped to visemes that were designed by a professional animator. Figure 11.3 shows examples of two visemes (Frames 3 and 10). The transitions between phonemes is done using cosine interpolation (see Fig. 11.3 frames 4–9). More precisely, the frame at point X between point A and point B is given as

$$F(X) = (1 - \cos(X * \Pi)) * 0.5 \qquad (11.1)$$

$$X = A * (1 - F(X) + B * (F(X)) \qquad (11.2)$$

Moreover, the robot cannot display a "O" mouth movement along with a "Smile." Therefore, if a forbidden transition is needed, a closing mouth movement is generated prior to display of the next viseme. Synchronization is done so that the predefined viseme position is reached at the end of each phoneme.

---

[8]http://www.cereproc.com/en/products/sdk.

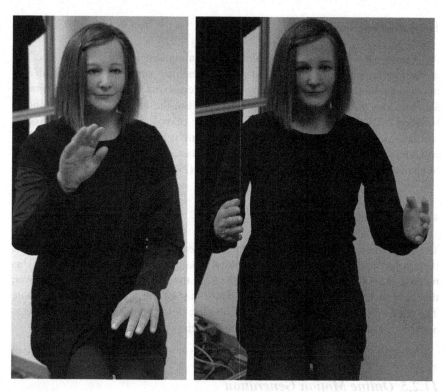

Fig. 11.4 Examples of body movements and facial expressions from the library of gestures

11.2.4.2 Predefined Gestures Database

In addition to the lip-synch animation generator, a professional animator designed predefined animations for the Nadine robot. This is used to display iconic gestures such as waving hand. The predefined gestures also include facial and bodily emotional expressions (Fig. 11.4). Other examples of iconic gestures in the library are head nods, head shake, etc.

11.2.4.3 Blending Mechanisms

Animations consist of joint trajectories. Each joint is treated independently. Providing they do not require the same joints, animations are dynamically combined to create richer display. In case concurrent joints are requested, the currently played animation is interrupted. This allows the Nadine robot to react promptly and adaptively to unpredicted situations during interactions.

11.2.4.4 Idle Behaviors

A professional animator designed a library of animations for idling behaviors. The animations are played repeatedly and include breathing patterns as well as small arm movements that are varied depending on the internal state of the robot. The library also includes different body poses that are used in the background for shifting in between body postures. The idle behaviors are played simultaneously with other animations. For instance, if a waving hand gesture is being displayed, the breathing behaviors are not interrupted. It should also be noted that the idle behaviors continue to be played on the joints that are not requested (Fig. 11.5).

11.2.4.5 Signaling Attention

To signal attention, the robot is able to move its head so that its face targets. To realize these behaviors, a geometrical solution based on tangent projection is employed. This method generates movements that turn the head toward specified points. Moreover, this geometrical solution takes the physical limits of the robot into consideration. The reader can refer to [62] for a more complete description. The head movements are blended and synchronized with all the behaviors of the robot.

11.2.5 Online Motion Generation

Humanoid social robots need to display coordinated and independent arm movements depending on the actual situation. To achieve this, inverse kinematics/dynamics approach are typically used that rely on precise mathematical modeling methods. However, analytic solutions work only for a few robots [41]. For redundant robots (i.e., robots with more degrees of freedom than needed for an end-effector task [60]), the traditional solutions are pseudoinverse-based approaches [57]. This typically implies computing matrix inverse, which is computationally expensive and may impair real-time systems. In addition, pseudoinverse-based approaches have an inner limitation that it cannot solve the inequality problems. In recent years, optimization methods are preferred and studied widely. For instance, Kim [27] proposed an optimization method for a whole-body robot which performs a throwing task. Zhang et al. propose quadratic program (QP)-based motion planning algorithms that can effectively solve the redundancy resolution problems for industrial robots [60, 64, 66]. More importantly, the above QP-based optimization schemes can be used in the dual-arms situation [65]. Hence, it was selected for the Nadine robot controller.

A kinematics model is necessary to generate motions dynamically. The kinematics model of the Nadine robot includes two parts, i.e., forward kinematics model and inverse kinematic model. The forward kinematics model outputs the end-effector (hand) trajectories of the robot if the joint vector of dual-arms is given, while the inverse kinematic model outputs joint vector of dual-arms if the end-effector (hand) path is known. Mathematically, given joint-space vector $\theta(t) \in R^n$, the end-effector

Fig. 11.5 Examples of emotional expressions from the library of postures

position/orientation vector $r(t) \in R^m$ can be formulated as the following forward kinematic equation:

$$r(t) = f(\theta(t)), \tag{11.3}$$

where $f(\cdot)$ is a smooth nonlinear function, which can be obtained if the structure and parameters of a robot are known; n is the dimension of joint space; m is the dimension of end-effector Cartesian space. Conversely, given end-effector position/orientation vector $r(t) \in R^m$, joint-space vector $\theta(t) \in R^n$ can be denoted as

$$\theta(t) = f^{-1}(r(t)), \tag{11.4}$$

where $f^{-1}(\cdot)$ is the inverse function of $f(\cdot)$ in Eq. (11.3). For a redundant arm system, i.e., $n > m$, the difficulty is that inverse kinematics equation (11.4) is usually nonlinear and under-determined, and difficult (impossible to date) to solve. The key of online motion generation is how to solve the inverse kinematics problem.

11.2.5.1 State of Art

The dual-arms of a humanoid robot is a redundant system. It is therefore difficult to obtain analytic solutions. Classical approaches for solving the redundancy-resolution problem are the pseudoinverse based methods, i.e., one minimum-norm particular solution plus a homogeneous solution [58]. Based on such a pseudoinverse-type solution, many optimization performance criteria have been exploited in terms of manipulator configurations and interaction with the environment, such as joint-limits avoidance [16, 36], singularity avoidance [49], and manipulability enhancement [35]. Recent research shows that the solutions to redundancy resolution problems can be enhanced using optimization techniques based on quadratic program (QP) methods [14, 17, 23, 26, 64]. Compared with conventional pseudoinverse-based solutions, such QP-based methods do not need to compute the inverse of the Jacobian matrix, and can deal with the inequality and/or bound constraints. Thus, QP-based methods have been employed. In [17], considering the physical limits, Cheng et al. proposed a compact QP method to resolve the constrained kinematic redundancy problem. In [66] Zhang and Zhang, implement a QP-based two-norm scheme on a planar six-DOF manipulator. However, the above methods only consider a single arm and are therefore not directly applicable for two-arms of the humanoid robot. Hence, a QP-based dual-arms kinematic motion generation scheme is proposed, and a simplified recurrent neural network is employed to solve the QP problem.

11.2.5.2 QP-Based Redundancy Resolution Scheme for Nadine Robot

In our setting, the robot is expected to generate social gestures and motions dynamically according to the situation. For instance, the handshake is commonly used as a greeting at the beginning and end of an interaction. Moreover, in the future, this will allow the robot to communicate through touch, which is common in human–human interaction. Such gestures cannot be included in the predefined library as they need to be adapted to the current user's position on-the-fly. In order to generate motion dynamically, the forward kinematic equations of dual-arms are first built. Then they are integrated into a quadratic programming formulation. A simplified recurrent neural network is used to solve the quadratic programming. Thanks to this method, the robot is able to stretch out its arm and touch the user's hand when needed.

The forward kinematics model considers the robot's arms. Each arm has 7 degrees of freedom. Given the left arm end-effector position vector $p_{\mathrm{endL}} \in R^m$, the right arm end-effector position vector $p_{\mathrm{endR}} \in R^m$ and their corresponding homogeneous representation $r_L = r_R \in R^{m+1}$ with superscript $^\mathrm{T}$ denoting the transpose of a vector or a matrix, we can obtain the homogeneous representations r_L and r_R from the following chain formulas, respectively.

$$r_L(t) = f_\mathrm{L}(\theta_\mathrm{L}) = {}_1^0T \cdot {}_2^1T \cdot {}_3^2T \cdot {}_4^3T \cdot {}_5^4T \cdot {}_6^5T \cdot {}_7^6T \cdot p_{\mathrm{endL}}, \qquad (11.5)$$

$$r_R(t) = f_\mathrm{R}(\theta_\mathrm{R}) = {}_8^0T \cdot {}_9^8T \cdot {}_{10}^9T \cdot {}_{11}^{10}T \cdot {}_{12}^{11}T \cdot {}_{13}^{12}T \cdot {}_{14}^{13}T \cdot p_{\mathrm{endR}}, \qquad (11.6)$$

where ${}_{i+1}^iT$ with $i = 0, 1, \ldots, 14$ denote the homogeneous transform matrixes. In this paper, $n = 7$ and $m = 3$.

Inspired by the work on one-arm redundant system [66], we try to build a model based on quadratic programming as shown below.

$$\text{minimize} \quad \dot{\vartheta}^\mathrm{T}(t) M \dot{\vartheta}(t)/2 \qquad (11.7)$$

$$\text{subject to} \quad J(\vartheta)\dot{\vartheta}(t) = \dot{\Upsilon}(t), \qquad (11.8)$$

$$\vartheta^-(t) \le \vartheta(t) \le \vartheta^+(t), \qquad (11.9)$$

$$\dot{\vartheta}^-(t) \le \dot{\vartheta}(t) \le \dot{\vartheta}^+(t), \qquad (11.10)$$

where $\vartheta(t) = [\theta_\mathrm{L}^\mathrm{T}, \theta_\mathrm{R}^\mathrm{T}]^\mathrm{T} \in R^{2n}$; $\vartheta^-(t) = [\theta_\mathrm{L}^{-\mathrm{T}}, \theta_\mathrm{R}^{-\mathrm{T}}]^\mathrm{T} \in R^{2n}$; $\vartheta^+(t) = [\theta_\mathrm{L}^{+\mathrm{T}}, \theta_\mathrm{R}^{+\mathrm{T}}]^\mathrm{T} \in R^{2n}$; $\dot{\vartheta}(t) = d\vartheta/dt = [\dot{\theta}_\mathrm{L}^\mathrm{T}, \dot{\theta}_\mathrm{R}^\mathrm{T}]^\mathrm{T} \in R^{2n}$; $\dot{\vartheta}^-(t) = [\dot{\theta}_\mathrm{L}^{-\mathrm{T}}, \dot{\theta}_\mathrm{R}^{-\mathrm{T}}]^\mathrm{T} \in R^{2n}$; $\dot{\vartheta}^+(t) = [\dot{\theta}_\mathrm{L}^{+\mathrm{T}}, \dot{\theta}_\mathrm{R}^{+\mathrm{T}}]^\mathrm{T} \in R^{2n}$. $\dot{\Upsilon}(t) = [\dot{r}_\mathrm{L}^\mathrm{T}; \dot{r}_\mathrm{R}^\mathrm{T}]^\mathrm{T} \in R^{2n}$. Matrix J is composed by Jacobian matrixes J_L and J_R; M is a $n \times n$ identity matrix. Specifically, $M \in R^{2n \times 2n}$ is an identity matrix, and

$$J = \begin{bmatrix} J_\mathrm{L} & \mathbf{0}_{m \times n} \\ \mathbf{0}_{m \times n} & J_\mathrm{R} \end{bmatrix} \in R^{2m \times 2n}.$$

For the sake of calculations, the QP-based coordinated dual-arm scheme can be formulated as the following expression constrained by an equality and an inequality:

$$\text{minimize} \quad \|\dot{\vartheta}(t)\|^2/2 \qquad (11.11)$$

$$\text{subject to} \quad J(\vartheta)\dot{\vartheta}(t) = \dot{\Upsilon}(t), \qquad (11.12)$$

$$\xi^-(t) \leqslant \dot{\vartheta}(t) \leqslant \xi^+(t), \qquad (11.13)$$

where $\| \cdot \|$ denotes the two norms of a vector or a matrix. Equation (11.11) is the simplification of Eq. (11.7). Equation (11.13) is transformed by Eqs. (11.9) and (11.10). In Eq. (11.13), the ith components of $\xi^-(t)$ and $\xi^+(t)$ are $\xi_i^-(t) = \max\{\dot{\vartheta}_i^-, \nu(\vartheta_i^-(t) - \vartheta_i)\}$ and $\xi_i^+(t) = \min\{\dot{\vartheta}_i^+, \nu(\vartheta_i^+(t) - \vartheta_i)\}$ with $\nu = 2$ being used to scale the feasible region of $\dot{\vartheta}$. $\vartheta^- = [\vartheta_L^{-T}, \vartheta_R^{-T}]^T \in R^{2n}$; $\vartheta^+ = [\vartheta_L^{+T}, \vartheta_R^{+T}]^T \in R^{2n}$. $\dot{\vartheta}^- = [\dot{\vartheta}_L^{-T}, \dot{\vartheta}_R^{-T}]^T \in R^{2n}$; $\dot{\vartheta}^+ = [\dot{\vartheta}_L^{+T}, \dot{\vartheta}_R^{+T}]^T \in R^{2n}$.

In the subsequent experiments, the physical limits $\vartheta_L^+ = [\pi/20, \pi/10, \pi/8, \pi/2, 0, 2\pi/3, \pi/2]^T$, $\vartheta_L^- = [0, -3\pi/10, -7\pi/120, 0, -131\pi/180, 0, \pi/9]^T$, $\vartheta_R^+ = [0, 3\pi/10, 7\pi/120, \pi, 0, 2\pi/3, -\pi/2]^T$, and $\vartheta_R^- = [-\pi/20, -\pi/10, -\pi/8, \pi/2, -131\pi/180, 0, -8\pi/9]^T$.

11.2.5.3 QP Conversion into PLE

According to [66], Eqs. (11.11)–(11.13) can be converted into a linear variational inequality. That is, to find a solution vector $u^* \in \Omega$ w.r.t.

$$(u - u^*)^T(\Gamma u^* + q) \geq 0, \ \forall u \in \Omega. \tag{11.14}$$

Equation (11.14) is equivalent to the following system of piecewise-linear equations (PLE) [66]:

$$\Phi_\Omega(u - (\Gamma u + q)) - u = 0, \tag{11.15}$$

where $\Phi_\Omega(\cdot): R^{2n+2m} \to \Omega$ is a projection operator, i.e.,

$$\begin{cases} u_i^-, & \text{if } u_i < u_i^-, \\ u_i, & \text{if } u_i^- \leqslant u_i \leqslant u_i^+, \ \forall i \in \{1, 2, \ldots, n+m\}. \\ u_i^+, & \text{if } u_i > u_i^+, \end{cases}$$

In addition, $\Omega = \{u \in R^{2n+2m} | u^- \leq u \leq u^+\} \subset R^{2n+2m}$; $u \in R^m$ is the primal-dual decision vector; $u^- \in R^m$ and $u^+ \in R^m$ are the lower and upper bounds of u, respectively; ω is usually set a sufficiently large value (e.g., in the simulations and experiments afterward, $\varpi := 10^{10}$). Specifically,

$$u = \begin{bmatrix} \vartheta(t) \\ \iota \end{bmatrix} \in R^{2n+2m}, \ u^+ = \begin{bmatrix} \zeta^+(t) \\ \omega 1_\iota \end{bmatrix} \in R^{2n+2m}, \ u^- = \begin{bmatrix} \zeta^-(t) \\ -\omega 1_\iota \end{bmatrix} \in R^{2n+2m},$$

$$\Gamma = \begin{bmatrix} M & -J^T \\ J & 0 \end{bmatrix} \in R^{(2n+2m)\times(2n+2m)}, q = \begin{bmatrix} 0 \\ -\dot{\Upsilon} \end{bmatrix} \in R^{n+m}, \ 1_v := [1, \ldots, 1]^T.$$

11.2.6 QP Solver

Being guided by dynamic-system-solver design experience [61, 63], we can adopt the following neural dynamics (the simplified recurrent neural network [63]) to solve Eq. (11.15).

$$\dot{u} = \gamma P_\Omega (u - (Mu + q)) - u, \tag{11.16}$$

where γ is a positive design parameter used to scale the convergence rate of the neural network. The lemma proposed in [63] guarantees the convergence of neural network formulated by Eq. (11.16) (with proof omitted due to space limitation).

  Lemma: Assume that the optimal solution $\vartheta^\star$ to the strictly convex QP problem formulated by Eqs. (11.11)–(11.13) exists. Being the first $2n$ elements of state $u(t)$, output $\vartheta(t)$ of the simplified recurrent neural network in Eq. (11.16) is globally exponentially convergent to $\vartheta^\star$. In addition, the exponential-convergence rate is proportional to the product of γ and the minimum eigenvalue of M [63].

11.3 Example of Research Applications

11.3.1 Signaling Awareness of Sound

An important aspect of research is to make robots aware of sounds within their environments. For instance, Chap. 3 presents methods for acoustic source localization. This allows the Nadine robot to know from which direction the voice is coming from and to classify different types of sounds such as impulsive (e.g., clapping hands) and nonimpulsive sound (e.g., phone ringing). In this case, the robot controller presented in this chapter is responsible for sending social signals and reacting to what is happening. For instance, if an object drops on the floor, the Nadine robot is able to speak, look at the object, and point toward the object in a highly synchronized way. Socially, she is able to signal to a user that she drops something and point in the direction of the fallen object. These highly synchronized social behaviors all result from the robot controller presented in Sect. 11.2.4.

11.3.2 Human–Robot Interaction with Upper Body Language Understanding

Chapter 3 introduces methods to understand gestures made by the user. Thanks to this work, the Nadine robot is able to understand gestures such as waving hands, shaking hands, head nods, and object manipulations. The new robot controller described in this chapter allows for Nadine to react socially and appropriately. For instance, if a user wishes to shake hands with it, the robot understands the intention and shakes hand with the user while synchronously verbally greeting her and looking at her. On the robot controller side, this is done using the methods described in Sect. 11.2.4. While the gesture recognition (Chap. 3) provides understanding of the users' communication intent, the robot controller provides the means to react to it. An envisioned scenario based on this research is to use a social robot for teaching where they need to understand the user's state and intention and react appropriately while delivering the lecture content.

11.3.3 Signaling Attention

An important aspect of social interaction is gaze. Indeed, gaze signal attention and should be displayed synchronously with ongoing actions. The robot controller allows for the synchronization of these movements. This can be used to signal attention, but also as described in the section above, to look at addressees when the robot is speaking. Eye movements are not yet part of the robot controller, however, they will be integrated in the near future. Indeed, eye movements within the robot controller should improve its capability to signal attention but also be carefully synchronized with speech to improve the realism and believability of the generated behaviors.

11.4 System Implementation

The robot controller is implemented using a framework called Integrated Integration Platform (I2P) that is specifically developed for integration. I2P was developed by the Institute for Media Innovation.[9] This framework allows for the link and integration of perception, decision, and action modules within an unified and modular framework. The platform uses client–server communications between the different components. Each component has an I2P interface and the communication between the client and servers is implemented using Thrift.[10] It should be noted that the framework is highly modular and components are extendable.

11.5 Conclusions

Throughout this chapter, the main areas of research for nonverbal behaviors generation are highlighted. There are still a number of research avenues that need to be addressed, the first being adaptivity. The nonverbal behaviour we display while

---

[9]http://imi.ntu.edu.sg/Pages/Home.aspx.

[10]http://thrift.apache.org/.

interacting is highly volatile. Indeed, the way we interact depends on the topic of the conversation, the surrounding context, the person with whom we interact, etc.We also vary our nonverbal behaviors while interacting with the same person in different contexts. Social robots are not yet able to display this kind of flexibility. The work presented in this chapter allows the Nadine robot to express herself using a combination of body movements, facial expressions, and verbal language simultaneously, aiming to give the users a vivid experience. The future work will aim at making these behaviors adaptive and peronalized to provide users with natural interactions.

References

1. Argyle M (1975) Bodily communication. Methuen, London
2. Aryel B, Lola C, Luisa D, Giacomo S, Fabio T, Piero C (2011) Children interpretation of emotional body language displayed by a robot. Soc Robot (2011-01-01):62–70
3. Atkinson AP, Dittrich WH, Gemmell AJ, Young AW (2004) Emotion perception from dynamic and static body expressions in point-light and full-light displays. Perception 33(6):717–746
4. Barakova El, Tourens T (2010) Expressing and interpreting emotional movements in social games with robots. Personal Ubiquitous Comput 14:457–467
5. Beck A, Cañamero L, Hiolle A, Damiano L, Cosi P, Tesser F, Sommavilla G (2013) Interpretation of emotional body language displayed by a humanoid robot: a case study with children. Int J Soc Robot 5(3):325–334
6. Beck A, Hiolle A, Cañamero L (2013) Using perlin noise to generate emotional expressions in a robot. In: Proceedings of annual meeting of the cognitive science society (Cog Sci 2013), pp 1845–1850
7. Beck A, Hiolle A, Mazel A, Cañamero L (2010) Interpretation of emotional body language displayed by robots. In: Proceedings of the 3rd international workshop on affective interaction in natural environments. ACM, pp 37–42
8. Beck A, Stevens B, Bard KA, Cañamero L (2012) Emotional body language displayed by artificial agents. ACM Trans Inter Intell Syst 2(1):2:1–2:29
9. Bee N, Haring M, Andre E (2011) Creation and evaluation of emotion expression with body movement, sound and eye color for humanoid robots. In: Ro-Man 2011, IEEE, pp 204–209
10. Belpaeme T, Baxter PE, Read R, Wood R, Cuayáhuitl H, Kiefer B, Racioppa S, Kruijff-Korbayová I, Athanasopoulos G, Enescu V et al (2012) Multimodal child-robot interaction: building social bonds. J Hum-Robot Inter 1(2):33–53
11. Bernhardt D (2010) Emotion inference from human body. PhD thesis, University of Cambridge, Computer Laboratory
12. Bethel CL, Murphy RR (2008) Survey of non-facial/non-verbal affective expressions for appearance-constrained robots. IEEE Trans Syst Man Cybern Part C: Appl Rev 38(1):83–92
13. Breazeal C (2002) Designing sociable robots. Intelligent robotics and autonomous agents. MIT press, Cambridge
14. Cai B, Zhang Y (2012) Different-level redundancy-resolution and its equivalent relationship analysis for robot manipulators using gradient-descent and zhang 's neural-dynamic methods. IEEE Trans Ind Electron 59(8):3146–3155
15. Camurri A, Mazzarino B, Volpe G (2003) Analysis of expressive gesture: the eyesweb expressive gesture processing library. In: Gesture-based communication in human-computer interaction. LNAI, pp 460–467
16. Chan TF, Dubey RV (1995) A weighted least-norm solution based scheme for avoiding joint limits for redundant joint manipulators. IEEE Trans Robot Autom 11(2):286–292
17. Cheng F-T, Chen T-H, Sun Y-Y (1994) Resolving manipulator redundancy under inequality constraints. IEEE Trans Robot Autom 10(1):65–71

18. Coombes SA, Cauraugh JH, Janelle CM (2006) Emotion and movement: activation of defensive circuitry alters the magnitude of a sustained muscle contraction. Neurosci Lett 396(3):192–196
19. Dautenhahn K (2007) Socially intelligent robots: dimensions of human-robot interaction. Philos Trans Royal Soc B: Biol Sci 362(1480):679–704
20. Dautenhahn K, Nehaniv CL, Walters ML, Robins B, Kose-Bagci H, Blow M (2009) Kaspar—a minimally expressive humanoid robot for human–robot interaction research. Appl Bionics Biomech 6(3, 4):369–397
21. De Silva PR, Bianchi-Berthouze N (2004) Modeling human affective postures: an information theoretic characterization of posture features. Comput Animation Virtual Worlds 15(3–4):269–276
22. Fong T, Nourbakhsh I, Dautenhahn K (2003) A survey of socially interactive robots. Robot Auton Syst 42(3):143–166
23. Guo D, Zhang Y (2012) A new inequality-based obstacle-avoidance mvn scheme and its application to redundant robot manipulators. IEEE Trans Syst Man Cybern Part C: Appl Rev 42(6):1326–1340
24. Hartmann B, Mancini M, Buisine S, Pelachaud C (2005) Design and evaluation of expressive gesture synthesis for embodied conversational agents. In: Proceedings of 4th international joint conference on autonomous agents and multiagent systems, AAMAS'05. ACM, New York, NY, USA, pp 1095–1096
25. Ho C-C, MacDorman KF, Pramono ZADD (2008) Human emotion and the uncanny valley: a glm, mds, and isomap analysis of robot video ratings. In: Proceedings of the 3rd ACM/IEEE international conference on human robot interaction, HRI'08. ACM, New York, NY, USA, pp 169–176
26. Kanoun O, Lamiraux F, Wieber PB (2011) Kinematic control of redundant manipulators: generalizing the task-priority framework to inequality task. IEEE Trans Robot 27(4):785–792
27. Kim HJ (2011) Optimization of throwing motion planning for whole-body humanoid mechanism: sidearm and maximum distance. Mech Mach Theory 46(4):438–453
28. Kleinsmith A, De Silva PR, Bianchi-Berthouze N (2006) Cross-cultural differences in recognizing affect from body posture. Interact Comput 18(6):1371–1389
29. Kleinsmith A, Bianchi-Berthouze N, Steed A (2011) Automatic recognition of non-acted affective postures. IEEE transactions on systems man, and cybernetics part B
30. Laban R, Ullmann L (1971) The mastery of movement. Plays, Inc, Boston
31. Leite I, Castellano G, Pereira A, Martinho C, Paiva A (2012) Modelling empathic behaviour in a robotic game companion for children: an ethnographic study in real-world settings. In: Proceedings of the seventh annual ACM/IEEE international conference on human-robot interaction, HRI'12. ACM, New York, NY, USA, pp 367–374
32. Lola C (2006) Did garbo care about the uncanny valley? commentary to K.F. Macdorman and H. Ishiguro, the uncanny advantage of using androids in cognitive and social science research. Inter Stud 7:355–359
33. Marc C (2004) Attributing emotion to static body postures: recognition accuracy, confusions, and viewpoint dependence. J Nonverbal Behav 28:117–139
34. Martin S, Christoph B (2010) Perception of affect elicited by robot motion. In: International Conference on Human Robot Interaction, ACM/IEEE
35. Martins AM, Dias AM, Alsina PJ (2006) Comments on manipulability measure in redundant planar manipulators. In: Proceedings of IEEE Latin American robotics symposium (LARS 06), pp 169–173
36. Ma S, Watanabe M (2002) Time-optimal control of kinematically redundant manipulators with limit heat characteristics of actuators. Adv Robot 16(8):735–749
37. Metta G, Sandini G, Vernon D, Natale L, Nori F (2008) The icub humanoid robot: an open platform for research in embodied cognition. In: Proceedings of the 8th workshop on performance metrics for intelligent systems, pp 50–56
38. Miyashita T, Ishiguro H (2004) Human-like natural behavior generation based on involuntary motions for humanoid robots. Robot Auton Syst 48(4):203–212
39. Mori M (1970) Bukimi no tani [the un-canny valley]. Energy 7:33–35

40. Nalin M, Baroni I, Kruijff-Korbayova I, Canamero L, Lewis M, Beck A, Cuayahuitl H, Sanna A (2012) Children's adaptation in multi-session interaction with a humanoid robot. In: International symposium on robot and human interactive communication (RO-MAN). IEEE
41. Nunez JV, Briseno A, Rodriguez DA, Ibarra JM, Rodriguez VM (2012) Explicit analytic solution for inverse kinematics of bioloid humanoid robot. In: Robotics symposium and Latin American robotics symposium (SBR-LARS), 2012 Brazilian, pp 33–38
42. Pierris G, Lagoudakis MG (2009) An interactive tool for designing complex robot motion patterns. In: Proceedings of IEEE international conference on robotics and automation (ICRA 09), pp 4013–4018
43. Read R, Belpaeme T (2013) People interpret robotic non-linguistic utterances categorically. In: 2013 8th ACM/IEEE international conference on Human-Robot Interaction (HRI), pp 209–210. March 2013
44. Robins B, Dautenhahn K (2007) Encouraging social interaction skills in children with autism playing with robots: a case study evaluation of triadic interactions involving children with autism, other people (peers and adults) and a robotic toy. ENFANCE 59:72–81
45. Roether CL, Omlor L, Christensen A, Giese MA (2009) Critical features for the perception of emotion from gait. J Vision 9(6):15
46. Rosenthal-von der Pütten AM, Krämer NC, Becker-Asano C, Ogawa K, Nishio S, Ishiguro H (2014) The uncanny in the wild. Analysis of unscripted human–android interaction in the field international. J Soc Robot 6(1):67–83
47. Saerbeck M, Bartneck C (2010) Attribution of affect to robot motion. In: 5th ACM/IEEE international conference on human-robot interaction (HRI2010). ACM, Osaka, pp 53–60
48. Smith LB, Breazeal C (2007) The dynamic lift of developmental process. Dev Sci 10(1):61–68
49. Taghirad HD, Nahon M (2008) Kinematic analysis of a macro-micro redundantly actuated parallel manipulator. Adv Robot 22(6–7):657–687
50. Takahashi Y, Kimura T, Maeda Y, Nakamura T (2012) Body mapping from human demonstrator to inverted-pendulum mobile robot for learning from observation. In: Proceedings of IEEE conference on fuzzy systems (FUZZ-IEEE 2012), pp 1–6
51. Thomas F, Johnston O (1995) The illusion of life. Abbeville-Press, New-York
52. Torta E, Oberzaucher J, Werner F, Cuijpers RH, Juola JF (2012) Attitudes towards socially assistive robots in intelligent homes: results from laboratory studies and field trials. Journal of Human-Robot. Interaction 1(2):76–99
53. van Breemen A, Yan X, Meerbeek B (2005) icat: an animated user-interface robot with personality. In: Proceedings of the fourth international joint conference on autonomous agents and multiagent systems, AAMAS'05. ACM, New York, NY, USA, pp 143–144
54. Wainer J, Dautenhahn K, Robins B, Amirabdollahian F (2014) A pilot study with a novel setup for collaborative play of the humanoid robot kaspar with children with autism. Int J Soc Robot 6(1):45–65
55. Wallbott HG (1998) Bodily expression of emotion. Eur J Soc Psychol 28(6):879–896
56. Walters ML, Dautenhahn K, Boekhorst RT, Koay KL, Syrdal DS, Nehaniv CL (2009) An empirical framework for human-robot proxemics. Procs of new frontiers in human-robot interaction
57. Wang J, Li Y (2009) Inverse kinematics analysis for the arm of a mobile humanoid robot based on the closed-loop algorithm. In: International conference on information and automation, 2009. ICIA'09. pp 516–521
58. Wang J, Li Y (2009) Inverse kinematics analysis for the arm of a mobile humanoid robot based on the closed-loop algorithm. In: Proceedings of international conference on information and automation (ICIA 2009), pp. 516–521
59. Xiao Y, Zhang Z, Beck A, Yuan J, Thalmann D (2014) Human-robot interaction by understanding upper body gestures. Presence 23(2):133–154
60. Zhang Z (2012) Motion planning and control of redundant manipulator from fixed base to mobile platfrom. Ph.D dissertation, Sun Yat-sen University (2012)
61. Zhang Y, Huarong W, Zhang Z, Xiao L, Guo Dongsheng (2013) Acceleration-level repetitive motion planning of redundant planar robots solved by a simplified lvi-based primal-dual neural network. Robot Comput-Integr Manuf 29(2):328–343

62. Zhang Z, Beck A, Thalmann NM Human-like behavior generation based on head-arms model for robot tracking external targets and body parts. IEEE Transaction on Cybernetics, Accepted for publication
63. Zhang Y, Tan Z, Yang Z, Lv X, Chen K (2008) A simplified lvi-based primal-dual neural network for repetitive motion planning of pa10 robot manipulator starting from different initial states. In: Proceedings of IEEE joint conference on neural networks (IJCNN 2008), pp. 19–24
64. Zhang Z, Zhang Y (2012) Acceleration-level cyclic-motion generation of constrained redundant robots tracking different paths. IEEE Trans Syst Man Cybern Part B: Cybern 42(4):1257–1269
65. Zhang Z, Zhang Y (2013) Equivalence of different-level schemes for repetitive motion planning of redundant robots. Acta Automatica Sinica 39(1):88–91
66. Zhang Z, Zhang Y (2013) Variable joint-velocity limits of redundant robot manipulators handled by quadratic programming. IEEE/ASME Trans Mechatron 18(2):674–686

Chapter 12
Multiple Virtual Human Interactions

Samuel Lemercier and Daniel Thalmann

Abstract Autonomous virtual humans need to be able to interact between each others in virtual environments. These interactions are essentials for the generation of realistic behaviours from virtual humans. This chapter presents a review about interactions between real and multiple virtual humans, as well as between themselves. After presenting the problematics and approaches raised by virtual humans interactions, different methods for simulating such interactions are discussed. Interactions between real and multiple virtual humans are presented first with a focus on virtual assistants and social phobia examples. Interactions between virtual humans are then adressed, particularly gaze attention of other characters and navigation interactions between multiple virtual humans.

12.1 Introduction

Autonomous virtual humans need to be able to interact between each other in virtual environments. These interactions are essential for generation of realistic behaviors from virtual humans.

Several properties are required to make good interaction between multiple virtual humans.

Performance is a key requirement as interactions have to be done in real time. Virtual humans have to immediately react to the user's actions. However, the more complicated the interaction is, the more time-consuming it is going to be. Moreover, the more the virtual humans, the more the interactions, and the more the time required.

Another important criteria is autonomy. Virtual humans are expected to be able to take decisions about any event that may happen during a simulation. While controlled virtual humans scrupulously follow the procedure provided by the scenario,

S. Lemercier (✉) · D. Thalmann
BeingThere Centre, Nanyang Technological University, Singapore, Singapore
e-mail: samuelemercier@hotmail.com

D. Thalmann
e-mail: danielthalmann@ntu.edu.sg

© Springer International Publishing Switzerland 2016
N. Magnenat-Thalmann et al. (eds.), *Context Aware Human-Robot and Human-Agent Interaction*, Human–Computer Interaction Series,
DOI 10.1007/978-3-319-19947-4_12

autonomous virtual humans are supposed to adapt their behaviors according to the situation in which they are.

Finally, virtual humans' realism is the main criteria as long as the interaction is performed in real time. Realism can be visual through the virtual human appearance. From a behavioral point of view, the aim is to get a virtual human that behaves in a natural way, such as a real human would. High realism has to be obtained for each individual; however, on another scale the behavior of the group or the population itself also has to be realistic. An important question that is still raised is how to evaluate the realism of virtual humans' behavior both at the individual and at the group or population scale.

Two approaches can be considered to generate such interactions:

- A centralized approach in which the virtual humans are driven by a central processing unit that is omniscient and drives all the virtual humans;
- An agent-based approach in which each virtual human has its own behavior and reacts to a situation according to its perception of the virtual environment.

This second approach is generally preferred as it provides more autonomy to virtual humans and allows more realism in their behavior, even if computation costs may increase.

This chapter presents a review of multiple virtual human interaction and focuses on how these interactions are modeled for navigation purposes.

12.2 Interactions Between Real and Virtual Humans

Interactions between real and multiple virtual humans have been addressed in some particular scenarios. Wang et al. [66] present an interactive multi-agent system that allows the user to interact in real time with a crowd of virtual humans in immersive environments. Through a natural interface using Kinect sensor device and gesture recognition, the agents can react to the virtual human's command by changing their moving behavior. Interaction with virtual humans has been studied in different contexts such as virtual storytelling [5], virtual assistants, or social phobia scenarios, for example.

12.2.1 Social Channel and Virtual Assistants

An Interactive Narrative Space [17] denotes a narrative environment allowing for interactive interventions from the participants side that affects the evolution of the story. The Interactive Narration Space should provide proper semantics allowing for expression and execution of simple interactive stories oriented toward pedagogical content. Although similar to storytelling engines, the Interactive Narrative Space concept is rather a pedagogical/therapeutic engine and relies on the synergy of storytelling and training/therapy.

In the context of virtual reality simulation, the social channel denotes an interaction paradigm relying on a direct and humanlike communication between the participant and virtual humans. In other words, interaction between the participant and the virtual reality environment is mediated through virtual humans, who execute orders, ask questions, speak about simulation states, etc. Their presence is seamlessly combined into the fabric of the pedagogical/therapeutic story, hence they are not perceived explicitly as an interaction method. These special virtual humans are called virtual assistants and they are semi-autonomous.

The social channel defines negotiation-based interactions, where virtual humans have the following roles:

- Virtual assistants can refuse to execute orders that would push the story into undesired directions (from the pedagogical/therapeutic viewpoint). However, such behaviors are not frustrating for the participant, as they take place in a social-interaction context (as opposed to human–machine interaction, which assumes absolute superiority of human over machine).
- Virtual assistants encourage, suggest, and prompt the user to perform certain actions. This allows the trainer/therapist to guide the participant through the interactive scenario.
- The Virtual assistant is perceived by the trainee/patient as an inherent element of the evolving scenario. At the same time, the virtual assistant's main role is to mediate the interactions between the Interactive Narrative Space and the subject. During the simulation, virtual assistants (decision executors) accompany the trainee/patient (the decision-maker). The latter navigates, assesses the situation, and makes decisions by issuing natural voice commands. Virtual assistants wait for commands and execute actions showing the expected skills.
- Finally, in case of lack of cooperation or too slow interaction from the participants' side, virtual assistants may make decisions by themselves. This again is acceptable from the social-behavior point of view, and may even have stimulating effects on the participant; encouraging him to take an active role can be used as a positive stress-generating factor. Negotiation and mediation are natural interaction modes for the trainee/patient, while the trainer/therapist can control the narration into pedagogically/therapeutically meaningful directions: the social channel forms the bridge that allows for compromising and masking of the inherent contradiction between interaction and narration.

12.2.1.1 Example: A Virtual Assistant for Basic Life Support

The goal of this scenario is to train for the Basic Life Support (BLS) medical procedure [36]. The trainee is immersed in a virtual space (in an office or in the street, as shown in Fig. 12.1) and discovers a man lying on the ground. He has to give BLS to the victim by giving orders to a young girl (the virtual assistant). She possesses all

Fig. 12.1 Basic life support at the office and in the street

the skills required (e.g., mouth-to-mouth, chest compression), but she is unsure and hesitates about the order in which to proceed; guiding her is the job of the trainee. The latter will interact with the virtual assistant and apply his theoretical knowledge about the BLS procedure, confronting it with tight time constraints in a semi-real experience. The user navigates the scene, assesses the situation, and makes decisions by issuing natural voice commands. The virtual assistant waits for commands and executes the actions. If the users commands are correct, the victim recovers. In cases where the user provides incorrect commands, the virtual assistant may refuse to do harm to the victim; in such situations, the virtual assistant may prompt the user for retrial, or may suggest an alternative possibility.

12.2.2 Virtual Humans in Social Phobia

There are also many applications where we need to simulate people and how to interact with them. For example, we can use virtual humans to train people who have social phobia [12, 25, 47] (see Fig. 12.2). A review of the first works proposed in this topic is presented by Krijn et al. [26].

The real patient will be able to discuss with them. The advantage is that we may easily change the type of people, their age, their sex, their attitude, which is not easy with real people.

A therapist is helping a patient overcome a fear of public speaking. To overcome this fear, the patient has to perform while immersed in a virtual environment consisting of a seminar room and a virtual audience, which can react to the user in an autonomous way. The therapist can choose the type of virtual audience (for instance, one that is aggressive or sexist) that will result in a more effective treatment for the patient. This framework [12] allows the real-time animation of a small group of characters. They are endowed with gaze control and facial animation. Scripts allow for interactive control of the characters in order to make them talk , for example; this consists in playing a prerecorded sound and animating the characters' face and eyes.

These scenarios can either be viewed on a monitor, in an HMD, or on a large back-projection screen. While using the HMD, the users' head can be tracked in order to modify the images with regard to head rotation for enhanced immersion. While using the back-projection screen, the user can be equipped with a coupled eye- and head-tracking device in order to determine where the user is looking on screen. The combination of the two allows freedom of movement in front of the screen.

Moreover, as in [16], an eye-tracking data visualization tool can be used. It is based on a gaze-map chromatic gradient coding. This allows representing the eye-tracked points on the virtual character even if it is dynamic. It therefore serves as assessment tool to analyze recorded eye-tracking data and illustrate possible eye contact avoidance behaviors. More details on this method can be found in [16].

12.2.2.1 Several Environments

The main scenes used in [12, 16] are depicted in Fig. 12.2. They were all designed to exercise public speaking.

The first scene is an office environment, depicted on the top left and top right of Fig. 12.2. Two different scenarios have been created with this environment; the first is an interview with the boss of a company. This was further diversified by letting the boss be either a man or a woman. The second scenario takes place in another room in the same environment and consists in sitting in front of five people from the company and having to give a speech.

The second environment, depicted in the middle left of Fig. 12.2 is a bar. The scenario consists of being seated facing a person in a bar. The user would have to imagine that this person is a new friend or a new colleague. Here as well, this character can be either a man or a woman. Other characters are seated at different tables in the bar. The third environment is a cafeteria, depicted in the middle right of Fig. 12.2. This scenario is actually very similar to that in the bar. Here as well, the user is seated facing a person, a man or a woman. Some social phobic people are unable to eat in front of others. Food was thus added on a plate in front of the user.

The last environment used in this context is an auditorium, illustrated at the bottom left and bottom right of Fig. 12.2. Various scenarios have also been created with this setup. In the first, the user is standing in the scene and has to give a speech or a presentation in front of a jury of five characters. In the second scenario, the user is also standing in the scene, but has to give a speech or a presentation in front of approximately 20 characters. Finally, in the last scenario, the user is seated at the back of the auditorium and has to ask questions to the character in the scene, presenting something. Here as well, approximately 20 other characters are seated in the auditorium.

12.3 Interactions Between Virtual Humans

12.3.1 Virtual Human Behavior

The virtual human's behavior is a result of the different interactions it has with its environment. Several cognitive models have been proposed to represent human decision-making such as SOAR [28], ACT-R [1], PECS [63], CLARION [61] or PMFs [58].

Fig. 12.2 Various VEs used for public speaking exercises. *Top left* Job interview simulation. *Top right* In an office, facing five people. *Middle left* Meeting in a bar. *Middle right* Meeting in a cafeteria. *Bottom left* Speech in front of an auditorium. *Bottom right* Sitting at the back of an auditorium

Cognitive models define how virtual humans perceive and interact with their environment, which includes other virtual humans. Paris and Donikian [44] propose a decision process based on Newell's [40] architecture in which virtual human interactions are separated into different abstraction layers, from physical to social interactions.

Virtual humans often interact with environments through events. The action of a virtual human can generate an event that will make another virtual human react and this will generate an interaction between virtual humans. The event can be directly sent to a particular virtual human through a message. Yu and Terzopulos [70] introduce a decision network framework for advanced behavioral modeling in virtual humans. Each virtual human is given a probability for a reactive decision to an event based on several features concerning the event and the agent. They use tables to store each possibility that can happen and give it a probability. Action selection is thus manually coded. Stocker et al. [60] introduced the notion of smart events. Smart events inform virtual humans about plausible actions to undertake. Different traits are given to the agents. Then a virtual human reacts to an event depending on both the nature of the event and the virtual human features. A similar work was realized with smart objects by [20]. Smart objects provide the expected behaviors to virtual humans about how they could be used.

In [33], virtual humans are guided by purposes. They differentiate three types of actions: scheduled, reactive, and need-based. They use the OCEAN psychological model [67] based on five factors (openness, conscientiousness, extroversion, agreeableness, and neuroticism) to manage need-based actions. Reactive actions are given high priority as they have to be done immediately after an event. Guy et al. [13] also use character traits, here to modify the locomotion behaviors of their virtual humans.

Virtual humans activity schedules can be represented in different ways: through finite state machines (FSM) [29, 60] or behavior trees [5, 57] for example.

12.3.2 Gaze Animation and Attention

Attentional behaviors should be added to the virtual human motion to increase realism and enhance considerably the interaction between virtual humans [11]. It can be achieved in two steps. The first step is to define the interest points, i.e., the points in the space that are considered as interesting and that therefore should attract the characters' attention. Several different methods can be used to do this depending on the result we want to obtain:

- The interest points can be defined as regions in space that have been described as interesting. In this case, they will be static.
- They can be defined as characters evolving in space. All characters may then potentially attract the attention of other characters as long as they are in their field of view. In this case, we have dynamic constraints, as the characters move around.
- They can be defined as a user if this user is tracked while interacting with the system. In this last case, a coupled head- and eye-tracking setup allows to define the position of the user in 3D space. Characters may then look at the user.

When considering characters attracting the attention of other characters, one method is to automatically detect the interest points for each character from the trajectories of the other characters. To do this, score functions may be used with the following components:

- Proximity: closer objects or people seem larger and attract attention more easily than those far away. Moreover, those that are closer occlude those that are further away.
- Relative speed: a person will be more prone to set his/her attention on something moving fast than on something moving slowly relative to his/her own velocity.
- Relative orientation: we are more attentive to objects coming toward us than those moving away from us. Moreover, something coming toward us seems to become larger.
- Periphery: we are sensitive to movements occurring in the peripheral vision. More specifically, to objects or people entering the field of view (see Fig. 12.3 left).

The second step to obtain the desired attentional behaviors consists in computing the displacement map that allows for the current character posture to achieve the gaze posture, i.e., to satisfy the gaze constraints (interest points) defined by the scoring function. Once the displacement map has been computed, it is dispatched to the various joints composing the eyes, head, and spine in order for each to contribute to the final posture. Finally, this displacement is propagated in time for looking at or looking away motions to be smooth, natural, and humanlike.

12.3.3 Interactions Through Navigation

The navigation task of virtual humans have also addressed the multiple virtual human interaction problem. Many kinds of models have been proposed to simulate the navigation of virtual humans in their environment. Agent-based models identify the interactions between each individual and its neighborhood to influence its behavior. Such models are thus related to our problematic, and different kinds of interactions have been modeled. Most of the models propose to directly control the velocity of the virtual humans, except force-based models.

Fig. 12.3 Example of attention and gaze animation

12.3.3.1 Collision Avoidance Behavior

Collision avoidance interaction is a research topic that has received much attention in the past years. Indeed, collision avoidance is a key factor for the behavioral realism perceived by the user. Moreover, increasing the number of simulated virtual humans brings problems of performance. Several approaches have been proposed to address these challenges.

Cellular automata models are based on a space discretization in cells. The principle is that each virtual human is on a cell and can only go to an empty cell. In general, the environment is represented by a bidimensional grid of cells. At each time step, each virtual human can reach an adjacent cell according to its preferred direction and a probabilistic approach [4, 54]. Kirchner et al. [24] looked after discretization effects and gave the possibility to virtual humans to fill more than one cell and to reach speeds higher than one cell per time step. Such an approach simplifies the expression of the interactions between virtual humans but the discrete aspect of the trajectories generates limitations in terms of realism and believability (Fig. 12.4).

Introduced by Helbing and Molnár [15], force-based models are inspired by Newtonian physics and consider that a virtual human is subject to attractive and repulsive forces that define its acceleration according to Newton's second law:

$$\sum \mathbf{F} = m \times \mathbf{a}, \tag{12.1}$$

where $\sum \mathbf{F}$ is the sum of the forces that are applied to a body of mass m, and $\mathbf{a}$. Attractive forces make the virtual human go toward a goal while repulsive forces solve collision avoidance issues between virtual humans. These models are efficient in terms of computation time but suffer from a lack of realism and the presence of many artifacts. Improvements have been proposed [19, 46] but there are still non-realistic behaviors, in particular, at the microscopic scale and with low densities of virtual humans.

While force-based models only take into account the position of the different obstacles, geometric models also take into account the obstacles' relative velocities

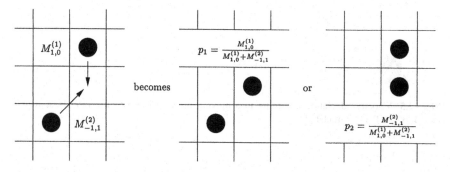

Fig. 12.4 Resolution of a collision conflict through the probabilistic approach presented in [4]

[22, 45, 49, 65]. These models are thus considered predictive as they are able to predict a future collision as long as the virtual human trajectory remains the same. Indeed, they determine which velocities will allow a virtual human to avoid a collision with the surrounding obstacles. Geometric models thus bring a high level of realism at the microscopic scale and are able to reproduce several macroscopic phenomena. There are still open questions about the combination of different interactions and on how to incorporate different sociocultural factors. The prediction proposed by these models is mainly linear and does not consider other virtual human intentions, which are however taken into account in real cases (Fig. 12.5).

Vision-based models introduce the perception-action loop into the virtual human behavior for its navigation task by simulating sensory perception [6, 9, 41–43, 51, 62]. They generally offer a high level of realism but suffer from efficiency issues, as ray-casting is a costly tool in terms of computation time. These models still need to be validated from real observations (Fig. 12.6).

In rule-based models, each virtual human behavior is subjected to rules that depend on the situation the virtual human is in. Very different rules can be defined and these models are quite heterogeneous [21, 30, 39, 53]. Rule-based models explicitly express the behavior of a rule. These rules generally come from observation and bring about realistic behaviors. However, challenges exist about how to combine these rules as well as about the effects of such combinations, and there are still open questions about the validity domain and the completeness of these models. Most of the models presented here only address the navigation task as a collision avoidance problem. Other kinds of interactions still exist in human behavior when navigating within a crowd. Rule-based models define in general more than only the collision avoidance interaction. They can also model following or group behaviors for example, and define in which conditions such interaction has to be applied to the virtual human (Fig. 12.7).

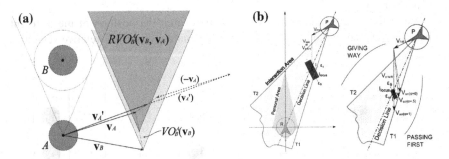

Fig. 12.5 Velocity adaptation according to a moving obstacle in geometric models. **a** RVO2 model [65]. **b** Pettré's model [49]

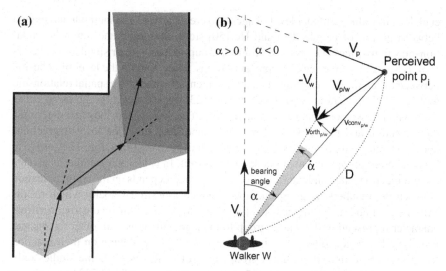

Fig. 12.6 Vision-based models. **a** Destination update according to the environment exploration [62]. **b** Velocity adaptation according to the mobile object perception [43]

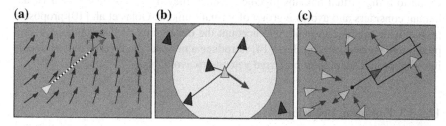

Fig. 12.7 Some behavior rules proposed by Reynolds [53]. **a** Flow following. **b** Separation. **c** Leader following

12.3.3.2 Group Behavior

Humans often move in groups rather than alone during their everyday life. Several works have been carried out on groups' behaviors during navigation. The first work was probably done by Reynolds [52], who simulated flocks, herds, and schools behaviors for animation purposes. Several models have been proposed to model group cohesion. These models are often integrated in collision avoidance simulations and are suited for a type of collision avoidance model such as cellular automata [35], force-based [3, 37], rule-based [39, 53], or velocity-based [23, 71] models.

Musse and Thalmann [39] present a system based on a multilevel hierarchy formed by crowd, groups, and agents on which they can manage the agents' degree of autonomy. They define rules to model flocking formation in groups. In [3, 37, 59], groups exist through an attractive force between the agents of the same group. Schuerman et al. [55] introduce a higher level of agents to create groups and facilitate navigation between groups of people. Qiu and Hu [50] store intragroup and intergroup relationships in matrices and produce different group shapes in their simulations. Peters et al. [48] also use matrices to represent groups. They contain the level of cohesion between the members of a group, i.e., their tendency to maintain a spatial relationship with each other. Karamouzas and Overmars [23] consider each group as an entity itself with its own position, velocity, and goal. At each time step, they first determine the formation and the velocity of the group and then solve the local interactions between agents with a velocity-based approach using a cost function. They strive to keep coherent groups and avoid making them split. In [71], each member is given a communication value and the formation of the group depends on the communication between its members. A group member is given a desired velocity which results from its goal and its willingness to stay in the group. They also construct a virtual character representing the whole group to manage collisions with other agents and propose a heterogeneous interaction between walkers by playing on their reaction flexibility. Their algorithm allows groups to split if necessary. Some studies only focus on simulating small groups of 2, 3, or 4 pedestrians [23, 37, 71].

Some recent works have also been realized on how a virtual human considers a group during its navigation task. These works do not focus on social groups by trying to bring virtual humans together. Rather, they try to simulate how a virtual human considers and avoids a group of virtual humans. Golas et al. [10] propose a probabilistic approach to take into account the uncertainty of long-range collision prediction. He and van den Berg [14] introduce a mesoscopic layer to cluster agents into groups and adapt their preferred velocity to avoid them.

12.3.3.3 Following Behavior

About following behavior, few models have been proposed so far. It has mainly been included in group behavior as several group behavior models propose a follow-the-leader approach [3, 34, 39]. In follow-the-leader approaches, each following virtual human tries to follow one leader while avoiding the other virtual humans, including the ones from the group.

Pelechano et al. [46] use influence areas to model following behavior; if a virtual human's influence area is free, then it can move on. Aw et al. [2] propose a road traffic model that could also be applied to walking virtual humans (Fig. 12.8).

Psychologists have also studied such behavior by studying humans breaking behavior through visual control [8, 31, 69].

In [53] a following behavior is also proposed by combining several rules. It consists of targeting a point located just behind the leader:

$$v(t + 1) = v_{\max} * \frac{d(t) - d_{\text{offset}}}{d_{\text{slow}}}, \tag{12.2}$$

Fig. 12.8 Simulating groups of people in [66]

where $v(t + 1)$ is the agent velocity at time $t + 1$, v_{max} the comfort velocity, $d(t)$ the distance to leader at time t, d_{offset} the offset distance, and d_{slow} the distance from which the follower starts to slow down.

Lemercier et al. [32] aim at modeling and simulating the following interactions between individuals moving in crowds. They built up a kinematic database to observe following behaviors during pedestrian groups movement from an original experimental process using motion capture. From this database they present a detailed analysis of these data by highlighting both the nature of the local interactions between participants and the global patterns that emerge from the combination of these interactions, in particular, the formation of propagating speed waves. Based on this analysis, they propose a realistic model of following behavior between pedestrians calibrated on the experimental data that controls the acceleration of the virtual human instead of directly controlling its velocity:

$$a(t) = C \cdot \Delta v(t - \tau) \cdot \rho^{\gamma}(t), \tag{12.3}$$

where $a(t)$ is the tangential acceleration at time t, $\Delta v(t)$ the relative speed between follower and leader at time t, τ a delay parameter, and ρ the local density ($\rho = 1/\Delta p$), which is the multiplicative inverse of the distance, C, and γ parameters.

Simulation results are evaluated on their capacity to reproduce the observed macroscopic patterns (Fig. 12.9).

Fig. 12.9 Waiting queue simulated in [32]

12.3.3.4 Evaluating Models

One of the main upcoming challenges is to be able to evaluate the quality of virtual human behaviors. Such evaluation would enable to compare the behavioral realism of different models.

A first way to evaluate the quality of virtual humans behaviors is through user studies, where real humans observe and rate the believability of virtual human behaviors [27].

In the navigation problematic, another approach is also used. Observations of real humans' behaviors have been carried out to evaluate navigation behaviors. Some studies have been realized about the formation of pedestrian lanes. Yamori [68] observed lane formation at a crosswalk while [38] studied their conditions of apparition in an experimental setup. Daamen and Hoogendoorn [7] carried out experiments to study unidirectional and bidirectional traffic, crossing situations and bottlenecks (Fig. 12.10).

Several studies have also been carried out on groups dynamics about their size, their shape, and their evolution according to the environment conditions [37, 48]. There have also been studies of following behaviors.

Several observations have been carried out in the context of unidirectional traffic to study the fundamental diagram that expresses the relation between human speed and their density [18, 56, 64] (Fig. 12.11). The dynamics of speed waves have also been addressed [18].

It is however still challenging to evaluate such behaviors due to the chaotic aspect of multiple humans' decisions, particularly when considering both microscopic and macroscopic scales.

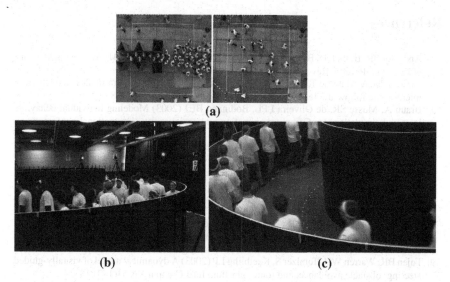

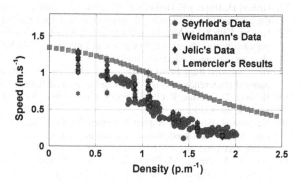

Fig. 12.10 Experimental studies on crowd dynamics. **a** Bottleneck and crossing observations by Daamen and Hoogendoorn [7]. **b** Observation of lane formation by Moussaïd et al. [38]. **c** Following behaviors observed by Jelić et al. [18]

Fig. 12.11 Fundamental diagram data acquired in [18, 56, 64] and simulation results obtained in [32]

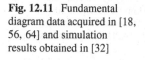

12.4 Conclusion

This chapter proposes a review of the interactions between real and multiple virtual humans. After a presentation of the problematics and approaches raised by virtual human interactions, different methods for simulating such interactions have been discussed. First, interactions between real and multiple virtual humans have been presented, with a focus on virtual assistants and social phobia examples. Then interactions between virtual humans have been adressed, particularly, gaze attention of other characters and navigation interactions between multiple virtual humans.

References

1. Anderson JR, Bothell D, Byrne MD, Douglass S, Lebiere C, Qin Y (2004) An integrated theory of the mind. Psychol Rev 111:1036–1060
2. Aw A, Klar A, Materne T, Rascle M (2002) Derivation of continuum traffic flow models from microscopic follow-the-leader models. SIAM J Appl Math 63:259–278
3. Braun A, Musse SR, de Oliveira LPL, Bodmann BEJ (2003) Modeling individual behaviors in crowd simulation. In: Computer animation and social agents, international conference on 2003, p 0:143
4. Burstedde C, Klauck K, Schadschneider A, Zittartz J (2001) Simulation of pedestrian dynamics using a two-dimensional cellular automaton. Physica A Stat Mech Appl 295:507–525
5. Cavazza M, Charles F, Mead SJ (2002) Character-based interactive storytelling. IEEE Intell Syst 17(4):17–24
6. Conde T, Thalmann D (2006) An integrated perception for autonomous virtual agents: active and predictive perception. Comput Anim Virtual Worlds 17:457–468
7. Daamen W, Hoogendoorn SP (2003) Qualitative results from pedestrian laboratory experiments. In: Pedestrian and evacuation dynamics, pp 121–132
8. Fajen BR (2007) Affordance-based control of visually guided action. Ecol Psychol 19:383–410
9. Fajen BR, Warren WH, Temizer S, Kaelbling LP (2003) A dynamical model of visually-guided steering, obstacle avoidance, and route selection. Int J Comput Vis 54(1–3):13–34
10. Golas A, Narain R, Lin M (2013) Hybrid long-range collision avoidance for crowd simulation. In: Proceedings of the ACM SIGGRAPH symposium on interactive 3D graphics and games, pp 29–36
11. Grillon H, Thalmann D (2009) Simulating gaze attention behaviors for crowds. Comput Anim Virtual Worlds 20:111–119
12. Grillon H, Riquier F, Herbelin B, Thalmann D (2006) Virtual reality as a therapeutic tool in the confines of social anxiety disorder treatment. Int J Disabil Hum Dev 5:243–250
13. Guy SJ, Kim S, Lin MC, Manocha D (2011) Simulating heterogeneous crowd behaviors using personality trait theory. In: Proceedings of the 2011 ACM SIGGRAPH/Eurographics symposium on computer animation, pp 43–52
14. He L, van den Berg J (2013) Meso-scale planning for multi-agent navigation. In: IEEE international conference on robotics and automation (ICRA) 2013, pp 2839–2844
15. Helbing D, Molnár P (1995) Social force model for pedestrian dynamics. Phys Rev E 51(5):4282–4286
16. Herbelin B, Benzaki P, Riquier F, Renault O, Thalmann D (2004) Using physiological measures for emotional assessment: a computer-aided tool for cognitive and behavioural therapy. ICDVRAT 2004:307–314
17. Herbelin B, Ponder M, Thalmann D (2005) Building exposure: synergy of interaction and narration through the social channel. Presence 14:234–246
18. Jelić A, Appert-Rolland C, Lemercier S, Pettré J (2012) Properties of pedestrians walking in line: fundamental diagrams. Phys Rev E 85:036111
19. Johansson A, Helbing D, Shukla PK (2007) Specification of the social force pedestrian model by evolutionary adjustment to video tracking data. Adv Complex Syst 10 (supp02):271–288
20. Kallmann M, Thalmann D (1999) Direct 3d interaction with smart objects. In: Proceedings of the ACM symposium on virtual reality software and technology, pp 124–130
21. Kapadia M, Singh S, Hewlett W, Faloutsos P (2009) Egocentric affordance fields in pedestrian steering. In: I3D'09: proceedings of the 2009 symposium on interactive 3D graphics and games, pp 215–223
22. Karamouzas I, Overmars M (2010) A velocity-based approach for simulating human collision avoidance. In: Intelligent virtual agents. Springer, Berlin, pp 180–186
23. Karamouzas I, Overmars M (2012) Simulating and evaluating the local behavior of small pedestrian groups. Vis Comput Graph IEEE Trans 18:394–406
24. Kirchner A, Klüpfel H, Nishinari K, Schadschneider A, Schreckenberg M (2004) Discretization effects and the influence of walking speed in cellular automata models for pedestrian dynamics. J Stat Mech: Theory Exp 10:P10011

25. Klinger E, Bouchard S, Légeron P, Roy S, Lauer F, Chemin I, Nugues P (2005) Virtual reality therapy versus cognitive behavior therapy for social phobia: a preliminary controlled study. Cyberpsychol Behav 8(1):76–88
26. Krijn M, Emmelkamp PMG, Olafsson RP, Biemond R (2004) Virtual reality exposure therapy of anxiety disorders: a review. Clinical psychol Rev 24(3):259–281
27. Kulpa R, Olivier A-H, Ondřej J, Pettré J (2011) Imperceptible relaxation of collision avoidance constraints in virtual crowds. ACM Trans Graph 30:138:1–138:10
28. Laird JE, Newell A, Rosenbloom PS (1987) Soar: an architecture for general intelligence. Artif Intell 33(1):1–64
29. Lamarche F, Donikian S (2002) Automatic orchestration of behaviours through the management of resources and priority levels. In: Proceedings of the first international joint conference on autonomous agents and multiagent systems: part 3, pp 1309–1316
30. Lamarche F, Donikian S (2004) Crowd of virtual humans: a new approach for real time navigation in complex and structured environments. Comput Graph Forum 23:509–518
31. Lee DN (1976) A theory of visual control of braking based on information about time-to-collision. Perception 5:437–459
32. Lemercier S, Jelic A, Kulpa R, Hua J, Fehrenbach J, Degond P, Appert-Rolland C, Donikian S, Pettré J (2012) Realistic following behaviors for crowd simulation. Comput Graph Forum 31:489–498
33. Li W, Allbeck JM (2011) Populations with purpose. In: Motion in games. Springer, Berlin, Heidelberg, pp 132–143
34. Li T-Y, Jeng Y-J, Chang S-I (2001) Simulating virtual human crowds with a leader-follower model. In: Proceedings of computer animation 2001. The fourteenth conference on computer animation, pp 93 –102
35. Loscos C, Marchal D, Meyer A (2003) Intuitive crowd behavior in dense urban environments using local laws. Theory Pract Comput Graph 2003:122–129
36. Manganas A, Tsiknakis M, Leisch E, Karefilaki L, Monsieurs K, Bossaert LL, Giorgini F (2004) Just in time health emergency interventions: an innovative approach to training the citizen for emergency situations using virtual reality techniques and advanced it tools (the web-cd). Studies in health technology and informatics, pp 315–326
37. Moussaïd M, Perozo N, Garnier S, Helbing D, Theraulaz G (2010) The walking behaviour of pedestrian social groups and its impact on crowd dynamics. PLoS ONE 5:10047
38. Moussaïd M, Guillot EG, Moreau M, Fehrenbach J, Chabiron O, Lemercier S, Pettré J, Appert-Rolland C, Degond P, Theraulaz G (2012) Traffic instabilities in self-organized pedestrian crowds. PLoS Comput Biol 8:1–10
39. Musse SR, Thalmann D (2001) Hierarchical model for real time simulation of virtual human crowds. Vis Comput Graph IEEE Trans 7(2):152–164
40. Newell A (1994) Unified theories of cognition. Harvard University Press, Cambridge
41. Noser H, Renault O, Thalmann D, Thalmann NM (1995) Navigation for digital actors based on synthetic vision, memory, and learning. Comput Graph 19:7–19
42. Noser H, Thalmann D (1998) Sensor-based synthetic actors in a tennis game simulation. Vis Comput 14:193–205
43. Ondřej J, Pettré J, Olivier A-H, Donikian S (2010) A synthetic-vision based steering approach for crowd simulation. ACM Trans Graph 29:123:1–123:9
44. Paris S, Donikian S (2009) Activity-driven populace: a cognitive approach to crowd simulation. IEEE Comput Graph Appl 29(4):34–43
45. Paris S, Pettré J, Donikian S (2007) Pedestrian reactive navigation for crowd simulation: a predictive approach. Eurographics'07. Comput Graph Forum 26:665–674
46. Pelechano N, Allbeck JM, Badler NI (2007) Controlling individual agents in high-density crowd simulation. In: SCA'07: proceedings of the 2007 ACM SIGGRAPH/Eurographics symposium on computer animation, pp 99–108
47. Pertaub DP, Slater M, Barker C (2001) An experiment on fear of public speaking in virtual reality. Studies in health technology and informatics, pp 372–378

48. Peters C, Ennis C (2009) Modeling groups of plausible virtual pedestrians. IEEE Comput Graph Appl 29:54–63
49. Pettré J, Ondřej J, Olivier A-H, Cretual A, Donikian S (2009) Experiment-based modeling, simulation and validation of interactions between virtual walkers. In: SCA'09: proceedings of the 2009 ACM SIGGRAPH/Eurographics symposium on computer animation, pp 189–198
50. Qiu F, Hu X (2010) Modeling group structures in pedestrian crowd simulation. Simul Modell Pract Theory 18:190–205
51. Renault O, Thalmann NM, Thalmann D (1990) A vision-based approach to behavioural animation. J Vis Comput Anim 1:18–21
52. Reynolds CW (1987) Flocks, herds and schools: a distributed behavioral model. In: SIG-GRAPH'87: proceedings of the 14th annual conference on computer graphics and interactive techniques, pp 25–34
53. Reynolds CW (1999) Steering behaviors for autonomous characters. In: Game developers conference. http://www.red3d.com/cwr/steer/gdc99
54. Schadschneider A (2001) Cellular automaton approach to pedestrian dynamics—theory. In: Pedestrian and evacuation dynamics, pp 75–86
55. Schuerman M, Singh S, Kapadia M, Faloutsos P (2010) Situation agents: agent-based externalized steering logic. Comput Anim Virtual Worlds 21:267–276
56. Seyfried A, Steffen B, Klingsch W, Boltes M (2005) The fundamental diagram of pedestrian movement revisited. J Stat Mech: Theory Exp 10:P10002
57. Shoulson A, Garcia FM, Jones M, Mead R, Badler NI (2011) Parameterizing behavior trees. In: Proceedings of the 4th international conference on motion in games, pp 144–155
58. Silverman BG, Johns M, Cornwell J, O'Brien K (2006) Human behavior models for agents in simulators and games: part I: enabling science with pmfserv. Presence: Teleoper Virtual Environ 15(2):139–162
59. Singh H, Arter R, Dodd L, Langston P, Lester E, Drury J (2009) Modelling subgroup behaviour in crowd dynamics DEM simulation. Appl Math Modell 33:4408–4423
60. Stocker C, Sun L, Huang P, Qin W, Allbeck JM, Badler NI (2010) Smart events and primed agents. In: Intelligent virtual agents. Springer, Berlin, pp 15–27
61. Sun R (2006) Cognition and multi-agent interaction: from cognitive modeling to social simulation, chapter the CLARION cognitive architecture: extending cognitive modeling to social simulation. Cambridge University Press, Cambridge, p 142
62. Turner A (2007) To move through space: lines of vision and movement. In: Proceedings, 6th international space syntax symposium
63. Urban C, Schmidt B (2001) Pecs—agent-based modelling of human behaviour. In: Emotional and intelligent II—the tangled knot of social cognition, AAAI fall symposium
64. Ulrich W (1993) Transporttechnik der fussgänger—transporttechnische eigenschaften des fuss-gängerverkehrs (literaturstudie). Technical report, Institut füer Verkehrsplanung, Transporttechnik, Strassen- und Eisenbahnbau IVT an der ETH Zürich, German
65. van den Berg J, Stephen G, Ming L, Dinesh M (2011) Reciprocal n-body collision avoidance. Robotics research, vol 70. Springer, Berlin, pp 3–19
66. Wang Y, Dubey R, Magnenat-Thalmann N, Thalmann D (2013) An immersive multi-agent system for interactive applications. Vis Comput 29:323–332
67. Wiggins JS (1996) The five-factor model of personality: theoretical perspectives. Guilford Press, New York
68. Yamori K (1998) Going with the flow: micro-macro dynamics in the macrobehavioral patterns of pedestrian crowds. Psychol Rev 105:530–557
69. Yilmaz EH, Warren WH (1995) Visual control of braking: a test of the τ hypothesis. J Exp Psychol: Hum Percept Perform 21(5):996–1014
70. Yu Q, Terzopoulos D (2007) A decision network framework for the behavioral animation of virtual humans. In: Proceedings of the 2007 ACM SIGGRAPH/Eurographics symposium on computer animation, pp 119–128
71. Zhang Y, Pettre J, Qin X, Donikian S, Peng Q (2011) A local behavior model for small pedestrian groups. In: 12th international conference on computer-aided design and computer graphics (CAD/Graphics), pp 275–281

Chapter 13
Multimodal and Multi-party Social Interactions

Zerrin Yumak and Nadia Magnenat-Thalmann

Abstract Virtual characters and robots interacting with people in social contexts should understand the users' behaviours and respond back with gestures, facial expressions and gaze. The challenges in this area are the estimation of high level user states fusing low level multi-modal sensory input, taking socially appropriate decisions using this partial sensory information and rendering synchronized and timely multi-modal behaviours based on taken decisions. Moreover, these characters should be able to communicate with multiple users and also among each other in multi-party group interactions. In this chapter, we provide an overview of the methods for multi-modal and multi-party interactions and discuss the challenges in this area. We also mention our current work and point out the future research directions.

13.1 Introduction

Personal assistants such as iPhone Siri and Microsoft Cortana have started to take part in our lives recently. However, these personal assistants are limited in social intelligence and are not yet capable of understanding the context, users' intentions, and emotions. We believe that, in the future, we will have more of these characters integrated in our daily lives as companions and assistants, and also in physical forms as virtual humans and social robots. In order for us to interact with them in a natural way, they are expected to behave according to social rules and norms and adapt to our human life.

Recognition of goals, intentions, and emotions of other people is a major aspect of communication between people. To give humanlike capabilities to artificial characters, they should be equipped with the ability to predict these user states. They should understand users' behaviors through various sensors and respond back using

Z. Yumak (✉) · N. Magnenat-Thalmann
BeingThere Centre, Nanyang Technological University, Singapore, Singapore
e-mail: zerrin.yumak@gmail.com

N. Magnenat-Thalmann
e-mail: nadiathalmann@ntu.edu.sg

© Springer International Publishing Switzerland 2016
N. Magnenat-Thalmann et al. (eds.), *Context Aware Human-Robot and Human-Agent Interaction*, Human–Computer Interaction Series,
DOI 10.1007/978-3-319-19947-4_13

multimodal output. Besides natural multimodal interaction, they should also be able to communicate with multiple users and among each other in multi-party group interactions. The challenges in this area include (1) estimating high-level user states based on low-level multimodal sensory input, (2) taking socially appropriate decisions using this partial sensory information, and (3) rendering synchronized and timely multimodal behaviors. In this chapter, we provide an overview of the previous work for multimodal and multi-party interactions and discuss the challenges in this area. First, in Sect. 13.2, we provide a general overview of methods in multimodal sensing, decision making, and multimodal behavior generation. Section 13.3 mentions in particular the challenges in multi-party interaction; finally, in Sect. 13.4, we present our proposed work, provide a discussion on the current results, and point out the future research directions.

13.2 Overview of Steps in Multimodal Interaction

Multimodality in human–computer interaction refers to natural interaction with a computer using speech, vision, facial expressions, and gestures. Two or more modalities are combined to infer the user's state with regard to the application. For example, in a multimodal speaker identification task, face recognition, and speaker identification techniques can be combined by processing audiovisual input. High-level emotional and cognitive states can be inferred using multiple modalities as a combination of facial expressions, voice, gestures, and posture. Multimodality can also be on the output side to generate the synchronized gestures, facial expressions, and gaze.

A standard pipeline for a multimodal interaction system consists of the following steps: (1) Individual low-level sensing modules (e.g., face recognition, skeleton tracking, sound localization, speech recognition), (2) multimodal tracking and fusion to combine information from individual trackers for making high-level inferences about the situation and the user state, (3) decision making and dialogue management to decide what to say and what to do given the partial sensory information, history of actions and the artificial character's internal state, (4) planning and synchronization of the output behavior to render the output decisions, and (5) actual realization of the planned behaviors at the level of motor controls for the robots and using computer animation techniques for virtual humans.

In this chapter, we are mainly interested in steps 2, 3, and 4, which stays between low-level sensing and behavior generation and deals with high-level user states, decisions, and behaviors. While the methods on the individual trackers and motion generation/animation side are pretty much established, the methods in the middle layers vary a lot according to the requirements of the applications. Thus, research in this area is still at its early stages due to the complexity of human behaviors in social contexts, the lack of human–computer interaction studies and data collection in real-world settings. In the following sections, we give an overview of the methods in steps 2, 3, and 4.

13.2.1 Multimodal Tracking and Fusion

The advantage of multimodal tracking is twofold. First, multiple modalities provide complementary information, i.e., information from sound localization and user tracking can be combined to decide which user is speaking. Second, multiple modalities can be useful in case one modality cannot be used efficiently due to environmental conditions, i.e. in case of poor lighting conditions, speaker identification from voice might be a better solution when face recognition results are not very accurate.

Multimodal fusion can be at the feature-level combining features at the low-level signal processing layer or can be at later stages at the semantic level. Atrey et al. [1] classify fusion techniques as below:

- *Early fusion* is suitable when input modalities are temporally synchronized, e.g., audiovisual speech recognition combining speech and lip movements. The features from multimodalities are combined into a single feature vector and classified.
- *Intermediate fusion* methods are used for inferring high-level states such as user intent, emotions, and activities, which are based on related but not always temporally aligned features. Methods such as probabilistic graphical models are used for fusing different sources of input.
- *Late fusion* works at the semantic level by fusing partial outputs from unimodal classifiers. It uses data structures such as frames to represent objects/relations and natural language processing tools such as typed feature structures for unification. Late fusion is appropriate for less temporally coupled modalities such as speech and pen input.

Various methods can be used for fusion depending on the synchronization between modalities [1]. *Rule-based* fusion methods include linear weighted fusion of individual decisions and are rather appropriate for early and intermediate fusion, e.g. MAX, MIN, AND, OR operations, and majority voting. At the semantic level, custom-defined application-dependent rules can be applied [36]. *Classification-based* methods classify multimodal observations into predefined classes. Support vector machines (SVMs), Dempster–Shafer theory, dynamic Bayesian networks (DBNs), neural networks (NNs) and maximum entropy model belong to this category. *Estimation-based* methods are used to estimate the state of a moving object or to combine input from multiple sensors. Kalman and Particle filters (also called sequential Monte Carlo method) are examples in this category. For an extensive analysis of these methods we refer to [1].

13.2.2 Decision Making for Social Interaction

The next step in the multimodal interaction pipeline is decision making and dialogue management. This step is related to the planning of the communicative intents and dialogue moves. It deals with high-level concepts such as who is communicating with whom, in which socio-cultural and situational context, the overall interaction history of the communication partners, the intention and content of the communication as well as personality and emotion of the communication partners [22]. However, these concepts are application dependent. Functional Mark-up Language (FML) is an attempt by the community for standardization. It provides an inventory of high-level concepts in social interaction. The basic building blocks of a communicative event according to FML description are the *communication partners* and *communication acts*. The tags for each are mentioned below [22]:

- *Communication partners*: person, name, gender, type of the character, appearance, voice, personality, mood, role in the given application, emotion felt, emotion expressed, and interpersonal stance (relation to the communicative partner).
- *Communication acts*: turn-taking, communicative acts (related to communicative function or goal such as provide–get information, improve relationship, maintain–gain power, cheat, lie), dialogue acts (verbal communication acts such as question, answer, assertion), information structure (what is being communicated (theme) and what is new (rheme)), nonverbal acts such as backchannels, producer of the communicative act, addressee and hearer of the communicative act, receiver of the communicative act (the one who feels addressed by the producer, the receiver and addressee might be different), perceiver of the communicative act (the overhearer of the communicative act).

Bickmore [3] introduced contextual tags to define the purpose of the interaction, e.g. task (information exchange), social (social chat, small talk), empathy (comforting interactions), and encouragement (coaching, motivating). Gaze is also subject to discussion as it is often defined at the behavior level in the previous work. However, Lee et al. [23] argue that gaze is a complex phenomenon reflecting the cognitive states such as task planning, dialogue, and emotions and should be defined at the communicative intent level. It has several roles such as conversation regulation, monitoring of expected/unexpected changes, or attention to a physical stimulant in the environment. Thus, they define gaze behavior tags which are indicators of the reason for the gaze behavior. Lee et al. [23] propose two different types of emotion tags: felt emotions that occur as a result of the appraisal process of events and intended emotions that are used as coping strategies. Developing computational models of these concepts has been an active research area recently. For instance, personality, mood, and emotions were modeled as three-layer models [12, 14]. Bickmore and Cassell [4] modeled relationships based on the trust concept. Gockley et al. [15] described an affective system based on emotion, mood, and attitudes toward users where attitudes were represented with dimensions like familiarity and affect. Kasap et al. [17] developed an emotion model that updates social relationship dimensions friendliness and dominance, using past interactions derived from an episodic memory.

Decision-making methods are typically goal based or utility based. Goal-based characters have a description of what is desirable and combine this with their perception in order to choose actions that achieve the goals. They provide an intelligent way of decision making using AI planning techniques. Belief-Desire-Intention (BDI) architecture is a widely used goal-based architecture, where *belief* stands for the characters knowledge about the world, *desires* are the objectives to be accomplished and *intentions* are what the characters have chosen to do [27]. In our previous work [16], we have combined finite-state-machines and hierarchical task networks to model interactions with an emotion and memory enabled virtual character and social robot. Utility-based approaches are useful when there are multiple ways to reach a goal or when there are conflicting goals. Decision-theoretic methods combine probability and utility theory and update current state by choosing the action with the highest expected utility, e.g., [34]. Strategies for decisions can be either based on handcrafted rules or they can be learned from data. The latter requires huge data collection effort, however, action or dialogue strategies are learned automatically and relieve the application developer from the burden of writing handcrafted rules. Thus, there is an increasing interest in the community to learn decision policies from data of human–human and human–machine interactions.

In contrast to the above systems that keep an internal variable state to model the decisions of an artificial character, behavior-based architectures model behaviors via sensory-motor links without having an explicit internal representation of the environment and the user. In other words, raw input obtained from the sensors is used to generate reactive behaviors and the character gradually learns to correct its actions by making mistakes. Subsumption architecture [10] is an early example of this method and is based on hierarchies of sub-behaviors which are triggered based on their priority. Behavior-based models can be used to model reactive behaviors such as obstacle avoidance and attention modeling based on a bottom-up approach. In contrast, state-based approaches work top-down and make high-level inferences about the world and user state.

13.2.3 Behavior Generation for Virtual Characters and Social Robots

Virtual characters and social robots use gaze, posture and hand-arm gestures while interacting with people. The synchronization among various body expressions, gestures, facial expressions, gaze, and head movements is a challenging task [21].

For generation of nonverbal behaviors, Lee et al. [24] mention two main approaches: literature-based and machine learning. The literature-based approach relies on the findings on human behavior understanding which are obtained through manual analysis of observations and recordings. The disadvantage of this method is its inadequacy to explain the full complexity of the mappings between behaviors and the communicative functions. For example, nonverbal behaviors might be affected by several factors such as emotion, personality, gender and social context, and the relations between them may not be understood very well through observation. On the other hand, machine learning approaches automatize this process and find regularities and dependencies between these factors using statistics, e.g., head movements generation [24] and gesture generation [20]. However, obtaining good annotated data remains a disadvantage. Behavior Expression Animation Toolkit (BEAT) [11] allows the animators to input typed text that they wish to be spoken by an animated character, similar to the way a text-to-speech system produces speech output from text. The text input is analyzed according to its linguistic and contextual features and a rule base is created to convert these features into appropriate behaviors. Clauses are divided into two parts called theme (the part of the clause that creates a coherent link with a preceding clause) and rheme (the part that contributes some new information). The novelty and contrast of the words and their semantic meaning are also taken into consideration. For example, if a rheme contains a new node, the system generates a beat gesture that coincides with the object phrase. Another work in the same direction is the Nonverbal Behavior Generator (NVBG) [25]. NVBG takes as input FML and produces in turn Behavior Mark-up Language (BML). BML is an XML-based language to coordinate speech, gesture, gaze, and body movements.

At the motion generation level, two main approaches are used to animate the computer generated characters and to program the movements of the robots: data-based methods that represent the animations as a trajectory of joints over time (keyframe-based animation, blend shapes, morph targets, motion capture, and variances of motion capture methods such as motion graphs) and parameter-based methods which set parameters to generate the animations (procedural animation, e.g. walking, inverse forward kinematics, physically-based animation). Individual animation controllers are often developed for each of these animations. However, the animations often happen at the same time and can effect the same body parts. This raises challenges in the synchronization and blending of animations. Existing game engines cannot handle complex character animations although they provide solutions for other real-time simulation problems [33]. Thus, this is an open research area which requires further attention.

13.3 Multi-party Interaction: Current State and Challenges

Multi-party interactions involve several participants organized in a certain way to interact with each other. Participants position and orient themselves in a way that allows them to address other participants. The analysis of group interaction and dynamics in human–human interaction has been subject to attention in the area of social pyschology and nonverbal communication. Kendon [19] mentions that people often group themselves into clusters, lines or circles or various other kinds of patterns. These patterns are called "formations." An F-formation is a special type of formation that happens when group members come together in a way that the space between them is shared allowing their equal contribution. It is the type of group interaction that happens everyday when people form a conversational group for casual talk. Participants stand so that they face inwards to a shared space in which they cooperate together. Figure 13.1a shows an F-formation with three participants. The region between the participants is called an o-space, while the region they occupy is called a p-space and the region behind them is called an r-space. In case of multi-party interactions with artificial characters, the area that people can interact in is

Fig. 13.1 F-formation for
agents. **a** F-formation.
b F-formation for humans

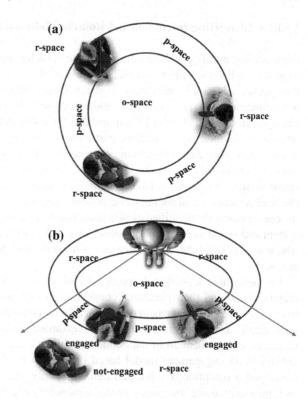

constrained by the field of view angle (FOV) of the camera used for detecting people. While human beings have a 180° horizontal FOV and 135° vertical FOV, cameras used for tracking often have limitations. In Fig. 13.1b, we see how o-space, r-space, and p-space change according to the field of view of the camera.

Previous work on interactive virtual humans and social robots mainly focusing on one-to-one interactions and multi-party interactions involving multiple users and multiple artificial characters has not been investigated enough. Although there has been research on modeling group and multi-party interactions in virtual reality applications [37], modeling of multi-party interactions in open and dynamic environments with multiple people requires further investigation. In this section, we will discuss the challenges and current approaches to multi-party interaction in three steps: tracking and fusion, decision making, and behavior generation.

13.3.1 Tracking and Fusion for Multi-party Interaction

For multi-party interaction a tracking system should be able to make continuous inferences about the current state of the scene. Below, we mention the challenges in tracking and fusion for multi-party interaction.

13.3.1.1 Identifying Intentions and Roles in Multi-party Interaction

For modeling multi-party interaction, the state of each participant needs to be tracked to identify who is willing to interact with whom. This includes the identification of the speaker, addressee, and detecting engagement intentions. The participants may have different roles such as speaker, addressee, side participants or overhearers. For example, Bohus and Horvitz [7] capture these roles by defining a signal source and addressees. In their representation, participants of the conversation are determined based on an engagement detection component. The people other than the engaged ones are considered overhearers. If there is a speech contribution in a detected conversation, a subset of the participants is defined as the addressees of the signal based on the head orientation and attention components. The ones that are not the addressees in the conversation are identified as side participants. Location features from the vision system and sound angle from the sound localization system are combined to decide which user is speaking. For addressee estimation, head pose and posture direction are used.

Engagement is defined as the process by which individuals in an interaction start, maintain, and end their perceived connection to one another [35]. There are two lines of research in engagement detection: rule-based methods that infer engagement heuristically using proximity and attention features and machine learning approaches that learn engagement from data collected through interactions. Peters et al. [31] developed an engagement model based on interest level. Michalowski et al. [28] developed a receptionist robot and defined people who were attending based on their proximity using four states: *present*, *attending*, *engaged*, and *interacting*. Their model was also based on heuristic rules but designed for the purpose of multi-user interaction. Foster et al. [13] described a data-driven engagement estimation method where the robot serves drinks to customers. They compared the machine learning approach with a rule-based hand-coded method derived from observations in a real bar. According to their findings the data-driven method outperforms the rule-based method. Engagement intentions of the user were determined based on the proximity of the user to the bar and eye contact with the bartender. The data collected were hand-labelled with three classes: *notSeekingEngagement*, *seekingEngagement* and *engaged*, and face and head coordinates were used as features. Bohus et al. [6] developed a dynamic engagement model where the dialogue system learned to predict engagement intentions in situ through interaction. They first applied a heuristic engagement estimation method assuming a person is engaged if there is a frontal face in front of the camera. Then the moments before engagement are labelled automatically as engagement intention to train the system without hand labelling. They applied a maximum entropy model to detect engagement intentions fusing several features such as location of the face, width and height, confidence score of the face, trajectory of location features, and manually labelled attention features.

One of the open research areas regarding engagement is the detection of group engagements. This happens when participants want to engage with a group of embodied characters rather than with only one character. In Sect. 13.4, we further discuss the challenges in engagement with multiple users and multiple embodied characters.

13.3.1.2 Interruptions and Overlaps During Speech

Most of the dialogue systems follow a "you-speak-then-I-speak" approach, which leads to an unnatural interaction experience [7]. In a multi-party interaction set-up, users can interrupt each other or they can also interrupt the system. In both cases it is necessary for the system to understand who is speaking at any moment, as the spoken signals may overlap. Audiovisual speaker diarization methods can be used to identify who is speaking. Speaker diarization helps to identify the speaker turn points and answer the question, "Who spoke when?" in an audio or video recording that contains an unknown amount of speakers. It is a method often applied for multimodal meeting analysis [38].

From the dialogue systems literature, allowing input during system speech is known as "barge-in." Speaker diarization systems can distinguish between speech and nonspeech sound segments and find out which user is speaking. However, system's own speech output (synthesized speech) can also be considered as an environmental noise during human–machine interaction. Echo cancellation and noise removal techniques are used for this by subtracting the system's own voice from the acoustic signal coming to the microphone array. In this way, the speaker can still be recognized while the speech synthesis keeps running [2]. Otherwise, speech recognition software may misinterpret the system output as user input and this may result in unnecessary dialogue exchanges.

Another point is the discrimination between barge-ins and backchanneling. The user might speak during system speech for two reasons. One of them is interrupting the system speech (barge-in) as we explained above. The second is backchanneling (e.g. uh-huh, hmmm, yeah, really? Wow!) to signal clarifications or interest on what is spoken but does not imply a request for the turn. These two can be distinguished as the overlapping speech will be shorter in case of backchanneling [2].

Finally, speech recognition based on complete recognition of a sentence may not be appropriate for multi-party interaction. Conventional speech recognition approaches usually wait until the user has finished talking before returning a recognition hypothesis. This results in spoken dialogue systems that are unable to react when the users are interrupted by the system. Incremental speech recognition (ISR), where partial recognized phrase results are returned during user speech, can be used to create more responsive systems [32].

13.3.2 Decision Making for Multi-party Interaction

Decision making for multi-party interaction involves decisions about when to engage with which user and when to take the turn. We discuss below the state-of-the-art models for engagement and turn-taking decisions.

13.3.2.1 Modeling Engagement Decisions

In Sect. 13.3.1, we discussed the engagement detection methods mainly related to tracking and fusion. Another issue is modeling of engagement decisions. This involves mappings from internal states to engagement decisions. Bohus and Horvitz [6] describe an engagement model that combines engagement detection with high-level engagement control decisions to decide whom to engage. The engagement actions (*engage, no-action, maintain, disengage*) are estimated based on a conditional probabilistic model based on the current engagement state of the user, previous character, and system actions and other additional sensory inputs (such as greeting and salutations or calling by name). They also define an *engagement control policy* and a *behavior control policy*. *Engagement control policy* includes high-level application-dependent goals of the users and other global contexts (history of the interactions, relationships between users). For example, the system might decide to refuse engagement for a while because it is already engaged in a high-priority interaction or it might try to engage with a person even though the user has no intention to engage. These policies can be authored manually to capture the desired system behavior or can be learned from data. *Behavior control policy* is to coordinate the output behaviors based on the engagement state, actions, and intentions of the users. For example, an engage action can trigger a sequence of behaviors: *establishAttention, greet*, and *monitor*. The action completes successfully if the character switches to the engaged state. Otherwise, engage system action completes with failure and this is signalled to the engagement control layer. Similar to the engagement sensing module, it is decoupled from the task at hand and reusable among application domains. The advantage of this method is that it separates the application-independent engagement control decisions and application-dependent high-level decisions.

Keizer et al. [18] learn dialogue strategies automatically based on multi-user human–robot social interactions using a bartender robot. Their system is composed of two parts: a *Social State Recognizer (SSR)* that fuses the sensory data and make high-level inferences and a *Social State Executor (SSE)* that takes the changes from the SSR and generates the output behavior. SSE is modeled using two Markov decision processes (MDPs) and the system is trained with a multi-user simulation environment. The first one is used for multi-user coordination, to manage the system's engagement decisions with the users: to decide whether to respond to the user's attention requests or to proceed with the current user. The second one is used for single-user interaction to decide what to say or do once engaged with a user and it is application dependent. The state features considered are whether the user is *present, engaged, close to the bar* and dialogue history such as whether they were *served drinks before* or *asked to wait*. The actions consist of asking a user to *wait, accepting bid for attention* from a particular user or *proceeding with the currently engaged user*. In comparison to the work of [6], their model learns decision strategies based on data and provides a systematic framework to do this. However, the disadvantage is that the engagement model is application dependent and needs extra work to be adapted to other domains.

13.3.2.2 Modeling Turn-Taking Behavior

Modeling turn-taking implies deciding "when it is my time to speak". Turn can be assigned to another person by the last speaker or a person in the group can voluntarily take the turn. In [7], a heuristic turn-taking model is described taking into account the turn-taking context: *floor states, actions,* and *intentions* of each participant. *Floor state* is a binary variable indicating whether or not the participant has the floor. *Floor management actions* include the floor action type (*take, release, hold, null*) and the set of participants to release the floor. *Floor intention* is also a binary variable and is tied to floor actions. They are modeled separately keeping in mind that they might be useful for predicting actions. The floor states are updated based on the joint floor actions of all participants. The system takes the turn when the floor is released to it or when the floor is released to someone else but is not taken by anyone for more than a threshold amount of time. Floor management actions are summarized as below [7]:

- If a participant has the floor already, it means she is performing a hold action if she is speaking.
- If a participant has the floor already and if she is not speaking, the floor is assigned to the set of addressees for the last spoken utterance.
- If a participant does not have the floor, she will perform a take action if speaking and a null action otherwise.
- If a participant performs a hold or take action, she has the intention of holding the floor.

While this method is based on heuristic rules, in [9] a decision-theoretic approach is proposed. It models turn-taking considering the uncertainties arising from state recognition and based on the system's own computational delays in perception and production of behavior. This improves the naturalness of spoken dialog taking into account the fine structure of timing of turns. For example, the system might be able to handle situations such as long silences after an utterance of the user, barge-ins by a system before a user has completed speaking and floor conflicts resulting from confusions about turns. The approach allows the system to continuously deliberate about uncertainties and delays and resolve trade-offs between waiting and taking the floor.

13.3.3 Behavior Generation for Multi-party Interaction

Besides tracking user states and modeling multi-party decision making, it is important how these decisions are rendered in terms of synchronized multimodal output as speech, gaze, and gestures. Bohus et al. [8] developed a heuristics-based gaze model based on the existing literature on gaze behavior. For example, during a hold behavior, the virtual human directed its gaze away from the addressee during the thematic part of the current output and toward the addressee during the rhematic part. In case of multiple participants, it first established eye contact with one addressee and then in turn with each of the other addressees. Then it turned back to the first addressee again and this time had a longer duration eye contact. Wang et al. [39] proposed a rule-based method to model the listening behavior of different roles (*addressee, side participant, overhearer,* and *eavesdropper*). The model is based on participation and comprehension goals. For example, addressees and side participants are considered to have positive participation goals, while bystanders have negative participation goals. Eavesdroppers have stronger intentions to understand the conversation, while overhearers do not intend to understand the conversation. Based on how each participant wants to proceed with their role, they take certain actions. Side participants do not care about understanding the speaker's utterance but the goal is to maintain the participation status, so they use glances toward the speaker. Mimicking and mirroring the speaker's behavior are also considered as acts to keep the current state. To change roles, the new set of behaviors for the appropriate role is performed to signal the role change. This model is in particular developed for multiple conversational characters in virtual worlds.

Regarding the machine learning approach, there are methods analyzing and modeling human–human interactions in meetings. These models can be applied to behavior generation of virtual characters and humanoid robots. For example, Otsuka et al. [30] propose a probabilistic model for cross-modal nonverbal interactions in multi-party face-to-face conversations. The model infers the casual relationships among participants' behaviors using interaction structures. These are defined to be the basic primitives in conversations that can reveal how messages are exchanged among people. On the other hand, research on multimodal behavior generation for human–machine interaction relies on wizard-of-oz studies. For instance, Mutlu et al. [29] studied conversational gaze mechanisms with a humanoid robot based on data collected in a wizard-of-oz setup and developed models of role-signalling, turn-taking, and topic signalling during multi-party interactions. They found that in a two-party conversation with one bystander, the speaker gazed toward the addressee 76 % of the time, looked at the bystander 8 % of the time and looked at the environment 16 % of the time. In the three-party conversations, the speaker looked at the addressees 71 % of the time and looked at the environment 29 % of the time. However, we could not find any existing work on full-fledged interactive systems working on using machine-learning based multi-party gaze behaviors. Thus, it still remains an interesting open research area.

13.4 Proposed Work: Multimodal and Multi-party Interactions Among Multiple Users and Multiple Agents

Previous work on multi-party interactions deal with systems either with multiple virtual humans in a virtual environment and a single user or multiple users, and a humanoid robot situated in the real world. Similar to the latter, we are interested in situated interaction in the real world but with two artificial characters and at least two users. The differences between these two cases is explained in the following section. We refer to [41] for further technical details.

13.4.1 Comparison to Previous Work

Figure 13.2 illustrates the possible configurations of interaction with a single artificial character and multiple users. Namely, the system can dynamically handle situations of one-to-one interaction, one character two-user interaction and the cases where the users just pass by without interacting. The system can also handle situations when there are bystanders waiting behind the interacting users or can interpret when two users are talking to each other.

The previous work decides on the engagement based on a single character's point-of-view, as the center of the F-formation remains on the same line as the torso orientation of the artificial character. However, in the case of two characters, the center of the F-formation shifts in between these two. Thus, the engagement model for one character is not applicable for the two character-based interaction. Figure 13.3 shows how the model of engagement with a single character does not apply to the two-characters case. While the blue circles show the F-formation for the two-characters case, the red circles with dashes illustrate the F-formation for the character on the left side (in bluish color). According to the single character interaction model, the user on the right is marked as not engaged. However, in reality the user is engaged in

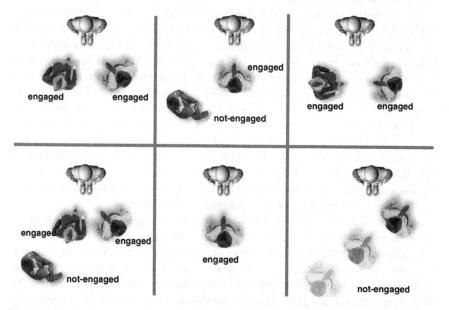

Fig. 13.2 Possible group interaction configurations in previous work

Fig. 13.3 Comparison of
F-formation with
multi-characters to previous
work

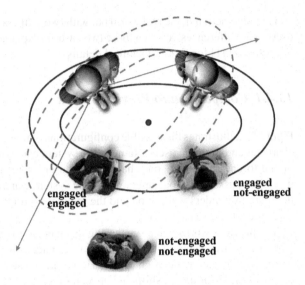

a group interaction with the virtual human, the robot, and the other user on the left
in a four-party interaction. Thus, for a situated character in real worlds to become
fully adaptive to multi-party interactions, it should have a dynamic understanding of
F-formations, by calculating in a dynamic way how other characters and other users
position themselves in the real world. To do this it needs good tracking capabilities,
mobility, and flexibility of head movements to make a model of the world from its
partial knowledge, as humans do.

To study the challenges regarding the multi-character, multi-user interaction system, we developed a prototype system with a virtual human, a humanlike robot, and
two users (Fig. 13.4). Both the virtual human and the robot can interact with the users
and engage in multi-party conversations. This requires that each character keep track
of the actions of other participants. In order to interpret the users' actions, they need
to understand the scene as a whole by fusing information from different channels
of information. In our case, one of the artificial characters is a virtual human. Its
gaze is modified to give the impression that it is looking at a point in the real world.
The virtual human is at the same scale with real people and we render it on a big
horizontal screen. Similarly, the robot is human-sized. It has limited head movement
capability and a camera in both the eyes. However, due to low resolution and the
eyelashes in the eye region, we prefer not to use the camera in the eye. Alternatively,
we use Kinect cameras due to their capabilities and low cost.

Ideally, two Kinect cameras could be used, one for each character placed on
top of their head as it also provides a wider horizontal field of view. However,
since Kinect 360 depth maps suffer from major quality degradation in overlapping
areas, we use a single Kinect as the eyes of two characters positioned between
them. Figure 13.5 illustrates the interaction environment. The virtual human and the
robot are positioned in a glass room so that visitors other than the ones interacting
can observe the interactions. The door is in the left opposite corner of the room.

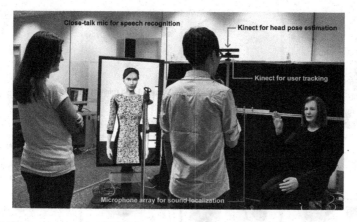

Fig. 13.4 System setup with the virtual human and the robot

Fig. 13.5 Our setup with two artificial characters and one Kinect

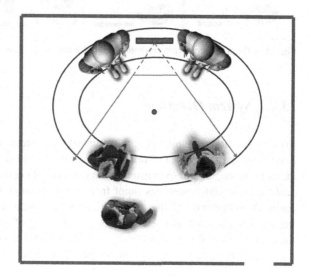

Interacting users engage and disengage with the characters by entering and leaving from the door.

There could also be cases where the users go outside the FOV of Kinect, by going too much to the left and right sides of the room. People might either just pass by or go somewhere at the back of the room. Another similar case is when a user passes by between the two characters. This was observed as a problem in our experiments when researchers wanted to get something from the room without an intention to interact with the virtual human or the robot [40]. Finally, there could be cases where people do not engage with the characters together in a group interaction but they might engage only with the virtual character or only with the robot. Figure 13.6 shows a set of these combinations.

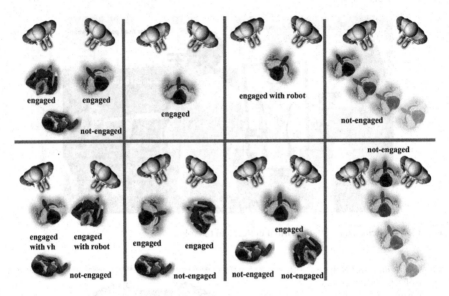

Fig. 13.6 Possible interaction configuration with multiple artificial characters and multiple users

13.4.2 System Overview

Figure 13.7 shows the overall architecture of the system. There are three main components in the system: (1) Multi-user tracking and fusion module, (2) multi-party dialogue manager, and (3) virtual human and robot controllers. *Multi-user tracking and fusion module* combines input from audiovisual components and make inferences about the state of the users which are then sent to the multi-party dialogue manager. *Multi-party dialogue manager* is the core of action selection process for the coordination of behaviors of the virtual character and the robot. Finally, *virtual human and robot controllers* generate speech and nonverbal behavior for the virtual

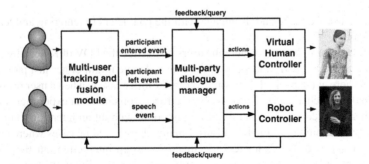

Fig. 13.7 Multi-party interaction architecture

character and the robot. They can give feedback to the fusion and dialogue modules to inform whether an action is completed successfully. They can also query the state of the world by sending messages to the multi-user tracking module (e.g., to retrieve the position of the users).

13.4.2.1 Multi-user Tracking and Fusion

Multi-party interaction requires the identification of the speaker and the addressee. In our current system, in order to make the virtual character and the robot understand the current scene, input from individual vision and audio processing components are fused. The fusion module allows to keep track of several information in real-time such as *the number of users in the scene, when they entered or left the scene, their positions, whether they are speaking, their names, to whom they are speaking* and *what they are saying.*

Situated-interaction taking into account the dynamics in the physical environment surrounding the artificial characters requires both being aware of the configuration of the characters and objects in the environment and keeping track of the movement trajectories of users. In order to make both the artificial characters and the human users interact in a common reference frame, we defined a model of the real world where each object in the interaction area is defined in terms of the real-world coordinates, the origin being the left top corner of the demo area. For the tracking of users, we use two Microsoft Kinect cameras as shown in Fig. 13.4. The Kinect at the bottom allows tracking of the full skeleton of two users. Kinect can detect position of six users and full skeleton of two users normally. Since we are interested in full tracking of the users, currently we are limiting the system to two users interaction. Kinect on the top is used for head pose estimation. For detecting the speech events in the environment, a microphone array with eight microphones is used to identify the speaker. It is placed half a meter below the Kinects. A close-talk microphone with a flexible cable is also available for speech recognition.

Figure 13.8 shows the architecture of the multi-user tracking and fusion module. It has three parts: (1) Multi-user tracking and visualization of the user states in real-time, (2) world model (e.g., position, orientation, name) of the objects in the world (static objects such as the screen, robot, and sensors or dynamic objects such as the users), and (3) fusion of the information coming from individual trackers, e.g., sound localization, speech recognition, and head pose estimation in order to identify the speaker and the addressee.

After combining the information from the individual trackers, fusion module produces three types of events: *participantEntered, participantLeft*, and *speech* as shown in (2.6). The first two events consist of three parameters: *event ID, person name*, and *location. Speech* event contains four parameters: *event ID, speaking person, speech content*, and *listening person.* These three events are sent to the multi-party dialogue manager module in order to decide what to do and what to say at each point in time.

Fig. 13.8 Multi-user tracking and fusion module

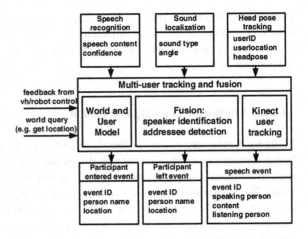

13.4.2.2 Multi-party Dialogue Manager

For natural interaction, dialogue manager should interpret the multimodal input, develop strategies for handling misinterpretations for a more robust interaction, and produce appropriate response taking into account the social context. Thus the role of the dialogue system is critical in two ways: Finding ways to handle error-prone multimodal input and modeling the social aspects of multi-user, multi-character interactions.

Figure 13.9 shows the architecture of the multi-party dialogue system. Events received from the fusion module are handled by the event listening thread of the multi-party dialogue manager as soon as they arrive. Participant model is created based on the *participantEntered* and *participantLeft* events and keep the list of current participants in the scene and their states. In addition to processing speech events and responding to them in a reactive manner, dialogue manager thread also checks the goals and action history of the virtual character and the robot and selects actions based on the goals for a mixed-initiative interaction.

Fig. 13.9 Multi-party dialogue manager

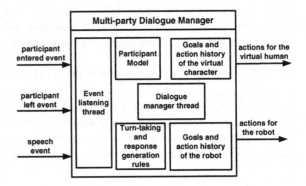

The system supports users engaging and leaving a conversation in a dynamic way considering four different cases: (1) One user interacting with the system, (2) one user interacting with the system and a newcomer joins, (3) one user leaves while two users are interacting with the system and the remaining user continues interaction, and (4) two users can enter and leave the scene at the same time. Sophie and Nadine take random turns to interact with the users unless they ask a question to a specific user and wait for an answer. For example, if they want to greet the user, they do a greet action in a random order at each interaction session. Some actions have a specific addressee due to their contextual meaning. For example, the question,"What is your name?" requires Sophie or Nadine to address a specific user by looking at this person. If there is only one user in the scene, both characters keep track of the user with their gaze as the user moves around regardless of the question. In the case of two users, Sophie and Nadine switch their gaze between these two users based on the dialogue context and speech event received. In case there is no specific user to look at, they look somewhere in between the two users.

13.4.3 Case Study and Results

We designed an experiment in order to get the users' feedback to the system and obtained promising results for the first prototype. The details regarding the experiment and the system can be found in [40]. We measured whether the users felt they were addressed by Sophie or Nadine and whether Sophie and Nadine could identify them correctly. We also asked in general how natural and comfortable was the interaction. The experiment was conducted with the research staff from the Computer Science and Biotechnology departments of Nanyang Technological University. 21 participants interacted with the system in 14 sessions. In half the sessions, both users were study participants. In the remaining 7 sessions, one user was the study participant while the other user was a researcher. Before the experiment, written consent of the participants were taken. They were instructed about the speech recognition vocabulary and the general flow of the interaction. They were not told when exactly a new user would join or when they had to leave the conversation keeping this aspect of the interaction rather dynamic. The experiment was conducted on 4 consecutive days. The total interaction time was 105 min being around 7.5 min on average. We video recorded all interactions for further analysis after the experiment. After the interaction, users were taken into separate rooms and filled in a questionnaire about their experience. The questionnaire was composed of two parts. The first part was based on the social presence questionnaire of Lombard et al. [26]. We added one more question to this section about how comfortable and natural was the interaction. The second part of the questionnaire was prepared by the researchers of this study and was inspired by [5]. The questions can be seen in Fig. 13.10. They were based on a seven-point Likert scale. We also had some open-ended questions to get further

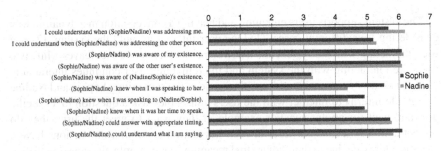

Fig. 13.10 Average value for the multi-party interaction questions

comments from the participants regarding their experience. We analyzed the video recordings in order to find out the percentage of speaker identification and addressee detection errors. Due to reverberations in the glass room and sound interference, the accuracy of the speaker identification was found as 82.3 %. Addressee detection accuracy was 81.4 %. The main problem of addressee detection was the loss of face tracking as soon as the users turned their head too much toward left or right. For addressee detection, the numbers were obtained by counting the number of times the system found the correct addressee, each time a user addressed Sophie or Nadine. The number of times the system identified the speaking user correctly was also counted from the video material. However, response generation was not only based on the accuracy of speaker identification and addressee detection but also depending on the accuracy of the speech recognition system. This decreased the overall accuracy of the system to around 60 % when the errors from three modules were considered together. We also asked users questions regarding the multi-party interaction experience. Figure 13.10 shows the results. The first impressions from the users indicate that the system is able to correctly identify speakers and addressees and can handle basic turn-taking functionality.

13.4.4 Future Research Directions

As we mentioned in Sect. 13.4.1, previous work focused on systems with one artificial character and multiple users. However, there could also be cases where there are multiple characters and multiple users interacting together and this is quite different from the first one. It is more complex in a sense that it requires coordination among not only multiple users but also multiple artificial characters. Based on the analysis of the previous work and methods in multi-party interaction research, we summarize below the three important future directions.

13.4.4.1 Engagement and Turn-Taking for Multi-character and Multi-user Interaction

Engagement detection and modeling in the open world with multiple users moving around freely is an active area of research. However, engagement detection methods with single artificial characters might not be directly applied to two characters case as the F-formation changes dynamically based on the size of the group. For studying these challenges, we developed a prototype system with two artificial characters and two users interacting together and will study the possible solutions for a more generic engagement intention detection method and engagement decision-making model. Regarding the turn-taking aspect, the flow of turns between two characters needs to be coordinated. Problems in sensing such as which user is interacting with which character must be resolved in a robust way using the perception components. Moreover, not only are there challenges on the sensing side but also the personality modeling aspect of the characters can effect the nature of the interactions and floor management. For example, while the virtual human chooses to respond immediately to an engagement request, the robot might prefer to first finish interaction with the active user. That might depend on their personality type and emotional state.

13.4.4.2 Interruption Enabled Multi-party Interaction

One aspect that is not addressed yet is the interruption handling during interaction. We would like to address a highly natural and dynamic situation where any of the real or artificial participants can interrupt each other or share overlapping speech segments. This requires discriminating between artificial and real voices as well as understanding which user is speaking at any point in time. Speech recognition with incremental understanding is also important as it is not very natural to wait until the users finish a whole phrase. These are the challenges mainly related to speech and sound processing. Another point is the decision-making based on overlapping partial input. Decisions-theoretic methods using probability of input states and utility of planned actions can be explored to develop more sophisticated decision-making capabilities.

13.4.4.3 Behavior Generation for Multi-party Interaction

Finally, on the behavior generation side, there is a lack of studies of how artificial characters behave in multi-party interactions to signal turn-taking or to convey their intentions. We are interested in a data-driven behavior generation method that can learn links between high-level intentions and output behaviors. Methods such as dynamic Bayesian networks (DBNs) can be appropriate for modeling multi-party behaviors. There are also issues at the lower motion control level to create smooth synchronized realistic behaviors. For example, in the case of interruptions an ongoing animation needs to be stopped and smoothly blended with the next animation sequence.

13.5 Conclusion

In this chapter, we gave an overview of previous work in multimodal and multi-party interactions and introduced the current challenges. We have also mentioned about our current efforts to handle multi-character and multi-user group interactions with a prototype system and results from a case study with real participants. Finally, we summarized the three important future directions of research based on our detailed analysis. We hope that the information provided in this chapter will be useful for other researchers in this field and encourage them to further investigate on the open research areas mentioned above.

References

1. Atrey PK, Hossain MA, Saddik AE, Kankanhalli MS (2010) Multimodal fusion for multimedia analysis: a survey. Multimedia Syst 16(6):345–379
2. Berton A, Kaltenmeier A, Haiber U, Schreiner O (2006) Speech recognition. In: Wahlster W (ed) SmartKom: foundations of multimodal dialogue systems. Springer, Berlin
3. Bickmore T (2008) Framing and interpersonal stance in relational agents. In: Why conversational agents do what they do. Functional representations for generating conversational agent behavior. AAMAS 2008, Estoril, Portugal
4. Bickmore TW, Picard RW (2005) Establishing and maintaining long-term human-computer relationships. ACM Trans Comput-Hum Interact 12:293–327
5. Bohus D, Horvitz E (2009) Dialog in the open world: platform and applications. In: Proceedings of the 2009 international conference on multimodal interfaces, ICMI-MLMI'09. ACM, New York, pp 31–38
6. Bohus D, Horvitz E (2009) Learning to predict engagement with a spoken dialog system in open-world settings. In: Proceedings of the SIGDIAL 2009 conference: the 10th annual meeting of the special interest group on discourse and dialogue. Association for computational linguistics, pp 244–252
7. Bohus D, Horvitz E (2010) Computational models for multiparty turn-taking. Technical report MSR-TR-2010-115, Microsoft technical report
8. Bohus D, Horvitz E (2010) Facilitating multiparty dialog with gaze, gesture, and speech. In: International conference on multimodal interfaces and the workshop on machine learning for multimodal interaction, ICMI-MLMI'10. ACM, New York, pp 5:1–5:8
9. Bohus D, Horvitz E (2011) Decisions about turns in multiparty conversation: from perception to action. In: Proceedings of the 13th international conference on multimodal interfaces, ICMI'11. ACM, New York, pp 153–160
10. Brooks RA (1985) A robust layered control system for a mobile robot. Technical report, Cambridge
11. Cassell J, Vilhjálmsson HH, Bickmore T (2001) BEAT: the behavior expression animation toolkit. In: Proceedings of the 28th annual conference on computer graphics and interactive techniques, SIGGRAPH'01. ACM, New York, pp 477–486

12. Egges A, Kshirsagar S, Magnenat-Thalmann N (2004) Generic personality and emotion simulation for conversational agents: research articles. Comput Animat Virtual Worlds 15:1–13
13. Foster ME, Gaschler A, Giuliani M (2013) How can i help you? comparing engagement classification strategies for a robot bartender. In: Proceedings of the 15th international conference on multimodal interaction (ICMI 2013)
14. Gebhard P (2005) ALMA: a layered model of affect. In: Proceedings of the fourth international joint conference on autonomous agents and multiagent systems, AAMAS'05. ACM, New York, pp 29–36
15. Gockley R, Forlizzi J, Simmons R (2006) Interactions with a moody robot. In: Proceedings of the 1st ACM SIGCHI/SIGART conference on human-robot interaction, HRI'06. ACM, New York, pp 186–193
16. Kasap Z, Thalmann NM (2010) Towards episodic memory based long-term affective interaction with a human-like robot. In: IEEE international symposium on robot and human interactive communication (RO-MAN). IEEE, pp 479–484
17. Kasap Z, Moussa MB, Chaudhuri P, Magnenat-Thalmann N (2009) Making them remember: emotional virtual characters with memory. IEEE Comput Graph Appl 29:20–29
18. Keizer S, Foster ME, Lemon O, Gaschler A, Giuliani M (2013) Training and evaluation of an MDP model for social multi-user human-robot interaction. In: Proceedings of the 14th annual SIGdial meeting on discourse and dialogue
19. Kendon A (2010) Spacing and orientation in co-present interaction. In: Proceedings of the second international conference on development of multimodal interfaces: active listening and synchrony, COST'09. Springer, Berlin, Heidelberg, pp 1–15
20. Kipp M, Neff M, Kipp KH, Albrecht I (2007) Towards natural gesture synthesis: evaluating gesture units in a data-driven approach to gesture synthesis. In: Pelachaud C, Martin J-C, André E, Chollet G, Karpouzis K, Pelé D (eds) Intelligent virtual agents. Lecture notes in computer science, vol 4722. Springer, Berlin, pp 15–28
21. Kopp S, Krenn B, Marsella S, Marshall AN, Pelachaud C, Pirker H, Thórisson KR, Vilhjálmsson H (2006) Towards a common framework for multimodal generation: the behavior markup language. In: Proceedings of the 6th international conference on intelligent virtual agents, IVA'06. Springer, Berlin, Heidelberg, pp 205–217
22. Krenn B, Sieber G (2008) Functional markup for behaviour planning: theory and practice. In: Proceedings of the AAMAS 2008 workshop FML: functional markup language. Why conversational agents do what they do, AAMAS'08
23. Lee J, DeVault D, Marsella S, Traum D (2008) Thoughts on fml: behavior generation in the virtual human communication architecture. In: Proceedings of the 1st functional markup language workshop
24. Lee J, Marsella S (2012) Modeling speaker behavior: a comparison of two approaches. In: Nakano Y, Neff M, Paiva A, Walker M (eds) Intelligent virtual agents. Lecture notes in computer science, vol 7502. Springer, Berlin, pp 161–174
25. Lee J, Marsella S (2006) Nonverbal behavior generator for embodied conversational agents. Intelligent virtual agents. Lecture notes in computer science, vol 4133. Springer, Berlin, pp 243–255
26. Lombard M, Ditton TB, Crane D, Davis B, Gil-Egui G, Horvath K, Rossman J, Park S (2000) Measuring presence: a literature-based approach to the development of a standardized paper-and-pencil instrument. In: IJsselsteijn W, Freeman J, de Ridder H (eds) Proceedings of the third international workshop on presence
27. Mascardi V, Demergasso D, Ancona D (2005) Languages for programming BDI-style agents: an overview. In: Woa'05
28. Michalowski MP (2006) A spatial model of engagement for a social robot. In: Proceedings of the 9th international workshop on advanced motion control (AMC 2006)
29. Mutlu B, Kanda T, Forlizzi J, Hodgins J, Ishiguro H (2012) Conversational gaze mechanisms for humanlike robots. ACM Trans Interact Intell Syst 1(2):12:1–12:33
30. Otsuka K, Sawada H, Yamato J (2007) Automatic inference of cross-modal nonverbal interactions in multiparty conversations: who responds to whom, when, and how? from gaze, head

gestures, and utterances. In: Proceedings of the 9th international conference on multimodal interfaces, ICMI'07. ACM, New York, pp 255–262

31. Peters C, Pelachaud C, Bevacqua E, Mancini M, Poggi I (2005) A model of attention and interest using gaze behavior. In: Intelligent virtual agents. Springer, London, pp 229–240

32. Selfridge EO, Arizmendi I, Heeman PA, Williams JD (2011) Stability and accuracy in incremental speech recognition. In: Proceedings of the SIGDIAL 2011 conference, SIGDIAL'11. Stroudsburg, Association for Computational Linguistics, pp 110–119

33. Shapiro A (2011) Building a character animation system. In: Motion in games. Springer, London, pp 98–109

34. Si M, Marsella SC, Pynadath DV (2006) Thespian: Modeling socially normative behavior in a decision-theoretic framework. In: Gratch J, Young M, Aylett R, Ballin D, Olivier P (eds) Intelligent virtual agents. Lecture notes in computer science, vol 4133. Springer, Berlin, pp 369–382

35. Sidner CL, Kidd CD, Lee C, Lesh N (2004) Where to look: a study of human-robot engagement. In: Proceedings of the 9th international conference on intelligent user interfaces, IUI'04. ACM, New York, pp 78–84

36. Stiefelhagen R, Ekenel HK, Fügen C, Gieselmann P, Holzapfel H, Kraft F, Nickel K, Voit M, Waibel A (2007) Enabling multimodal human-robot interaction for the karlsruhe humanoid robot. IEEE Trans Robot 23(5):840–851

37. Traum D (2004) Issues in multi-party dialogues. In: Dignum F (ed) Advances in agent communication, pp 201–211

38. Vijayasenan D, Valente F, Bourlard H (2012) Multistream speaker diarization of meetings recordings beyond mfcc and tdoa features. Speech Commun 54(1):55–67

39. Wang Z, Lee J, Marsella SC (2013) Multi-party, multi-role comprehensive listening behavior. J Auton Agents Multi-Agent Syst

40. Yumak Z, Ren J, Magnenat-Thalmann N, Yuan J (2014) Modelling multi-party interactions among virtual characters, robots and humans. MIT presence: teleoperators and virtual environments (presence), vol 23(2). MIT Press, Cambridge, pp 172–190

41. Yumak Z, Ren J, Thalmann NM, Yuan J (2014) Tracking and fusion for multiparty interaction with a virtual character and a social robot. In: SIGGRAPH Asia 2014 autonomous virtual humans and social robot for telepresence. ACM, New York, p 3

Printed in the United States
By Bookmasters